An Introduction to Network Programming with Java

Jan Graba

An Introduction to Network Programming with Java

Java 7 Compatible

Third Edition

Jan Graba
Department of Computing
Sheffield Hallam University
Sheffield, South Yorkshire, UK

Additional material to this book can be downloaded from http://extras.springer.com.

ISBN 978-1-4471-5253-8 ISBN 978-1-4471-5254-5 (eBook)
DOI 10.1007/978-1-4471-5254-5
Springer London Heidelberg New York Dordrecht

Library of Congress Control Number: 2013946037

Printed on acid-free paper

Springer is part of Springer Science+Business Media (www.springer.com)

Preface to Third Edition

It is now 7 years since I wrote the second edition of *An Introduction to Network Programming with Java* and so, when approached to produce a third edition, I felt that it was an appropriate time to agree to do so (possibly rather later than it should have been). One of the very first things that I did after being approached was examined the literature to find out what texts had been produced in the Java/network programming area in the interim period, and so what the current state of the competition was. (Though I had had a strong interest in this area for a considerable number of years, I had also been involved in other areas of software development, of course, and hadn't had cause to examine the literature in this area for some time.) To my great surprise, I found that virtually nothing of any consequence had been produced in this area during those years! Of course, this was a very welcome surprise and provided further impetus to go ahead with the project.

The changes in this third edition are not as profound as those in the second edition, largely because Java 5 brought in major language changes (both network and non-network) that needed to be reflected in the second edition, whereas neither Java 6 nor Java 7 has had such an impact, particularly in the area of network programming. One major change that did occur during this time, and is worth mentioning, was Sun's takeover by Oracle in April of 2009, but this has had no significant effect on the way in which Java has been developed.

Since the changes that have been necessary since the second edition are somewhat more small-scale than those that were desirable after the first edition, I think that it would be useful to give a chapter-by-chapter indication of what has been changed, what has been introduced that wasn't there before and, in some cases, what has been removed completely (the last of these hopefully resulting in a more 'streamlined' product). Consequently, the great bulk of the remainder of this preface will comprise a chapter-by-chapter breakdown of those changes.

Chapter 1

- Updating of browsers and browser versions used (along with associated updating of screenshots).
- Updating of the comparison between TCP and UDP.

Chapter 2

- Removal of Sect. 2.4 ('Downloading Web Pages'), felt by me to be of little use to most people.
- Some very minor changes to lines of code.

Chapter 3

- Extra text devoted to the differing strategies for determining which thread from a group of competing threads is to be given use of the processor at any given time.

Chapter 4

- Addition of *ArrayList*s and associated relegation of *Vector*s (with consequent modification of example program).
- Comparison of *Vector*s and *ArrayList*s.

Chapter 5

- Removal of step 2 in 5.3 (compiling with *rmic*), which has actually been unnecessary since Java 5.
- *Vector* references replaced with *ArrayList* ones in bank example of 5.4.

Chapter 6

- Some very minor URL changes.

Chapter 7

- Statement of redundancy of the loading of the database driver (for all JDBC4-compatible drivers), with consequent removal from examples. (JDBC4 was part of Java 6, which was introduced in December of 2006.)
- Addition of material on Apache Derby/Java DB, which came in with Java 6. This material introduced in a new Sect. 7.6, with consequent re-numbering of the old 7.6 and all later sections in this chapter.
- Information about Jakarta's retirement on 21/12/11 (and consequent direct control of Jakarta's sub-projects by Apache).
- Changes to the steps required in the new Sect. 7.12 (previously 7.11) for using the *DataSource* interface and creating a DAO (this method having changed somewhat since 2006), with consequent changes to the code of the example.
- Modification of the steps required for downloading and extracting DBCP files.

Chapter 8

- Updating of the Servlet API installation instructions.
- Removal of references to Tomcat's ROOT folder (now no longer in existence).
- Introduction of servlet annotation lines (introduced in Java 6).

Chapter 9

- Replacement of some HTML code with HTML-5 compatible CSS.
- Some very minor changes to lines of code.

Chapter 10

- Removal of Sect. 10.1, due to the Bean Builder now being defunct and no replacement for this software having appeared.
- Removal of the requirement that beans implement the *Serializable* interface, since this is (now?) unnecessary, with associated removal of the clause *implements Serializable* from the examples.
- Introduction of CSS into examples, to make examples HTML-5 compatible.

(Old) Chapter 11

- **Removal** of this entire chapter (with consequent re-numbering of later chapters). This has been done partly because EJPs are no longer of such importance since the emergence of frameworks such as Hibernate and Spring and partly because I felt that the complexity of EJBs probably didn't warrant their inclusion in this text.

New 'Chapter 11' (Previously 'Chapter 12')

- Very minor changes of wording.

New 'Chapter 12' (Previously 'Chapter 13')

- Updating of browsers used.

In keeping with the society-wide move towards Internet storage, there is now no CD accompanying this text. Model solutions for end-of-chapter exercises are accessible by lecturers and other authorised individuals through access/application form via http://springer.com/978-1-4471-5253-8. Also included at this URL is a Word document called *Java Environment Installation* that provides downloading and installation instructions for Java 7 and all associated software required to complete the end-of-chapter exercises. (The instructions will not refer to the latest update of Java 7, so please download whatever is the latest update.)

At a second URL (http://extras.springer.com) are the items listed below, which can be found by searching for the book's ISBN (978-1-4471-5253-8).

- Chapter examples
- Supplied code
- GIF files

- JPEG files
- Sound files
- Videos

All that remains now is for me to wish you luck and satisfaction in your programming endeavours. Good luck!

Sheffield, South Yorkshire, UK
27 March 2013

Jan Graba

Contents

Chapter 1
Basic Concepts, Protocols and Terminology

Learning Objectives

After reading this chapter, you should:

- have a high level appreciation of the basic means by which messages are sent and received on modern networks;
- be familiar with the most important protocols used on networks;
- understand the addressing mechanism used on the Internet;
- understand the basic principles of client/server programming.

The fundamental purpose of this opening chapter is to introduce the underpinning network principles and associated terminology with which the reader will need to be familiar in order to make sense of the later chapters of this book. The material covered here is entirely generic (as far as any programming language is concerned) and it is not until the next chapter that we shall begin to consider how Java may be used in network programming. If the meaning of any term covered here is not clear when that term is later encountered in context, the reader should refer back to this chapter to refresh his/her memory.

It would be very easy to make this chapter considerably larger than it currently is, simply by including a great deal of dry, technical material that would be unlikely to be of any practical use to the intended readers of this book. However, this chapter is intentionally brief, the author having avoided the inclusion of material that is not of relevance to the use of Java for network programming. The reader who already has a sound grasp of network concepts may safely skip this chapter entirely.

1.1 Clients, Servers and Peers

The most common categories of network software nowadays are *clients* and *servers*. These two categories have a symbiotic relationship and the term *client/server programming* has become very widely used in recent years. It is important to

J. Graba, *An Introduction to Network Programming with Java: Java 7 Compatible*,
DOI 10.1007/978-1-4471-5254-5_1,

distinguish firstly between a server and the machine upon which the server is running (called the *host* machine), since I.T. workers often refer loosely to the host machine as 'the server'. Though this common usage has no detrimental practical effects for the majority of I.T. tasks, those I.T. personnel who are unaware of the distinction and subsequently undertake network programming are likely to be caused a significant amount of conceptual confusion until this distinction is made known to them.

A server, as the name implies, provides a service of some kind. This service is provided for clients that connect to the server's host machine specifically for the purpose of accessing the service. Thus, it is the clients that initiate a dialogue with the server. (These clients, of course, are also programs and are **not** human clients!) Common services provided by such servers include the 'serving up' of Web pages (by Web servers) and the downloading of files from servers' host machines via the File Transfer Protocol (FTP servers). For the former service, the corresponding client programs would be Web browsers (such as Firefox, Chrome or Internet Explorer). Though a client and its corresponding server will normally run on different machines in a real-world application, it is perfectly possible for such programs to run on the *same* machine. Indeed, it is often very convenient (as will be seen in subsequent chapters) for server and client(s) to be run on the same machine, since this provides a very convenient 'sandbox' within which such applications may be tested before being released (or, more likely, before final testing on separate machines). This avoids the need for multiple machines and multiple testing personnel.

In some applications, such as messaging services, it is possible for programs on users' machines to communicate directly with each other in what is called *peer-to-peer* (or *P2P*) mode. However, for many applications, this is either not possible or prohibitively costly in terms of the number of simultaneous connections required. For example, the World Wide Web simply does not allow clients to communicate directly with each other. However, some applications use a server as an intermediary, in order to provide 'simulated'peer-to-peer facilities. Alternatively, both ends of the dialogue may act as both client and server. Peer-to-peer systems are beyond the intended scope of this text, though, and no further mention will be made of them.

1.2 Ports and Sockets

These entities lie at the heart of network communications. For anybody not already familiar with the use of these terms in a network programming context, the two words very probably conjure up images of hardware components. However, although they are closely associated with the hardware communication links between computers within a network, *ports* and *sockets* are not themselves hardware elements, but abstract concepts that allow the programmer to make use of those communication links.

A port is a *logical* connection to a computer (as opposed to a physical connection) and is identified by a number in the range 1–65535. This number has no correspondence with the number of physical connections to the computer, of which there may be only one (even though the number of ports used on that machine may be much greater than this). Ports are implemented upon all computers attached to a network, but it is only those machines that have server programs running on them for which the network programmer will refer explicitly to port numbers. Each port may be dedicated to a particular server/service (though the number of available ports will normally greatly exceed the number that is actually used). Port numbers in the range 1–1023 are normally set aside for the use of specified standard services, often referred to as 'well-known' services. For example, port 80 is normally used by Web servers. Some of the more common well-known services are listed in Sect. 1.4. Application programs wishing to use ports for non-standard services should avoid using port numbers 1–1023. (A range of 1024–65535 should be more than enough for even the most prolific of network programmers!).

For each port supplying a service, there is a server program waiting for any requests. All such programs run together in parallel on the host machine. When a client attempts to make connection with a particular server program, it supplies the port number of the associated service. The host machine examines the port number and passes the client's transmission to the appropriate server program for processing.

In most applications, of course, there are likely to be multiple clients wanting the same service at the same time. A common example of this requirement is that of multiple browsers (quite possibly thousands of them) wanting Web pages from the same server. The server, of course, needs some way of distinguishing between clients and keeping their dialogues separate from each other. This is achieved via the use of *sockets*. As stated earlier, a socket is an abstract concept and **not** an element of computer hardware. It is used to indicate one of the two end-points of a communication link between two processes. When a client wishes to make connection to a server, it will create a socket at its end of the communication link. Upon receiving the client's initial request (on a particular port number), the server will create a new socket at its end that will be dedicated to communication with that particular client. Just as one hardware link to a server may be associated with many ports, so too may one port be associated with many sockets. More will be said about sockets in Chap. 2.

1.3 The Internet and IP Addresses

An internet (lower-case 'i') is a collection of computer networks that allows any computer on any of the associated networks to communicate with any other computer located on any of the other associated networks (or on the same network, of course). The protocol used for such communication is called the Internet Protocol (IP). *The* Internet (upper-case 'I') is the world's largest IP-based network. Each computer on the Internet has a unique IP address, the current version of which is still, for most people, IPv4 (Internet Protocol version 4), though this is likely to change at some point during the next few years. This represents machine addresses in what is called **quad notation**. This is made up of four eight-bit numbers (i.e., numbers in the decimal range 0–255), separated by dots. For example, 131.122.3.219 would be one such address. Due to a growing shortage of IPv4 addresses, IPv4 is due to be replaced with IPv6, the draft standard for which was published on the 10th of August, 1998. IPv6 uses 128-bit addresses, which provide massively more addresses. Many common Internet applications already work with IPv6 and it is expected that IPv6 will gradually replace IPv4, with the two coexisting for a number of years during a transition period.

Recent years have witnessed an explosion in the growth and use of the Internet. As a result, there has arisen a need for a programming language with features designed specifically for network programming. Java provides these features and does so in a platform-independent manner, which is vital for a heterogeneous network such as the Internet. Java is sometimes referred to as 'the language of the Internet' and it is the use of Java in this context that has had a major influence on the popularisation of the language. For many programmers, the need to program for the Internet is one of the main reasons, if not *the* reason, for learning to program in Java.

1.4 Internet Services, URLs and DNS

Whatever the service provided by a server, there must be some established *protocol* governing the communication that takes place between server and client. Each end of the dialogue must know what may/must be sent to the other, the format in which it should be sent, the sequence in which it must be sent (if sequence matters) and, for 'open-ended' dialogues, how the dialogue is to be terminated. For the standard services, such protocols are made available in public documents, usually by either the Internet Engineering Task Force (IETF) or the World Wide Web Consortium (W3C). Some of the more common services and their associated ports are shown in Table 1.1. For a more esoteric or 'bespoke' service, the application writer must establish a protocol and convey it to the intended users of that service.

Table 1.1 Some well-known network services

Protocol name	Port number	Nature of service
Echo	7	The server simply echoes the data sent to it. This is useful for testing purposes
Daytime	13	Provides the ASCII representation of the current date and time on the server
FTP-data	20	Transferring files. (FTP uses two ports.)
FTP	21	Sending FTP commands like PUT and GET
Telnet	23	Remote login and command line interaction
SMTP	25	E-mail. (Simple Mail Transfer Protocol.)
HTTP	80	HyperText Transfer Protocol (the World Wide Web protocol)
NNTP	119	Usenet. (Network News Transfer Protocol.)

A URL (Uniform Resource Locator) is a unique identifier for any resource located on the Internet. It has the following structure (in which BNF notation is used):

```
<protocol>://<hostname>[:<port>][/<pathname>]
[/<filename>[#<section>]]
```

For example:

```
http://www.oracle.com/technetwork/java/javase/down-
loads/index.html
```

For a well-known protocol, the port number may be omitted and the default port number will be assumed. Thus, since the example above specifies the HTTP protocol (the protocol of the Web) and does not specify on which port of the host machine the service is available, it will be assumed that the service is running on port 80 (the default port for Web servers). If the file name is omitted, then the server sends a default file from the directory specified in the path name. (This default file will commonly be called *index.html* or *default.html*.) The 'section' part of the URL (not often specified) indicates a named 'anchor' in an HTML document. For example, the HTML anchor in the tag

```
<A HREF="#summary">Summary of Report</A>
```

would be referred to as `summary` by the section component of the URL.

Since human beings are generally much better at remembering meaningful strings of characters than they are at remembering long strings of numbers, the Domain Name System was developed. A *domain name*, also known as a *host name*, is the user-friendly equivalent of an IP address. In the previous example of a URL, the domain name was `www.oracle.com`. The individual parts of a domain name don't correspond to the individual parts of an IP address. In fact, domain names don't always have four parts (as IPv4 addresses must have).

Normally, human beings will use domain names in preference to IP addresses, but they can just as well use the corresponding IP addresses (if they know what they are!). The *Domain Name System* provides a mapping between IP addresses and domain names and is held in a distributed database. The IP address system and the DNS are governed by ICANN (the Internet Corporation for Assigned Names and Numbers), which is a non-profitmaking organisation. When a URL is submitted to a browser, the DNS automatically converts the domain name part into its numeric IP equivalent.

1.5 TCP

In common with all modern computer networks, the Internet is a **packet-switched** network, which means that messages between computers on the Internet are broken up into blocks of information called **packets**, with each packet being handled separately and possibly travelling by a completely different route from that of other such packets from the same message. IP is concerned with the **routing** of these packets through an internet. Introduced by the American military during the Cold War, it was designed from the outset to be robust. In the event of a military strike against one of the network routers, the rest of the network **had** to continue to function as normal, with messages that would have gone through the damaged router being re-routed. IP is responsible for this re-routing. It attaches the IP address of the intended recipient to each packet and then tries to determine the most efficient route available to get to the ultimate destination (taking damaged routers into account).

However, since packets could still arrive out of sequence, be corrupted or even not arrive at all (without indication to either sender or intended recipient that anything had gone wrong), it was decided to place another protocol layer on top of IP. This further layer was provided by TCP (Transmission Control Protocol), which allowed each end of a connection to acknowledge receipt of IP packets and/or request retransmission of lost or corrupted packets. In addition, TCP allows the packets to be rearranged into their correct sequence at the receiving end. IP and TCP are the two commonest protocols used on the Internet and are almost invariably coupled together as TCP/IP. TCP is the higher level protocol that uses the lower level IP.

For Internet applications, a four-layer model is often used, which is represented diagrammatically in Fig. 1.1 below. The transport layer will often comprise the TCP protocol, but may be UDP (described in the next section), while the internet layer will always be IP. Each layer of the model represents a different level of abstraction, with higher levels representing higher abstraction. Thus, although applications may appear to be communicating directly with each other, they are actually communicating directly only with their transport layers. The transport and internet layers, in their turn, communicate directly only with the layers immediately above and below them, while the host-to-network layer communicates directly only with the IP layer at each end of the connection. When a message is sent by the application layer at one end of the connection, it passes through each of the lower layers. As it does so, each layer adds further protocol data specific to the particular protocol at that level. For the TCP layer, this process involves breaking up the data packets into TCP segments and adding sequence numbers and checksums; for the IP layer, it involves placing the TCP segments into IP packets called **datagrams** and adding the routing details. The host-to-network layer then converts the digital data into an analogue form suitable for transmission over the carrier wire, sends the data and converts it back into digital form at the receiving end.

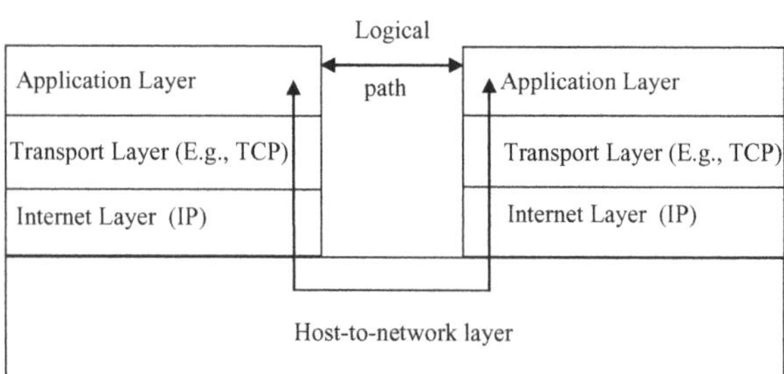

Fig. 1.1 The 4-layer network model

At the receiving end, the message travels up through the layers until it reaches the receiving application layer. As it does so, each layer converts the message into a form suitable for receipt by the next layer (effectively reversing the corresponding process carried out at the sending end) and carries out checks appropriate to its own protocol. If recalculation of checksums reveals that some of the data has been corrupted or checking of sequence numbers shows that some data has not been received, then the transport layer requests re-transmission of the corrupt/missing data. Otherwise, the transport layer acknowledges receipt of the packets. All of this is completely transparent to the application layer. Once all the data has been received, converted and correctly sequenced, it is presented to the recipient application layer as though that layer had been in direct communication with the sending application layer. The latter may then send a response in exactly the same manner (and so on). In fact, since TCP provides full duplex transmission, the two ends of the connection may be sending data simultaneously.

The above description has deliberately hidden many of the low-level details of implementation, particularly the tasks carried out by the host-to-network layer. In addition, of course, the initial transmission may have passed through several routers and their associated layers before arriving at its ultimate destination. However, this high-level view covers the basic stages that are involved and is quite sufficient for our purposes.

Another network model that is often referred to is the seven-layer Open Systems Interconnection (OSI) model. However, this model is an unnecessarily complex one for our purposes and is better suited to non-TCP/IP networks anyway.

1.6 UDP

Most Internet applications use TCP as their transport mechanism. In contrast to TCP, User Datagram Protocol (UDP) is an unreliable protocol, since:

(i) it doesn't guarantee that each packet of data will arrive;
(ii) it doesn't guarantee that packets will be in the right order.

UDP doesn't re-send a packet if it fails to arrive or there is some other error and it doesn't re-assemble packets into the correct sequence at the receiving end. However, the TCP overhead of providing facilities such as confirmation of receipt and re-transmission of lost or corrupted packets used to mean that UDP was significantly *faster* than TCP. For many applications (e.g., file transfer), this didn't really matter greatly. As far as these applications were concerned, it was much more important that the data arrived intact and in the correct sequence, both of which were guaranteed by TCP. For some applications, however, the relatively slow throughput speed offered by TCP was simply not feasible. Such applications included the *streaming* of audio and video files (i.e., the playing of those files while they were being downloaded). Such applications didn't use TCP, because of its large overhead. Instead, they used UDP, since their major objective was to keep playing the sound/video without interruption and losing a few bytes of data was much better than waiting for re-transmission of the missing data.

Nowadays, network transmission speeds are considerably greater than they were only a few years ago, meaning that UDP is now a feasible transport mechanism for applications in which it would not once have been considered. In addition to this, it is much easier for TCP packets to get through firewalls than it is for UDP packets to do so, since Web administrators tend to allow TCP packets from remote port 80s to pass through unchallenged. For these reasons, the choice of whether to use TCP or UDP for speed-critical applications is not nearly as clear cut as it used to be.

Chapter 2
Starting Network Programming in Java

Learning Objectives

After reading this chapter, you should:

- know how to determine the host machine's IP address via a Java program;
- know how to use TCP sockets in both client programs and server programs;
- know how to use UDP sockets in both client programs and server programs;
- appreciate the convenience of Java's stream classes and the consistency of the interface afforded by them;
- appreciate the ease with which GUIs can be added to network programs;
- know how to check whether ports on a specified machine are running services.

Having covered fundamental network protocols and techniques in a generic fashion in Chap. 1, it is now time to consider how those protocols may be used and the techniques implemented in Java. Core package *java.net* contains a number of very useful classes that allow programmers to carry out network programming very easily. Package *javax.net*, introduced in J2SE 1.4, contains factory classes for creating sockets in an implementation-independent fashion. Using classes from these packages (primarily from the former), the network programmer can communicate with any server on the Internet or implement his/her own Internet server.

2.1 The *InetAddress* Class

One of the classes within package *java.net* is called *InetAddress*, which handles Internet addresses both as host names and as IP addresses. Static method *getByName* of this class uses DNS (Domain Name System) to return the Internet address of a specified host name as an *InetAddress* object. In order to display the IP address from this object, we can simply use method *println* (which will cause the object's *toString* method to be executed). Since method *getByName* throws the checked exception

J. Graba, *An Introduction to Network Programming with Java: Java 7 Compatible*, DOI 10.1007/978-1-4471-5254-5_2, © Springer-Verlag London 2013

UnknownHostException if the host name is not recognised, we must either throw this exception or (preferably) handle it with a `catch` clause. The following example illustrates this.

Example

```
import java.net.*;
import java.util.*;

public class IPFinder
{
    public static void main(String[] args)
    {
        String host;
        Scanner input = new Scanner(System.in);
        InetAddress address;

        System.out.print("\n\nEnter host name: ");
        host = input.next();
        try
        {
            address = InetAddress.getByName(host);
            System.out.println("IP address: "
                                    + address.toString());
        }

        catch (UnknownHostException uhEx)
        {
            System.out.println("Could not find " + host);
        }
    }
}
```

The output from a test run of this program is shown in Fig. 2.1.

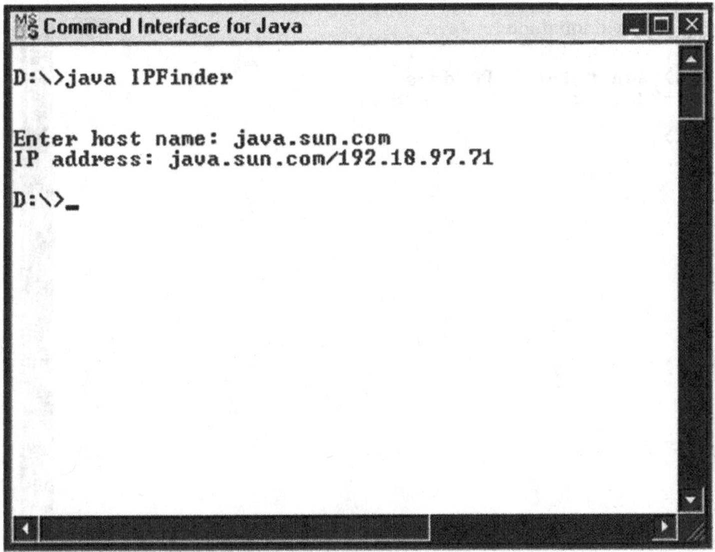

Fig. 2.1 Using method *getByName* to retrieve IP address of a specified host

It is sometimes useful for Java programs to be able to retrieve the IP address of the current machine. The example below shows how to do this.

Example

```
import java.net.*;

public class MyLocalIPAddress
{
    public static void main(String[] args)
    {
        try
        {
            InetAddress address =
                          InetAddress.getLocalHost();
            System.out.println(address);
        }
        catch (UnknownHostException uhEx)
        {
            System.out.println(
                       "Could not find local address!");
        }
    }
}
```

Output from this program when run on the author's office machine is shown in Fig. 2.2.

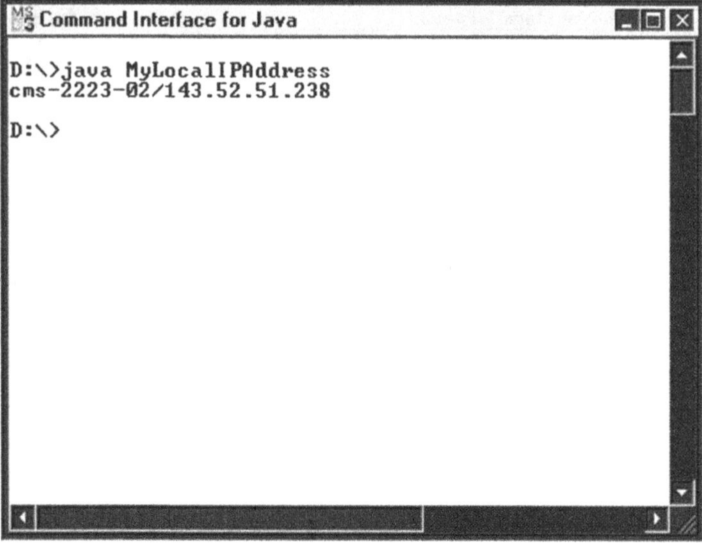

Fig. 2.2 Retrieving the current machine's IP address

2.2 Using Sockets

As described in Chap. 1, different processes (programs) can communicate with each other across networks by means of sockets. Java implements both **TCP/IP** sockets and **datagram** sockets (UDP sockets). Very often, the two communicating processes will have a *client/server* relationship. The steps required to create client/server programs via each of these methods are very similar and are outlined in the following two sub-sections.

2.2.1 TCP Sockets

A communication link created via TCP/IP sockets is a **connection-orientated** link. This means that the connection between server and client remains open throughout the duration of the dialogue between the two and is only broken (under normal circumstances) when one end of the dialogue formally terminates the exchanges (via an agreed protocol). Since there are two separate types of process involved (client and server), we shall examine them separately, taking the server first. Setting up a server process requires five steps…

1. Create a ServerSocket object.

The *ServerSocket* constructor requires a port number (1024–65535, for non-reserved ones) as an argument. For example:

```
ServerSocket serverSocket = new ServerSocket(1234);
```

In this example, the server will await ('listen for') a connection from a client on port 1234.

2. Put the server into a waiting state.
The server waits indefinitely ('blocks') for a client to connect. It does this by calling method *accept* of class *ServerSocket*, which returns a *Socket* object when a connection is made. For example:

```
Socket link = serverSocket.accept();
```

3. Set up input and output streams.
Methods *getInputStream* and *getOutputStream* of class *Socket* are used to get references to streams associated with the socket returned in step 2. These streams will be used for communication with the client that has just made connection. For a non-GUI application, we can wrap a *Scanner* object around the *InputStream* object returned by method *getInputStream*, in order to obtain string-orientated input (just as we would do with input from the standard input stream, *System.in*). For example:

```
Scanner input = new Scanner(link.getInputStream());
```

Similarly, we can wrap a *PrintWriter* object around the *OutputStream* object returned by method *getOutputStream*. Supplying the *PrintWriter* constructor with a second argument of `true` will cause the output buffer to be flushed for every call of *println* (which is usually desirable). For example:

```
PrintWriter output =
        new PrintWriter(link.getOutputStream(),true);
```

4. Send and receive data.
Having set up our *Scanner* and *PrintWriter* objects, sending and receiving data is very straightforward. We simply use method *nextLine* for receiving data and method *println* for sending data, just as we might do for console I/O. For example:

```
output.println("Awaiting data…");
String input = input.nextLine();
```

5. Close the connection (after completion of the dialogue).
This is achieved via method *close* of class *Socket*. For example:

```
link.close();
```

The following example program is used to illustrate the use of these steps.

Example

In this simple example, the server will accept messages from the client and will keep count of those messages, echoing back each (numbered) message. The main protocol for this service is that client and server must alternate between sending and receiving (with the client initiating the process with its opening message, of course). The only details that remain to be determined are the means of indicating when the dialogue is to cease and what final data (if any) should be sent by the server. For this simple example, the string "***CLOSE***" will be sent by the client when it wishes to close down the connection. When the server receives this message, it will confirm the number of preceding messages received and then close its connection to this client. The client, of course, must wait for the final message from the server before closing the connection at its own end.

Since an *IOException* may be generated by any of the socket operations, one or more `try` blocks must be used. Rather than have one large `try` block (with no variation in the error message produced and, consequently, no indication of precisely what operation caused the problem), it is probably good practice to have the opening of the port and the dialogue with the client in separate `try` blocks. It is also good practice to place the closing of the socket in a `finally` clause, so that, whether an exception occurs or not, the socket will be closed (unless, of course, the exception is generated when actually closing the socket, but there is nothing we can do about that). Since the `finally` clause will need to know about the *Socket* object, we shall have to declare this object within a scope that covers both the `try` block handling the dialogue and the `finally` block. Thus, step 2 shown above will be broken up into separate declaration and assignment. In our example program, this will also mean that the *Socket* object will have to be explicitly initialised to `null` (as it will not be a global variable).

Since a server offering a public service would keep running indefinitely, the call to method *handleClient* in our example has been placed inside an 'infinite' loop, thus:

```
do
{
    handleClient();
}while (true);
```

In the code that follows (and in later examples), port 1234 has been chosen for the service, but it could just as well have been any integer in the range 1024–65535. Note that the lines of code corresponding to each of the above steps have been clearly marked with emboldened comments.

```
//Server that echoes back client's messages.
//At end of dialogue, sends message indicating
//number of messages received. Uses TCP.

import java.io.*;
import java.net.*;
import java.util.*;

public class TCPEchoServer
{
   private static ServerSocket serverSocket;
   private static final int PORT = 1234;

   public static void main(String[] args)
```

```
{
   System.out.println("Opening port…\n");
   try
   {
     serverSocket = new ServerSocket(PORT);//Step 1.
   }
   catch(IOException ioEx)
   {
      System.out.println(
                       "Unable to attach to port!");
      System.exit(1);
   }
   do
   {
      handleClient();
   }while (true);
}

private static void handleClient()
{
   Socket link = null;                         //Step 2.

   try
   {

      link = serverSocket.accept();             //Step 2.

      Scanner input =
        new Scanner(link.getInputStream());//Step 3.
      PrintWriter output =
           new PrintWriter(
             link.getOutputStream(),true); //Step 3.

      int numMessages = 0;
      String message = input.nextLine();    //Step 4.
      while (!message.equals("***CLOSE***"))
      {

         System.out.println("Message received.");
         numMessages++;
         output.println("Message " + numMessages
                             + ": " + message); //Step 4.
         message = input.nextLine();
      }
      output.println(numMessages
                   + " messages received.");//Step 4.
   }
```

```
        catch(IOException ioEx)
        {
             ioEx.printStackTrace();
        }
        finally
        {
           try
           {
              System.out.println(
                          "\n* Closing connection... *");
              link.close();                          //Step 5.
           }
           catch(IOException ioEx)
           {
               System.out.println(
                              "Unable to disconnect!");
             System.exit(1);
           }
        }
    }
}
```

Setting up the corresponding client involves four steps…

1. Establish a connection to the server.
We create a *Socket* object, supplying its constructor with the following two arguments:

- the server's IP address (of type *InetAddress*);
- the appropriate port number for the service.
  (The port number for server and client programs must be the same, of course!)

For simplicity's sake, we shall place client and server on the same host, which will allow us to retrieve the IP address by calling static method *getLocalHost* of class *InetAddress*. For example:

```
Socket link =
        new Socket(InetAddress.getLocalHost(),1234);
```

2. Set up input and output streams.
These are set up in exactly the same way as the server streams were set up (by calling methods *getInputStream* and *getOutputStream* of the *Socket* object that was created in step 2).

3. Send and receive data.
The *Scanner* object at the client end will receive messages sent by the *PrintWriter* object at the server end, while the *PrintWriter* object at the client end will send messages that are received by the *Scanner* object at the server end (using methods *nextLine* and *println* respectively).

4. Close the connection.
This is exactly the same as for the server process (using method *close* of class *Socket*).

The code below shows the client program for our example. In addition to an input stream to accept messages from the server, our client program will need to set up an input stream (as another *Scanner* object) to accept user messages from the keyboard. As for the server, the lines of code corresponding to each of the above steps have been clearly marked with emboldened comments.

```
import java.io.*;
import java.net.*;
import java.util.*;

public class TCPEchoClient
{
    private static InetAddress host;
    private static final int PORT = 1234;

    public static void main(String[] args)
    {
        try
        {
            host = InetAddress.getLocalHost();
        }
        catch(UnknownHostException uhEx)
        {
            System.out.println("Host ID not found!");
            System.exit(1);
        }
        accessServer();
    }
    private static void accessServer()
    {
        Socket link = null;                           //Step 1.

        try
        {
           link = new Socket(host,PORT);         //Step 1.

           Scanner input =
              new Scanner(link.getInputStream());
                                                      //Step 2.
           PrintWriter output =
              new PrintWriter(
                link.getOutputStream(),true);    //Step 2.

           //Set up stream for keyboard entry...
           Scanner userEntry = new Scanner(System.in);
```

```
            String message, response;
            do
            {
                System.out.print("Enter message: ");
                message = userEntry.nextLine();
                output.println(message);        //Step 3.
                response = input.nextLine();   //Step 3.
                System.out.println("\nSERVER> "+response);
            }while (!message.equals("***CLOSE***"));
        }
        catch(IOException ioEx)
        {
            ioEx.printStackTrace();
        }

        finally
        {
            try
            {
                System.out.println(
                            "\n* Closing connection... *");
                link.close();                    //Step 4.
            }
            catch(IOException ioEx)
            {
                System.out.println(
                              "Unable to disconnect!");
                System.exit(1);
            }
        }
    }
}
```

For the preceding client–server application to work, TCP/IP must be installed and working. How are you to know whether this is the case for your machine? Well, if there is a working Internet connection on your machine, then TCP/IP **is** running. In order to start the application, first open two command windows and then start the server running in one window and the client in the other. (Make sure that the server is running first, in order to avoid having the client program crash!) The example screenshots in Figs. 2.3 and 2.4 show the dialogues between the server and two consecutive clients for this application. Note that, in order to stop the TCPEchoServer program, Ctrl-C has to be entered from the keyboard.

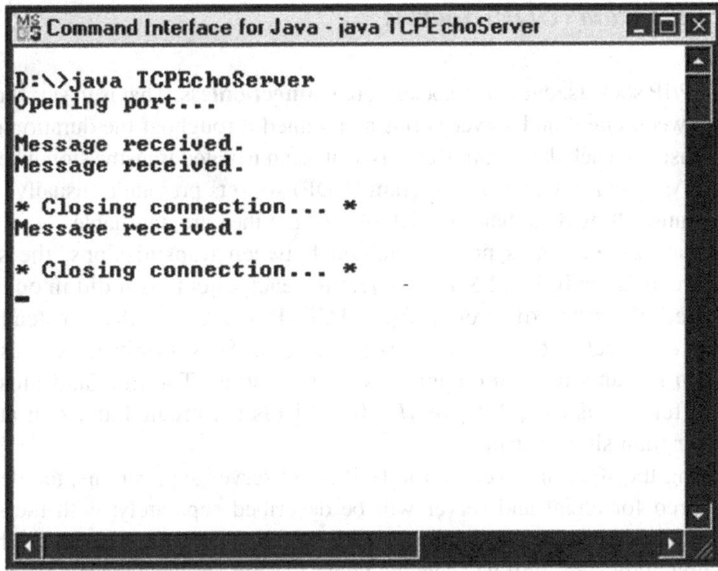

Fig. 2.3 Example output from the TCPEchoServer program

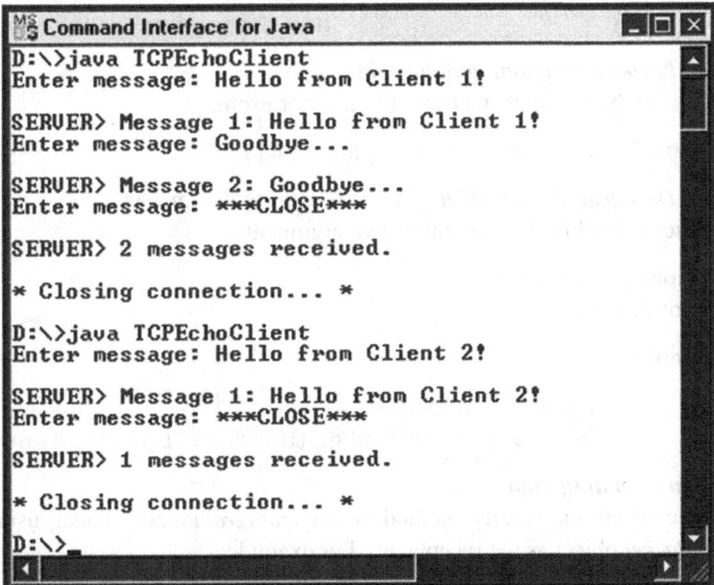

Fig. 2.4 Example output from the TCPEchoClient program

2.2.2 Datagram (UDP) Sockets

Unlike TCP/IP sockets, datagram sockets are **connectionless**. That is to say, the connection between client and server is **not** maintained throughout the duration of the dialogue. Instead, each datagram packet is sent as an isolated transmission whenever necessary. As noted in Chap. 1, datagram (UDP) sockets provide a (usually) faster means of transmitting data than TCP/IP sockets, but they are unreliable.

Since the connection is not maintained between transmissions, the server does not create an individual *Socket* object for each client, as it did in our TCP/IP example. A further difference from TCP/IP sockets is that, instead of a *ServerSocket* object, the server creates a *DatagramSocket* object, as does each client when it wants to send datagram(s) to the server. The final and most significant difference is that *DatagramPacket* objects are created and sent at both ends, rather than simple strings.

Following the style of coverage for TCP client/server applications, the detailed steps required for client and server will be described separately, with the server process being covered first. This process involves the following nine steps, though only the first eight steps will be executed under normal circumstances…

1. Create a DatagramSocket object.
Just as for the creation of a *ServerSocket* object, this means supplying the object's constructor with the port number. For example:

```
DatagramSocket datagramSocket =
                        new DatagramSocket(1234);
```

2. Create a buffer for incoming datagrams.
This is achieved by creating an array of bytes. For example:

```
byte[] buffer = new byte[256];
```

3. Create a DatagramPacket object for the incoming datagrams.
The constructor for this object requires two arguments:

- the previously-created byte array;
- the size of this array.

For example:

```
DatagramPacket inPacket =
        new DatagramPacket(buffer, buffer.length);
```

4. Accept an incoming datagram.
This is effected via the *receive* method of our *DatagramSocket* object, using our *DatagramPacket* object as the receptacle. For example:

```
datagramSocket.receive(inPacket);
```

5. Accept the sender's address and port from the packet.

Methods *getAddress* and *getPort* of our *DatagramPacket* object are used for this. For example:

```
InetAddress clientAddress = inPacket.getAddress();
int clientPort = inPacket.getPort();
```

6. Retrieve the data from the buffer.

For convenience of handling, the data will be retrieved as a string, using an overloaded form of the *String* constructor that takes three arguments:

- a byte array;
- the start position within the array (= 0 here);
- the number of bytes (= full size of buffer here).

For example:

```
String message =  new String(inPacket.getData(),
                            0,inPacket.getLength());
```

7. Create the response datagram.

Create a *DatagramPacket* object, using an overloaded form of the constructor that takes four arguments:

- the byte array containing the response message;
- the size of the response;
- the client's address;
- the client's port number.

The first of these arguments is returned by the *getBytes* method of the *String* class (acting on the desired *String* response). For example:

```
DatagramPacket outPacket =
   new DatagramPacket(response.getBytes(),
     response.length(),clientAddress, clientPort);
```

(Here, *response* is a *String* variable holding the return message.)

8. Send the response datagram.

This is achieved by calling method *send* of our *DatagramSocket* object, supplying our outgoing *DatagramPacket* object as an argument. For example:

```
datagramSocket.send(outPacket);
```

Steps 4–8 may be executed indefinitely (within a loop).

Under normal circumstances, the server would probably not be closed down at all. However, if an exception occurs, then the associated *DatagramSocket* should be closed, as shown in step 9 below.

9. Close the DatagramSocket.

This is effected simply by calling method *close* of our *DatagramSocket* object. For example:

```
datagramSocket.close();
```

To illustrate the above procedure and to allow easy comparison with the equivalent TCP/IP code, the example from Sect. 2.2.1 will be employed again. As before, the lines of code corresponding to each of the above steps are indicated via emboldened comments. Note that the *numMessages* part of the message that is returned by the server is somewhat artificial, since, in a real-world application, many clients could be making connection and the overall message numbers would not mean a great deal to individual clients. However, the cumulative message-numbering will serve to emphasise that there are no separate sockets for individual clients.

There are two other differences from the equivalent TCP/IP code that are worth noting, both concerning the possible exceptions that may be generated:

- the *IOException* in *main* is replaced with a *SocketException*;
- there is no checked exception generated by the *close* method in the `finally` clause, so there is no `try` block.

Now for the code…

```
//Server that echoes back client's messages.
//At end of dialogue, sends message indicating number of
//messages received. Uses datagrams.

import java.io.*;
import java.net.*;

public class UDPEchoServer
{
     private static final int PORT = 1234;
     private static DatagramSocket datagramSocket;
     private static DatagramPacket inPacket, outPacket;
     private static byte[] buffer;

     public static void main(String[] args)
     {
          System.out.println("Opening port…\n");
          try
          {
             datagramSocket =
                  new DatagramSocket(PORT);
                                                  //Step 1.
          }
          catch(SocketException sockEx)
          {
             System.out.println("Unable to open port!");
             System.exit(1);
          }
          handleClient();
     }
```

```
private static void handleClient()
{
    try
    {
        String messageIn,messageOut;
        int numMessages = 0;
        InetAddress clientAddress = null;
        int clientPort;

        do
        {
            buffer = new byte[256];          //Step 2.
            inPacket =
                new DatagramPacket(
                    buffer, buffer.length);
                                             //Step 3.
            datagramSocket.receive(inPacket);
                                             //Step 4.

            clientAddress = inPacket.getAddress();
                                             //Step 5.

            clientPort = inPacket.getPort();
                                             //Step 5.

            messageIn =
                new String(inPacket.getData(),
                    0,inPacket.getLength());
                                             //Step 6.

            System.out.println("Message received.");
            numMessages++;
            messageOut = "Message " + numMessages
                           + ": " + messageIn;
            outPacket =
             new DatagramPacket(messageOut.getBytes(),
                messageOut.length(),clientAddress,
                  clientPort);               //Step 7.
            datagramSocket.send(outPacket); //Step 8.
        }while (true);
    }
    catch(IOException ioEx)
      {
        ioEx.printStackTrace();
      }
```

```
            finally    //If exception thrown, close
                                              connection.
            {
               System.out.println(
                           "\n* Closing connection... *");
               datagramSocket.close();          //Step 9.
            }
      }
}
```

Setting up the corresponding client requires the eight steps listed below.

1. Create a DatagramSocket object.
This is similar to the creation of a DatagramSocket object in the server program, but with the important difference that the constructor here requires no argument, since a default port (at the client end) will be used. For example:

```
DatagramSocket datagramSocket = new DatagramSocket();
```

2. Create the outgoing datagram.
This step is exactly as for step 7 of the server program. For example:

```
DatagramPacket outPacket =
       new DatagramPacket(message.getBytes(),
               message.length(), host, PORT);
```

3. Send the datagram message.
Just as for the server, this is achieved by calling method *send* of the *DatagramSocket* object, supplying our outgoing *DatagramPacket* object as an argument. For example:

```
datagramSocket.send(outPacket);
```

Steps 4–6 below are exactly the same as steps 2–4 of the server procedure.

4. Create a buffer for incoming datagrams.
For example:

```
byte[] buffer = new byte[256];
```

5. Create a DatagramPacket object for the incoming datagrams.
For example:

```
DatagramPacket inPacket =
        new DatagramPacket(buffer, buffer.length);
```

6. Accept an incoming datagram.
For example:

```
datagramSocket.receive(inPacket);
```

7. Retrieve the data from the buffer.
This is the same as step 6 in the server program. For example:

```
String response =
            new String(inPacket.getData(),0,
                              inPacket.getLength());
```

Steps 2–7 may then be repeated as many times as required.

8. Close the DatagramSocket.
This is the same as step 9 in the server program. For example:

```
datagramSocket.close();
```

As was the case in the server code, there is no checked exception generated by the above *close* method in the `finally` clause of the client program, so there will be no `try` block. In addition, since there is no inter-message connection maintained between client and server, there is no protocol required for closing down the dialogue. This means that we do not wish to send the final '***CLOSE***' string (though we shall continue to accept this from the user, since we need to know when to stop sending messages at the client end). The line of code (singular, this time) corresponding to each of the above steps will be indicated via an emboldened comment.

Now for the code itself…

```
import java.io.*;
import java.net.*;
import java.util.*;

public class UDPEchoClient
{
    private static InetAddress host;
    private static final int PORT = 1234;
    private static DatagramSocket datagramSocket;
    private static DatagramPacket inPacket, outPacket;
    private static byte[] buffer;

    public static void main(String[] args)
    {
        try
        {
            host = InetAddress.getLocalHost();
        }
        catch(UnknownHostException uhEx)
        {
            System.out.println("Host ID not found!");
            System.exit(1);
        }
```

```
        accessServer();
    }
    private static void accessServer()
    {
        try
        {
            //Step 1...
            datagramSocket = new DatagramSocket();

            //Set up stream for keyboard entry...
            Scanner userEntry = new Scanner(System.in);

            String message="", response="";
            do
            {
                System.out.print("Enter message: ");
                message = userEntry.nextLine();
                if (!message.equals("***CLOSE***"))
                {
                    outPacket = new DatagramPacket(
                                message.getBytes(),
                                message.length(),
                                host,PORT);
                                                  //Step 2.
                    //Step 3...
                    datagramSocket.send(outPacket);
                    buffer = new byte[256];   //Step 4.
                    inPacket =
                     new DatagramPacket(
                     buffer, buffer.length);//Step 5.
                    //Step 6...
                    datagramSocket.receive(inPacket);
                    response =
                     new String(inPacket.getData(),
                       0, inPacket.getLength());
                                                  //Step 7.
                    System.out.println(
                                "\nSERVER> "+response);
                }
            }while (!message.equals("***CLOSE***"));
        }
        catch(IOException ioEx)
        {
            ioEx.printStackTrace();
        }
```

```
        finally
        {
              System.out.println(
                          "\n* Closing connection... *");
              datagramSocket.close();
                                                  //Step 8.
        }
    }
}
```

For the preceding application to work, UDP must be installed and working on the host machine. As for TCP/IP, if there is a working Internet connection on the machine, then UDP **is** running. Once again, in order to start the application, first open two command windows and then start the server running in one window and the client in the other. (Start the server *before* the client!) As before, the example screenshots in Figs. 2.5 and 2.6 show the dialogues between the server and two clients. Observe the differences in output between this example and the corresponding TCP/IP example. (Note that the change at the client end is simply the rather subtle one of cumulative message-numbering.)

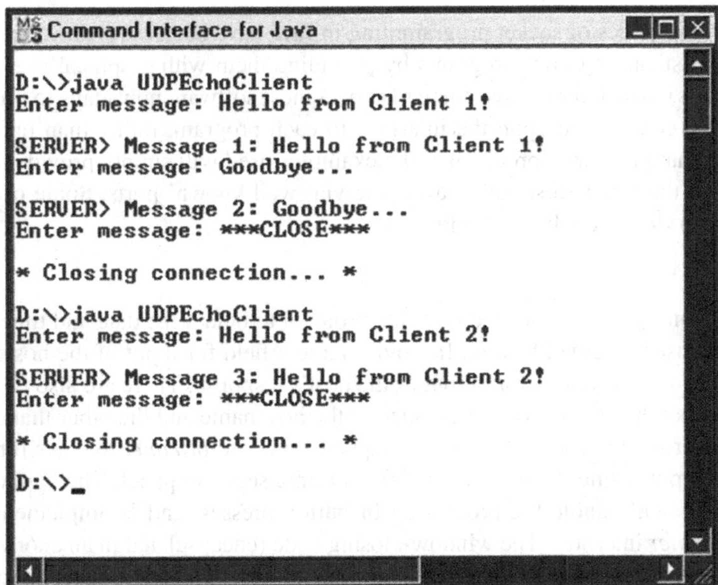

Fig. 2.6 Example output from the UDPEchoClient program (with two clients connecting separately)

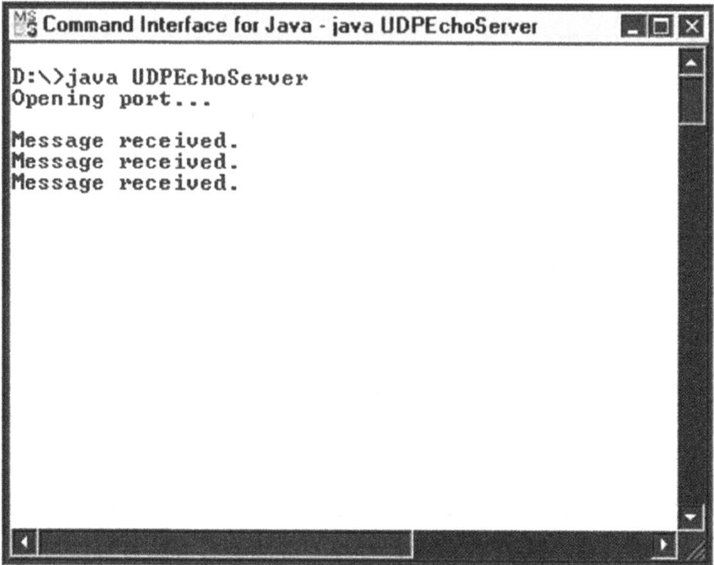

Fig. 2.5 Example output from the UDPEchoServer program

2.3 Network Programming with GUIs

Now that the basics of socket programming in Java have been covered, we can add some sophistication to our programs by providing them with graphical user interfaces (GUIs), which users have come to expect most software nowadays to provide. In order to concentrate upon the interface to each program, rather than upon the details of that program's processing, the examples used will simply provide access to some of the standard services, available via 'well known' ports. Some of these standard services were listed in Fig. 1.1.

<u>Example</u>

The following program uses the *Daytime* protocol to obtain the date and time from port 13 of user-specified host(s). It provides a text field for input of the host name by the user and a text area for output of the host's response. There are also two buttons, one that the user presses after entry of the host name and the other that closes down the program. The text area is 'wrapped' in a *JScrollPane*, to cater for long lines of output, while the buttons are laid out on a separate panel. The application frame itself will handle the processing of button presses, and so implements the *ActionListener* interface. The window-closing code (encapsulated in an anonymous *WindowAdapter* object) ensures that any socket that has been opened is closed before exit from the program.

```
import java.awt.*;
import java.awt.event.*;
```

```
import javax.swing.*;
import java.net.*;
import java.io.*;
import java.util.*;

public class GetRemoteTime extends JFrame
                    implements ActionListener
{
     private JTextField hostInput;
     private JTextArea display;
     private JButton timeButton;
     private JButton exitButton;
     private JPanel buttonPanel;
     private static Socket socket = null;

     public static void main(String[] args)
     {
          GetRemoteTime frame = new GetRemoteTime();
          frame.setSize(400,300);
          frame.setVisible(true);

          frame.addWindowListener(
              new WindowAdapter()
              {
                  public void windowClosing(
                                    WindowEvent event)
                  {
                       //Check whether a socket is open…
                       if (socket != null)
                       {
                             try
                             {
                                 socket.close();
                             }
                             catch (IOException ioEx)
                             {
                                System.out.println(
                                      "\nUnable to close
                                              link!\n");
                                System.exit(1);
                             }
                         }
                         System.exit(0);
                  }
              }
          );
     }
```

```
    public GetRemoteTime()
    {
        hostInput = new JTextField(20);
        add(hostInput, BorderLayout.NORTH);

        display = new JTextArea(10,15);

        //Following two lines ensure that word-wrapping
        //occurs within the JTextArea…
        display.setWrapStyleWord(true);
        display.setLineWrap(true);

        add(new JScrollPane(display),
                          BorderLayout.CENTER);

        buttonPanel = new JPanel();

        timeButton = new JButton("Get date and time ");
        timeButton.addActionListener(this);
        buttonPanel.add(timeButton);

        exitButton = new JButton("Exit");
        exitButton.addActionListener(this);
        buttonPanel.add(exitButton);

        add(buttonPanel,BorderLayout.SOUTH);
    }

    public void actionPerformed(ActionEvent event)
    {
        if (event.getSource() == exitButton)
           System.exit(0);

        String theTime;

        //Accept host name from the user…
        String host = hostInput.getText();
        final int DAYTIME_PORT = 13;

        try
        {
            //Create a Socket object to connect to the
            //specified host on the relevant port…
            socket = new Socket(host, DAYTIME_PORT);

            //Create an input stream for the above Socket
            //and add string-reading functionality…
            Scanner input =
                 new Scanner(socket.getInputStream());

            //Accept the host's response via the
```

```
            //above stream...
            theTime = input.nextLine();

            //Add the host's response to the text in
            //the JTextArea...
            display.append("The date/time at " + host
                            + " is " + theTime + "\n");
            hostInput.setText("");
        }
        catch (UnknownHostException uhEx)
        {
          display.append("No such host!\n");
          hostInput.setText("");
        }
        catch (IOException ioEx)
        {
          display.append(ioEx.toString() + "\n");
        }

        finally
        {
          try
          {
             if (socket!=null)
                 socket.close(); //Close link to host.
          }
          catch(IOException ioEx)
          {
               System.out.println(
                             "Unable to disconnect!");
               System.exit(1);
            }
         }
      }
   }
```

If we run this program and enter *ivy.shu.ac.uk* as our host name in the client's GUI, the result will look something like that shown in Fig. 2.7.

Unfortunately, it is rather difficult nowadays to find a host that is running the *Daytime* protocol. Even if one does find such a host, it may be that the user's own firewall blocks the output from the remote server. If this is the case, then the user will be unaware of this until the connection times out—which may take some time! The user is advised to terminate the program (with Ctrl-C) if the waiting time appears to be excessive. One possible way round this problem is to write one's own 'daytime server'…

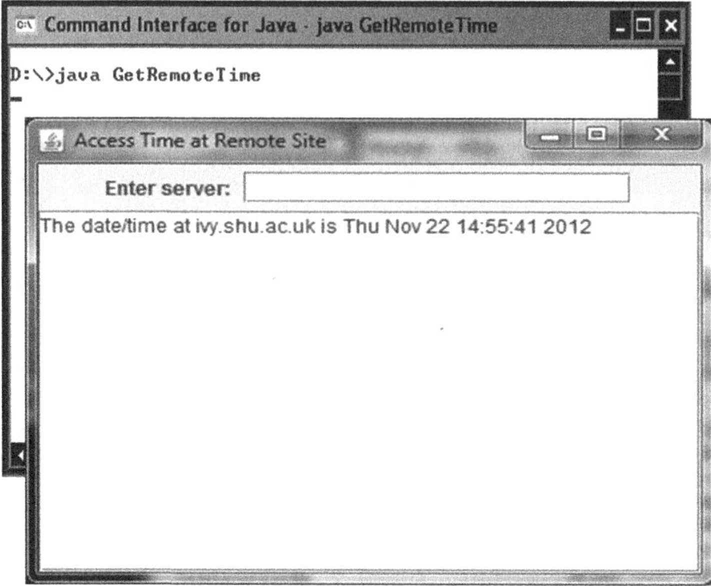

Fig. 2.7 Example output from the GetRemoteTime program

To illustrate just how easy it is to provide a server that implements the *Daytime* protocol, example code for such a server is shown below. The program makes use of class *Date* from package *java.util* to create a *Date* object that will automatically hold the current day, date and time on the server's host machine. To output the date held in the *Date* object, we can simply use *println* on the object and its *toString* method will be executed implicitly (though we could specify *toString* explicitly, if we wished).

```
import java.net.*;
import java.io.*;
import java.util.Date;
public class DaytimeServer
{
   public static void main(String[] args)
   {
      ServerSocket server;
      final int DAYTIME_PORT = 13;
      Socket socket;

      try
      {
         server = new ServerSocket(DAYTIME_PORT);

         do
```

```
            {
               socket = server.accept();
               PrintWriter output =
                     new PrintWriter(
                          socket.getOutputStream(),true);
               Date date = new Date();
               output.println(date);
               //Method toString executed in line above.

               socket.close();
            }while (true);
         }
         catch (IOException ioEx)
         {
            System.out.println(ioEx);
         }
      }
   }
```

The server simply sends the date and time as a string and then closes the connection. If we run the client and server in separate command windows and enter *localhost* as our host name in the client's GUI, the result should look similar to that shown in Fig. 2.7. Unfortunately, there is still a potential problem on some systems: since a low-numbered port (i.e., below 1024) is being used, the user may not have sufficient system rights to make use of the port. The solution in such circumstances is simple: change the port number (in both server and client) to a value above 1024. (E.g., change the value of *DAYTIME_PORT* from 13 to 1300.)

Now for an example that checks a range of ports on a specified host and reports on those ports that are providing a service. This works by the program trying to create a socket on each port number in turn. If a socket is created successfully, then there is an open port; otherwise, an *IOException* is thrown (and ignored by the program, which simply provides an empty `catch` clause). The program creates a text field for acceptance of the required URL(s) and sets this to an initial default value. It also provides a text area for the program's output and buttons for checking the ports and for exiting the program.

```
import java.awt.*;
import java.awt.event.*;
import javax.swing.*;
import java.net.*;
import java.io.*;

public class PortScanner extends JFrame
                            implements ActionListener
```

```
{
   private JLabel prompt;
   private JTextField hostInput;
   private JTextArea report;
   private JButton seekButton, exitButton;
   private JPanel hostPanel, buttonPanel;
   private static Socket socket = null;

   public static void main(String[] args)
   {
      PortScanner frame = new PortScanner();

      frame.setSize(400,300);
      frame.setVisible(true);
      frame.addWindowListener(
          new WindowAdapter()
          {
              public void windowClosing(
                                      WindowEvent event)
              {
                 //Check whether a socket is open…
                 if (socket != null)
                 {
                    try
                    {
                       socket.close();
                    }
                    catch (IOException ioEx)
                    {
                       System.out.println(
                         "\nUnable to close link!\n");
                       System.exit(1);
                    }
                 }
                 System.exit(0);
              }
          }
      );
   }
   public PortScanner()
   {
       hostPanel = new JPanel();

       prompt = new JLabel("Host name: ");
       hostInput = new JTextField("ivy.shu.ac.uk", 25);
       hostPanel.add(prompt);
```

```
        hostPanel.add(hostInput);
        add(hostPanel,BorderLayout.NORTH);

        report = new JTextArea(10,25);
        add(report,BorderLayout.CENTER);

        buttonPanel = new JPanel();

        seekButton = new JButton("Seek server ports ");
        seekButton.addActionListener(this);
        buttonPanel.add(seekButton);

        exitButton = new JButton("Exit");
        exitButton.addActionListener(this);
        buttonPanel.add(exitButton);

        add(buttonPanel,BorderLayout.SOUTH);
    }
    public void actionPerformed(ActionEvent event)
    {
        if (event.getSource() == exitButton)
            System.exit(0);
        //Must have been the 'seek' button that was
        //pressed, so clear the output area of any
        //previous output…
        report.setText("");

        //Retrieve the URL from the input text field…
        String host = hostInput.getText();

        try
        {
            //Convert the URL string into an INetAddress
            //object…
            InetAddress theAddress =
                          InetAddress.getByName(host);
            report.append("IP address: "
                               + theAddress + "\n");

            for (int i = 0; i < 25; i++)
            {

                try
                {
                    //Attempt to establish a socket on
                    //port i…
                    socket = new Socket(host, i);
                    //If no IOException thrown, there must
                    //be a service running on the port…
```

```
                    report.append(
                          "There is a server on port "
                                           + i + ".\n");
                    socket.close();
                }
                catch (IOException ioEx)
                {}// No server on this port
            }
        }
        catch (UnknownHostException uhEx)
        {
            report.setText("Unknown host!");
        }
    }
}
```

When the above program was run for the default server (which is on the author's local network), the output from the GUI was as shown in Fig. 2.8. Unfortunately, remote users' firewalls may block output from most of the ports for this default server (or any other remote server), causing the program to wait for each of these port accesses to time out. This is likely to take a **very** long time indeed! The reader is strongly advised to use a local server for the testing of this program (and to get clearance from your system administrator for port scanning, to be on the safe side). Even when running the program with a suitable local server, **be patient** when waiting for output, since this may take a minute or so, depending upon your system.

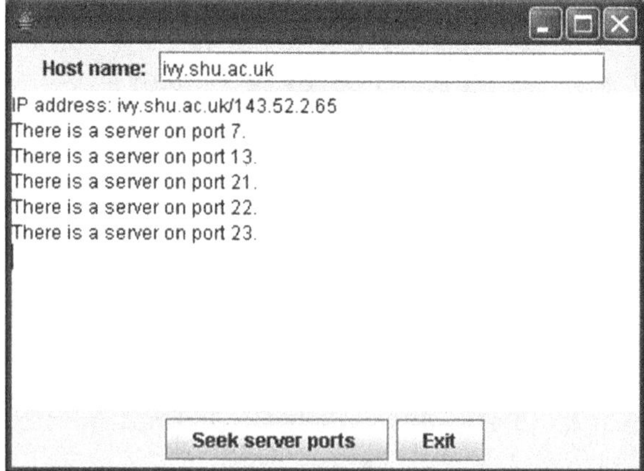

Fig. 2.8 Example output from the PortScanner program

Exercises

2.1 If you haven't already done so, compile programs *TCPEchoServer* and *TCPEchoClient* from Sect. 2.2.1 and then run them as described at the end of that section.

2.2 This exercise converts the above files into a simple email server and email client respectively. The server conversion has been done for you and is contained in file *EmailServer.java*, a printed version of which appears on the following pages for ease of reference. Some of the code for the client has also been provided for you and is held in file *EmailClient.java*, a printed version of which is also provided.

You are to complete the coding for the client and then run the server program in one command window and the client program **consecutively** in each of two further command windows. For the first client, log in with one of the names specified below (i.e., 'Dave' or 'Karen') and send a few emails (fewer than 10) to the other user. Then quit and run the client program again, this time logging in as the other user and selecting reading of his/her emails. The full details of this simplified client–server application are given below.

- The server recognises only two users, called 'Dave' and 'Karen'.
- Each of the above users has a message box on the server that can accept a maximum of 10 messages.
- Each user may either send a one-line message to the other or read his/her own messages.
- A count is kept of the number of messages in each mailbox. As another message is received, the appropriate count is incremented (if the maximum has not been reached). When messages are read, the appropriate count is reduced to zero.
- When sending a message, the client sends three things: the user's name, the word 'send' and the message itself.
- When requesting reading of mail, the client sends two things: the user's name and the word 'read'.
- As each message is received by the server, it is added to the appropriate mailbox (if there is room). If the mailbox is full, the message is ignored.
- When a read request is received, the server first sends an integer indicating the number of messages (possibly 0) that will be sent and then transmits the messages themselves (after which it reduces the appropriate message count to 0).
- Each user is to be allowed to 'send' and/or 'read' as many times as he/she wishes, until he/she decides to quit.
- When the user selects the 'quit' option, the client sends two things: the user's name and then the word 'quit'.

2.3 If you haven't already done so, compile and run the server program *DayTimeServer* and its associated client, *GetRemoteTime*, from Sect. 2.3.

2.4 Program *Echo* is similar to program *TCPEchoClient* from Sect. 2.2.1, but has a GUI front-end similar to that of program *GetRemoteTime* from Sect. 2.3. It provides an implementation of the **echo** protocol (on port 7). This implementation sends one-line messages to a server and uses the following components:

- a text field for input of messages (in addition to the text field for input of host name);
- a text area for the (cumulative) echoed responses from the server;
- a button to close the connection to the host.

Some of the code for this program has been provided for you in file *Echo.java*, a printed copy of which appears at the end of this chapter. Examine this code and make the necessary additions in the places indicated by the commented lines. When you have completed the program, run it and supply the name of any convenient server when prompted for a server name. If you don't have access to a convenient server use *localhost*, having changed the port number of *TCPEchoServer* (Sect. 2.2.1) to 7 and then started that program running.

```
//For use with exercise 2.2.

import java.io.*;
import java.net.*;
import java.util.*;

public class EmailServer
{
   private static ServerSocket serverSocket;
   private static final int PORT = 1234;
   private static final String client1 = "Dave";
   private static final String client2 = "Karen";
   private static final int MAX_MESSAGES = 10;
   private static String[] mailbox1 =
                              new String[MAX_MESSAGES];
   private static String[] mailbox2 =
                              new String[MAX_MESSAGES];
   private static int messagesInBox1 = 0;
   private static int messagesInBox2 = 0;
   public static void main(String[] args)
   {
      System.out.println("Opening connection…\n");
      try
      {
         serverSocket = new ServerSocket(PORT);
      }
      catch(IOException ioEx)
```

```
    {
       System.out.println(
                   "Unable to attach to port!");
       System.exit(1);
    }
    do
    {
       try
       {
          runService();
       }
       catch (InvalidClientException icException)
       {
         System.out.println("Error: " + icException);
       }
       catch (InvalidRequestException irException)
       {
         System.out.println("Error: " + irException);
       }
    }while (true);
 }

 private static void runService()
                   throws InvalidClientException,
                          InvalidRequestException
 {
    try
    {
       Socket link = serverSocket.accept();

       Scanner input =
               new Scanner(link.getInputStream());
       PrintWriter output =
           new PrintWriter(
                     link.getOutputStream(),true);

       String name = input.nextLine();
       String sendRead = input.nextLine();
       if (!name.equals(client1) &&
                            !name.equals(client2))
          throw new InvalidClientException();
       if (!sendRead.equals("send") &&
                            !sendRead.equals("read"))
          throw new InvalidRequestException();
       System.out.println("\n" + name + " "
                         + sendRead + "ing mail…");
       if (name.equals(client1))
```

```
            {
               if (sendRead.equals("send"))
               {
                  doSend(mailbox2,messagesInBox2,input);
                  if (messagesInBox2<MAX_MESSAGES)
                     messagesInBox2++;
               }
               else
               {
                  doRead(mailbox1,messagesInBox1,output);
                  messagesInBox1 = 0;
               }
            }
            else   //From client2.
            {
               if (sendRead.equals("send"))
               {
                  doSend(mailbox1,messagesInBox1,input);
                  if (messagesInBox1<MAX_MESSAGES)
                        messagesInBox1++;
               }
               else
               {
                  doRead(mailbox2,messagesInBox2,output);
                  messagesInBox2 = 0;
               }
            }
            link.close();
         }
         catch(IOException ioEx)
         {
            ioEx.printStackTrace();
         }
      }

      private static void doSend(String[] mailbox,
                        int messagesInBox, Scanner input)
      {
         /*
         Client has requested 'sending', so server must
         read message from this client and then place
         message into message box for other client (if
         there is room).
         */
```

```
      String message = input.nextLine();
      if (messagesInBox == MAX_MESSAGES)
         System.out.println("\nMessage box full!");
      else
         mailbox[messagesInBox] = message;
   }

   private static void doRead(String[] mailbox,
                 int messagesInBox, PrintWriter output)
   {
      /*
      Client has requested 'reading', so server must
      read messages from other client's message box and
      then send those messages to the first client.
      */
      System.out.println("\nSending " + messagesInBox
                                 + " message(s).\n");
      output.println(messagesInBox);
      for (int i=0; i<messagesInBox; i++)
         output.println(mailbox[i]);
   }
}

class InvalidClientException extends Exception
{
   public InvalidClientException()
   {
      super("Invalid client name!");
   }
   public InvalidClientException(String message)
   {
      super(message);
   }
}
class InvalidRequestException extends Exception
{
   public InvalidRequestException()
   {
      super("Invalid request!");
   }
   public InvalidRequestException(String message)
   {
      super(message);
   }
}
```

```
//For use with exercise 2.2.

import java.io.*;
import java.net.*;
import java.util.*;

public class EmailClient
{
   private static InetAddress host;
   private static final int PORT = 1234;
   private static String name;
   private static Scanner networkInput, userEntry;
   private static PrintWriter networkOutput;

   public static void main(String[] args)
                                  throws IOException
   {
      try
      {
         host = InetAddress.getLocalHost();
      }
      catch(UnknownHostException uhEx)
      {
         System.out.println("Host ID not found!");
         System.exit(1);
      }

      userEntry = new Scanner(System.in);
      do
      {
         System.out.print(
                 "\nEnter name ('Dave' or 'Karen'): ");
         name = userEntry.nextLine();
      }while (!name.equals("Dave")
                          && !name.equals("Karen"));
      talkToServer();
   }
   private static void talkToServer() throws IOException
   {
      String option, message, response;

      do
      {
/*******************************************************
    CREATE A SOCKET, SET UP INPUT AND OUTPUT STREAMS,
    ACCEPT THE USER'S REQUEST, CALL UP THE APPROPRIATE
    METHOD (doSend OR doRead), CLOSE THE LINK AND THEN
```

```
    ASK IF USER WANTS TO DO ANOTHER READ/SEND.
*****************************************************/
      }while (!option.equals("n"));

   }

   private static void doSend()
   {
      System.out.println("\nEnter 1-line message: ");
      String message = userEntry.nextLine();
      networkOutput.println(name);
      networkOutput.println("send");
      networkOutput.println(message);
   }

   private static void doRead() throws IOException
   {

      /*********************************
      BODY OF THIS METHOD REQUIRED
      *********************************/

   }
}
```

```
//For use with exercise 2.4.

import java.awt.*;
import java.awt.event.*;
import javax.swing.*;
import java.net.*;
import java.io.*;
import java.util.*;

public class Echo extends JFrame
                              implements ActionListener
 {
   private JTextField hostInput,lineToSend;
   private JLabel hostPrompt,messagePrompt;
   private JTextArea received;
   private JButton closeConnection;
   private JPanel hostPanel,entryPanel;
   private final int ECHO = 7;
   private static Socket socket = null;
   private Scanner input;
   private PrintWriter output;

   public static void main(String[] args)
```

```
{
   Echo frame = new Echo();
   frame.setSize(600,400);
   frame.setVisible(true);

   frame.addWindowListener(
      new WindowAdapter()
      {
         public void windowClosing(WindowEvent e)
         {
            if (socket != null)
            {
               try
               {
                  socket.close();
               }
               catch (IOException ioEx)
               {
                  System.out.println(
                   "\n* Unable to close link! *\n");
                  System.exit(1);
               }
               System.exit(0);
            }
         }
      }
   );
}

public Echo()
{
   hostPanel = new JPanel();

   hostPrompt = new JLabel("Enter host name:");
   hostInput = new JTextField(20);
   hostInput.addActionListener(this);
   hostPanel.add(hostPrompt);
   hostPanel.add(hostInput);
   add(hostPanel, BorderLayout.NORTH);
   entryPanel = new JPanel();

   messagePrompt = new JLabel("Enter text:");
   lineToSend = new JTextField(15);

   //Change field to editable when
   // host name entered…
   lineToSend.setEditable(false);
```

```
      lineToSend.addActionListener(this);

      /*******************************************
      * ADD COMPONENTS TO PANEL AND APPLICATION FRAME *
      *******************************************/

      /****************************************
      * NOW SET UP TEXT AREA AND THE CLOSE BUTTON *
      ****************************************/
   }

   public void actionPerformed(ActionEvent event)
   {
      if (event.getSource() == closeConnection)
      {
         if (socket != null)
         {
            try
            {
               socket.close();
            }
            catch(IOException ioEx)
            {
               System.out.println(
                     "\n* Unable to close link!*\n");
               System.exit(1);
            }
            lineToSend.setEditable(false);
            hostInput.grabFocus();
         }
         return;
      }

      if (event.getSource() == lineToSend)
      {
         /*****************/
         * SUPPLY CODE HERE *
         ******************/

      }

      //Must have been entry into host field...
      String host = hostInput.getText();
      try
      {

         /******************
         * SUPPLY CODE HERE *
```

```
         ******************/
      }
      catch (UnknownHostException uhEx)
      {
         received.append("\n*** No such host! ***\n");
         hostInput.setText("");
      }
      catch (IOException ioEx)
      {
         received.append("\n*** " + ioEx.toString()
                                        + " ***\n");
      }
   }
}
```

Chapter 3
Multithreading and Multiplexing

Learning Objectives

After reading this chapter, you should:

- understand what is meant by a **thread** (in a programming context);
- appreciate the need for multithreaded programming;
- be aware of typical circumstances under which multithreading might be appropriate;
- know how to implement threads in Java;
- know how to implement locking of variables in Java;
- be aware of the danger posed by deadlock;
- know what Java methods to use in order to improve thread efficiency and reduce the likelihood of deadlock;
- know how to implement a multithreaded server;
- know how to implement a non-blocking server via multiplexing.

It is often the case nowadays that programs need to carry out more than one significant task at the same time (i.e., 'concurrently'). For example, a GUI-driven program may be displaying a background animation while processing the user's foreground interactions with the interface, or a Web browser may need to download and display the contents of a graphics file while rendering the rest of the associated Web page. The popularity of client/server applications over the past decade has exacerbated this demand enormously, with server programs sometimes having to process the needs of several hundreds of clients at the same time.

Some years ago, each client that connected to a server would have caused a new process to be spawned on the server. The problem with this approach is that a fresh block of memory is set aside for each such process. While the number of clients connecting to the server remained reasonably low, this presented no difficulties. However, as the use of the Internet mushroomed, servers that created a new process for each client would grind to a halt as hundreds, possibly thousands, of clients attempted to access their services simultaneously. A way of significantly alleviating this problem is to use what are called **threads**, instead of processes.

J. Graba, *An Introduction to Network Programming with Java: Java 7 Compatible*,
DOI 10.1007/978-1-4471-5254-5_3,

Though the use of threads cannot guarantee that a server will not crash, it greatly reduces the likelihood of it happening by significantly increasing the number of client programs that can be handled concurrently.

3.1 Thread Basics

A **thread** is a flow of control through a program. Unlike a process, a thread does not have a separate allocation of memory, but shares memory with other threads created by the same application. This means that servers using threads do not exhaust their supply of available memory and collapse under the weight of excessive demand from clients, as they were prone to do when creating many separate processes. In addition, the threads created by an application can share global variables, which is often highly desirable. This does not prevent each thread from having its own local variables, of course, since it will still have its own stack for such variables.

Though it has been entirely transparent to us and we have had to make no explicit programming allowance for it, we have already been making use of threads in our Java programming. In fact, we cannot avoid using threads in Java, since each program will have at least one thread that is launched automatically by our machine's JVM when that program is executed. Such a thread is created when *main* is started and 'killed' when *main* terminates. If we wish to make use of further threads, in order to 'offload' processing tasks onto them, then we have to program such threads explicitly. Using more than one thread in this way is called **multithreading**.

Of course, unless we have a multiprocessor system, it is not possible to have more than one task being executed simultaneously. The operating system, then, must have some strategy for determining which thread is to be given use of the processor at any given time. There are two major factors…

- Thread priority (1–10, in increasing order of importance) in Java
- Whether scheduling is **pre-emptive** or **cooperative**.

A **pre-emptive** scheduler will determine when a thread has had its fair share of CPU time (possibly via simple time allocation) and will then pause it (temporarily). A **cooperative** scheduler, on the other hand, will wait for the running thread to pause itself before giving control of the CPU to another thread. A JVM using cooperative scheduling is thus much more susceptible to thread **starvation** (from uncooperative, high-priority threads 'hogging' the processor).

On PCs, threads with the same priority are each given an equal *time-slice* or time *quantum* for execution on the processor. When the quantum expires, the first thread is suspended and the next thread in the queue is given the processor, and so on. If some threads require more urgent attention than others, then they may be assigned higher priorities (allowing **pre-emption** to occur). Under the Solaris operating system, a thread runs either to completion or until another higher-priority thread becomes ready. If the latter occurs first, then the second thread pre-empts the first and is given control of the processor. For threads with the same priority, time-slicing is used, so that a thread does not have to wait for another thread with the same priority to end.

3.2 Using Threads in Java

Java is unique amongst popular programming languages in making multithreading directly accessible to the programmer, without him/her having to go through an operating system API. Unfortunately, writing multithreaded programs can be rather tricky and there are certain pitfalls that need to be avoided. These pitfalls are caused principally by the need to coordinate the activities of the various threads, as will be seen in Sect. 3.4.

In Java, an object can be run as a thread if it implements the inbuilt interface *Runnable*, which has just one method: *run*. Thus, in order to implement the interface, we simply have to provide a definition for method *run*. Since the inbuilt class *Thread* implements this interface, there are two fundamental methods for creating a thread class:

- create a class that extends *Thread*;
- create a class that does not extend *Thread* and specify explicitly that it implements *Runnable*.

Of course, if the application class already has a superclass (other than *Object*), extending *Thread* is not an option, since Java does not support multiple inheritance. The following two sub-sections consider each of the above methods in turn.

3.2.1 Extending the Thread *Class*

The *run* method specifies the actions that a thread is to execute and serves the same purpose for the process running on the thread as method *main* does for a full application program. Like *main*, *run* may not be called directly. The containing program calls the *start* method (inherited from class *Thread*), which then automatically calls *run*.

Class *Thread* has seven constructors, the two most common of which are:

- *Thread()*
- *Thread(String<name>)*

The second of these provides a name for the thread via its argument. If the first is used, the system generates a name of the form *Thread-n,* where n is an integer starting at zero and increasing in value for further threads. Thus, if three threads are created via the first constructor, they will have names *Thread-0*, *Thread-1* and *Thread-2* respectively. Whichever constructor is used, method *getName* may be used to retrieve the name.

<u>Example</u>

```
Thread firstThread = new Thread();
Thread secondThread = new Thread("namedThread");
System.out.println(firstThread.getName());
System.out.println(secondThread.getName());
```

The output from the above lines would be:

```
Thread-0
namedThread
```

Note that the name of the variable holding the address of a thread is **not** the same as the name of the thread! More often than not, however, we do not need to know the latter.

Method *sleep* is used to make a thread pause for a specified number of milliseconds. For example:

```
myThread.sleep(1500);   //Pause for 1.5 seconds.
```

This suspends execution of the thread and allows other threads to be executed. When the sleeping time expires, the sleeping thread returns to a *ready* state, waiting for the processor.

Method *interrupt* may be used to interrupt an individual thread. In particular, this method may be used by other threads to 'awaken' a sleeping thread before that thread's sleeping time has expired. Since method *sleep* will throw a checked exception (an *InterruptedException*) if another thread invokes the *interrupt* method, it must be called from within a `try` block that catches this exception.

In the next example, static method *random* from core class *Math* is used to generate a random sleeping time for each of two threads that simply display their own names ten times. If we were to run the program without using a randomising element, then it would simply display alternating names, which would be pretty tedious and would give no indication that threads were being used. Method *random* returns a random decimal value in the range 0–0.999…, which is then multiplied by a scaling factor of 3000 and typecast into an *int*, producing a final integer value in the range 0–2999. This randomising technique is also used in later thread examples, again in order to avoid producing the same pattern of output from a given program.

Note the use of *extends Thread* in the opening line of the class. Though this class already implements the *Runnable* interface (and so has a definition of method *run*), the default implementation of *run* does nothing and must be overridden by a definition that we supply.

Example

```
public class ThreadShowName extends Thread
{
   public static void main (String[] args)
   {
      ThreadShowName thread1, thread2;

      thread1 = new ThreadShowName();
      thread2 = new ThreadShowName();

      thread1.start();   //Will call run.
      thread2.start();   //Will call run.
   }
```

```
    public void run()
    {
        int pause;
        for (int i=0; i<10; i++)
        {
            try
            {
                System.out.println(
                        getName()+" being executed.");
                pause = (int)(Math.random()*3000);
                sleep(pause);     //0-3 seconds.
            }
            catch (InterruptedException interruptEx)
            {
                System.out.println(interruptEx);
            }
        }
    }
}
```

Example output from the above program is shown in Fig. 3.1 below.

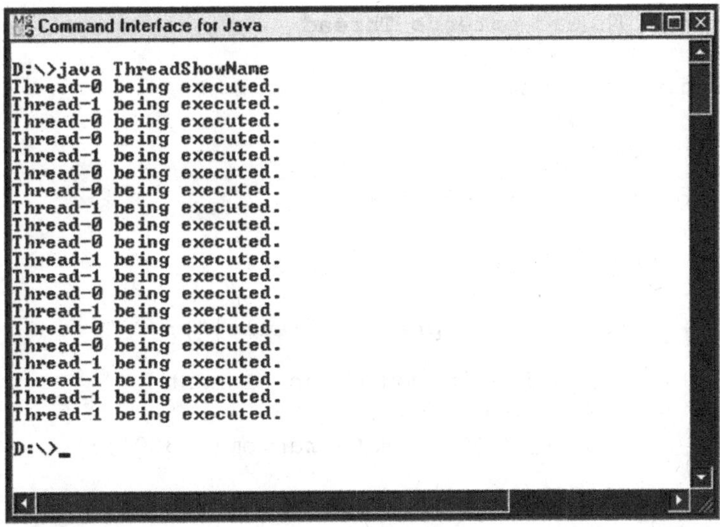

Fig. 3.1 Example output from the ThreadShowName program

In the above program, each of the two threads was carrying out exactly the same task, which meant that each of them could be created from the same *Thread* class and make use of exactly the same *run* method. In practice, of course, different threads will normally carry out different tasks. If we want the threads to carry out actions different from each other's, then we must create a separate class for each thread (each with its own *run* method), as shown in the next example.

Example

In this example, we shall again create two threads, but we shall have one thread display the message 'Hello' five times and the other thread output integers 1–5. For the first thread, we shall create a class called *HelloThread*; for the second, we shall create class *CountThread*. Note that it is **not** the main application class (*ThreadHelloCount*, here) that extends class *Thread* this time, but each of the two subordinate classes, *HelloThread* and *CountThread*. Each has its own version of the *run* method.

```
public class ThreadHelloCount
{
   public static void main(String[] args)
   {
      HelloThread hello = new HelloThread();
      CountThread count = new CountThread();
      hello.start();
      count.start();
   }
}

class HelloThread extends Thread
{
   public void run()
   {
      int pause;

      for (int i=0; i<5; i++)
      {
         try
         {
            System.out.println("Hello!");

            //Again, introduce an element
            //of randomness...
            pause = (int)(Math.random()*3000);

            sleep(pause);
         }
         catch (InterruptedException interruptEx)
         {
            System.out.println(interruptEx);
         }
      }
```

```
    }
}
class CountThread extends Thread
{
    int pause;
    public void run()
    {
        for (int i=0; i<5; i++)
        {
            try
            {
                System.out.println(i);
                pause=(int)(Math.random()*3000);
                sleep (pause);
            }
            catch (InterruptedException interruptEx)
            {
                System.out.println(interruptEx);
            }
        }
    }
}
```

An example of this program's output is shown below (Fig. 3.2).

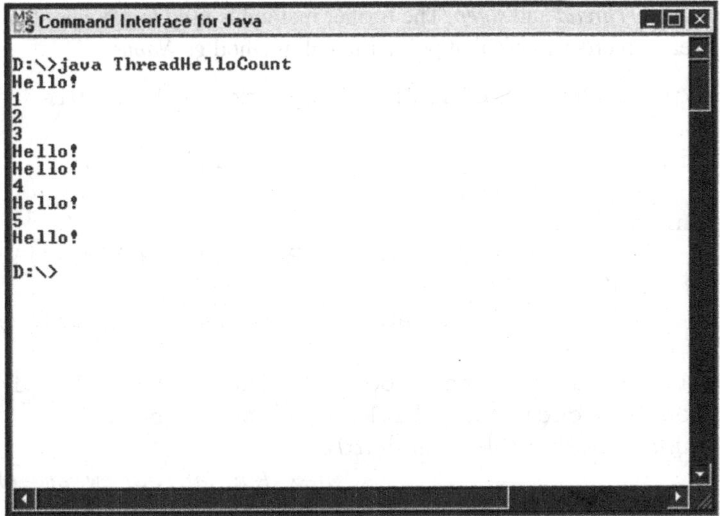

Fig. 3.2 Example output from the ThreadHelloCount program

3.2.2 *Explicitly Implementing the* Runnable *Interface*

This is very similar to the technique described in the previous sub-section. With this method, however, we first create an application class that explicitly implements the *Runnable* interface. Then, in order to create a thread, we instantiate an object of our *Runnable* class and 'wrap' it in a *Thread* object. We do this by creating a *Thread* object and passing the *Runnable* object as an argument to the *Thread* constructor. (Recall that the *Thread* class has seven constructors.) There are two *Thread* constructors that allow us to do this:

- *Thread (Runnable<object>)*
- *Thread(Runnable<object>, String<name>)*
  (The second of these allows us also to name the thread.)

When either of these constructors is used, the *Thread* object uses the *run* method of the *Runnable* object in place of its own (empty) *run* method.

Once a *Runnable* object has been used as an argument in the *Thread* constructor, we may never again need to refer to it. If this is the case, we can create such an object anonymously and dynamically by using the operator `new` in the argument supplied to the *Thread* constructor, as shown in the example below. However, some people may prefer to create a named *Runnable* object first and then pass that to the *Thread* constructor, so the alternative code is also shown. The second method employs about twice as much code as the first, but might serve to make the process clearer.

Example (Same effect as that of *ThreadShowName*)

Note that, since the thread objects in this example are not of class *Thread* (since *RunnableShowName* does **not** extend *Thread*), they cannot make direct use of methods *getName* and *sleep*, but must go through class *Thread* to make use of static methods *currentThread* and *sleep*. The former method is used to get a pointer to the current thread, in order to use that pointer to call method *getName*.

```
public class RunnableShowName implements Runnable
{
   public static void main(String[] args)
   {
      Thread thread1 =
                 new Thread(new RunnableShowName());
      Thread thread2 =
                 new Thread(new RunnableShowName());
/*
As an alternative to the above 2 lines, the following
(more long-winded) code could have been used:
      RunnableShowName runnable1 =
                             new RunnableShowName();
      RunnableShowName runnable2 =
                             new RunnableShowName();
      Thread thread1 = new Thread(runnable1);
      Thread thread2 = new Thread(runnable2);
*/
```

```
        thread1.start();
        thread2.start();
    }

    public void run()
    {
        int  pause;

        for (int i=0; i<10; i++)
        {
            try
            {
                //Use static method currentThread to get
                //reference to current thread and then call
                //method getName on that reference...
                System.out.println(
                        Thread.currentThread().getName()
                                + " being executed.");
                pause = (int)(Math.random() * 3000);

                //Call static method sleep...
                Thread.sleep(pause);
            }
            catch (InterruptedException interruptEx)
            {
                System.out.println(interruptEx);
            }
        }
    }
}
```

As another way of implementing the above program, we could declare *thread1* and *thread2* to be properties of a class that implements the *Runnable* interface, create an object of this class within *main* and have the constructor for this class create the threads and start them running. The constructor for each of the *Thread* objects still requires a *Runnable* argument, of course. It is the instance of the surrounding *Runnable* class that has been created (identified as *this*) that provides this argument, as shown in the code below.

```
public class RunnableHelloCount implements Runnable
{
    private Thread thread1, thread2;

    public static void main(String[] args)
    {
        RunnableHelloCount threadDemo =
                                    new RunnableHelloCount();
    }
```

```
    public RunnableHelloCount()
    {
      //Since current object implements Runnable, it can
      //be used as the argument to the Thread
      //constructor for each of the member threads...
      thread1 = new Thread(this);
      thread2 = new Thread(this);

      thread1.start();
      thread2.start();
    }

    public void run()
    {
       int  pause;

       for (int i=0; i<10; i++)
       {
          try
          {
             System.out.println(
                      Thread.currentThread().getName()
                                 + " being executed.");
             pause = (int)(Math.random()*3000);
             Thread.sleep(pause);
          }
          catch (InterruptedException interruptEx)
          {
             System.out.println(interruptEx);
          }
       }
    }
}
```

3.3 Multithreaded Servers

There is a fundamental and important limitation associated with all the server programs encountered so far:

- they can handle only one connection at a time.

This restriction is simply not feasible for most real-world applications and would render the software useless. There are two possible solutions:

- use a non-blocking server;
- use a multithreaded server.

Before J2SE 1.4, there was no specific provision for non-blocking I/O in Java, so the multithreaded option was the only feasible one for Java programmers. The introduction of non-blocking I/O in 1.4 was a major advance for Java network programmers and will be covered in the latter part of this chapter. For the time being, though, we shall restrict our attention to the more long-standing (and still widely used) implementation of servers via multithreading.

Though inferior to the non-blocking approach, the multithreaded technique has a couple of significant benefits:

- it offers a 'clean' implementation, by separating the task of allocating connections from that of processing each connection;
- it is robust, since a problem with one connection will not affect other connections.

The basic technique involves a two-stage process:

1. the main thread (the one running automatically in method *main*) allocates individual threads to incoming clients;
2. the thread allocated to each individual client then handles all subsequent interaction between that client and the server (via the thread's *run* method).

Since each thread is responsible for handling all further dialogue with its particular client, the main thread can 'forget' about the client once a thread has been allocated to it. It can then concentrate on its simple tasks of waiting for clients to make connection and allocating threads to them as they do so. For each client-handling thread that is created, of course, the main thread must ensure that the client-handling thread is passed a reference to the socket that was opened for the associated client.

The separation of responsibilities means that, if a problem occurs with the connection to a particular client, it has no effect on the connections to other clients and there is no general loss of service. This is a major benefit, of course.

Example

This is another echo server implementation, but one that uses multithreading to return messages to multiple clients. It makes use of a support class called *ClientHandler* that extends class *Thread*. Whenever a new client makes connection, a *ClientHandler* thread is created to handle all subsequent communication with that particular client. When the *ClientHandler* thread is created, its constructor is supplied with a reference to the relevant socket.

Here's the code for the server…

```
import java.io.*;
import java.net.*;

public class MultiEchoServer
{
   private static ServerSocket serverSocket;
   private static final int PORT = 1234;
```

```
   public static void main(String[] args)
                                          throws IOException
   {
      try
      {
         serverSocket = new ServerSocket(PORT);
      }
      catch (IOException ioEx)
      {
         System.out.println("\nUnable to set up port!");
         System.exit(1);
      }

      do
      {
         //Wait for client…
         Socket client = serverSocket.accept();

         System.out.println("\nNew client accepted.\n");

         //Create a thread to handle communication with
         //this client and pass the constructor for this
         //thread a reference to the relevant socket…
         ClientHandler handler =
                                    new ClientHandler(client);
         handler.start();//As usual, method calls run.
      }while (true);
   }
}

class ClientHandler extends Thread
{
   private Socket client;
   private Scanner input;
   private PrintWriter output;

   public ClientHandler(Socket socket)
   {
      //Set up reference to associated socket…
      client = socket;

      try
      {
        input = new Scanner(client.getInputStream());
        output = new PrintWriter(
                              client.getOutputStream(),true);
      }
      catch(IOException ioEx)
```

```
        {
            ioEx.printStackTrace();
        }
    }

    public void run()
    {
        String received;

        do
        {
            //Accept message from client on
            //the socket's input stream...
            received = input.nextLine();

            //Echo message back to client on
            //the socket's output stream...
            output.println("ECHO: " + received);

            //Repeat above until 'QUIT' sent by client...
        }while (!received.equals("QUIT"));

        try
        {
            if (client!=null)
            {
                System.out.println(
                            "Closing down connection...");
                client.close();
            }
        }
        catch(IOException ioEx)
        {
            System.out.println("Unable to disconnect!");
        }
    }
}
```

The code required for the client program is exactly that which was employed in the *TCPEchoClient* program from the last chapter. However, since (i) there was only a modest amount of code in the *run* method for that program, (ii) we should avoid confusion with the *run* method of the *Thread* class and (iii) it'll make a change (!) without being harmful, all the executable code has been placed inside *main* in the *MultiEchoClient* program below.

```
import java.io.*;
import java.net.*;
import java.util.*;
```

```
public class MultiEchoClient
{
    private static InetAddress host;
    private static final int PORT = 1234;

    public static void main(String[] args)
    {
        try
        {
            host = InetAddress.getLocalHost();
        }
        catch(UnknownHostException uhEx)
        {
            System.out.println("\nHost ID not found!\n");
            System.exit(1);
        }
        sendMessages();
    }

    private static void sendMessages()
    {
        Socket socket = null;

        try
        {
            socket = new Socket(host,PORT);

            Scanner networkInput =
                    new Scanner(socket.getInputStream());
            PrintWriter networkOutput =
               new PrintWriter(
                         socket.getOutputStream(),true);

            //Set up stream for keyboard entry…
            Scanner userEntry = new Scanner(System.in);

            String message, response;
            do
            {
                System.out.print(
                    "Enter message ('QUIT' to exit): ");
                message =  userEntry.nextLine();

                //Send message to server on the
                //socket's output stream…

                //Accept response from server on the
                //socket's intput stream…
                networkOutput.println(message);
```

```
                response = networkInput.nextLine();

                //Display server's response to user...
                System.out.println(
                                  "\nSERVER> " + response);
            }while (!message.equals("QUIT"));
        }
        catch(IOException ioEx)
        {
            ioEx.printStackTrace();
        }
        finally
        {
            try
            {
                System.out.println(
                                  "\nClosing connection...");
                socket.close();
            }
            catch(IOException ioEx)
            {
                System.out.println(
                                  "Unable to disconnect!");
                System.exit(1);
            }
        }
    }
}
```

If you wish to test the above application, you should start the server running in one command window and then start up two clients in separate command windows. Sample output from such an arrangement is shown in Fig. 3.3.

3.4 Locks and Deadlock

As mentioned at the start of Sect. 3.2, writing multithreaded programs can present some awkward problems, primarily caused by the need to coordinate the activities of the various threads that are running within an application. In order to illustrate what can go wrong, consider the situation illustrated in Fig. 3.4, where *thread1* and *thread2* both need to update a running total called *sum*.

If the operation that each thread is trying to execute were an **atomic** operation (i.e., one that could not be split up into simpler operations), then there would be no problem. Though this might at first appear to be the case, this is not so. In order to update *sum*, each thread will need to complete the following series of smaller

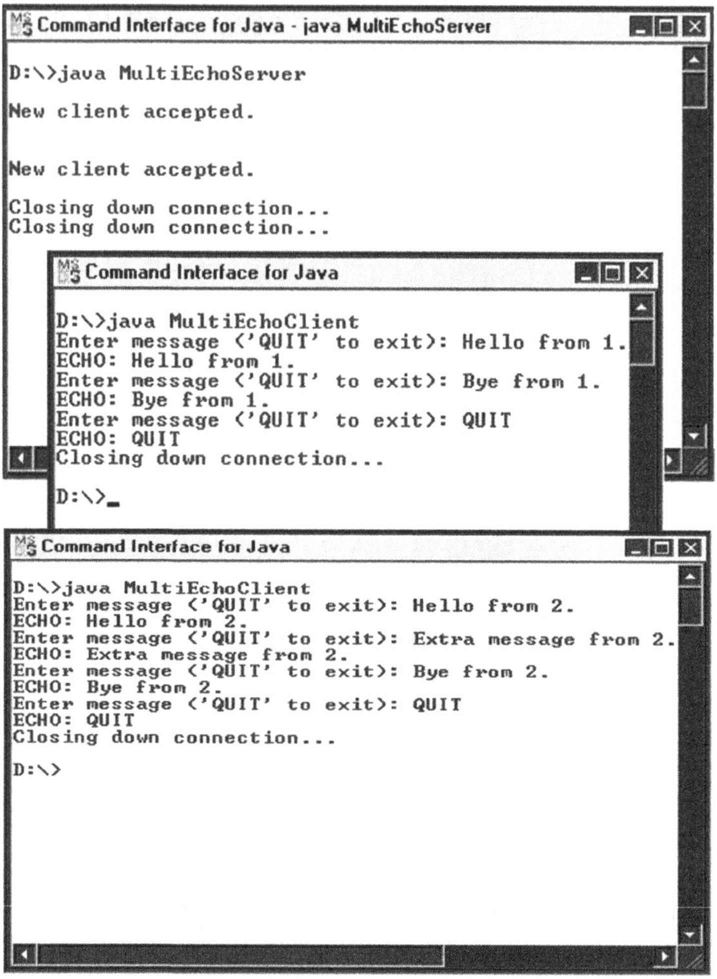

```
Command Interface for Java - java MultiEchoServer

D:\>java MultiEchoServer

New client accepted.


New client accepted.

Closing down connection...
Closing down connection...
```

```
Command Interface for Java

D:\>java MultiEchoClient
Enter message ('QUIT' to exit): Hello from 1.
ECHO: Hello from 1.
Enter message ('QUIT' to exit): Bye from 1.
ECHO: Bye from 1.
Enter message ('QUIT' to exit): QUIT
ECHO: QUIT
Closing down connection...

D:\>_
```

```
Command Interface for Java

D:\>java MultiEchoClient
Enter message ('QUIT' to exit): Hello from 2.
ECHO: Hello from 2.
Enter message ('QUIT' to exit): Extra message from 2.
ECHO: Extra message from 2.
Enter message ('QUIT' to exit): Bye from 2.
ECHO: Bye from 2.
Enter message ('QUIT' to exit): QUIT
ECHO: QUIT
Closing down connection...

D:\>
```

Fig. 3.3 Example output from a multithreaded server and two connected clients

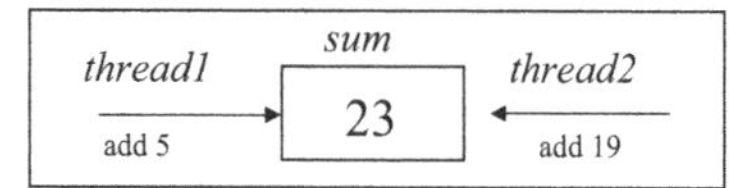

Fig. 3.4 Two threads attempting to update the same variable at the same time

operations: read the current value of *sum*, create a copy of it, add the appropriate amount to this copy and then write the new value back. The final value from the two original update operations, of course, should be 47 (=23 + 5 + 19). However, if both reads occur before a write takes place, then one update will overwrite the other and the result will be either 28 (=23 + 5) or 42 (=23 + 19). The problem is that the sub-operations from the two updates may overlap each other.

In order to avoid this problem in Java, we can require a thread to obtain a **lock** on the object that is to be updated. Only the thread that has obtained the lock may then update the object. Any other (updating) thread must wait until the lock has been released. Once the first thread has finished its updating, it should release the lock, making it available to other such threads. (Note that threads requiring read-only access do not need to obtain a lock.)

One unfortunate possibility with this system, however, is that **deadlock** may occur. A state of deadlock occurs when threads are waiting for events that will never happen. Consider the example illustrated in Fig. 3.5. Here, *thread1* has a lock on resource *res1*, but needs to obtain a lock on *res2* in order to complete its processing (so that it can release its lock on *res1*). At the same time, however, *thread2* has a lock on *res2*, but needs to obtain a lock on *res1* in order to complete *its* processing. Unfortunately, only good design can avoid such situations. In the next section, we consider how locks are implemented in Java.

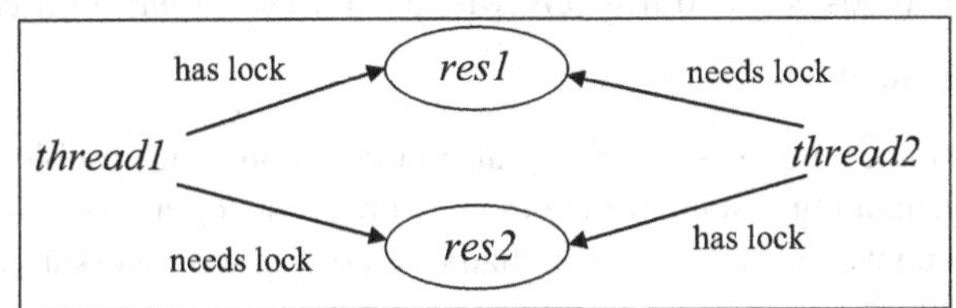

Fig. 3.5 An illustration of deadlock

3.5 Synchronising Threads

Locking is achieved by placing the keyword `synchronized` in front of the method definition or block of code that does the updating.

<u>Example</u>

```
public synchronized void updateSum(int amount)
{
   sum+=amount;
}
```

If *sum* is not locked when the above method is invoked, then the lock on *sum* is obtained, preventing any other thread from executing *updateSum*. All other threads attempting to invoke this method must wait. Once the method has finished execution, the lock is released and made available to other threads. If an object has more than one `synchronized` method associated with it, then only one may be active at any given time.

In order to improve thread efficiency and to help avoid deadlock, the following methods are used:

- *wait();*
- *notify();*
- *notifyAll().*

If a thread executing a `synchronized` method determines that it cannot proceed, then it may put itself into a waiting state by calling method *wait*. This releases the thread's lock on the shared object and allows other threads to obtain the lock. A call to *wait* may lead to an *InterruptedException*, which must either be caught or declared to be thrown by the containing (`synchronized`) method.

When a `synchronized` method reaches completion, a call may be made to *notify*, which will 'wake up' a thread that is in the waiting state. Since there is no way of specifying which thread is to be woken, this is only really appropriate if there is only one waiting thread. If all threads waiting for a lock on a given object are to be woken, then we use *notifyAll*. However, there is still no way of determining which thread gets control of the object. The JVM will make this decision.

Methods *wait*, *notify* and *notifyAll* may only be called when the current thread has a lock on the object (i.e., from within a `synchronized` method or from within a method that has been called by a `synchronized` method). If any of these methods is called from elsewhere, an *IllegalMonitorStateException* is thrown.

<u>Example</u>

This example is the classical producer-consumer problem, in which a producer is generating instances of some resource (cars on a production line, chocolate bars on a conveyor belt, wooden chairs in a carpenter's workshop or whatever) and a consumer is removing instances of the resource. Though this is largely a theoretical example, rather than a practical example of a service that might be provided by a server program, it could be modified to involve a server providing some network resource, such as a printing facility (though the server would probably be working with a fixed 'pool' of printers, rather than creating new ones).

The resource will be modelled by a *Resource* class, while the producer and consumer will be modelled by a *Producer* class and a *ConsumerClient* class respectively. The *Producer* class will be a thread class, extending class *Thread*. The server program, *ResourceServer*, will create a *Resource* object and then a *Producer* thread, passing the constructor for this thread a reference to the *Resource* object. The server will then start the thread running and begin accepting connections from *ConsumerClient*s. As each client makes connection, the server will create an instance of *ClientThread* (another *Thread* class), which will be responsible for handling all subsequent dialogue with the client. The code for *ResourceServer* is shown below.

```
import java.io.*;
import java.net.*;

public class ResourceServer
{
   private static ServerSocket serverSocket;
   private static final int PORT = 1234;

   public static void main(String[] args)
                                    throws IOException
   {
```

```
        try
        {
           serverSocket = new ServerSocket(PORT);
        }
        catch (IOException e)
        {
           System.out.println("\nUnable to set up port!");
           System.exit(1);
        }

        //Create a Resource object with
        //a starting resource level of 1…
        Resource item = new Resource(1);

        //Create a Producer thread, passing a reference
        //to the Resource object as an argument to the
        //thread constructor…
        Producer producer = new Producer(item);

        //Start the Producer thread running…
        producer.start();

        do
        {
           //Wait for a client to make connection…
           Socket client = serverSocket.accept();
           System.out.println("\nNew client accepted.\n");

           //Create a ClientThread thread to handle all
           //subsequent dialogue with the client, passing
           //references to both the client's socket and
           //the Resource object…
           ClientThread handler =
                            new ClientThread(client,item);

           //Start the ClientThread thread running…
           handler.start();
        }while (true);     //Server will run indefinitely.
     }
}
```

Method *addOne* of *Resource* will be called by a *Producer* object and will attempt to add one item to the resource level. Method *takeOne* of *Resource* will be called by a *ConsumerClient* object and will attempt to remove/consume one item. Both of these methods will return the new resource level. Since each of these methods will modify the resource level, they must both be declared with the keyword `synchronized`.

The code for the *Producer* class is shown below. As in previous examples, a randomising feature has been included. This causes the producer to wait 0–5 s between successive (attempted) increments of the resource level, so that it does not produce so quickly that it is always at maximum (or, very briefly, one below maximum).

```
class Producer extends Thread
{
   private Resource item;

   public Producer(Resource resource)
   {
      item = resource;
   }

   public void run()
   {
      int pause;
      int newLevel;

      do
      {
         try
         {
            //Add 1 to level and return new level…
            newLevel = item.addOne();
            System.out.println(
                  "<Producer> New level: " + newLevel);
            pause = (int)(Math.random() * 5000);

            //'Sleep' for 0-5 seconds…
            sleep(pause);
         }
         catch (InterruptedException interruptEx)
         {
            System.out.println(interruptEx);
         }
      }while (true);
   }
}
```

Just as a factory may not produce more than it can either sell or store, so the producer normally has some maximum resource level beyond which it must not produce. In this simple example, the resource level will not be allowed to exceed 5. Once the resource level has reached 5, production must be suspended. This is done from method *addOne* by calling *wait* from within a loop that continuously checks whether the resource level is still at maximum. The calling of *wait* suspends the *Producer* thread and releases the lock on the shared resource level variable, allowing any *ConsumerClient* to obtain it. When the resource level is below the maximum, *addOne* increments the level and then calls method *notify* to 'wake up' any waiting *ConsumerClient* thread.

At the other extreme, the consumer must not be allowed to consume when there is nothing to consume (i.e., when the resource level has reached zero). Thus, if the resource level is at zero when method *takeOne* is executed, *wait* is called from within a loop that continuously checks that the level is still at zero. The calling of *wait* suspends the *ConsumerClient* thread and releases the lock on the shared resource level variable, allowing any *Producer* to obtain it. When the resource level is above zero, *takeOne* decrements the level and then calls method *notifyAll* to 'wake up' any waiting *Producer* thread.

The code for class *Resource* is shown below. Note that *ResourceServer* must have access to the code for both *Producer* and *Resource*.

```
class Resource
{
   private int numResources;
   private final int MAX = 5;

   public Resource(int startLevel)
   {
      numResources = startLevel;
   }

   public int getLevel()
   {
      return numResources;
   }

   public synchronized int addOne()
   {
      try
      {
         while (numResources >= MAX)
            wait();
         numResources++;

         //'Wake up' any waiting consumer…
         notifyAll();
      }
      catch (InterruptedException interruptEx)
      {
         System.out.println(interruptEx);
      }
      return numResources;
   }

   public synchronized int takeOne()
   {
      try
      {
         while (numResources == 0)
```

```
            wait();
         numResources--;

         //'Wake up' waiting producer…
         notify();
      }
      catch (InterruptedException interruptEx)
      {
         System.out.println(interruptEx);
      }
      return numResources;
   }
}
```

The *ClientThread* objects created by *ResourceServer* handle all resource requests from their respective clients. In this simplified example, clients will be allowed to request only one item at a time from the resource 'pile', which they will do simply by sending a '1'. When a client wishes to disconnect from the service, it will send a '0'. The code for *ClientThread* is shown below. Just as for classes *Producer* and *Resource*, this code must be accessible by *ResourceServer*. Note that, although *ClientThread* calls *takeOne* to 'consume' an item of resource on behalf of the client, the only thing that is actually sent to the client is a symbolic message of confirmation that the request has been granted. Only when the material on serialisation has been covered at the end of the next chapter will it be clear how general resource 'objects' may actually be sent to a client.

```
import java.io.*;
import java.net.*;
import java.util.*;

class ClientThread extends Thread
{
   private Socket client;
   private Resource item;
   private Scanner input;
   private PrintWriter output;

   public ClientThread(Socket socket, Resource resource)
   {
      client = socket;
      item = resource;

      try
      {
         //Create input and output streams
         //on the socket…
         input = new Scanner(client.getInputStream());
         output = new PrintWriter(
                           client.getOutputStream(),true);
      }
```

```
        catch(IOException ioEx)
        {
            ioEx.printStackTrace();
        }
    }

    public void run()
    {
        String request = "";

        do
        {
            request = input.nextLine();
            if (request.equals("1"))
            {
                item.takeOne();//If none available,
                               //wait until resource(s)
                               //available (and thread is
                               //at front of thread queue).
                output.println("Request granted.");
            }
        }while (!request.equals("0"));

        try
        {
            System.out.println(
                        "Closing down connection...");
            client.close();
        }
        catch(IOException ioEx)
        {
            System.out.println(
                "Unable to close connection to client!");
        }
    }
}
```

All that remains to be done now is to produce the code for the *ConsumerClient* class. However, the required code for this class is very similar in structure to that of *MultiEchoClient* from Sect. 3.3 (as, indeed, it would be to most client programs), and so production of this code is one of the exercises at the end of the chapter. In the meantime, the screenshots in Figs. 3.6 and 3.7 show example output from *ResourceServer* and two *ConsumerClients*.

```
Command Interface for Java - java ResourceServer

D:\>java ResourceServer
<Producer> New level: 2

New client accepted.


New client accepted.

<Producer> New level: 1
<Producer> New level: 2
Closing down connection...
<Producer> New level: 2
Closing down connection...
<Producer> New level: 2
<Producer> New level: 3
<Producer> New level: 4
<Producer> New level: 5
```

Fig. 3.6 Example output from *ResourceServer* (with two clients connecting)

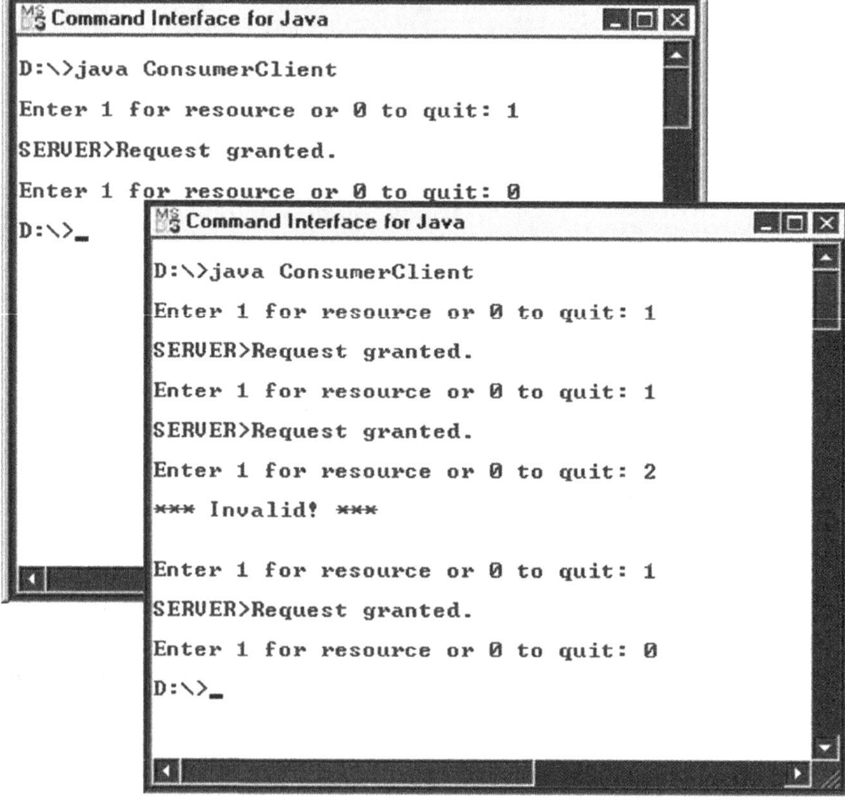

Fig. 3.7 Output from two *ConsumerClient*s connected to *ResourceServer* of Fig. 3.6

3.6 Non-blocking Servers

3.6.1 Overview

Before J2SE 1.4, we could *simulate* non-blocking I/O by using method *available* of class *InputStream*. The signature for this method is as follows:

```
int available() throws IOException
```

For an *InputStream* object attached to a network connection, this method returns the number of bytes received via that connection (and now in memory), but not yet read. In order to simulate non-blocking I/O, we could create a separate connection (on the same port) for each incoming client and repeatedly 'poll' clients in turn, using method *available* to check for data on each connection. However, this is a poor substitute for true non-blocking I/O and has never been used much.

J2SE 1.4 introduced the New Input/Output API, often abbreviated to NIO. This API is implemented by package *java.nio* and a handful of sub-packages, the most notable of which is *java.nio.channels*. Instead of employing Java's traditional stream mechanism for I/O, NIO makes use of the **channel** concept. Essentially, rather than being byte-orientated, as Java streams are, channels are **block-orientated**. This means that data can be transferred in large blocks, rather than as individual bytes, leading to significant speed gains. As will be seen shortly, each channel is associated with a **buffer**, which provides the storage area for data that is written to or read from a particular channel. It is even possible to make use of what are called **direct buffers**, which avoid the use of intermediate Java buffers wherever possible, allowing system level operations to be performed directly, leading to even greater speed gains.

Of greater relevance to the title of this section, though, is the mechanism for handling multiple clients. Instead of allocating an individual thread to each client, NIO uses **multiplexing** (the handling of multiple connections simultaneously by a single entity). This is based on the use of a **selector** (the single entity) to monitor both new connections and data transmissions from existing connections. Each of our channels simply registers with the selector the type(s) of event in which it is interested. It is possible to use channels in either blocking or non-blocking mode, but we shall be using them in non-blocking mode. The use of a selector to monitor events means that, instead of having a separate thread allocated to each connection, we can have one thread (or more, if we wish) monitoring several channels at once. This avoids problems such as operating system limits, deadlocks and thread safety violations that may occur with the one thread per connection approach.

Though the multiplexing approach offers significant advantages over the multi-threaded one, its implementation is notably more complex. However, most of the original I/O classes have, in fact, been redesigned to use channels as their underlying mechanism, which means that developers may reap some of the benefits of NIO without changing their programming. If greater speed is required, though, it will be necessary to employ NIO directly. The next sub-section provides the necessary detail to allow you to do this.

3.6.2 Implementation

The channels associated with *Sockets* and *ServerSockets* are, unsurprisingly, called *SocketChannels* and *ServerSocketChannels* respectively. Classes *SocketChannel* and *ServerSocketChannel* are contained in package *java.nio.channels*. By default, the sockets associated with such channels will operate in blocking mode, but may be configured as non-blocking sockets by calling method *configureBlocking* with an argument of `false`. This method is a method of the channel classes and needs to be called on a channel object **before** the associated socket is created. Once this has been done, the socket itself may be generated by calling method *socket* on the channel socket. The code below shows these steps. In this code and elsewhere in this section, the prior declaration of *Socket*, SocketChannel, *ServerSocket* and *ServerSocketChannel* objects with names *socket*, *socketChannel*, *serverSocket* and *serverSocketChannel* respectively is assumed. Note that a *ServerSocketChannel* object is created not via a constructor, but via static method *open* of the *ServerSocketChannel* class. This generates an instance of a platform-specific subclass that is hidden from the programmer.

```
serverSocketChannel = ServerSocketChannel.open();
serverSocketChannel.configureBlocking(false);
serverSocket = serverSocketChannel.socket();
.........................................
//The lines below will occur rather later in the
//program, of course.
socketChannel = serverSocketChannel.accept();
socketChannel.configureBlocking(false);
socket = socketChannel.socket();
```

Once the *ServerSocketChannel* and *ServerSocket* objects have been created, the *ServerSocket* object needs to be bound to the port on which the server is to be run. This involves the creation of an object of class *InetSocketAddress*, which is another class introduced in J2SE 1.4 and is defined in package *java.net*. The lines required to create the *InetSocketAddress* object and bind the *ServerSocket* object to the port are shown below. The pre-declaration of a constant *PORT* holding the port number is assumed.

```
InetSocketAddress netAddress =
                        new InetSocketAddress(PORT);
serverSocket.bind(netAddress);   //Bind socket to port.
```

It is now appropriate to create an instance of class *Selector*, which is another of the classes in package *java.nio.channels*. This object will be responsible for monitoring both new connections and the transmission of data from and to existing connections. Each channel (whether *SocketChannel* or *ServerSocketChannel*) must register with the *Selector* object the type of event in which the channel is interested via method *register*. There are four static constants of class *SelectionKey* (package *java.nio.channels*) that are used to identify the type of event that may be monitored:

- *SelectionKey.OP_ACCEPT*
- *SelectionKey.OP_CONNECT*
- *SelectionKey.OP_READ*
- *SelectionKey.OP_WRITE*

These constants are *int*s with bit patterns that may be OR-ed together to form the second argument for the *register* method. The two most commonly required constants (and the ones that we shall be using) are *SelectionKey.OP_ACCEPT* and *SelectionKey.OP_READ*. These will allow us to monitor new connections and data transmissions from existing connections respectively. The first will be of interest to our *ServerSocketChannel* object, of course, while the second will be of interest to our *SocketChannel* object.

The code for creating the *Selector* object and registering the respective interests of our two channel objects is shown below. Note that, as with the *ServerSocketChannel* object, a *Selector* object is created not via a constructor, but via static method *open* that again creates an instance of a platform-specific sub-class that is hidden from the programmer. Here and elsewhere in this section, the pre-declaration of a *Selector* object called *selector* is assumed.

```
selector = Selector.open();
serverSocketChannel.register(selector,
                                SelectionKey.OP_ACCEPT);
.........................................
//The line below will occur rather later in the
//program, of course.
socketChannel.register(selector,
                                SelectionKey.OP_ READ);
```

The final 'top level' step that needs to be carried out is the setting up of a *Buffer* object (package *java.nio*) to provide the shared data structure for the *SocketChannel*s associated with connecting clients. Class *Buffer* itself is an abstract class, and so no objects of this class can be created, but it has seven sub-classes from which objects may be created:

- *ByteBuffer*
- *CharBuffer*
- *IntBuffer*
- *LongBuffer*
- *ShortBuffer*
- *FloatBuffer*
- *DoubleBuffer*

The last six of these are type-specific, but *ByteBuffer* supports reading and writing of the other six types. This class is easily the most commonly used and is the type that we shall be using. It has at its heart an array for storing the data and we can specify the size of this array via method *allocate*, a static method of each of the *Buffer* classes. The code below shows how this may be done. Of course, the size allocated will depend upon a number of factors related to the demands of the particular application and the operating system for the particular platform, but, for efficiency's sake, should be on a kilobyte boundary. A 2 KB buffer allocation has been chosen for the example and the pre-declaration of a *ByteBuffer* called *buffer* has been assumed.

```
buffer = ByteBuffer.allocate(2048);
```

There is also a method called *allocateDirect* that may be used to set up a buffer. This attempts to allocate the required memory as direct memory, so that data does not need to be copied to an intermediate buffer before being written to disc. This means that there is the potential for I/O operations to be performed considerably more quickly. Whether the use of direct buffers is appropriate or desirable (and there will be a cost associated with the use of them, in terms of system resources) depends upon the needs of the particular application and the characteristics of the underlying operating system. In practice, multiple buffers and multiple threads (in thread pools) will be needed for heavily used servers.

Once all of the above preparatory steps have been executed, the server will enter a traditional `do…while(true)` loop that accepts connecting clients and processes their data. The first step within this loop is a call to method *select* on the *Selector* object. This returns the number of events of the type(s) that are being monitored and have occurred. This method is very efficient and appears to be based on the Unix system call of the same name. Here's an example of its use, employing the same *Selector* object called *selector* as was used previously in this section:

```
int numKeys = selector.select();
```

If no events have occurred since the last call of *select*, then execution loops back to this call until there is at least one event detected.

For each event that is detected on a particular call to *select*, an object of class *SelectionKey* (package *java.nio.channels*) is generated and contains all the information pertaining to the particular event. The set of *SelectionKey*s created by a given call to *select* is called the **selected set**. The selected set is generated by a call to method *selectedKeys* of the *Selector* object and is placed into a Java *Set* object. An *Iterator* object associated with the selected set is then created by a call to the *Set* object's *iterator* method. The lines to generate the selected set and its iterator are shown below.

```
Set eventKeys = selector.selectedKeys();
Iterator keyCycler = eventKeys.iterator();
```

Using the above *Iterator* object, we can now work our way through the individual *SelectionKey* objects, making use of the *Iterator* methods *hasNext* and *next*. As we retrieve each *SelectionKey* from the set, we need to typecast from type *Object* (which is how each key is held within the *Set* object) into type *SelectionKey*. Here is the code required for detection and retrieval of each key:

```
while (keyCycler.hasNext())
```

```
{
    SelectionKey key =
                  (SelectionKey)keyCycler.next();
```

At this point, we don't know the type of event with which this *SelectionKey* is associated. To find this out, we need to retrieve the set of ready operations for the current key by calling the *SelectionKey* method *readyOps*. This method returns the set of operations as a bit pattern held in an *int*. By AND-ing this integer with specific *SelectionKey* operation constants, we can determine whether those particular events have been generated. For our program, of course, the only two event types of interest are *SelectionKey.OP_ACCEPT* and *SelectionKey.OP_READ*. If the former is detected, we shall process a new connection, whilst detection of the latter will lead to the processing of incoming data. The code for determination of event type and the initiation of processing (but not the details of such processing just yet) appears below.

```
int keyOps = key.readyOps();
if ((keyOps & SelectionKey.OP_ACCEPT) ==
                                SelectionKey.OP_ACCEPT)
{
    acceptConnection(key);        //Pass key to
                                  //processing method.
    continue; //Back to start of key-processing loop.
}
if ((keyOps & SelectionKey.OP_READ) ==
                                SelectionKey.OP_READ)
{
    acceptData(key); //Pass key to processing method.
}
```

The processing required for a new connection has already been specified in this section, split across two separate locations in the text, but is now brought together for the sake of clarity:

```
socketChannel = serverSocketChannel.accept();
socketChannel.configureBlocking(false);
socket = socketChannel.socket();
socketChannel.register(selector,
                           SelectionKey.OP_READ);
```

The only additional operation that is required is the removal of the current *SelectionKey* from the selected set, in order to avoid re-processing it the next time through the loop as though it represented a new event. This is effected by calling method *remove* on the selected set, a reference to which may be obtained by calling method *selectedKeys* again. The *remove* method will have the *SelectionKey* as its single argument, of course:

```
selector.selectedKeys().remove(key);
```

The processing of data from an existing connection involves making use of the *ByteBuffer* object created earlier. Buffer method *clear* (the purpose of which is self-evident) should be called before each fresh reading of data into the buffer from its associated channel. A reference to the channel is obtained by calling method *channel* on the current *SelectionKey* and again typecasting the *Object* reference that is returned. The reading itself is carried out by method *read* of the *SocketChannel* class. This method takes the buffer as its single argument and returns an integer that indicates the number of bytes read. The lines to obtain the *SocketChannel* reference, clear the *ByteBuffer* and read data from the channel into the buffer are as follows:

```
socketChannel = (SocketChannel)key.channel();
buffer.clear();
int numBytes = socketChannel.read(buffer);
```

In order to write the data from the buffer to the channel, it is necessary to call *Buffer* method *flip* to reset the buffer pointer to the start of the buffer and then call method *write* on the channel object, supplying the buffer as the single argument. In the example at the end of this section (which will contain all the code accumulated within the section), the data received will simply be echoed back to the client. Since it may not be possible to send the entire contents of the buffer in one operation, a `while` loop will be used, with *Buffer* method *remaining* being called to determine whether there are any bytes still to be sent. Since an *IOException* may be generated, this code will need to be contained within a `try` block, but the basic code (without the `try`) is shown below.

```
buffer.flip();
while (buffer.remaining()>0)
    socketChannel.write(buffer);
```

Note that whereas, with the multithreading approach, we had separate streams for input and output, the *SocketChannel* is a two-way conduit and provides all the I/O requirements between server and client. Note also that reading and writing is specified with respect to the **channel**. It can be very easy at first viewing to interpret `socketChannel.read(buffer)` as being 'read from buffer' and `socketChannel.write(buffer)` as being 'write to buffer', whereas this is precisely the **opposite** of what is actually happening.

The link between client and server can break down, of course, possibly because the connection has been closed at the client end or possibly because of some error situation. Whatever the reason, this must be taken into account when attempting to read from the *SocketChannel*. If a breakdown occurs, then the call to method *read* will return –1. When this happens, the registration of the current *SelectionKey* with the *Selector* object must be rescinded. This is done by calling method *cancel* on the *SelectionKey* object. The socket associated with the client should also be closed. Before this can be done, it is necessary to get a reference to the *Socket* object by calling method *socket* on the *SocketChannel* object. The (attempted) closure of the socket may fail and needs to be executed within a `try` block, but the example program places this code within a (programmer-defined) method called *closeSocket* (which takes the *Socket* object as its single argument). The code to handle the communication breakdown as described above is shown here:

```
socket = socketChannel.socket();

if (numBytes==-1)
{
    key.cancel();
    closeSocket(socket);
```

Now that all the required steps for implementation of a non-blocking server have been covered, this section will finish with an example that brings together all those individual steps…

Example

This example is the multiplexing equivalent of *MultiEchoServer* from Sect. 3.3 and will allow you to compare the coding requirements of the multithreading approach with those of the multiplexing approach. The code for the equivalent client is not shown, since this (of course) will be identical to that shown for *MultiEchoClient*. As before, the server simply echoes back all transmissions from the client(s).

```
import java.io.*;
import java.net.*;
import java.nio.*;
import java.nio.channels.*;
import java.util.*;

public class MultiEchoServerNIO
{
    private static ServerSocketChannel
                                 serverSocketChannel;
    private static final int PORT = 1234;

    private static Selector selector;
    /*
    Above Selector used both for detecting new
    connections (on the ServerSocketChannel) and for
    detecting incoming data from existing connections
    (on the SocketChannel).
    */

    public static void main(String[] args)
    {
       ServerSocket serverSocket;

       System.out.println("Opening port...\n");

       try
       {
```

```
        serverSocketChannel =
                        ServerSocketChannel.open();
        serverSocketChannel.configureBlocking(false);
        serverSocket = serverSocketChannel.socket();
        /*
        ServerSocketChannel created before
        ServerSocket largely in order to configure
        latter as a non-blocking socket by calling
        the configureBlocking method of the
        ServerSocketChannel with argument of 'false'.

        (ServerSocket will have a ServerSocketChannel
        only if latter is created first.)
        */

        InetSocketAddress netAddress =
                        new InetSocketAddress(PORT);

        //Bind socket to port...
        serverSocket.bind(netAddress);

        //Create a new Selector object for detecting
        //input from channels...
        selector = Selector.open();

        //Register ServerSocketChannel with Selector
        //for receiving incoming connections...
        serverSocketChannel.register(selector,
                            SelectionKey.OP_ACCEPT);
     }
     catch(IOException ioEx)
     {
        ioEx.printStackTrace();
        System.exit(1);
     }

     processConnections();
  }

  private static void processConnections()
  {
     do
     {
        try
        {
           //Get number of events (new connection(s)
           //and/or data transmissions from existing
           //connection(s))...
           int numKeys = selector.select();
```

```
        if (numKeys > 0)
        {
            //Extract event(s) that have been
            //triggered …
            Set eventKeys =
                          selector.selectedKeys();

            //Set up Iterator to cycle though set
            //of events…
            Iterator keyCycler =
                            eventKeys.iterator();

            while (keyCycler.hasNext())
            {
              SelectionKey key =
                 (SelectionKey)keyCycler.next();

              //Retrieve set of ready ops for
              //this key (as a bit pattern)…
              int keyOps = key.readyOps();

              if (
               (keyOps & SelectionKey.OP_ACCEPT)
                     == SelectionKey.OP_ACCEPT)
              {//New connection.
                 acceptConnection(key);
                 continue;
              }
              if (
                (keyOps & SelectionKey.OP_READ)
                      == SelectionKey.OP_READ)
              {//Data from existing client.
                 acceptData(key);
              }
            }
        }
     }
     catch(IOException ioEx)
     {
        ioEx.printStackTrace();
        System.exit(1);
     }
  }while (true);
}

private static void acceptConnection(
               SelectionKey key) throws IOException
{//Accept incoming connection and add to list.
```

```
      SocketChannel socketChannel;
      Socket socket;

      socketChannel = serverSocketChannel.accept();
      socketChannel.configureBlocking(false);
      socket = socketChannel.socket();
      System.out.println("Connection on "
                                    + socket + ".");

      //Register SocketChannel for receiving data…
      socketChannel.register(selector,
                              SelectionKey.OP_READ);

      //Avoid re-processing this event as though it
      //were a new one (next time through loop)…
      selector.selectedKeys().remove(key);
   }

   private static void acceptData(SelectionKey key)
                                    throws IOException
   {//Accept data from existing connection.
      SocketChannel socketChannel;
      Socket socket;
      ByteBuffer buffer = ByteBuffer.allocate(2048);
      //Above used for reading/writing data from/to
      //SocketChannel.

      socketChannel = (SocketChannel)key.channel();
      buffer.clear();
      int numBytes = socketChannel.read(buffer);
      System.out.println(numBytes + " bytes read.");
      socket = socketChannel.socket();

      if (numBytes==-1)
      //OP_READ event also triggered by closure of
      //connection or error of some kind. In either
      //case, numBytes = -1.
      {
         //Request that registration of this key's
         //channel with its selector be cancelled…
         key.cancel();

         System.out.println("\nClosing socket "
                                 + socket + "…");
         closeSocket(socket);
      }
      else
      {
         try
```

```
            {
               /*
               Reset buffer pointer to start of buffer,
               prior to reading buffer's contents and
               writing them to the SocketChannel…
               */
               buffer.flip();
               while (buffer.remaining()>0)
                  socketChannel.write(buffer);
            }
            catch (IOException ioEx)
            {
               System.out.println("\nClosing socket "
                                    + socket + "…");
               closeSocket(socket);
            }
         }
         //Remove this event, to avoid re-processing it
         //as though it were a new one…
         selector.selectedKeys().remove(key);
      }

      private static void closeSocket(Socket socket)
      {
         try
         {
            if (socket != null)
               socket.close();
         }
         catch (IOException ioEx)
         {
            System.out.println(
                  "*** Unable to close socket! ***");
         }
      }
   }
```

3.6.3 Further Details

Though the preceding sub-section provides enough information to allow the reader to implement a basic non-blocking server, there are other methods that are often required in more sophisticated implementations. Not all of the remaining methods associated with Java's NIO will be covered in this section, but the reader should find that those that are covered are the only additional ones that are needed for many

NIO applications. They are certainly the only methods not already covered that will be needed for implementation of the chat server in Exercise 3.6 at the end of this chapter. In fact, of the six new methods mentioned below, only four are NIO methods. The other two are methods of the *String* class. In all the examples within this section, *buffer* is assumed to be a pre-declared *ByteBuffer*.

Though methods *read* and *write* are the usual methods for transferring data to and from buffers, there are occasions when it is necessary to implement I/O at the byte level. This is particularly so when the programmer wishes to place particular values into a buffer or to remove all or part of the data from the buffer in order to carry out further processing on that data (possibly prior to re-writing the processed data back to the buffer). The methods to read and write a single byte from/to a buffer are *get* and *put* respectively.

Examples

- `byte oneByte = buffer.get();`
- `buffer.put(anotherByte);`

As was stated in the previous sub-section, each *ByteBuffer* has at its heart an array for storing the data that is to be read from or written to a particular channel. Sometimes, it is desirable to access the contents of this array directly. Method *array* of class *ByteBuffer* allows us to do just this by returning the array of bytes holding the data. For example:

```
byte[] bufferArray = buffer.array();
```

If the data that is being transferred is of type *String*, then we may wish to convert this array of bytes into a *String*. This may be achieved by using an overloaded form of the *String* constructor that has this form:

```
String(<byteArray>, <offset>, <numBytes>)
```

In the above signature, 'offset' is an integer specifying the byte number at which to start in the array of bytes, while 'numBytes' specifies the number of bytes from the array that are to be used (counting from position 'offset'). Obviously, we need to know how many bytes of data there are in the array. The reader's first inclination may be to assume that this can be derived from the array's *length* property. However, this will not work, since it will simply show the size that was allocated to the *ByteBuffer* by the programmer, not the number of bytes that have been used. In order to determine how many data bytes have been written to the buffer, one must use the *ByteBuffer*'s *position* method **following the latest writing to the buffer** (i.e., before the buffer is 'flipped' for reading).

Example

```
int numBytes = buffer.position();
byte[] bufferArray = buffer.array();
String dataString =
          new String(bufferArray, 0, numBytes);
```

The above example copies the entire contents of the buffer's array and converts that copy into a *String*. Another method of the *String* class that can be very useful when processing data within a *ByteBuffer* does the opposite of the above. Method *getBytes* converts a specified *String* into an array of bytes, which may then be written to the buffer.

Example

```
String myStringData = "Just an example";
byte[] byteData = myStringData.getBytes();
buffer.put(byteData);
```

Exercises

3.1 Take a copy of example *ThreadHelloCount* (Sect. 3.2.1). Examine the code and then compile and run the program, observing the results.

3.2 Modify the above code to use the alternative method for multithreading (i.e., implementing the *Runnable* interface). Name your main class *RunnableHelloBye* and your subsidiary classes *Hello* and *Goodbye* respectively. The first should display the message 'Hello!' ten times (with a random delay of 0–2 s between consecutive displays), while the second should do the same with the message 'Goodbye!'.

Note that it will NOT be the main class that implements the Runnable **interface, but each of the two subsidiary classes.**

3.3 Take a copy of *ResourceServer* (Sect. 3.5), examine the code and run the program.

3.4 Take a copy of *MultiEchoClient* (Sect. 3.3), re-naming it *ConsumerClient*. Using this file as a template, modify the code so that the program acts as a client of *ResourceServer*, as shown in the screenshots at the end of Sect. 3.5. (Ensure that the user can pass only 0 or 1 to the server.) Test the operation of the server with two clients.

Note that exercises 3.5 and 3.6 (especially the latter) are rather substantial tasks.

3.5 Implement a basic electronic chatroom application that employs a multithreaded server. Both server and client will need to be implemented and brief details of these programs are provided below.

The multithreaded chat server must broadcast each message it receives to all the connected clients, of course. It should also maintain a dynamic list of *Socket* references associated with those clients. Though you **could** use an array to hold the list (with an appropriate over-allocation of array cells, to cater for a potentially large number of connections), the use of a *Vector* object would be much more realistic. (If you are unfamiliar with *Vector*s, then refer to Sect. 4.8 in the next chapter.)

The client must be implemented as a GUI that can send and receive messages until it sends the string 'Bye'. A separate thread will be required to receive messages from the server and add them cumulatively to a text area. The first two things that this thread should do are (i) accept the user's chatroom nickname (probably via an input dialogue box) and (ii) send this name to the server. All other messages should be sent via a text area and associated button. As a simplification, assume that no two clients will select the same nickname.

Note

It is likely that a *NoSuchElementException* will be generated at the line that reads from the socket's input stream when the user's socket is closed (after sending 'Bye'), so place this reading line inside a `try` and have an empty `catch`.

3.6 Implement the same electronic chatroom application that you did for exercise 3.5 above, but this time using Java's non-blocking I/O on the server. You may very well be able to make use of your original client program, but have the client close its socket only after it has received (and displayed) its own 'Bye' message sent back from the server. You can also now get rid of the code dealing with any *NoSuchElementException*.

At the server end, you will probably find it useful to maintain two *Vector*s, the first of these holding references to all *SocketChannel*s of newly-connected clients for which no data has been processed and the second holding references to instances/objects of class *ChatUser*. Each instance of this class should hold references to the *SocketChannel* and chatname (a *String*) associated with an individual chatroom user, with appropriate 'get' methods to retrieve these references. As the first message from a given user (the one holding the user's chatroom nickname) is processed, the user's *SocketChannel* reference should be removed from the first *Vector* and a *ChatUser* instance created and added to the second *Vector*.

It will probably be desirable to have separate methods to deal with the following:

(i) a user's entry into the chatroom;
(ii) a normal message;
(iii) a user's exit from the chatroom (after sending 'Bye').

Signatures for the first and last of these are shown below.

```
public static void announceNewUser(
            SocketChannel userSocketChannel,
            ByteBuffer buffer)

public static void announceExit(String name)
```

The method for processing an ordinary message has been done for you and is shown below.

```
public static void broadcastMessage(String chatName,
                                    ByteBuffer buffer)
{
   String messagePrefix = chatName + ": ";
   byte[] messagePrefixBytes = messagePrefix.getBytes();
   final byte[] CR = "\n".getBytes();//Carriage return.

   try
   {
      int messageSize = buffer.position();
      byte[] messageBytes = buffer.array();
      byte[] messageBytesCopy = new byte[messageSize];

      for (int i=0; i<messageSize; i++)
      {
         messageBytesCopy[i] = messageBytes[i];
```

```
            }
            buffer.clear();
            //Concatenate message text onto message prefix…
            buffer.put(messagePrefixBytes);
            for (int i=0; i<messageSize; i++)
            {
               buffer.put(messageBytesCopy[i]);
            }
            buffer.put(CR);
            SocketChannel chatSocketChannel;
            for (ChatUser chatUser:allUsers)
            {
               chatSocketChannel =
                               chatUser.getSocketChannel();
               buffer.flip();
               //Write full message (with user's name)…
               chatSocketChannel.write(buffer);
            }
         }
         catch (IOException ioEx)
         {
            ioEx.printStackTrace();
         }
      }
```

Chapter 4
File Handling

Learning Objectives

After reading this chapter, you should:

- know how to create and process serial files in Java;
- know how to create and process random access files in Java;
- know how to redirect console input and output to disc files;
- know how to construct GUI-based file-handling programs;
- know how to use command line parameters with Java programs;
- understand the concept and importance of Java's serialisation mechanism and know how to implement it;
- know how to make use of *ArrayLists* for convenient packaging of serialised objects.

With all our programs so far, there has been a very fundamental limitation: all data accepted is held only for as long as the program remains active. As soon as the program finishes execution, any data that has been entered and the results of processing such data are thrown away. Of course, for very many real-life applications (banking, stock control, financial accounting, etc.), this limitation is simply not realistic. These applications demand **persistent** data storage. That is to say, data must be maintained in a permanent state, such that it is available for subsequent further processing. The most common way of providing such persistent storage is to use disc files. Java provides such a facility, with the access to such files being either **serial** or **random**. The following sections explain the use of these two file access methods, firstly for non-GUI applications and later for GUI applications. In addition, the important and often neglected topic of **serialisation** is covered.

4.1 Serial Access Files

Serial access files are files in which data is stored in physically adjacent locations, often in no particular logical order, with each new item of data being added to the end of the file.

J. Graba, *An Introduction to Network Programming with Java: Java 7 Compatible*,
DOI 10.1007/978-1-4471-5254-5_4, © Springer-Verlag London 2013

[Note that serial files are often mis-named *sequential* files, even by some authors who should know better. A sequential file is a serial file in which the data are stored in some particular order (e.g., in account number order). A sequential file is a serial file, but a serial file is not necessarily a sequential file.]

Serial files have a number of distinct disadvantages (as will be pointed out in 4.2), as a consequence of which they are often used only to hold relatively small amounts of data or for temporary storage, prior to processing, but such files are simpler to handle and are in quite common usage.

The internal structure of a serial file can be either **binary** (i.e., a compact format determined by the architecture of the particular computers on which the file is to be used) or **text** (human-readable format, almost invariably using ASCII). The former stores data more efficiently, but the latter is much more convenient for human beings. Coverage here will be devoted exclusively to **text** files.

Before Java SE 5, a text file required a *FileReader* object for input and a *FileWriter* object for output. As of Java 5, we can often use just a *File* object for either input or output (though not for both at the same time). The *File* constructor takes a *String* argument that specifies the name of the file as it appears in a directory listing.

Examples

```
(i)  File inputFile = new File("accounts.txt");
(ii) String fileName = "dataFile.txt";
     ..................................
     File outputFile = new File(fileName);
```

N.B. If a string literal is used (e.g., `"results.txt"`), the full pathname may be included, but double backslashes are then required in place of single backslashes (since a single backslash would indicate an escape sequence representing one of the invisible characters, such as tab). For example:

```
File resultsFile = new File("c:\\data\\results.txt");
```

Incidentally, we can (of course) call our files anything we like, but we should follow good programming practice and give them meaningful names. In particular, it is common practice to denote text data files by a suffix of `.txt` (for 'text').

Class *File* is contained within package *java.io*, so this package should be imported into any file-handling program. Before Java SE 5, it was necessary to wrap a *BufferedReader* object around a *FileReader* object in order to read from a file. Likewise, it was necessary to wrap a *PrintWriter* object around a *FileWriter* object in order to write to the file. Now we can wrap a *Scanner* object around a *File* object for input and a *PrintWriter* object around a *File* object for output. (The *PrintWriter* class is also within package *java.io*.)

Examples

```
(i) Scanner input =
                      new Scanner(new File("inFile.txt"));
```

```
(ii)    PrintWriter output =
                  new PrintWriter(new File("outFile.txt"));
```

We can then make use of methods *next, nextLine, nextInt, nextFloat*, … for input and methods *print* and *println* for output.

Examples (using objects *input* and *output*, as declared above)

```
(i)     String item = input.next();
(ii)    output.println("Test output");
(iii)   int number = input.nextInt();
```

Note that we need to know the type of the data that is in the file before we attempt to read it! Another point worth noting is that we may choose to create anonymous *File* objects, as in the examples above, or we may choose to create named *File* objects.

Examples

```
(i)  File inFile = new File("inFile.txt");
     Scanner input = new Scanner(inFile);

(ii) File outFile = new File("outFile.txt");
     PrintWriter output = new PrintWriter(outFile);
```

Creating a named *File* object is slightly longer than using an anonymous *File* object, but it allows us to make use of the *File* class's methods to perform certain checks on the file. For example, we can test whether an input file actually exists. Programs that depend upon the existence of such a file in order to carry out their processing **must** use named *File* objects. (More about the *File* class's methods shortly.)

When the processing of a file has been completed, the file should be closed via the *close* method, which is a member of both the *Scanner* class and the *PrintWriter* class. For example:

```
input.close();
```

This is particularly important for output files, in order to ensure that the file buffer has been emptied and all data written to the file. Since file output is buffered, it is not until the output buffer is full that data will normally be written to disc. If a program crash occurs, then any data still in the buffer will not have been written to disc. Consequently, it is good practice to close a file explicitly if you have finished writing to it (or if your program does not need to write to the file for anything more than a very short amount of time). Closing the file causes the output buffer to be flushed and any data in the buffer to be written to disc. No such precaution is relevant for a file used for input purposes only, of course.

Note that we cannot move from reading mode to writing mode or vice versa without first closing our *Scanner* object or *PrintWriter* object and then opening a *PrintWriter* object or *Scanner* object respectively and associating it with the file.

Now for a simple example program to illustrate file output…

Example

Writes a single line of output to a text file.

```
import java.io.*;

public class FileTest1
{

   public static void main(String[] args)
                                    throws IOException
   {
      PrintWriter output =
               new PrintWriter(new File("test1.txt"));
      output.println("Single line of text!");
      output.close();
   }
}
```

Note that there is no 'append' method for a serial file in Java. After execution of the above program, the file 'test1.txt' will contain **only** the specified line of text. If the file already existed, its initial contents will have been overwritten. This may or may not have been your intention, so take care! If you need to add data to the contents of an existing file, you still (as before Java SE 5) need to use a *FileWriter* object, employing either of the following constructors with a second argument of `true`:

- `FileWriter(String` <fileName>, `boolean` <append>`)`
- `FileWriter(File` <fileName>, `boolean` <append>`)`

For example:

```
FileWriter addFile = new FileWriter("data.txt", true);
```

In order to send output to the file, a *PrintWriter* would then be wrapped around the *FileWriter*:

```
PrintWriter output = new PrintWriter(addFile);
```

These two steps may, of course, be combined into one:

```
PrintWriter output =
     new PrintWriter(
             new FileWriter("data.txt", true);
```

It would be a relatively simple matter to write Java code to read the data back from a text file to which it has been written, but a quick and easy way of checking that the data has been written successfully is to use the relevant operating system command. For example, on a PC, open up an MS-DOS command window and use the MS-DOS *type* command, as below.

```
type test1.dat
```

Often, we will wish to accept data from the user during the running of a program. In addition, we may also wish to allow the user to enter a name for the file. The next example illustrates both of these features. Since there may be a significant delay between consecutive file output operations while awaiting input from the user, it is good programming practice to use *File* method *flush* to empty the file output buffer. (Remember that, if the program crashes and there is still data in the file output buffer, that data will be lost!)

Example

```
import java.io.*;
import java.util.*;

public class FileTest2
{

    public static void main(String[] args)
                              throws IOException
    {
        String fileName;
        int mark;
        Scanner input= new Scanner(System.in);

        System.out.print("Enter file name: ");
        fileName = input.nextLine();
        PrintWriter output =
                 new PrintWriter(new File(fileName));
        System.out.println("Ten marks needed.\n");
        for (int i=1; i<11; i++)
        {
            System.out.print("Enter mark " + i + ": ");
            mark = input.nextInt();
            //* Should really validate entry! *
            output.println(mark);
            output.flush();
        }
        output.close();
    }
}
```

Example output from this program is shown in Fig. 4.1.

When reading data from any text file, we should not depend upon being able to read a specific number of values, so we should read until the end of the file is reached. Programming languages differ fundamentally in how they detect an end-of-file situation. With some, a program crash will result if an attempt is made to read beyond the end of a file; with others, you **must** attempt to read beyond the end of the file in order for end-of-file to be detected. Before Java SE 5, Java fell into the latter category and it was necessary to keep reading until the string read (and **only** strings were read then)

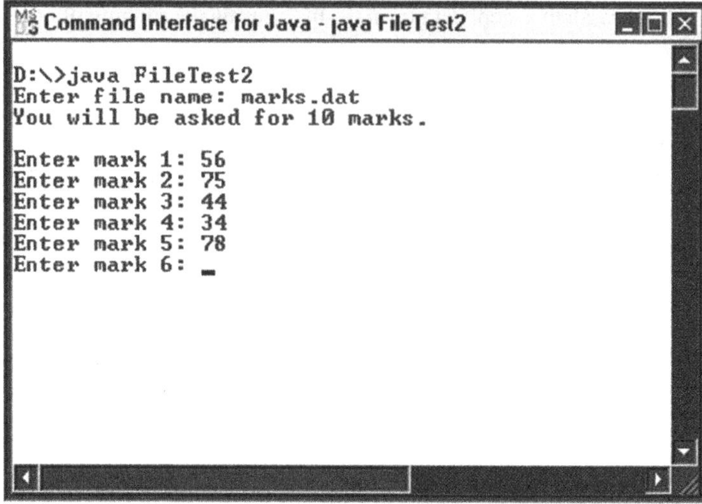

Fig. 4.1 Accepting serial file input from the user

had a `null` reference. As of Java 5, we must **not** attempt to read beyond the end-of-file if we wish to avoid the generation of a *NoSuchElementException*. Instead, we have to check ahead to see whether there is more data to be read. This is done by making use of the *Scanner* class's *hasNext* method, which returns a Boolean result indicating whether or not there is any more data.

Example

```
import java.io.*;
import java.util.*;

public class FileTest3
{
    public static void main(String[] args)
                                    throws IOException
    {
        int mark, total=0, count=0;
        Scanner input =
                    new Scanner(new File("marks.txt"));

        while (input.hasNext())
        {
            mark = input.nextInt();
            total += mark;
            count++;
        }
        input.close();
```

```
        System.out.println("Mean = "
                                   + (float)total/count);
    }
}
```

Note that there is no structure imposed upon a file by Java. It is the programmer's responsibility to impose any required logical structuring upon the file. 'Records' on the file are not physical units determined by Java or the operating system, but logical units set up and maintained by the programmer. For example, if a file is to hold details of customer accounts, each logical record may comprise the following:

- account number;
- customer name;
- account balance.

It is the programmer's responsibility to ensure that each logical record on the file holds exactly these three fields and that they occur in the order specified.

4.2 File Methods

Class *File* has a large number of methods, the most important of which are shown below.

- ***boolean canRead()***
  Returns *true* if file is readable and *false* otherwise.
- ***boolean canWrite()***
  Returns *true* if file is writeable and *false* otherwise.
- ***boolean delete()***
  Deletes file and returns *true/false* for success/failure.
- ***boolean exists()***
  Returns *true* if file exists and *false* otherwise.
- ***String getName()***
  Returns name of file.
- ***boolean isDirectory()***
  Returns *true* if object is a directory/folder and *false* otherwise.
  (Note that *File* objects can refer to ordinary files or to directories.)
- ***boolean isFile()***
  Returns *true* if object is a file and *false* otherwise.
- ***long length()***
  Returns length of file in bytes.
- ***String[] list()***
  If object is a directory, array holding names of files within directory is returned.

- ***File[] listFiles()***
  Similar to previous method, but returns array of *File* objects.
- ***boolean mkdir()***
  Creates directory with name of current *File* object.
  Return value indicates success/failure.

The following example illustrates the use of some of these methods.

Example

```
import java.io.*;
import java.util.*;

public class FileMethods
{
    public static void main(String[] args)
                                throws IOException
    {
        String filename;
        Scanner input = new Scanner(System.in);

        System.out.print(
                      "Enter name of file/directory ");
        System.out.print("or press <Enter> to quit: ");
        filename = input.nextLine();

        while (!filename.equals("")) //Not <Enter> key.
        {
            File fileDir = new File(filename);

            if (!fileDir.exists())
            {
                System.out.println(filename
                                  + " does not exist!");
                break; //Get out of loop.
            }

            System.out.print(filename + " is a ");
            if (fileDir.isFile())
                System.out.println("file.");
            else
                System.out.println("directory.");

            System.out.print("It is ");
            if (!fileDir.canRead())
                System.out.print("not ");
            System.out.println("readable.");

            System.out.print("It is ");
            if (!fileDir.canWrite())
                System.out.print("not ");
```

```
            System.out.println("writeable.");
            if (fileDir.isDirectory())
            {
                System.out.println("Contents:");
                String[] fileList  = fileDir.list();
                //Now display list of files in
                //directory…
                for (int i=0;i<fileList.length;i++)
                    System.out.println("      "
                                       + fileList[i]);
            }
            else
            {
                System.out.print("Size of file: ");
                System.out.println(fileDir.length()
                                          + " bytes.");
            }
            System.out.print(
               "\n\nEnter name of next file/directory ");
            System.out.print(
                         "or press <Enter> to quit: ");
            filename   = input.nextLine();
        }
        input.close();
    }
}
```

Figure 4.2 shows example output from the above program.

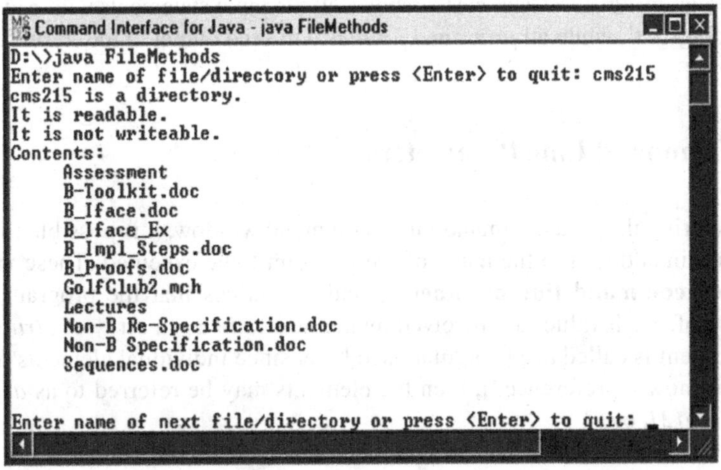

```
Command Interface for Java - java FileMethods
D:\>java FileMethods
Enter name of file/directory or press <Enter> to quit: cms215
cms215 is a directory.
It is readable.
It is not writeable.
Contents:
      Assessment
      B-Toolkit.doc
      B_Iface.doc
      B_Iface_Ex
      B_Impl_Steps.doc
      B_Proofs.doc
      GolfClub2.mch
      Lectures
      Non-B Re-Specification.doc
      Non-B Specification.doc
      Sequences.doc

Enter name of next file/directory or press <Enter> to quit: _
```

Fig. 4.2 Outputting file properties

4.3 Redirection

By default, the standard input stream *System.in* is associated with the keyboard, while the standard output stream *System.out* is associated with the VDU. If, however, we wish input to come from some other source (such as a text file) or we wish output to go to somewhere other than the VDU screen, then we can **redirect** the input/output. This can be **extremely** useful when debugging a program that requires anything more than a couple of items of data from the user. Instead of re-entering the data each time we run the program, we simply create a text file holding our items of data on separate lines (using a text editor or wordprocessor) and then re-direct input to come from our text file. This can save a **great deal** of time-consuming, tedious and error-prone re-entry of data when debugging a program.

We use '<' to specify the new source of input and '>' to specify the new output destination.

Examples

```
java ReadData < payroll.txt
java WriteData > results.txt
```

When the first of these lines is executed, program 'ReadData(.class)' begins execution as normal. However, whenever it encounters a file input statement (via *Scanner* method *next*, *nextLine*, *nextInt*, etc.), it will now take as its input the next available item of data in file 'payroll.txt'. Similarly, program 'WriteData(.class)' will direct the output of any *print* and *println* statements to file 'results.txt'.

We can use redirection of both input and output with the same program, as the example below shows. For example:

```
java ProcessData < readings.txt > results. txt
```

For program 'ProcessData(.class)' above, all file input statements will read from file 'readings.txt', while all *print*s and *println*s will send output to file 'results.txt'.

4.4 Command Line Parameters

When entering the *java* command into a command window, it is possible to supply values in addition to the name of the program to be executed. These values are called **command line parameters** and are values that the program may make use of. Such values are received by method *main* as an array of *String*s. If this argument is called *arg* [Singular used here, since individual elements of the array will now be referenced], then the elements may be referred to as *arg[0]*, *arg[1]*, *arg[2]*, etc.

<u>Example</u>

Suppose a compiled Java program called *Copy.class* copies the contents of one file into another. Rather than prompting the user to enter the names of the files (which would be perfectly feasible, of course), the program may allow the user to specify the names of the two files as command line parameters:

```
java Copy source.dat dest.dat
```

(Please ignore the fact that MS-DOS has a perfectly good *copy* command that could do the job without the need for our Java program!)

Method *main* would then access the file names through *arg[0]* and *arg[1]*:

```
import java.io.*;
import java.util.*;

public class Copy
{
    public static void main(String[] arg)
                                    throws IOException
    {
        //First check that 2 file names have been
        //supplied...
        if (arg.length < 2)
        {
            System.out.println(
                       "You must supply TWO file names.");
            System.out.println("Syntax:");
            System.out.println(
              "        java Copy <source> <destination>");
            return;
        }

        Scanner source = new Scanner(new File(arg[0]));
        PrintWriter destination =
                       new PrintWriter(new File(arg[1]));

        String input;
        while (source.hasNext())
        {
            input = source.nextLine();
            destination.println(input);
        }

        source.close();
        destination.close();
    }
}
```

4.5 Random Access Files

Serial access files are simple to handle and are quite widely used in small-scale applications or as a means of providing temporary storage in larger-scale applications. However, they do have two distinct disadvantages, as noted below.

(i) We can't go directly to a specific record. In order to access a particular record, it is necessary to physically read past all the preceding records. For applications containing thousands of records, this is simply not feasible.
(ii) It is not possible to add or modify records within an existing file. (The whole file would have to be re-created!)

Random access files (probably more meaningfully called **direct access** files) overcome both of these problems, but do have some disadvantages of their own...

(i) In common usage, all the (logical) records in a particular file must be of the same length.
(ii) Again in common usage, a given string field must be of the same length for all records on the file.
(iii) Numeric data is not in human-readable form.

However, the speed and flexibility of random access files often greatly outweigh the above disadvantages. Indeed, for many real-life applications, there is no realistic alternative to some form of direct access.

To create a random access file in Java, we create a *RandomAccessFile* object. The constructor takes two arguments:

- a string or *File* object identifying the file;
- a string specifying the file's access mode.

The latter of these may be either "r" (for read-only access) or "rw" (for read-and-write access). For example:

```
RandomAccessFile ranFile =
      new RandomAccessFile("accounts.dat","rw");
```

Before reading or writing a record, it is necessary to position the **file pointer**. We do this by calling method *seek*, which requires a single argument specifying the byte position within the file. Note that the first byte in a file is byte **0**. For example:

```
ranFile.seek(500);
//Move to byte 500 (the 501st byte).
```

In order to move to the correct position for a particular record, we need to know two things:

- the size of records on the file;
- the algorithm for calculating the appropriate position.

The second of these two factors will usually involve some kind of **hashing function** that is applied to the key field. We shall avoid this complexity and assume that records have keys 1, 2, 3,... and that they are stored sequentially. However, we still need to calculate the record size. Obviously, we can decide upon the size of each *String* field ourselves. For numeric fields, though, the byte allocations are fixed by Java (in a platform-independent fashion) and are as shown below.

`int`	4 bytes
`long`	8 bytes
`float`	4 bytes
`double`	8 bytes

Class *RandomAccessFile* provides the following methods for manipulating the above types:

readInt, readLong, readFloat, readDouble
writeInt, writeLong, writeFloat, writeDouble

It also provides similarly-named methods for manipulating the other primitive types. In addition, it provides a method called *writeChars* for writing a (variable-length) string. Unfortunately, no methods for reading/writing a string of fixed size are provided, so we need to write our own code for this. In doing so, we shall need to make use of methods *readChar* and *writeChar* for reading/writing the primitive type *char*.

Example

Suppose we wish to set up an accounts file with the following fields:

- account number (*long*);
- surname (*String*);
- initials (*String*);
- balance (*float*).

N.B. When calculating the number of bytes for a *String* field, do not make the mistake of allocating only one byte per character. Remember that Java is based on the unicode character set, in which each character occupies **two** bytes.

Now let's suppose that we decide to allocate 15 (unicode) characters to surnames and 3 (unicode) characters to initials. This means that each surname will be allocated 30 (i.e., 15 × 2) bytes and each set of initials will be allocated 6 (i.e., 3 × 2) bytes. Since we know that a *long* occupies precisely 8 bytes and a *float* occupies precisely 4 bytes, we now know that record size=(8+30+6+4) bytes=48 bytes. Consequently, we shall store records starting at byte positions 0, 48, 96, etc. The formula for calculating the position of any record on the file is then:

(Record No. –1) × 48

For example, suppose our *RandomAccessFile* object for the above accounts file is called *ranAccts*. Then the code to locate the record with account number 5 is:

```
ranAccts.seek(192);    //(5-1)x48 = 192
```

Since method *length* returns the number of bytes in a file, we can always work out the number of records in a random access file by dividing the size of the file by the size of an individual record. Consequently, the number of records in file *ranAccts* at any given time = *ranAccts.length()/48*.

Now for the code…

```
import java.io.*;
import java.util.*;

public class RanFile1
{
   private static final int REC_SIZE = 48;
   private static final int SURNAME_SIZE = 15;
   private static final int NUM_INITS = 3;
   private static long acctNum = 0;
   private static String surname, initials;
   private static float balance;

   public static void main(String[] args)
                                       throws IOException
   {
      RandomAccessFile ranAccts =
         new RandomAccessFile("accounts.dat", "rw");

      Scanner input = new Scanner(System.in);

      String reply = "y";

      do
      {
         acctNum++;
         System.out.println(
            "\nAccount number " + acctNum + ".\n");
         System.out.print("Surname: ");
         surname = input.nextLine();
         System.out.print("Initial(s): ");
         initials = input.nextLine();
         System.out.print("Balance: ");
         balance = input.nextFloat();

         //Now get rid of carriage return(!)…
         input.nextLine();

         writeRecord(ranAccts); //Method defined below.

         System.out.print(
            "\nDo you wish to do this again (y/n)? ");
         reply = input.nextLine();
      }while (reply.equals("y")||reply.equals("Y"));

      System.out.println();
      showRecords(ranAccts);     //Method defined below.
```

```
}

public static void writeRecord(RandomAccessFile file)
                                    throws IOException
{
   //First find starting byte for current record...
   long filePos = (acctNum-1) * REC_SIZE;

   //Position file pointer...
   file.seek(filePos);

   //Now write the four (fixed-size) fields.
   //Note that a definition must be provided
   //for method writeString...
   file.writeLong(acctNum);
   writeString(file, surname, SURNAME_SIZE);
   writeString(file, initials, NUM_INITS);
   file.writeFloat(balance);
}

public static void writeString(RandomAccessFile file,
       String text, int fixedSize) throws IOException
{
   int size = text.length();

   if (size<=fixedSize)
   {
      file.writeChars(text);

      //Now 'pad out' the field with spaces...
      for (int i=size; i<fixedSize; i++)
          file.writeChar(' ');
   }
   else    //String is too long!
      file.writeChars(text.substring(0,fixedSize));
   //Write to file the first fixedSize characters of
   //string text, starting at byte zero.
}

public static void showRecords(RandomAccessFile file)
                                    throws IOException
{
   long numRecords = file.length()/REC_SIZE;

   file.seek(0);      //Go to start of file.
   for (int i=0; i<numRecords; i++)
   {
      acctNum = file.readLong();
      surname = readString(file, SURNAME_SIZE);
```

```
            //readString defined below.
            initials = readString(file, NUM_INITS);
            balance = file.readFloat();

            System.out.printf("" + acctNum
                            + "    " + surname
                            + "   " + initials + "    "
                            + "%.2f %n",balance);
        }
    }

    public static String readString(
                RandomAccessFile file, int fixedSize)
                                throws IOException
    {
        String value = "";      //Set up empty string.
        for (int i=0; i<fixedSize; i++)
        //Read character and concatenate it onto value...
            value+=file.readChar();

        return value;
    }
}
```

Note that methods *readString* and *writeString* above may be used *without modification* in any Java program that needs to transfer strings from/to a random access file.

The following screenshot demonstrates the operation of this program (Fig. 4.3).

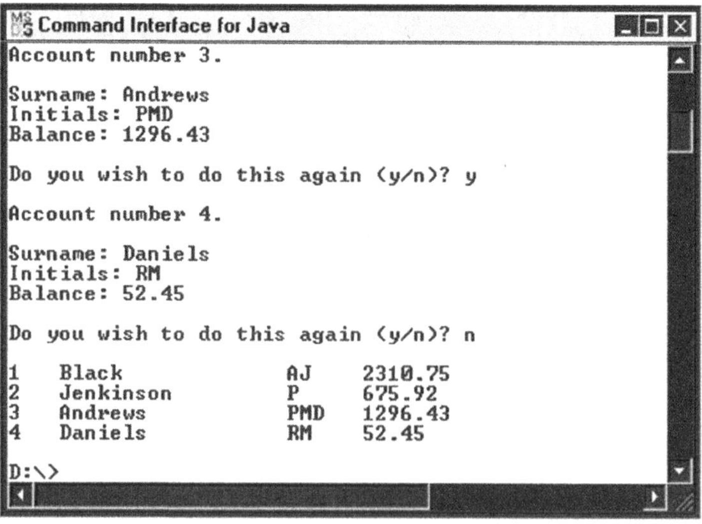

Fig. 4.3 Creating a simple random access file and displaying its contents

The above example does not adequately demonstrate the direct access capabilities of a *RandomAccessFile* object, since we have processed the whole of the file from start to finish, dealing with records in the order in which they are stored on the file. We should also be able to retrieve individual records from anywhere in the file and/or make modifications to those records. The next example shows how this can be done for our accounts file.

Example

```
//Allows the user to retrieve individual account
//records and modify their balances.

import java.io.*;
import java.util.*;

public class RanFile2
{
    private static final int REC_SIZE=48;
    private static final int SURNAME_SIZE=15;
    private static final int NUM_INITS=3;
    private static long acctNum=0;
    private static String surname, initials;
    private static float balance;

    public static void main(String[] args)
                                    throws IOException
    {
        Scanner input = new Scanner(System.in);
        RandomAccessFile ranAccts =
            new RandomAccessFile("accounts.dat", "rw");
        long numRecords = ranAccts.length()/REC_SIZE;
        String reply;
        long currentPos;       //File pointer position.

        do
        {
            System.out.print("\nEnter account number: ");
            acctNum = input.nextLong();
            while ((acctNum<1) || (acctNum>numRecords))
            {
                System.out.println(
                        "\n*** Invalid number! ***\n");
                System.out.print(
                            "\nEnter account number: ");
                acctNum = input.nextLong();
            }
```

```
            showRecord(ranAccts);     //Defined below.
            System.out.print("\nEnter new balance: ");
            balance = input.nextFloat();

            input.nextLine();
            //Get rid of carriage return!

            currentPos = ranAccts.getFilePointer();
            ranAccts.seek(currentPos-4); //Back 4 bytes.
            ranAccts.writeFloat(balance);
            System.out.print(
                     "\nModify another balance (y/n)? ");
            reply = (input.nextLine()).toLowerCase();
        }while (reply.equals("y"));
        //(Alternative to method in previous example.)

        ranAccts.close();
    }

    public static void showRecord(RandomAccessFile file)
                                        throws IOException
    {
        file.seek((acctNum-1)*REC_SIZE);
        acctNum = file.readLong();
        surname = readString(file, SURNAME_SIZE);
        initials = readString(file, NUM_INITS);
        balance = file.readFloat();

        System.out.println("Surname:  " + surname);
        System.out.println("Initials: " + initials);
        System.out.printf("Balance:  %.2f %n",balance);
    }

    public static String readString(
                RandomAccessFile file, int fixedSize)
                                        throws IOException
    {
        //Set up empty buffer before reading from file...
        StringBuffer buffer = new StringBuffer();

        for (int i=0; i<fixedSize; i++)
        //Read character from file and append to buffer.
            buffer.append(file.readChar());
       return buffer.toString(); //Convert into String.
    }
}
```

4.6 Serialisation [U.S. Spelling Serialization]

As seen in the preceding sections, transferring data of the primitive types to and from disc files is reasonably straightforward. Transferring string data presents a little more of a challenge, but even this is not a particularly onerous task. However, how do we go about transferring objects of classes? (*String* is a class, of course, but it is treated rather differently from other classes.) One way of saving an object to a file would be to decompose the object into its constituent fields (strings and numbers) and write those individual data members to the file. Then, when reading the values back from the file, we could re-create the original objects by supplying those values to the appropriate constructors. However, this is a rather tedious and long-winded method. In addition, since the data members of an object may themselves include other objects (some of whose data members may include further objects, some of whose members…), this method would not be generally applicable.

Unlike other common O-O languages, Java provides an inbuilt solution: **serialisation**. Objects of any class that implements the Serializable interface may be transferred to and from disc files as whole objects, with no need for decomposition of those objects. The *Serializable* interface is, in fact, nothing more than a marker to tell Java that objects of this class may be transferred on an object stream to and from files. Implementation of the *Serializable* interface need involve no implementation of methods. The programmer merely has to ensure that the class to be used includes the declaration '*implements Serializable*' in its header line.

Class *ObjectOutputStream* is used to save entire objects directly to disc, while class *ObjectInputStream* is used to read them back from disc. For output, we wrap an object of class *ObjectOutputStream* around an object of class *FileOutputStream*, which itself is wrapped around a *File* object or file name. Similarly, input requires us to wrap an *ObjectInputStream* object around a *FileInputStream* object, which in turn is wrapped around a *File* object or file name.

Examples

```
(i)  ObjectOutputStream outStream =
           new ObjectOutputStream(
               new FileOutputStream("personnel.dat"));
(ii) ObjectInputStream inStream =
           new ObjectInputStream(
               new FileInputStream("personnel.dat"));
```

Methods *writeObject* and *readObject* are then used for the actual output and input respectively. Since these methods write/read objects of class *Object* (the ultimate superclass), any objects read back from file must be **typecast** into their original class before we try to use them. For example:

```
Personnel person = (Personnel)inStream.readObject();
//(Assuming that inStream is as declared above.)
```

In addition to the possibility of an *IOException* being generated during I/O, there is also the possibility of a *ClassNotFoundException* being generated, so we must either handle this exception ourselves or throw it. A further consideration that needs to be made is how we detect end-of-file, since there is no equivalent of the *Scanner* class's *hasNext* method for use with object streams. We **could** simply use a `for` loop to read back the number of objects we believe that the file holds, but this would be very bad practice in general (especially as we may often not know how many objects a particular file holds).

The only viable option there appears to be is to catch the *EOFException* that is generated when we read past the end of the file. This author feels rather uneasy about having to use this technique, since it conflicts with the fundamental ethos of exception handling. Exception handling (as the term implies) is designed to cater for exceptional and erroneous situations that we do not expect to happen if all goes well and processing proceeds as planned. Here, however, we are going to be using exception handling to detect something that we not only know will happen eventually, but also are **dependent** upon happening if processing is to reach a successful conclusion. Unfortunately, there does not appear to be any alternative to this technique.

Example

This example creates three objects of a class called *Personnel* and writes them to disc file (as objects). It then reads the three objects back from file (employing a typecast to convert them into their original type) and makes use of the 'get' methods of class *Personnel* to display the data members of the three objects. We must, of course, ensure that class *Personnel* implements the *Serializable* interface (which involves nothing more than including the phrase *implements Serializable*). In a real-life application, class *Personnel* would be defined in a separate file, but it has been included in the main application file below simply for convenience.

```
import java.io.*;

public class Serialise
{
    public static void main(String[] args)
        throws IOException, ClassNotFoundException
    {
        ObjectOutputStream outStream =
           new ObjectOutputStream(
                new FileOutputStream("personnel.dat"));

        Personnel[] staff =
            {new Personnel(123456,"Smith", "John"),
             new Personnel(234567,"Jones", "Sally Ann"),
             new Personnel(999999,"Black", "James Paul")};

        for (int i=0; i<staff.length; i++)
            outStream.writeObject(staff[i]);
```

```
        outStream.close();

        ObjectInputStream inStream =
                new ObjectInputStream(
                 new FileInputStream("personnel.dat"));

        int staffCount = 0;

        try
        {
            do
            {
                Personnel person =
                      (Personnel)inStream.readObject();
                staffCount++;

                System.out.println(
                      "\nStaff member " + staffCount);
                System.out.println("Payroll number: "
                                + person.getPayNum());
                System.out.println("Surname: "
                                + person.getSurname());
                System.out.println("First names: "
                            + person.getFirstNames());
            }while (true);
        }
        catch (EOFException eofEx)
        {
            System.out.println(
               "\n\n*** End of file ***\n");
            inStream.close();
        }
    }
}

class Personnel implements Serializable
//No action required by Serializable interface.
{
    private long payrollNum;
    private String surname;
    private  String firstNames;

    public Personnel(long payNum,String sName,
                                      String fNames)
    {
        payrollNum = payNum;
        surname = sName;
```

```
        firstNames = fNames;
    }

    public long getPayNum()
    {
        return payrollNum;
    }

    public String getSurname()
    {
        return surname;
    }

    public String getFirstNames()
    {
        return firstNames;
    }

    public void setSurname(String sName)
    {
        surname = sName;
    }
}
```

Output from the above program is shown in Fig. 4.4.

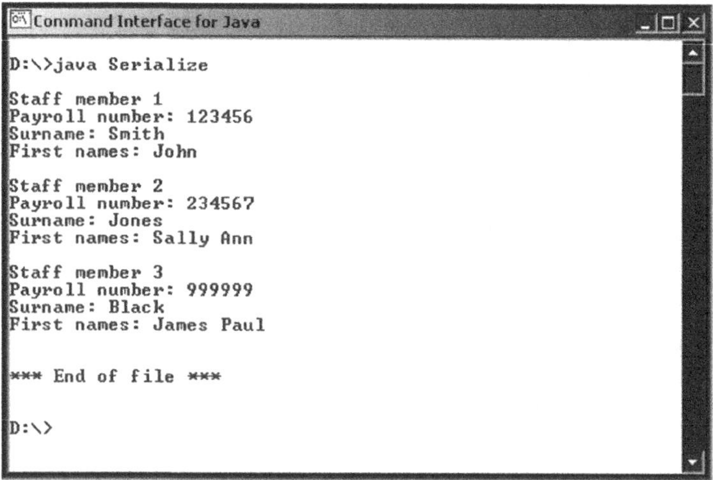

Fig. 4.4 Displaying the contents of a small file of serialised objects

4.7 File I/O with GUIs

Since the majority of applications nowadays have GUI interfaces, it would be nice to provide such an interface for our file handling programs. The reader will almost certainly have used file handling applications that provide such an interface. A particularly common feature of such applications is the provision of a dialogue box that allows the user to navigate the computer's file system and select either an existing file for opening or the destination directory for a file that is to be created. By employing Swing class *JFileChooser*, we can display a dialogue box that will allow the user to do just that.

A *JFileChooser* object opens a modal dialogue box ['Modal' means that the window must be dismissed before further processing may be carried out] that displays the system's directory structure and allows the user to traverse it. Once a *JFileChooser* object has been created, method *setFileSelectionMode* may be used to specify whether files and/or directories are selectable by the user, via the following constants:

JFileChooser.FILES_ONLY
JFileChooser.DIRECTORIES_ONLY
JFileChooser.FILES_AND_DIRECTORIES

Example

```
JFileChooser fileChooser = new JFileChooser();
fileChooser.setFileSelectionMode(
                                JFileChooser.FILES_ONLY);
```

We can then call either *showOpenDialog* or *showSaveDialog*. The former displays a dialogue box with 'Open' and 'Cancel' buttons, while the latter displays a dialogue box with 'Save' and 'Cancel' buttons. Each of these methods takes a single argument and returns an integer result. The argument specifies the *JFileChooser*'s parent component, i.e. the window over which the dialogue box will be displayed. For example:

```
fileChooser.showOpenDialog(this);
```

The above will cause the dialogue box to be displayed in the centre of the application window. If *null* is passed as an argument, then the dialogue box appears in the centre of the screen.

The integer value returned may be compared with either of the following inbuilt constants:

JFileChooser.CANCEL_OPTION
JFileChooser.APPROVE_OPTION

Testing against the latter of these constants will return 'true' if the user has selected a file.

Example

```
int selection = fileChooser.showOpenDialog(null);
if (selection == JFileChooser.APPROVE_OPTION)
   ..............................................
   //Specifies action taken if file chosen.)
```

If a file has been selected, then method *getSelectedFile* returns the corresponding *File* object. For example:

```
File file = fileChooser.getSelectedFile();
```

For serial I/O of strings and the primitive types, we would then wrap either a *Scanner* object (for input) or a *PrintWriter* object (for output) around the *File* object, as we did in 4.1.

Example

```
Scanner fileIn = new Scanner(file);
PrintWriter fileOut = new PrintWriter(file);
```

We can then make use of methods *next, nextInt*, etc. for input and methods *print* and *println* for output.

Similarly, for serial I/O of objects, we would wrap either an *ObjectInputStream* object plus *FileInputStream* object or an *ObjectOutputStream* object plus *FileOutputStream* object around the *File* object.

Example

```
ObjectInputStream fileIn =
          new ObjectInputStream(
                 new FileInputStream(file));

ObjectOutputStream fileOut =
          new ObjectOutputStream(
                 new FileOutputStream(file));
```

We can then make use of methods *readObject* and *writeObject*, as before. Of course, since we are now dealing with a GUI, we need to implement *ActionListener*, in order to process our button selections.

Example

This example is a simple application for reading a file of examination marks and displaying the results of individual students, one at a time. The file holding results will be a simple serial file, with each student's data held as three fields in the following sequence: surname, first name(s) and examination mark. We shall firstly allow the user to navigate the computer's file system and select the desired file (employing a *JFileChooser* object). Once a file has been selected, our program will open the file, read the first (logical) record and display its contents within the text fields of a panel we have set up. This panel will also contain two buttons, one to allow the user to open another file and the other to allow the user to move on to the next record in the file.

In order to read an individual record, we shall define a method called *readRecord* that reads in the surname, first name(s) and examination mark for an individual student.

Before looking at the code, it is probably useful to look ahead and see what the intended output should look like. In order that the *JFileChooser* object may be viewed as well, the screenshot in Fig. 4.5 shows the screen layout after one file has been opened and then the 'Open File' button has been clicked on by the user.

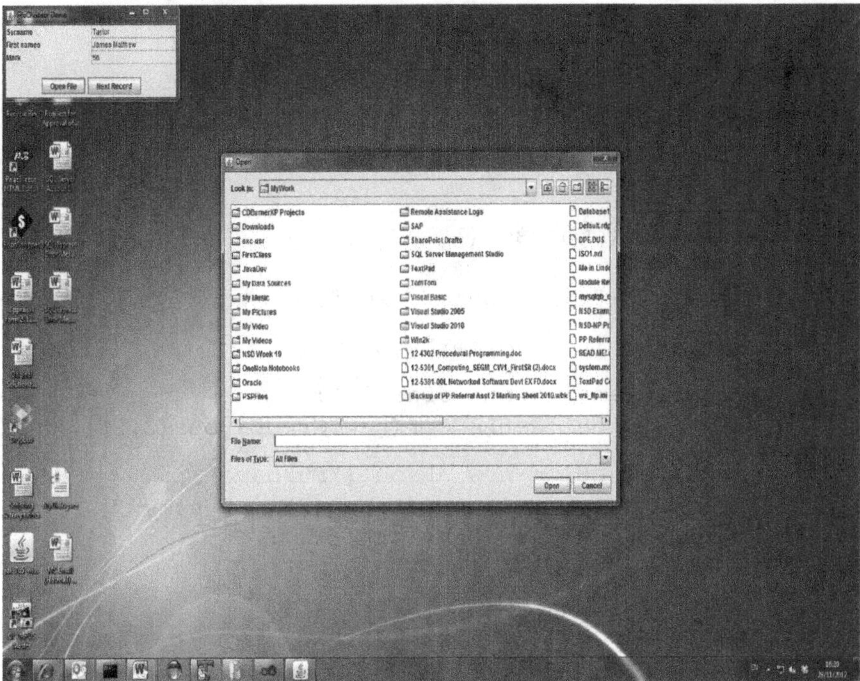

Fig. 4.5 A *JFileChooser* object being used to select a file

The code for this application is shown below. If the reader wishes to create a serial file for testing this program, this may be done very easily by using any text editor to enter the required three fields for each of a series of students (each field being followed by a carriage return).

```
import java.awt.*;
import java.awt.event.*;
import javax.swing.*;
import java.io.*;
import java.util.*;

public class UseFileChooser extends JFrame
                              implements ActionListener
```

```
{
    private JPanel displayPanel, buttonPanel;
    private JLabel surnameLabel, firstNamesLabel,
                                        markLabel;
    private JTextField surnameBox, firstNamesBox,
                                        markBox;
    private JButton openButton, nextButton;
    private Scanner input;

    public static void main(String[] args)
    {
        UseFileChooser frame = new UseFileChooser();
        frame.setSize(350,150);
        frame.setVisible(true);
    }

    public UseFileChooser()
    {
        setTitle("FileChooser Demo");

        setLayout(new BorderLayout());

        displayPanel = new JPanel();
        displayPanel.setLayout(new GridLayout(3,2));

        surnameLabel = new JLabel("Surname");
        firstNamesLabel = new JLabel("First names");
        markLabel = new JLabel("Mark");
        surnameBox= new JTextField();
        firstNamesBox = new JTextField();
        markBox = new JTextField();

        //For this application, user should not be able
        //to change any records…
        surnameBox.setEditable(false);
        firstNamesBox.setEditable(false);
        markBox.setEditable(false);

        displayPanel.add(surnameLabel);
        displayPanel.add(surnameBox);
        displayPanel.add(firstNamesLabel);
        displayPanel.add(firstNamesBox);
        displayPanel.add(markLabel);
        displayPanel.add(markBox);

        add(displayPanel, BorderLayout.NORTH);

        buttonPanel = new JPanel();
        buttonPanel.setLayout(new FlowLayout());

        openButton = new JButton("Open File");
```

```
        openButton.addActionListener(this);
        nextButton = new JButton("Next Record");
        nextButton.addActionListener(this);
        nextButton.setEnabled(false);
        //(No file open yet.)

        buttonPanel.add(openButton);
        buttonPanel.add(nextButton);

        add(buttonPanel, BorderLayout.SOUTH);

        addWindowListener(
            new WindowAdapter()
            {
                public void windowClosing(
                                     WindowEvent event)
                {
                  if (input != null)    //A file is open.
                      input.close();
                  System.exit(0);
                }
            }
        );
    }

    public void actionPerformed(ActionEvent event)
    {
        if (event.getSource() == openButton)
        {
            try
            {
                openFile();
            }
            catch(IOException ioEx)
            {
                JOptionPane.showMessageDialog(this,
                               "Unable to open file!");
            }
        }
        else
        {
            try
            {
                readRecord();
            }
            catch(EOFException eofEx)
            {
                nextButton.setEnabled(false);
```

```
                //(No next record.)
                JOptionPane.showMessageDialog(this,
                                "Incomplete record!\n"
                              + "End of file reached.");
            }
            catch(IOException ioEx)
            {
                JOptionPane.showMessageDialog(this,
                                "Unable to read file!");
            }
        }
    }

    public void openFile() throws IOException
    {
        if (input != null)    //A file is already open, so
                              //needs to be closed first.
        {
            input.close();
            input = null;
        }
        JFileChooser fileChooser = new JFileChooser();
        fileChooser.setFileSelectionMode(
                              JFileChooser.FILES_ONLY);

        int selection = fileChooser.showOpenDialog(null);
        //Window opened in centre of screen.

        if (selection == JFileChooser.CANCEL_OPTION)
            return;

        File results = fileChooser.getSelectedFile();
        if (results ==
                    null||results.getName().equals(""))
        //No file name entered by user.
        {
            JOptionPane.showMessageDialog(this,
                                "Invalid selection!");
            return;
        }
        input = new Scanner(results);
        readRecord(); //Read and display first record.
        nextButton.setEnabled(true);    //(File now open.)
    }

    public void readRecord() throws IOException
    {
        String surname, firstNames, textMark;
```

```
        //Clear text fields...
        surnameBox.setText("");
        firstNamesBox.setText("");
        markBox.setText("");

        if (input.hasNext()) //Not at end of file.
        {
            surname = input.nextLine();
            surnameBox.setText(surname);
        }
        else
        {
            JOptionPane.showMessageDialog(this,
                                    "End of file reached.");
            nextButton.setEnabled(false);//No next record.
            return;
        }
        //Should cater for possibility of incomplete
        //records...

        if (!input.hasNext())
            throw (new EOFException());

        //Otherwise...
        firstNames = input.nextLine();
        firstNamesBox.setText(firstNames);

        if (!input.hasNext())
            throw (new EOFException());

        //Otherwise...
        textMark = input.nextLine();
        markBox.setText(textMark);
    }
}
```

Note that neither *windowClosing* nor *actionPerformed* can throw an exception, since their signatures do not contain any *throws* clause and we cannot change those signatures. Consequently, any exceptions that do arise must be handled explicitly either by these methods themselves or by methods called by them (as with method *closeFile*).

4.8 ArrayLists

An object of class *ArrayList* is like an array, but can dynamically increase or decrease in size according to an application's changing storage requirements and can hold only references to objects, not values of primitive types. As of Java

SE 5, an individual *ArrayList* can hold only references to instances of a single, specified class. (This restriction can be circumvented by specifying the base type to be *Object*, the ultimate superclass, if a heterogeneous collection of objects is truly required.) Class *ArrayList* is contained within package *java.util*, so this package should be imported by any program wishing to make use of *ArrayList*s.

Constructor overloading allows us to specify the initial size if we wish, but the simplest form of the constructor takes no arguments and assumes an initial capacity of ten. In common with the other member classes of Java's Collection Framework, the class of elements that may be held in an *ArrayList* structure is specified in angle brackets after the collection class name, both in the declaration of the *ArrayList* and in its creation. For example, the following statement declares and creates an *ArrayList* that can hold *String*s:

```
ArrayList<String> stringArray = new ArrayList<String>();
```

This syntax was applicable up to Java SE 6 and is accepted in Java SE 7, but the latter also allows a shortened version of the above syntax, in which the type of elements held inside the collection class is not repeated. Instead, the angle brackets immediately preceding the brackets for the collection class constructor are left empty:

```
ArrayList<String> nameList = new ArrayList<>();
```

Objects are added to the end of an *ArrayList* via method *add* and then referenced/retrieved via method *get*, which takes a single argument that specifies the object's position within the *ArrayList* (numbering from zero, of course). Since the elements of an *ArrayList* (and of any other collection class) are stored as *Object* references (i.e., as references to instances of class *Object*) whilst in the *ArrayList*, it used to be the case that elements of the *ArrayList* had to be typecast back into their original type when being retrieved from the *ArrayList*, but the 'auto-unboxing' feature introduced by Java SE 5 means that they can be retrieved directly now.

Example (Assumes that *ArrayList* is empty at start)

```
String name1 = "Jones";
nameList.add(name1);
String name2 = nameList.get(0);
```

After execution of the above lines, *name1* and *name2* will both reference the string 'Jones'.

An object may be added at a specific position within an *ArrayList* via an overloaded form of the *add* method that takes two arguments, the first of which specifies the position at which the element is to be added.

Example

```
nameList.add(2, "Patterson"); //3rd position.
```

4.9 ArrayLists and Serialisation

It is much more efficient to save a single *ArrayList* to disc than it is to save a series of individual objects. Placing a series of objects into a single *ArrayList* is a very neat way of packaging and transferring our objects. This technique carries another significant advantage: we shall have some form of **random access**, via the *ArrayList* class's *get* method (albeit based on knowing each element's position within the *ArrayList*). Without this, we have the considerable disadvantage of being restricted to serial access only.

Example

This example creates three objects of class *Personnel* (as featured in the example at the end of Sect. 4.6) and uses the *add* method of class `ArrayList` to place the objects into an `ArrayList`. It then employs a 'for-each' loop and the 'get' methods of class *Personnel* to retrieve the data properties of the three objects.

We could use the same `ArrayList` object for sending objects out to the file and for receiving them back from the file, but two `ArrayList` objects have been used below simply to demonstrate beyond any doubt that the values have been read back in (and are not simply the original values, still held in the `ArrayList` object).

```
import java.io.*;
import java.util.*;

public class ArrayListSerialise
{
    public static void main(String[] args)
          throws   IOException, ClassNotFoundException
    {
        ObjectOutputStream outStream =
            new ObjectOutputStream(
              new FileOutputStream("personnelList.dat"));
        ArrayList<Personnel> staffListOut =
                                new ArrayList<>();
        ArrayList<Personnel> staffListIn =
                                new ArrayList<>();

        Personnel[] staff =
            {new Personnel(123456,"Smith", "John"),
            new Personnel(234567,"Jones", "Sally Ann"),
            new Personnel(999999,"Black", "James Paul")};

        for (int i=0; i<staff.length; i++)
            staffListOut.add(staff[i]);

        outStream.writeObject(staffListOut);

        outStream.close();
        ObjectInputStream inStream =
```

```
            new ObjectInputStream(
              new FileInputStream("personnelList.dat"));
        int staffCount = 0;
        try
        {
            staffListIn =
              (ArrayList<Personnel>)inStream.readObject();
            //The compiler will issue a warning for the
            //above line, but ignore this!
            for (Personnel person:staffListIn)
            {
                staffCount++;
                System.out.println(
                       "\nStaff member " + staffCount);
                System.out.println("Payroll number: "
                                   + person.getPayNum());
                System.out.println("Surname: "
                                   + person.getSurname());
                System.out.println("First names: "
                              + person.getFirstNames());
            }
            System.out.println("\n");
        }
        catch (EOFException eofEx)
        {
            System.out.println(
                           "\n\n*** End of file ***\n");
            inStream.close();
        }
    }
}

class Personnel implements Serializable
{
    private long payrollNum;
    private String surname;
    private String firstNames;

    public Personnel(long payNum,String sName,
                                      String fNames)
    {
        payrollNum = payNum;
        surname = sName;
        firstNames = fNames;
    }
```

```
    public long getPayNum()
    {
        return payrollNum;
    }

    public String getSurname()
    {
        return surname;
    }

    public String getFirstNames()
    {
        return firstNames;
    }

    public void setSurname(String sName)
    {
        surname = sName;
    }
}
```

Using methods covered in Chap. 2, the above code may be adapted very easily to produce a simple client–server application in which the server supplies personnel details in response to client requests. The only difference is that, instead of sending a series of strings from the server to the client(s), we shall now be passing an *ArrayList*. Consequently, we shall not be making use of a *PrintWriter* object in our server. Instead, we shall need to create an *ObjectOutputStream* object. We do this by passing the *OutputStream* object returned by our server's *Socket* object to the *ObjectOutputStream* constructor, instead of to the *PrintWriter* constructor (as was done previously).

Example

Suppose that the *Socket* object is called *socket* and the output object is called *out*. Then, instead of

```
PrintWriter out =
     new PrintWriter(socket.getOutputStream(),true);
```

we shall have:

```
ObjectOutputStream out =
  new ObjectOutputStream(socket.getOutputStream());
```

Though class *Personnel* was shown in previous examples as being in the same file as the main code, this was merely for convenience of reference. Normally, of course, we would hold this class in a separate file, in order to avoid code duplication and to allow the class's reusability by other applications. The code for the server (*PersonnelServer.java*) and the client (*PersonnelClient.java*) is shown below. You will find that the code for the server is an amalgamation of the first half of *MessageServer.java* from Chap. 2 and the early part of *ArrayListSerialise.java* from this section, while the code for the client is an amalgamation of the first part of *MessageClient.java* (Chap. 2) and the remainder of *ArrayListSerialise.java*.

As with earlier cases, this example is unrealistically simple, but serves to illustrate all the required steps of a socket-based client–server application for transmitting whole objects, without overwhelming the reader with unnecessary detail. Upon receiving the message 'SEND PERSONNEL DETAILS' from a client, the server simply transmits the *ArrayList* containing the three *Personnel* objects used for demonstration purposes in this section.

```
import java.io.*;
import java.net.*;
import java.util.*;

public class PersonnelServer
{
    private static ServerSocket serverSocket;
    private static final int PORT = 1234;
    private static Socket socket;
    private static ArrayList<Personnel> staffListOut;
    private static Scanner inStream;
    private static ObjectOutputStream outStream;

    public static void main(String[] args)
    {
        System.out.println("Opening port…\n");

        try
        {
            serverSocket = new ServerSocket(PORT);
        }
        catch(IOException ioEx)
        {
            System.out.println(
                             "Unable to attach to port!");
            System.exit(1);
        }

        staffListOut = new ArrayList<Personnel>();

        Personnel[] staff =
          {new Personnel(123456,"Smith", "John"),
           new Personnel(234567,"Jones", "Sally Ann"),
           new Personnel(999999,"Black", "James Paul")};

        for (int i=0; i<staff.length; i++)
            staffListOut.add(staff[i]);
        startServer();
    }
```

```
    private static void startServer()
    {
        do
        {
            try
            {
                socket = serverSocket.accept();

                inStream =
                  new Scanner(socket.getInputStream());

                outStream =
                    new ObjectOutputStream(
                             socket.getOutputStream());
              /*
              The above line and associated declaration
              are the only really new code featured in
              this example.
              */

                String message = inStream.nextLine();
                if (message.equals(
                             "SEND PERSONNEL DETAILS"))
                {
                   outStream.writeObject(staffListOut);
                    outStream.close();
                }

                System.out.println(
                         "\n* Closing connection... *");
                socket.close();
            }
            catch(IOException ioEx)
            {
                ioEx.printStackTrace();
            }
        }while (true);
    }
}
```

The only new point worthy of note in the code for the client is the necessary inclusion of `throws ClassNotFoundException`, both in the method that directly accesses the *ArrayList* of *Personnel* objects (the *run* method) and in the method that calls this one (the *main* method)…

```
import java.io.*;
import java.net.*;
import java.util.*;
```

```
public class PersonnelClient
{
    private static InetAddress host;
    private static final int PORT = 1234;

    public static void main(String[] args)
                              throws ClassNotFoundException
    {
        try
        {
            host = InetAddress.getLocalHost();
        }
        catch(UnknownHostException uhEx)
        {
            System.out.println("Host ID not found!");
            System.exit(1);
        }
        talkToServer();
    }

    private static void talkToServer()
                              throws ClassNotFoundException
    {
        try
        {
            Socket socket = new Socket(host,PORT);

            ObjectInputStream inStream =
                       new ObjectInputStream(
                              socket.getInputStream());

            PrintWriter outStream =
                new PrintWriter(
                        socket.getOutputStream(),true);

            //Set up stream for keyboard entry...
            Scanner userEntry = new Scanner(System.in);

            outStream.println("SEND PERSONNEL DETAILS");
            ArrayList<Personnel> response =
            (ArrayList<Personnel>)inStream.readObject();
            /*
            As in ArrayListSerialise, the compiler will
            issue a warning for the line above.
            Simply ignore this warning.
            */

            System.out.println(
                       "\n* Closing connection... *");
            socket.close();
```

```
            int staffCount = 0;

            for (Personnel person:response)
            {
                staffCount++;
                System.out.println(
                       "\nStaff member " + staffCount);
                System.out.println("Payroll number: "
                                  + person.getPayNum());
                System.out.println("Surname: "
                                 + person.getSurname());

                System.out.println("First names: "
                              + person.getFirstNames());
            }
            System.out.println("\n\n");
        }
        catch(IOException ioEx)
        {
            ioEx.printStackTrace();
        }
    }
}
```

The only change required to the code for the *Personnel* class (now in its separate file) will be the inclusion of `java.io.Serializable` in the header line (since it is no longer subject to the import of package *java.io*):

```
class Personnel implements java.io.Serializable
```

Figure 4.6 shows a client accessing the server, while Fig. 4.7 shows the corresponding output at the server end.

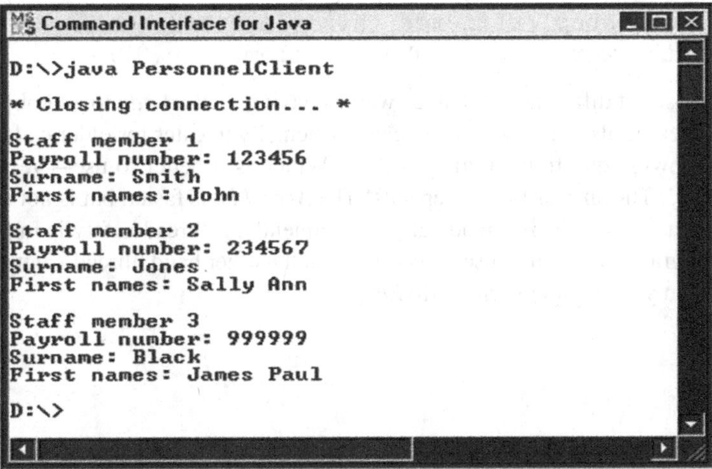

Fig. 4.6 Client using *ObjectInputStreams* to retrieve '*ArrayListed*' data from a server

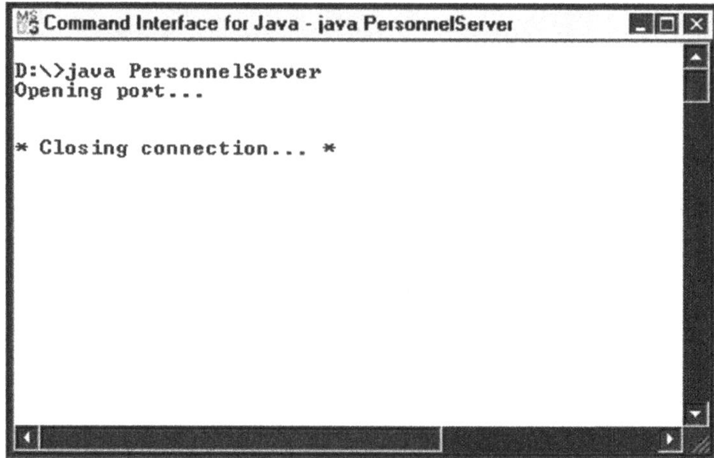

Fig. 4.7 Server providing '*Vector*ised' data to client in preceding screenshot

4.10 Vectors Versus ArrayLists

As an alternative to using an *ArrayList* to 'wrap up' our class objects, we could choose to use a *Vector*. This class existed in Java before the Collection Framework came into existence and was 'retro-fitted' to take its place alongside the other Collection classes. The only significant difference is that, instead of using method *get* to retrieve an object from a *Vector*, we need to use method *elementAt*.

Example

```
Vector<String> stringVector = new Vector<>();

stringVector.add("Example");
//Next step retrieves this element.
String word = stringVector.elementAt(0);
```

Another slight difference is that, as well as having method *add* to add objects to a *Vector*, there is also method *addElement*, principally to cater for older code.

The following question naturally arises: 'Which is it better to use—Vectors or ArrayLists?'. The answer is… it depends! The *ArrayList* is faster, but is not thread-safe, whereas the *Vector* **is** thread-safe. Consequently, if thread-safety is important to your program, you should use a *Vector*. If, on the other hand, thread-safety is not a factor, then you should use an *ArrayList*.

Exercises

4.1 Using a text editor or wordprocessor, create a text file holding a series of surnames and payroll numbers (at least five of each). For example:

Smith
123456
Jones
987654
Jenkins
555555
…
…

Now write a Java program that uses a *while* loop to read values from the above text file and displays then in a table under the headings 'Surname' and 'Payroll No.'. (Don't be too concerned about precise alignment of the columns.)

4.2 Take a copy of the above program, rename the class and modify the appropriate line so that the program accepts input from the standard input stream (i.e., using a *Scanner* around the standard input stream, *System.in*). Then use redirection to feed the values from your payroll text file into your program (displaying the contents as before).

4.3 Write a (very short) program that creates a serial text file holding just two or three names of your own choosing. After compiling and running the program, use the MS-DOS command `type` (or the equivalent command for your platform) to display the file's contents. For example:

```
type names.txt
```

4.4 Using a text editor or word processor, create a text file containing a series of five surnames and examination marks, each item on a separate line. For example:

Smith
47
Jones
63
…
…

By extending the code given below, create a random access file called *results.dat*, accepting input from the standard input stream (via a *Scanner* object) and redirecting input from the above text file. Each record should comprise a student surname and examination mark. When all records have been written, reposition the file pointer to the start of the file and then read each record in turn, displaying its contents on the screen.

```
import java.io.*;
import java.util.*;
public class FileResults

{
   private static final long REC_SIZE = 34;
   private static final int SURNAME_SIZE = 15;
   private static String surname;
   private static int mark;

   public static void main(String[] args)
                                  throws IOException
   {
      /*****************************************
            *** SUPPLY CODE FOR main! ***
      *****************************************/
   }

   public static void writeString(
                RandomAccessFile file, String text,
                int fixedSize) throws IOException
   {
      int size = text.length();

      if (size<=fixedSize)
      {
          file.writeChars(text);
          for (int i=size; i<fixedSize; i++)
            file.writeChar(' ');
      }
      else
         file.writeChars(text.substring(
                                    0,fixedSize));
   }

   public static String readString(
                RandomAccessFile file, int fixedSize)
                                  throws IOException
   {
      String value = "";
      for (int i=0; i<fixedSize; i++)
         value+=file.readChar();
      return value;
   }
}
```

4.5 Making use of class *Results* shown below, repeat the above program, this time writing/reading objects of class *Result*. (When displaying the names and marks that have been read, of course, you must make use of the methods of class *Result*.) Once again, redirect initial input to come from your text file.

```
class Result implements java.io.Serializable
{
   private String surname;
   private int mark;

   public Result(String name, int score)
   {
     surname = name;
     mark = score;
   }

   public String getName()
   {
     return surname;
   }

   public void setName(String name)
   {
     surname = name;
   }

   public int getMark()
   {
     return mark;
   }

   public void setMark(int score)
   {
      if ((score>=0) && (score<=100))
         mark = score;
   }
}
```

4.6 Using class *Personnel* from Sect. 4.9, create a simple GUI-based program called *ChooseSaveFile.java* that has no components, but creates an instance of itself within *main* and has the usual window-closing code (also within *main*). Within the constructor for the class, declare and initialise an array of three *Personnel* objects (as in program *ArrayListSerialise.java* from Sect. 4.9) and write the objects from the array to a file (using an *ObjectOutputStream*). The name and location of the file should be chosen by the user via a *JFileChooser* object. Note that you will need to close down the (empty) application window by clicking on the window close box.

4.7 Take a copy of the above program, rename it *ReadFile.java* and modify the code to make use of a *JFileChooser* object that allows a file to be selected for reading. Use the *JFileChooser* object to read from the file created above and get your program to use method *getSurname* of class *Personnel* to display the surnames of all the staff whose details were saved.

Chapter 5
Remote Method Invocation (RMI)

Learning Objectives

After reading this chapter, you should:

- understand the fundamental purpose of RMI;
- understand how RMI works;
- be able to implement an RMI client/server application involving *.class* files that are available locally;
- appreciate the potential danger presented by *.class* files downloaded from remote locations;
- know how security managers may be used to overcome the above danger.

With all our method calls so far, the objects upon which such methods have been invoked have been **local**. However, in a distributed environment, it is often desirable to be able to invoke methods on **remote** objects (i.e., on objects located on other systems). **RMI** (*Remote Method Invocation*) provides a platform-independent means of doing just this. Under RMI, the networking details required by explicit programming of streams and sockets disappear and the fact that an object is located remotely is almost transparent to the Java programmer. Once a reference to the remote object has been obtained, the methods of that object may be invoked in exactly the same way as those of local objects. Behind the scenes, of course, RMI will be making use of byte streams to transfer data and method invocations, but all of this is handled automatically by the RMI infrastructure. RMI has been a core component of Java from the earliest release of the language, but has undergone some evolutionary changes since its original specification.

5.1 The Basic RMI Process

Though the above paragraph referred to obtaining a reference to a remote object, this was really a simplification of what actually happens. The server program that has control of the remote object registers an interface with a naming service, thereby making this interface accessible by client programs. The interface contains the

J. Graba, *An Introduction to Network Programming with Java: Java 7 Compatible*, DOI 10.1007/978-1-4471-5254-5_5, © Springer-Verlag London 2013

signatures for those methods of the object that the server wishes to make publicly available. A client program can then use the same naming service to obtain a reference to this interface in the form of what is called a **stub**. This stub is effectively a local surrogate (a 'stand-in' or placeholder) for the remote object. On the remote system, there will be another surrogate called a **skeleton**. When the client program invokes a method of the remote object, it appears to the client as though the method is being invoked directly on the object. What is actually happening, however, is that an equivalent method is being called in the stub. The stub then forwards the call and any parameters to the skeleton on the remote machine. Only primitive types and those reference types that implement the *Serializable* interface may be used as parameters. (The serialising of these parameters is called **marshalling**.)

Upon receipt of the byte stream, the skeleton converts this stream into the original method call and associated parameters (the deserialisation of parameters being referred to as **unmarshalling**). Finally, the skeleton calls the implementation of the method on the server. The stages of this process are shown diagrammatically in Fig. 5.1. Even this is a simplification of what is actually happening at the network level, however, since the transport layer and a special layer called the **remote reference layer** will also be involved at each end of the transmission. In fact, the skeleton was removed entirely in J2SE 1.2 and server programs now communicate directly with the remote reference layer. However, the basic principles remain the same and Fig. 5.1 still provides a useful graphical representation of the process.

Fig. 5.1 Using RMI to invoke a method of a remote object

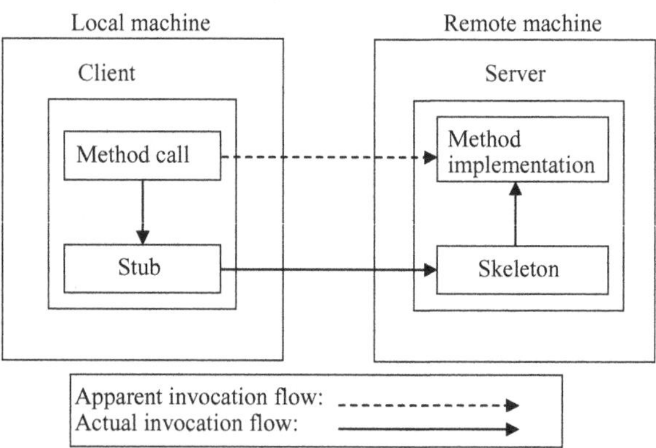

If the method has a return value, then the above process is reversed, with the return value being serialised on the server (by the skeleton) and deserialised on the client (by the stub).

5.2 Implementation Details

The packages used in the implementation of an RMI client–server application are ***java.rmi***, ***java.rmi.server*** and ***java.rmi.registry***, though only the first two need to be used explicitly. The basic steps are listed below.

1. Create the interface.
2. Define a class that implements this interface.
3. Create the server process.
4. Create the client process.

Simple Example

This first example application simply displays a greeting to any client that uses the appropriate interface registered with the naming service to invoke the associated method implementation on the server. In a realistic application, there would almost certainly be more methods and those methods would belong to some class (as will be shown in a later example). However, we shall adopt a minimalistic approach until the basic method has been covered. The required steps will be numbered as above…

1. Create the interface.
This interface should import package *java.rmi* and must extend interface *Remote*, which (like *Serializable*) is a 'tagging' interface that contains no methods. The interface definition for this example must specify the signature for method *getGreeting*, which is to be made available to clients. This method must declare that it throws a *RemoteException*. The contents of this file are shown below.

```
import java.rmi.*;

public interface Hello extends Remote
{
   public String getGreeting() throws RemoteException;
}
```

2. Define a class that implements this interface.
The implementation file should import packages *java.rmi* and *java.rmi.server*. The implementation class must extend class *RemoteObject* or one of *RemoteObject*'s subclasses. In practice, most implementations extend subclass *UnicastRemoteObject*, since this class supports point-to-point communication using TCP streams. The implementation class must also implement our interface *Hello*, of course, by providing an executable body for the single interface method *getGreeting*. In addition, we **must** provide a constructor for our implementation object (even if we simply give this constructor an empty body, as below). Like the method(s) declared in the interface, this constructor must declare that it throws a *RemoteException*. Finally, we shall adopt the common convention of appending *Impl* onto the name of our interface to form the name of the implementation class.

```
import java.rmi.*;
import java.rmi.server.*;

public class HelloImpl extends UnicastRemoteObject
                                      implements Hello
{
   public HelloImpl() throws RemoteException
   {
      //No action needed here.
   }
```

```
    public String getGreeting() throws RemoteException
    {
        return ("Hello there!");
    }
}
```

3. Create the server process.

The server creates object(s) of the above implementation class and registers them with a naming service called the **registry**. It does this by using static method *rebind* of class *Naming* (from package *java.rmi*). This method takes two arguments:

- a *String* that holds the name of the remote object as a URL with protocol *rmi*;
- a reference to the remote object (as an argument of type *Remote*).

The method establishes a connection between the object's name and its reference. Clients will then be able to use the remote object's name to retrieve a reference to that object via the registry.

The URL string, as well as specifying a protocol of *rmi* and a name for the object, specifies the name of the remote object's host machine. For simplicity's sake, we shall use *localhost* (which is what RMI assumes by default anyway). The default port for RMI is 1099, though we can change this to any other convenient port if we wish. The code for our server process is shown below and contains just one method: *main*. To cater for the various types of exception that may be generated, this method declares that it throws *Exception*.

```
import java.rmi.*;

public class HelloServer
{
    private static final String HOST = "localhost";

    public static void main(String[] args)
                                  throws Exception
    {
        //Create a reference to an
        //implementation object...
        HelloImpl temp = new HelloImpl();

        //Create the string URL holding the
        //object's name...
        String rmiObjectName = "rmi://" + HOST + "/Hello";
        //(Could omit host name here, since 'localhost'
        //would be assumed by default.)

        //'Bind' the object reference to the name...
        Naming.rebind(rmiObjectName,temp);

        //Display a message so that we know the process
        //has been completed...
```

```
        System.out.println("Binding complete...\n");
    }
}
```

4. Create the client process.

The client obtains a reference to the remote object from the registry. It does this by using method *lookup* of class *Naming*, supplying as an argument to this method the same URL that the server did when binding the object reference to the object's name in the registry. Since *lookup* returns a *Remote* reference, this reference must be typecast into an *Hello* reference (**not** an *HelloImpl* reference!). Once the *Hello* reference has been obtained, it can be used to call the solitary method that was made available in the interface.

```
import java.rmi.*;

public class HelloClient
{
   private static final String HOST = "localhost";

   public static void main(String[] args)
   {
      try
      {
        //Obtain a reference to the object from the
        //registry and typecast it into the appropriate
        //type...
        Hello greeting =
            (Hello)Naming.lookup("rmi://"
                                    + HOST + "/Hello");
        //Use the above reference to invoke the remote
        //object's method...
        System.out.println("Message received: "
                               + greeting.getGreeting());
      }
      catch(ConnectException conEx)
      {
         System.out.println(
                    "Unable to connect to server!");
         System.exit(1);
      }
      catch(Exception ex)
      {
         ex.printStackTrace();
         System.exit(1);
      }
   }
}
```

Note that some authors choose to combine the implementation and server into one class. This author, however, feels that the separation of the two probably results in a clearer delineation of responsibilities.

The method required for running the above application is provided in the next section.

5.3 Compilation and Execution

There are several steps that need to be carried out, as described below.

1. Compile all files with javac.
This is straightforward…

```
javac Hello.java
javac HelloImpl.java
javac HelloServer.java
javac HelloClient.java
```

[Note that, before Java SE 5, it was necessary to compile the implementation class (yes, compile a .class file!) with the rmic compiler thus:

```
rmic HelloImpl
```

This would generate both a stub file and a skeleton file. However, this stage is no longer required.]

2. Start the RMI registry.

```
rmiregistry
```

Enter the following command:
When this is executed, the only indication that anything has happened is a change in the command window's title. For the author's Java implementation, the change is as shown in Fig. 5.2.

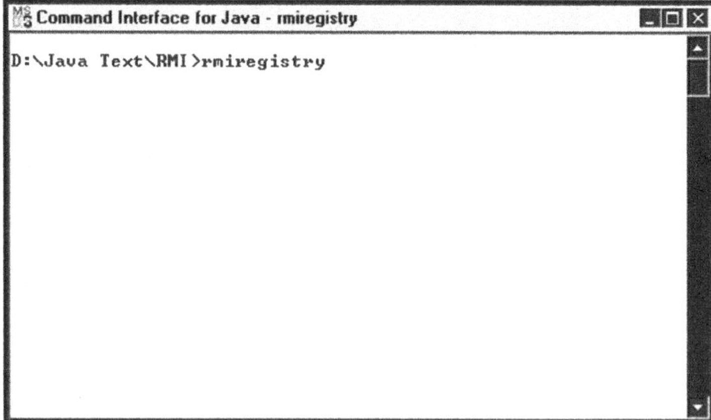

Fig. 5.2 Starting the RMI registry

3. Open a new window and run the server.
From the new window, invoke the Java compiler:

```
java HelloServer
```

Server output is shown in Fig. 5.3.

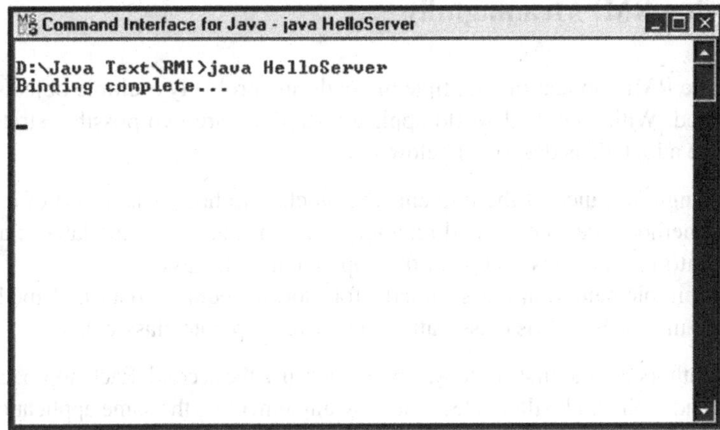

Fig. 5.3 Output from the *HelloServer* RMI program

4. Open a third window and run the client.
Again, invoke the Java compiler:

```
java HelloClient
```

Output is as shown in Fig. 5.4.

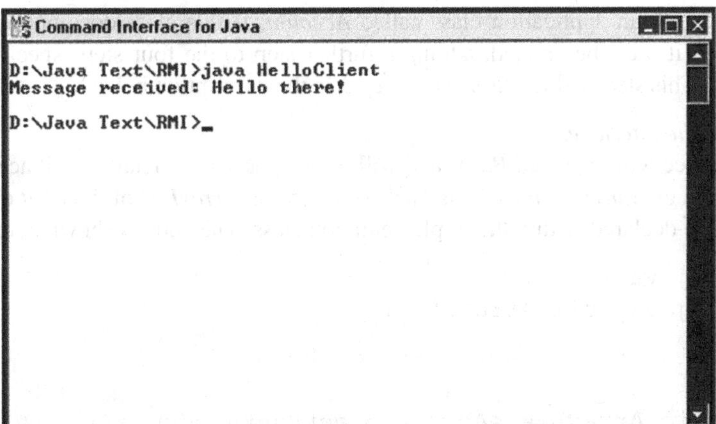

Fig. 5.4 Output from the *HelloClient* RMI program

Since the server process and the RMI registry will continue to run indefinitely after the client process has finished, they will need to be closed down by entering Ctrl-C in each of their windows.

Now that the basic process has been covered, the next section will examine a more realistic application of RMI.

5.4 Using RMI Meaningfully

In a realistic RMI application, multiple methods and probably multiple objects will be employed. With such real-world applications, there are two possible strategies that may be adopted, as described below.

- Use a single instance of the implementation class to hold instance(s) of a class whose methods are to be called remotely. Pass instance(s) of the latter class as argument(s) of the constructor for the implementation class.
- Use the implementation class directly for storing required data and methods, creating instances of **this** class, rather than using separate class(es).

Some authors use the first strategy, while others use the second. Each approach has its merits and both will be illustrated below by implementing the same application, so that the reader may compare the two techniques and choose his/her own preference.

Example

This application will make bank account objects available to connecting clients, which may then manipulate these remote objects by invoking their methods. For simplicity's sake, just four account objects will be created and the practical considerations relating to security of such accounts will be ignored completely!

Each of the above two methods will be implemented in turn…

Method 1

Instance variables and associated methods for an individual account will be encapsulated within an application class called *Account*. If this class does not already exist, then it must be created, adding a further step to the four steps specified in Sect. 5.2. This step will be inserted as step 3 in the description below.

1. Create the interface.

Our interface will be called *Bank1*and will provide access to details of all accounts via method *getBankAccounts*. This method returns an *ArrayList* of *Account* objects that will be declared within the implementation class. The code is shown below:

```
import java.rmi.*;
import java.util.ArrayList;

public interface Bank1 extends Remote
{
   public ArrayList<Account> getBankAccounts()
                                     throws RemoteException;
}
```

2. Define the implementation.
The code for the implementation class provides both a definition for the above method and the definition for a constructor to set up the *ArrayLists* of *Account* objects:

```
import java.rmi.*;
import java.rmi.server.*;
import java.util.ArrayList;

public class Bank1Impl extends UnicastRemoteObject
                                             implements Bank1
{
   //Declare the ArrayList that will hold Account
   //objects…
   private ArrayList<Account> acctInfo;
   //The constructor must be supplied with an ArrayList
   //of Account objects…
   public Bank1Impl(ArrayList<Account> acctVals)
                                throws RemoteException
   {
      acctInfo = acctVals;
   }
   //Definition for the single interface method…
   public ArrayList<Account> getBankAccounts()
                                throws RemoteException
   {
      return acctInfo;
   }
}
```

3. Create any required application classes.
In this example, there is only class *Account* to be defined. Since it is to be used in the return value for our interface method, it must be declared to implement the *Serializable* interface (contained in package *java.io*).

```
public class Account implements java.io.Serializable
{
   //Instance variables…
   private int acctNum;
   private String surname;
   private String firstNames;
   private double balance;

   //Constructor…
   public Account(int acctNo, String sname,
                               String fnames, double bal)
   {
      acctNum = acctNo;
```

```
        surname = sname;
        firstNames = fnames;
        balance = bal;
    }

    //Methods...

    public int getAcctNum()
    {
        return acctNum;
    }
    public String getName()
    {
        return (firstNames + " " + surname);
    }

    public double getBalance()
    {
        return balance;
    }

    public double withdraw(double amount)
    {
        if ((amount>0) && (amount<=balance))
            return amount;
        else
            return 0;
    }

    public void deposit(double amount)
    {
        if (amount > 0)
            balance += amount;
    }
}
```

4. Create the server process.
The code for the server class sets up an *ArrayList* holding four initialised *Account* objects and then creates an implementation object, using the *ArrayList* as the argument of the constructor. The reference to this object is bound to the programmer-chosen name *Accounts* (which must be specified as part of a URL identifying the host machine) and placed in the registry. The server code is shown below.

```
import java.rmi.*;
import java.util.ArrayList;

public class Bank1Server
{
    private static final String HOST = "localhost";
```

```
    public static void main(String[] args)
                                        throws Exception
    {
        //Create an initialised array of four Account
        //objects…
        Account[] account =
         {new Account(111111,"Smith","Fred James",112.58),
          new Account(222222,"Jones","Sally",507.85),
          new Account(234567,"White","Mary Jane",2345.00),
          new Account(666666,"Satan","Beelzebub",666.00)};
        ArrayList<Account> acctDetails =
                                new ArrayList<Account>();
        //Insert the Account objects into the ArrayList…
        for (int i=0; i<account.length; i++)
           acctDetails.add(account[i]);

        //Create an implementation object, passing the
        //above ArrayList to the constructor…
        Bank1Impl temp = new Bank1Impl(acctDetails);

        //Save the object's name in a String…
        String rmiObjectName =
                        "rmi://" + HOST + "/Accounts";
        //(Could omit host name, since 'localhost' would be
        //assumed by default.)

        //Bind the object's name to its reference…
        Naming.rebind(rmiObjectName,temp);

        System.out.println("Binding complete…\n");
     }
}
```

5. Create the client process.
The client uses method *lookup* of class *Naming* to obtain a reference to the remote object, typecasting it into type *Bank1*. Once the reference has been retrieved, it can be used to execute remote method *getBankAccounts*. This returns a reference to the *ArrayList* of *Account* objects which, in turn, provides access to the individual *Account* objects. The methods of these *Account* objects can then be invoked as though those objects were local.

```
import java.rmi.*;
import java.util.ArrayList;

public class Bank1Client
{
    private static final String HOST = "localhost";

    public static void main(String[] args)
```

```
    {
        try
        {
          //Obtain a reference to the object from the
          //registry and typecast it into the appropriate
          //type…
          Bank1 temp = (Bank1)Naming.lookup(
                              "rmi://" + HOST + "/Accounts");

          ArrayList<Account> acctDetails =
                                      temp.getBankAccounts();
          //Simply display all acct details…
          for (int i=0; i<acctDetails.size(); i++)
          {
              //Retrieve an Account object from the
              //ArrayList…
              Account acct = acctDetails.get(i);

              //Now invoke methods of Account object
              //to display its details…
              System.out.println("\nAccount number: "
                                     + acct.getAcctNum());
              System.out.println("Name: "
                                       + acct.getName());
              System.out.println("Balance: "
                                     + acct.getBalance());
          }
        }
        catch(ConnectException conEx)
        {
           System.out.println(
                              "Unable to connect to server!");
           System.exit(1);
        }
        catch(Exception ex)
        {
           ex.printStackTrace();
           System.exit(1);
        }
    }
}
```

The steps for compilation and execution are the same as those outlined in the previous section for the *Hello* example, with the minor addition of compiling the source code for class *Account*. The steps are shown below.

1. Compile all files with javac.
This time, there are five files…

```
javac Bank1.java
javac Bank1Impl.java
javac Account.java
javac Bank1Server.java
javac Bank1Client.java
```

2. Start the RMI registry.
Enter the following command:

```
rmiregistry
```

The contents of the registry window will be identical to the screenshot shown in Fig. 5.2.

3. Open a new window and run the server.
From the new window, invoke the Java interpreter:

```
java Bank1Server
```

Server output is as shown in Fig. 5.3.

4. Open a third window and run the client.
Again, invoke the Java interpreter:

```
java Bank1Client
```

Output is shown in Fig. 5.5 below.

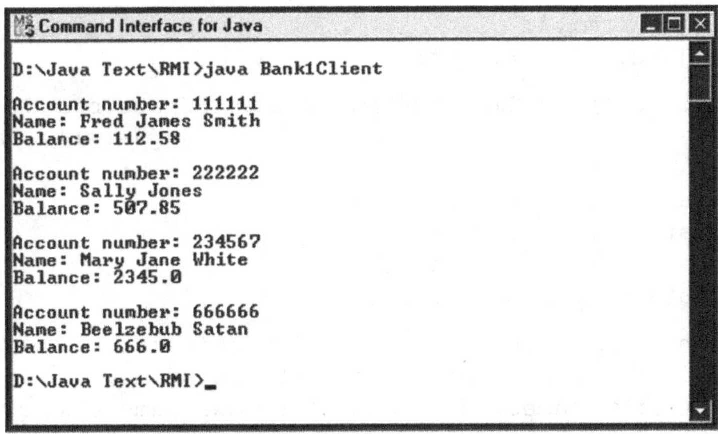

Fig. 5.5 Output from the *Bank1Client* RMI program

Once again, the server process and the RMI registry will need to be closed down by entering Ctrl-C in each of their windows.

Method 2

For this method, no separate *Account* class is used. Instead, the data and methods associated with an individual account will be defined directly in the implementation class. The interface will make the methods available to client processes. The same four steps as were identified in Sect. 5.2 must be carried out, as described below.

1. Create the interface.

The same five methods that appeared in class *Account* in *Method 1* are declared, but with each now declaring that it throws a *RemoteException*.

```
import java.rmi.*;

public interface Bank2 extends Remote
{
    public int getAcctNum()throws RemoteException;
    public String getName()throws RemoteException;
    public double getBalance()throws RemoteException;
    public double withdraw(double amount)
                                 throws RemoteException;
    public void deposit(double amount)
                                 throws RemoteException;
}
```

2. Define the implementation.

As well as holding the data and method implementations associated with an individual account, this class defines a constructor for implementation objects. The method definitions will be identical to those that were previously held within the *Account* class, of course.

```
import java.rmi.*;
import java.rmi.server.*;

public class Bank2Impl extends UnicastRemoteObject
                                          implements Bank2
{
   private int acctNum;
   private String surname;
   private String firstNames;
   private double balance;

   //Constructor for implementation objects...
   public Bank2Impl(int acctNo, String sname,
      String fnames, double bal) throws RemoteException
   {
      acctNum = acctNo;
      surname = sname;
      firstNames = fnames;
      balance = bal;
   }
```

```
    public int getAcctNum() throws RemoteException
    {
       return acctNum;
    }

    public String getName() throws RemoteException
    {
       return (firstNames + " " + surname);
    }

    public double getBalance() throws RemoteException
    {
       return balance;
    }

    public double withdraw(double amount)
                                      throws RemoteException
    {
          if ((amount>0) && (amount<=balance))
             return amount;
          else
             return 0;
    }

    public void deposit(double amount)
                                      throws RemoteException
    {
       if (amount > 0)
          balance += amount;
    }
}
```

3. Create the server process.

The server class creates an array of implementation objects and binds each one individually to the registry. The name used for each object will be formed from concatenating the associated account number onto the word 'Account' (forming 'Account111111', etc.).

```
import java.rmi.*;

public class Bank2Server
{
    private static final String HOST = "localhost";

    public static void main(String[] args)
                                         throws Exception
    {
       //Create array of initialised implementation
```

```
        //objects…
        Bank2Impl[] account =
           {new Bank2Impl(111111,"Smith",
                                    "Fred James",112.58),
            new Bank2Impl(222222,"Jones","Sally",507.85),
            new Bank2Impl(234567,"White",
                                    "Mary Jane",2345.00),
            new Bank2Impl(666666,"Satan",
                                    "Beelzebub",666.00)};
        for (int i=0; i<account.length; i++)
        {
           int acctNum = account[i].getAcctNum();
           /*
           Generate each account name (as a concatenation
           of 'Account' and the account number) and bind
           it to the appropriate object reference in the
           array…
           */
           Naming.rebind("rmi://" + HOST + "/Account"
                                   + acctNum, account[i]);
        }
        System.out.println("Binding complete…\n");
    }
}
```

4. Create the client process.

The client again uses method *lookup*, this time to obtain references to individual accounts (held in separate implementation objects):

```
import java.rmi.*;

public class Bank2Client
{
   private static final String HOST = "localhost";
   private static final int[] acctNum =
                       {111111,222222,234567,666666};
   public static void main(String[] args)
   {
      try
      {
         //Simply display all account details…
         for (int i=0; i<acctNum.length; i++)
         {
            /*
            Obtain a reference to the object from the
            registry and typecast it into the
            appropriate type…
```

```
            */
            Bank2 temp =
                (Bank2)Naming.lookup("rmi://" + HOST
                              + "/Account" + acctNum[i]);
            //Now invoke the methods of the interface to
            //display details of associated account…
            System.out.println("\nAccount number: "
                                    + temp.getAcctNum());
            System.out.println("Name: "
                                     + temp.getName());
            System.out.println("Balance: "
                                    + temp.getBalance());
         }
      }
      catch(ConnectException conEx)
      {
         System.out.println(
                          "Unable to connect to server!");
         System.exit(1);
      }
      catch(Exception ex)
      {
         ex.printStackTrace();
         System.exit(1);
      }
   }
}
```

Output for this client will be exactly as shown in Fig. 5.5 for *Method 1*.

5.5 RMI Security

If both the client and server processes have direct access to the same class files, then there is no need to take special security precautions, since no security holes can be opened up by such an arrangement. However, an application receiving an object for which it does **not** have the corresponding class file can try to load that class file from a remote location and instantiate the object in its JVM. Unfortunately, an object passed as an RMI argument from such a remote source can attempt to initiate execution on the client's machine immediately upon deserialisation—without the user/programmer doing anything with it! Such a security breach is not permitted to occur, of course. The loading of this file is handled by an object of class *SecureClassLoader*, which **must** have security restrictions defined for it. File *java.policy* defines these security restrictions, while file *java.security* defines the security properties. Implementation of the security policy is controlled by an object of class *RMISecurityManager* (a subclass of *SecurityManager*). The *RMISecurityManager* creates the same 'sandbox' rules that govern applets. Without such an object, a Java application will not even attempt to load classes that are not from its local file system.

Though the security policy can be modified by use of the Java utility *policytool*, this can be done only for individual hosts, so it is probably more straightforward to write and install one's own security manager. There is a default *RMISecurityManager*, but this relies on the system's default security policy, which is far too restrictive to permit the downloading of class files from a remote site. In order to get round this problem, we must create our own security manager that extends *RMISecurityManager*. This security manager must provide a definition for method *checkPermission*, which takes a single argument of class *Permission* from package *java.security*. For simplicity's sake and because the complications involved with specifying security policies go beyond the scope of this text, we shall illustrate the procedure with the simplest possible security manager—one that allows everything! The code for this security manager is shown below.

```
import java.rmi.*;
import java.security.*;
public class ZeroSecurityManager
                              extends RMISecurityManager
{
   public void checkPermission(Permission permission)
   {
       System.out.println("checkPermission for : "
                                + permission.toString());
   }
}
```

As with all our associated RMI application files, this file must be compiled with *javac*. The client program must install an object of this class by invoking method *setSecurityManager*, which is a static method of class *System* that takes a single argument of class *SecurityManager* (or a subclass of *SecurityManager*, of course). For illustration purposes, the code for our *HelloClient* program is reproduced below, now incorporating a call to *setSecurityManager*. This call is shown in emboldened text.

```
import java.rmi.*;

public class HelloClient
{
   private static final String HOST = "localhost";

   public static void main(String[] args)
   {
       //Here's the new code...
       if (System.getSecurityManager() == null)
       {
          System.setSecurityManager(
                        new ZeroSecurityManager());
```

```
        }

        try
        {
           Hello greeting =
                 (Hello)Naming.lookup(
                              "rmi://" + HOST + "/Hello");

           System.out.println("Message received: "
                               + greeting.getGreeting());
        }
        catch(ConnectException conEx)
        {
           System.out.println(
                          "Unable to connect to server!");
           System.exit(1);
        }
        catch(Exception ex)
        {
           ex.printStackTrace();
           System.exit(1);
        }
    }
}
```

When executing the server, we need to specify where the required *.class* files are located, so that clients may download them. To do this, we need to set the *java.rmi.server.codebase* property to the URL of this location, at the same time that the server is started. This is achieved by using the *-D* command line option to specify the setting of the codebase property. For example, if the URL of the file location is http://java.shu.ac.uk/rmi/, then the following line would set our *HelloServer* program running and would set the codebase property to the required location at the same time:

```
java  -Djava.rmi.server.codebase=http://java.shu.ac.uk/
rmi/ HelloServer
```

It is very easy to make a slip during the above process that will cause the application to fail, but coverage of these problems goes beyond the scope of this text.

Exercises

5.1 Using class *Result* (shown below) and making the minor modification that will ensure that objects of this class are serialisable, make method *getResults* available via an RMI interface. This method should return an *ArrayList* containing initialised *Result* objects that are set up by a server program (also to be written by you) and made available via an implementation object placed in the RMI registry by the server. The server should store two *Result* objects in the *ArrayList* contained within the implementation object. Access this implementation object via a client program and use the methods of the *Result* class to display the surname and examination mark for each of the two *Result* objects. (I.e., employ 'Method 1' from Sect. 5.4.)

You should find the solution to the above problem relatively straightforward by simply modifying the code for the *Bank* example application from this chapter.

```
class Result implements java.io.Serializable
{
   private String surname;
   private int mark;
   public Result(String name, int score)
   {
      surname = name;
      mark = score;
   }
   public String getName()
   {
      return surname;
   }
   public void setName(String name)
   {
      surname = name;
   }
   public int getMark()
   {
      return mark;
   }
   public void setMark(int score)
   {
      if ((score>=0) && (score<=100))
         mark = score;
   }
}
```

5.2 Repeat the above exercise, this time without using a separate *Result* class, but holding the result methods directly in the implementation class. (I.e., use 'Method 2' from Sect. 5.4.) Store the implementation objects remotely under the names *result1* and *result2*. Access these objects via a client program and use the methods of the implementation class to display the surnames and examination marks for each of the two objects.

Chapter 6
CORBA

Learning Objectives

After reading this chapter, you should:

- understand the basic principles of CORBA;
- appreciate the importance of CORBA in providing a method for implementing distributed objects in a platform-independent and language-independent manner;
- know how to create IDL specifications;
- know how to create server processes for use with the *Java IDL* ORB;
- know how to create client processes for use with the *Java IDL* ORB;
- know how to create and use CORBA factory objects.

Though RMI is a powerful mechanism for distributing and processing objects in a platform-independent manner, it has one significant drawback—it works only with objects that have been created using Java. Convenient though it might be if Java were the only language used for creating software objects, this simply is not the case in the real world. A more generic approach to the development of distributed systems is offered by CORBA (Common Object Request Broker Architecture), which allows objects written in a variety of programming languages to be accessed by client programs which themselves may be written in a variety of programming languages.

6.1 Background and Basics

CORBA is a product of the OMG (Object Management Group), a consortium of over 800 companies spanning most of the I.T. industry (with the notable exception of Microsoft!) that is dedicated to defining and promoting industry standards for object technology. The first version of CORBA appeared in 1991 and the current version (at the time of writing) is 3.3, which was released in November of 2012. In keeping with the ethos of the OMG, CORBA is not a specific implementation, but a specification for creating and using distributed objects. An individual

J. Graba, *An Introduction to Network Programming with Java: Java 7 Compatible*, DOI 10.1007/978-1-4471-5254-5_6, © Springer-Verlag London 2013

implementation of this specification constitutes an ORB (Object Request Broker) and there are several such implementations currently available on the market. *Java IDL* (Interface Definition Language) is the ORB that constitutes one of the core packages of the Java SE (from J2SE 1.2 upwards) and is the ORB that will be used for all the examples in this chapter. Whereas RMI ORBs use a protocol called JRMP (Java Remote Method Protocol), CORBA ORBs use IIOP (Internet Inter-Orb Protocol), which is based on TCP/IP. It is IIOP that provides interoperability between ORBs from different vendors.

Another fundamental difference between RMI and CORBA is that, whereas RMI uses Java to define the interfaces for its objects, CORBA uses a special language called **Interface Definition Language (IDL)** to define those interfaces. Although this language has syntactic similarities to C++, it is not a full-blown programming language. In order for any ORB to provide access to software objects in a particular programming language, the ORB has to provide a *mapping* from the IDL to the target language. Mappings currently specified include ones for Java, C++, C, Smalltalk, COBOL and Ada.

At the client end of a CORBA interaction, there is a code **stub** for each method that is to be called remotely. This stub acts as a proxy (a 'stand-in') for the remote method. At the server end, there is **skeleton** code that also acts as a proxy for the required method and is used to translate the incoming method call and any parameters into their implementation-specific format, which is then used to invoke the method implementation on the associated object. Method invocation passes through the stub on the client side, then through the ORB and finally through the skeleton on the server side, where it is executed on the object. For a client and server using the same ORB, Fig. 6.1 shows the process.

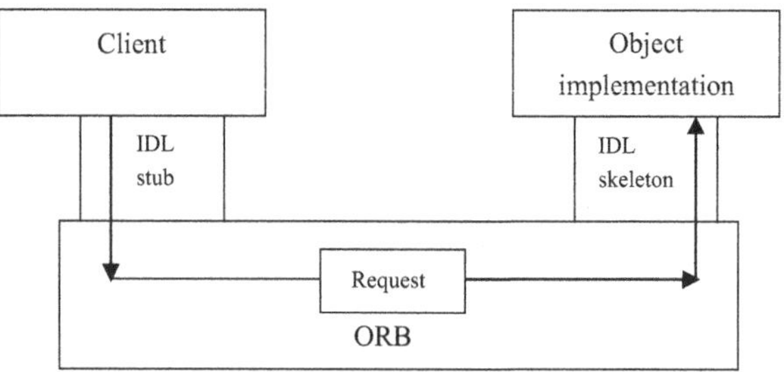

Fig. 6.1 Remote method invocation when client and server are using the same ORB

Figure 6.2 shows the same interaction for client and server processes operating on different ORBs.

6.2 The Structure of a *Java IDL* Specification

Java IDL includes an OMG-compliant version of the IDL and the corresponding mapping from this IDL into Java. Some unnecessary confusion is caused by the name *Java IDL*, which seems to imply that the product comprises *just* an IDL.

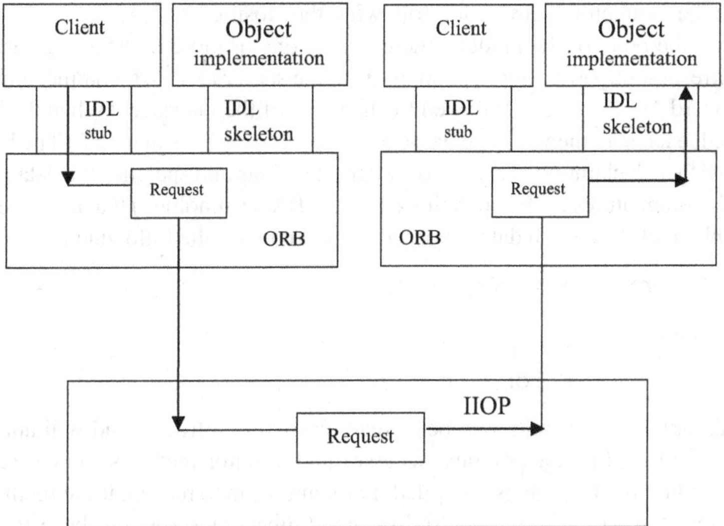

Fig. 6.2 Remote invocation when client and server are using different ORBs

Indeed, some of the pages on the old Sun site referred to the IDL model and the *Java ORB* as being separate entities. Mostly, however, *Java IDL* is referred to as the ORB itself, with this taken to include the IDL-to-Java mapping.

IDL supports a class hierarchy, at the root of which is class *Object*. This is **not** the same as the Java language's *Object* class and is identified as *org.omg.CORBA. Object* (a subclass of *java.lang.Object*) in Java. Some CORBA operations (such as name lookup) return an object of class *org.omg.CORBA.Object*, which must then be 'narrowed' explicitly (effectively, typecast into a more specific class). This is achieved by using a 'helper' class that is generated by the *idlj* compiler (along with stubs, skeletons and other files).

An IDL specification is contained within a file with the suffix .idl. The surrounding structure within this file is normally a *module* (though it may be an *interface*), which corresponds to a package in Java (and will cause a Java `package` statement to be generated when the IDL is compiled). The module declaration commences with the keyword `module`, followed by the name of the specific module (beginning with a capital letter, even though the Java convention is for a package name to begin with a lower-case letter). The body of the module declaration is enclosed by curly brackets and, like C++ (but unlike Java), is terminated with a semi-colon. For a module called *Sales*, then, the top level structure would look like this:

```
module Sales
{
    .....................;
    .....................;
    .....................;
};
```

Note the mandatory semi-colon following the closing bracket!

Within the body of the module, there will be one or more *interface* declarations, each corresponding to an application class on the server and each commencing with the keyword `interface`, followed by the name of the interface. (When the IDL is compiled, each statement will generate a Java `interface` statement.) The body of each interface declaration is enclosed by curly brackets and specifies the data properties and the signatures of the operations (in CORBA terminology) that are to be made accessible to clients. Each data property is declared with the following syntax:

```
attribute <type> <name>;
```

For example:

```
attribute long total;
```

By default, this attribute will be a 'read-and-write' attribute and will automatically be mapped to a pair of Java accessor and mutator methods ('get' and 'set') methods when the IDL file is compiled. For some strange reason, these methods do not contain the words 'get' and 'set' or any equivalent verbs, but have the same names as their (noun) attributes. [This is **not** good programming practice, at least as far as the 'set' method is concerned!] The accessor and mutator methods for a given attribute have exactly the same name, then, but are distinguished from each other by having different signatures. The 'get' method takes no arguments and simply returns the value of the attribute, while the 'set' method takes an argument of the corresponding Java type and has a return type of `void` (though only the different argument lists are significant for the compiler, of course). For the example above, the accessor and mutator methods have the following signatures:

```
int total();              //Accessor.
void total(int i);        //Mutator.
```

If we wish to make an attribute read-only (i.e., non-modifiable), then we can do this by using the modifier `readonly`. For example:

```
readonly attribute long total;
```

This time, only the accessor method will be created when the file is compiled. The full set of basic types that may be used in attribute declarations is shown in Table 6.1, with the corresponding Java types alongside. The complete table can be found at the following URL:

http://docs.oracle.com/javase/1.4.2/docs/guide/idl/mapping/jidlMapping.html

Within each operation signature, the basic types available for the return type are as above, but with the addition of **`void`**. Types `short`, `long` and `long long` may also be preceded by the qualifier `unsigned`, but this will not affect the targets of their mappings. The qualifier `const` may also be used (though this generates an initialised variable in Java, rather than a constant indicated by the Java qualifier `final`).

Parameters may have any of the basic types that data properties have, of course. In addition to this, each parameter declaration commences with `in` (for an input parameter), `out` (for an output parameter) or `inout` (for an update parameter).

Table 6.1 IDL types and their Java equivalents

IDL type	Java type
`boolean`	`boolean`
`char` and `wchar`	`char`
`octet`	`byte`
`string` and `wstring`	`String`
`short`	`short`
`long`	`int`
`long long`	`long`
`double`	`double`
fixed	`java.math.BigDecimal`

Example

```
module Sales
{
   interface StockItem
   {
      readonly attribute string code;
      attribute long currentLevel;

      long addStock(in long incNumber);
      long removeStock(in long decNumber);
   };

   interface .....
   {
      ...................;
      ...................;
   };
   ........(Etc.)......
   ........(Etc.)......
};
```

(Again, notice the semi-colons after closing brackets!)

If only one interface is required, then some programmers may choose to omit the `module` level in the *.idl* file.

In addition to the basic types, there are six structured types that may be specified in IDL: `enum`, `struct`, `union`, `exception`, `sequence` and `array`. The first four of these are mapped to *classes* in Java, while the last two are mapped to *arrays*. (The difference between a `sequence` and an `array` in IDL is that a sequence does not have a fixed size.) Since `enum`, `struct` and `union` are used only infrequently, they will not be given further coverage here.

IDL exceptions are of two types: system exceptions and user-defined exceptions. The former inherit (indirectly) from *java.lang.RuntimeException* and are unchecked exceptions (i.e., can be ignored, if we wish), while the latter inherit (indirectly) from *java.lang.Exception* via *org.omg.CORBA.UserException* and are checked exceptions (i.e., must be either caught and handled or be thrown for the runtime environment to handle). To specify that a method may cause an exception to be generated, the keyword `raises` is used. For example:

```
void myMethod(in dummy) raises (MyException);
```

(Note that brackets are required around the exception type.)

Obviously, `raises` maps to `throws` in Java.

One final IDL keyword worth mentioning is `typedef`. This allows us to create new types from existing ones. For example:

```
typedef sequence<long> IntSeq;
```

This creates a new type called IntSeq, which is equivalent to a sequence/array of integers. This new type can then be used in data property declarations. For example:

```
attribute IntSeq numSeq;
```

N.B. If a structured type (array, sequence, etc.) is required as a data attribute or parameter, then we cannot declare it directly as a structured type, but must use `typedef` to create the new type and then use that new type. Thus, a declaration such as

```
attribute sequence<long> numSeq;
```

would be rejected.

6.3 The *Java IDL* Process

At the heart of *Java IDL* is a compiler that translates the programmer's IDL into Java constructs, according to the IDL-to-Java mapping. Prior to J2SE 1.3, this compiler was called *idltojava* and was available as a separate download. As of J2SE 1.3, the compiler is called *idlj* and is part of the core Java download. The stub and skeleton files (and a number of other files) are generated by the *idlj* compiler for each object type that is specified in the *.idl* file. Once these files have been generated, the Java implementation files may be written, compiled and linked with the *idlj-generated* files and the ORB library to create an object server, after which client program(s) may be written to access the service provided.

Although the preceding two sentences summarise the basic procedure, there are several steps required to set up a CORBA client/server application. These steps are listed below.

1. Use the *idlj* compiler to compile the above file, generating up to six files for each interface defined.
2. Implement each interface as a 'servant'.
3. Create the server (incorporating servants).
4. Compile the server and the *idlj*-generated files.
5. Create a client.
6. Compile the client.
7. Run the application.

Simple Example

This first example application simply displays a greeting to any client that uses the appropriate interface registered with the *Java IDL* ORB to invoke the associated method implementation on the server. The steps will be numbered as above…

1. Create the IDL file.
The file will be called *Hello.idl* and will hold a module called *SimpleCORBAExample*. This module will contain a single interface called *Hello* that holds the signature for operation *getGreeting*. The contents of this file are shown below.

```
module SimpleCORBAExample
{
    interface Hello
    {
        string getGreeting();
    };
};
```

2. Compile the IDL file.
The *idlj* compiler defaults to generating only the client-side bindings. To vary this default behaviour, the *–f* option may be used. This is followed by one of three possible specifiers: *client*, *server* and *all*. If client and server are to be run on the same machine, then ***all*** is appropriate and the following command line should be entered:

```
idlj -fall Hello.idl
```

This causes a sub-directory with the same name as the module (i.e., *SimpleCORBAExample*) to be created, holding the six files listed below.

- *Hello.java*
  Contains the Java version of our IDL interface. It extends interface *HelloOperations* [See below], as well as org.*omg.CORBA.Object* (providing standard CORBA object functionality) and *org.omg.CORBA.portable.IDLEntity*.

- *HelloHelper.java*
  Provides auxiliary functionality, notably the *narrow* method required to cast CORBA object references into *Hello* references.

- *HelloHolder.java*
  Holds a public instance member of type *Hello*. If there were any `out` or `inout` arguments (which CORBA allows, but which do not map easily onto Java), this file would also provide operations for them.

- *HelloOperations.java*
  Contains the Java method signatures for all operations in our IDL file. In this application, it contains the single method *getGreeting*.

- *_HelloImplBase.java*
  An abstract class comprising the server skeleton. It provides basic CORBA functionality for the server and implements the *Hello* interface. Each servant (interface implementation) that we create for this service must extend *_HelloImplBase*.

- *_HelloStub.java*
  This is the client stub, providing CORBA functionality for the client. Like _ *HelloImplBase.java*, it implements the *Hello* interface.

Prior to J2SE 1.3, the method signatures would have been specified within *Hello.java*, but are now held within *HelloOperations.java*.

3. Implement the interface.
Here, we specify the Java implementation of our IDL interface. The implementation of an interface is called a 'servant', so we shall name our implementation class HelloServant. This class must extend *_HelloImplBase*. Here is the code:

```
class HelloServant extends _HelloImplBase
{
   public String getGreeting()
   {
      return ("Hello there!");
   }
}
```

This class will be placed inside the same file as our server code.

4. Create the server.
Our server program will be called *HelloServer.java* and will subsume the servant created in the last step. It will reside in the directory immediately above directory *SimpleCORBAExample* and will import package *SimpleCORBAExample* and the following three standard CORBA packages:

- *org.omg.CosNaming* (for the naming service);
- *org.omg.CosNaming.NamingContextPackage* (for special exceptions thrown by the naming service);
- *org.omg.CORBA* (needed by all CORBA applications).

There are several steps required of the server…

(i) *Create and initialise the ORB.*
This is effected by calling static method *init* of class *ORB* (from package *org.omg.CORBA*). This method takes two arguments: a *String* array and a *Properties* object. The first of these is usually set to the argument list received by *main*, while the second is almost invariably set to `null`:

```
ORB orb = ORB.init(args,null);
```

[The argument *args* is not used here (or in many other such programs) in a Windows environment, but it is simpler to supply it, since replacing it with *null* causes an error message, due to ambiguity with an overloaded form of *init* that takes an *Applet* argument and a *Properties* argument.]

(ii) *Create a servant.*
Easy enough:

```
HelloServant servant = new HelloServant();
```

(iii) *Register the servant with the ORB.*
This allows the ORB to pass invocations to the servant and is achieved by means of the ORB class's *connect* method:

```
orb.connect(servant);
```

(iv) *Get a reference to the root naming context.*
Method *resolve_initial_references* of class *ORB* is called with the *String* argument "NameService" (defined for all CORBA ORBs) and returns a CORBA *Object* reference that points to the naming context:

```
org.omg.CORBA.Object objectRef =
   orb.resolve_initial_references("NameService");
```

(v) *'Narrow' the context reference.*
In order for the generic *Object* reference from the previous step to be usable, it must be 'narrowed' (i.e., typecast 'down' into its appropriate type). This is achieved by the use of method *narrow* of class *NamingContextHelper* (from package *org.omg.CosNaming*):

```
NamingContext namingContext =
            NamingContextHelper.narrow(objectRef);
```

(vi) *Create a NameComponent object for our interface.*
The *NameComponent* constructor takes two *String* arguments, the first of which supplies a name for our service. The second argument can be used to specify a category (usually referred to as a 'kind') for the first argument, but is typically left as an empty string. In our example, the service will be called 'Hello':

```
NameComponent nameComp =
                     new NameComponent("Hello", "");
```

(vii) *Specify the path to the interface.*
This is effected by creating an array of *NameComponent* objects, each of which is a component of the path (in 'descending' order), with the last component specifying the name of the *NameComponent* reference that points to the service. For a service in the same directory, the array will contain a single element, as shown below.

```
NameComponent[] path = (nameComp};
```

(viii) *Bind the servant to the interface path.*
The *rebind* method of the *NamingContext* object created earlier is called with arguments that specify the path and service respectively:

```
namingContext.rebind(path,servant);
```

(ix) *Wait for client calls.*
Unlike our previous server programs, this is **not** achieved via an explicitly 'infinite' loop. A call is made to method *wait* of (Java class) *Object*. This call is isolated within a code block that is declared `synchronized`, as shown below.

```
java.lang.Object syncObj = new java.lang.Object();
synchronized(syncObj)
{
   syncObj.wait();
}
```

All of the above code will be contained in the server's *main* method. Since various CORBA system exceptions may be generated, all the executable code will be held within a `try` block.

Now for the full program…

```
import SimpleCORBAExample.*;

import org.omg.CosNaming.*;
import org.omg.CosNaming.NamingContextPackage.*;
import org.omg.CORBA.*;

public class HelloServer
{
   public static void main(String[] args)
   {
      try
      {
         ORB orb = ORB.init(args,null);

         HelloServant servant = new HelloServant();

         orb.connect(servant);

         org.omg.CORBA.Object objectRef =
          orb.resolve_initial_references("NameService");

         NamingContext namingContext =
                 NamingContextHelper.narrow(objectRef);

         NameComponent nameComp =
                      new NameComponent("Hello", "");
         NameComponent[] path = {nameComp};

         namingContext.rebind(path,servant);
         java.lang.Object syncObj =
                                new java.lang.Object();
         synchronized(syncObj)
```

```
            {
                syncObj.wait();
            }
        }
        catch (Exception ex)
        {
            System.out.println("*** Server error! ***");
            ex.printStackTrace();
        }
    }
}
class HelloServant extends _HelloImplBase
{
    public String getGreeting()
    {
        return ("Hello there!");
    }
}
```

5. Compile the server and the idlj-generated files.

From the directory above directory *SimpleCORBAExample*, execute the following command within a command window:

```
javac HelloServer.java SimpleCORBAExample\*.java
```

(Correct errors and recompile, as necessary.)

6. Create a client.

Our client program will be called *HelloClient.java* and, like the server program, will import package *SimpleCORBAExample*. It should also import two of the three CORBA packages imported by the server: *org.omg.CosNaming* and *org.omg.CORBA*. There are several steps required of the client, most of them being identical to those required of the server, so the explanations given for the server in step 4 above are not repeated here…

(i) *Create and initialise the ORB*.

```
ORB orb = ORB.init(args,null);
```

(ii) *Get a reference to the root naming context*.

```
org.omg.CORBA.Object objectRef =
     orb.resolve_initial_references("NameService");
```

(iii) *'Narrow' the context reference*.

```
NamingContext namingContext =
        NamingContextHelper.narrow(objectRef);
```

(iv) *Create a NameComponent object for our interface*.

```
NameComponent nameComp =
                   new NameComponent("Hello", "");
```

(v) *Specify the path to the interface.*

```
NameComponent[] path = (nameComp};
```

(vi) *Get a reference to the interface.*
This is achieved by passing the above interface path to our naming context's *resolve* method, which returns a CORBA *Object* reference:

```
org.omg.CORBA.Object objectRef =
                      namingContext.resolve(path);
```

(vii) *'Narrow' the interface reference.*
We 'downcast' the reference from the previous step into a *Hello* reference via static method *narrow* of the *idlj*-generated class *HelloHelper*:

```
Hello helloRef = HelloHelper.narrow(objectRef);
```

(viii) *Invoke the required method(s) and display results.*
We use the reference from the preceding step to invoke the required method, just as though the call were being made to a local object:

```
System.out.println("Message received: "
                                      + greeting);
```

As was the case with the server, our client may then generate CORBA system exceptions, and so all the executable code will be placed inside a `try` block.

The full program is shown below.

```
import SimpleCORBAExample.*;

import org.omg.CosNaming.*;
import org.omg.CORBA.*;

public class HelloClient
{
   public static void main(String[] args)
   {
      try
      {
         ORB orb = ORB.init(args,null);

         org.omg.CORBA.Object objectRef =
             orb.resolve_initial_references(
                                        "NameService");
         NamingContext namingContext =
                 NamingContextHelper.narrow(objectRef);
         NameComponent nameComp =
                    new NameComponent("Hello", "");
         NameComponent[] path = {nameComp};

         //Re-use existing object reference...
```

```
            objectRef = namingContext.resolve(path);
            Hello helloRef = HelloHelper.narrow(objectRef);
            String greeting = helloRef.getGreeting();
            System.out.println("Message received: "
                                                + greeting);
        }
        catch (Exception ex)
        {
            System.out.println("*** Client error! ***");
            ex.printStackTrace();
        }
    }
}
```

7. Compile the client.
From the directory above directory *SimpleCORBAExample*, execute the following command:

```
javac HelloClient.java
```

8. Run the application.
This requires three steps...

(i) *Start the CORBA naming service.*
This is achieved via the following command:

```
tnameserv
```

Example output is shown in Fig. 6.3 below.

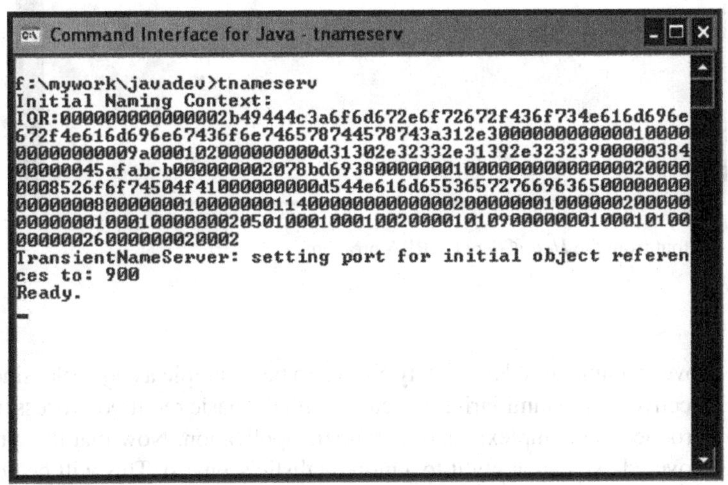

Fig. 6.3 Starting the CORBA naming service under Java IDL

The above command starts up the *Java IDL Transient Nameservice* as an object server that assumes a default port of 900. To use a different port (which would normally be necessary under Sun's Solaris operating system for ports below 1024), use the *ORBInitialPort* option to specify the port number. For example:

```
tnameserv -ORBInitialPort 1234
```

(ii) *Start the server in a new command window.*
For our example program, the command will be:

```
java HelloServer
```

(Since there is no screen output from the server, no screenshot is shown here.)
Again, a port other than the default one can be specified. For example:

```
java HelloServer -ORBInitialPort 1234
```

(iii) *Start the client in a third command window.*
For our example program, the command will be:

```
java HelloClient
```

(As above, a non-default port can be specified.)

The expected output should appear in the client window, as shown in Fig. 6.4.

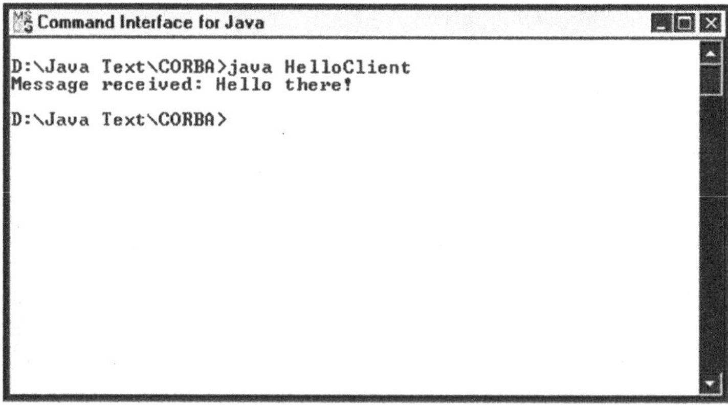

Fig. 6.4 Output from the *HelloClient* CORBA program

The above example was deliberately chosen to be as simple as possible, since the central objective was to familiarise the reader with the basic required process, rather than to introduce the complexities of a realistic application. Now that this process has been covered, we can apply it to a more realistic scenario. This will be done in the next section.

6.4 Using Factory Objects

In real-world applications, client programs often need to create CORBA objects, rather than simply using those that have already been set up. The only way in which this can be done is to go through a published *factory object* interface on the ORB. For each type of object that needs to be created, a factory object interface must be defined in the IDL specification (on the ORB) and implemented on the server. The usual naming convention for such interfaces is to append the word *Factory* to the name of the object type that is to be created. For example, an object of interface *Account* would be created by an *AccountFactory* object. The *AccountFactory* object will contain a creation method that allows connecting clients to create *Account* objects. The name of this creation method may be anything that we wish, but it is convenient to prepend the word 'create' onto the type of the object to be created. Thus, the *AccountFactory*'s creation method could meaningfully be called *createAccount*. Assuming that an *Account* object requires only an account number and account name at creation time, the *AccountFactory* interface in the IDL specification would look something like this:

```
interface AccountFactory
{
  Account createAccount(in long acctNum,
                        in string acctName);
};
```

This method's implementation will make use of the `new` operator to create the *Account* object. Like our other interface implementations, this implementation must extend the appropriate *idlj*-generated 'ImplBase' class (which, in this case, is _*AccountFactoryImplBase*). Following the convention of appending the word 'Servant' to such implementations, we would name the implementation *AccountFactoryServant*. Thus, the implementation would have a form similar to that shown below.

```
class AccountFactoryServant
               extends _AccountFactoryImplBase
{
   public Account createAccount(int acctNum,
                                String acctName)
   {
      return (new AccountServant(
                          acctNum, acctName));
   }
}
```

However, it would appear that we have merely moved the object creation problem on to the factory interface. Connecting clients cannot create factory objects, so how can they gain access to the creation methods within such objects? The simple answer is that the server will create a factory object for each factory interface and register that object with the ORB. Clients can then get a reference to the factory object and use the creation method of this object to create CORBA application objects. Assuming that a client has obtained a reference to the *AccountFactory* object created by the server and that this reference is held in the variable *acctFactoryRef*, the client could create an *Account* object with account number 12345 and account name 'John Andrews' with the following code:

```
Account acct = acctFactoryRef.createAccount(
                                  12345,"John Andrews");
```

For non-persistent objects, methods to destroy CORBA objects should also be defined (though we shall not be doing so).

To illustrate the use of factory interfaces and their associated factory objects, the rest of this section will be taken up by a specific example.

Example

We shall consider how *Java IDL* may be used to provide platform-independent access to stock items. Although only one item of stock will be used for illustration purposes, this could easily be extended to as many items of stock as might be required by a real-world application. The same basic steps will be required here as were used in the simple CORBA application of the last section, and the same numbering will be used here to indicate those steps.

1. Create the IDL file.

The file will be called *StockItem.idl* and will hold a module called *Sales*. This module will contain interfaces called *StockItem* and *StockItemFactory*. The former will hold the attributes and operations associated with an individual item of stock. For simplicity's sake, the attributes will be stock code and current level, while the operations will be ones to increase and decrease the stock level of this particular stock item. Since the stock code should never be changed, it will be declared read-only. The *StockItemFactory* interface will hold method *createStockItem*, which will be used to create a *StockItem* object with specified stock code and stock level (as indicated by the parameters of this operation). The contents of *StockItem.idl* are shown below.

```
module Sales
{
   interface StockItem
   {
      readonly attribute string code;
      attribute long currentLevel;
      long addStock(in long incNumber);
      long removeStock(in long decNumber);
   };

   interface StockItemFactory
   {
```

```
        StockItem createStockItem(in string newCode,
                                  in long newLevel);
    };
};
```

2. Compile the IDL file.

As in the previous example, client and server will be run on the same machine, so the -f flag will be followed by *all*. The command to execute the *idlj* compiler, then, is:

```
idlj -fall StockItem.idl
```

This causes a sub-directory with the same name as the module (i.e., *Sales*) to be created, holding the following 12 files (six each for the two interfaces):

- *StockItem.java*
- *StockItemHelper.java*
- *StockItemHolder.java*
- *StockItemOperations.java*
- *_StockItemImplBase.java*
- *_StockItemStub.java*
- *StockItemFactory.java*
- *StockItemFactoryHelper.java*
- *StockItemFactoryHolder.java*
- *StockItemFactoryOperations.java*
- *_ StockItemFactoryImplBase.java*
- *_ StockItemFactoryStub.java*

3. Implement the interfaces.

Once again, we shall follow the convention of appending the word 'servant' to each of our interface names to form the names of the corresponding implementation classes. This results in classes *StockItemServant* and *StockItemFactoryServant*, which must extend classes *_StockItemImplBase* and *_StockItemFactoryImplBase* respectively. The code is shown below. Note that both 'get' and 'set' methods for attribute currentLevel must be supplied and must have the same name as this attribute, whereas only the 'get' method for the read-only attribute *code* must be supplied.

```
class StockItemServant extends _StockItemImplBase
{
    //Declare and initialise instance variables…
    private String code = "";
    private int currentLevel = 0;

    //Constructor…
    public StockItemServant(String newCode, int newLevel)
    {
        code = newCode;
        currentLevel = newLevel;
    }
```

```
   public int addStock(int incNumber)
   {
      currentLevel += incNumber;
      return currentLevel;
   }

   public int removeStock(int decNumber)
   {
      currentLevel -= decNumber;
      return currentLevel;
   }

   //Must supply following 'get' and 'set' methods…

   //Accessor method ('get' method) for stock code…
   public String code()
   {
      return code;
   }

   //Accessor method ('get' method) for stock level…
   public int currentLevel()
   {
      return currentLevel;
   }

   //Mutator method ('set' method) for stock level…
   public void currentLevel(int newLevel)
   {
      currentLevel = newLevel;
   }
}

class StockItemFactoryServant
                  extends _StockItemFactoryImplBase
{
   /*
   Method to create a StockItemServant object and return
   a reference to this object (allowing clients to
   create StockItem objects from the servant)…
   */
   public StockItem createStockItem(String newCode,
                                         int newLevel)
   {
      return (new StockItemServant(newCode,newLevel));
   }
}
```

As in the first example, these classes will be placed inside the same file as our server code.

4. Create the server.
Our server program will be called *StockItemServer.java* and will subsume the servants created in the last step. It will import package *Sales* and (as in the previous example) the following three standard CORBA packages:

- *org.omg.CosNaming*;
- *org.omg.CosNaming.NamingContextPackage*;
- *org.omg.CORBA*.

The same basic sub-steps as were featured in the previous example will again be required, of course. Rather than reiterate these steps formally in the text, they will be indicated by comments within the code. The additional code involves the creation of a *StockItemFactoryServant* object and the associated registration of this object with the ORB, creation of an associated *NameComponent* object and so forth. Once again, comments within the code indicate the meaning of individual program lines.

```
import Sales.*;

import org.omg.CosNaming.*;
import org.omg.CosNaming.NamingContextPackage.*;
import org.omg.CORBA.*;

public class StockItemServer
{
   public static void main(String[] args)
   {
      try
      {
         //Create and initialise the ORB...
         ORB orb = ORB.init(args,null);

         //Create a StockItemServant object...
         StockItemServant stockServant =
                    new StockItemServant("S0001", 100);

         //Register the object  with the ORB...
         orb.connect(stockServant);

         //Create a StockItemFactoryServant object...
         StockItemFactoryServant factoryServant =
                         new StockItemFactoryServant();

         //Register the object  with the ORB...
         orb.connect(factoryServant);

         //Get a reference to the root naming context...
         org.omg.CORBA.Object objectRef =
          orb.resolve_initial_references("NameService");
```

```
        //'Narrow' ('downcast') context reference…
        NamingContext namingContext =
                NamingContextHelper.narrow(objectRef);
        //Create a NameComponent object for the
        //StockItem interface…
        NameComponent nameComp =
                      new NameComponent("Stock", "");
        //Specify the path to the interface…
        NameComponent[] stockPath = {nameComp};
        //Bind the servant to the interface path…
        namingContext.rebind(stockPath,stockServant);
        //Create a NameComponent object for the
        //StockFactory interface…
        NameComponent factoryNameComp =
                new NameComponent("StockFactory", "");
        //Specify the path to the interface…
        NameComponent[] factoryPath =
                                  {factoryNameComp};
        //Bind the servant to the interface path…
        namingContext.rebind(
                       factoryPath,factoryServant);
        System.out.print("\nServer running…");
        java.lang.Object syncObj =
                             new java.lang.Object();
        synchronized(syncObj)
        {
           syncObj.wait();
        }
     }
     catch (Exception ex)
     {
        System.out.println("*** Server error! ***");
        ex.printStackTrace();
     }
  }
}

class StockItemServant extends _StockItemImplBase
{
   //Code as shown in step 3 above.
}
```

```
class StockItemFactoryServant
                          extends _StockItemFactoryImplBase
{
   //Code as shown in step 3 above.
}
```

5. Compile the server and the idl-generated files.
From the directory above directory *Sales*, execute the following command within a command window:

```
javac StockItemServer.java Sales\*.java
```

(Correct errors and recompile, as necessary.)

6. Create a client.
Our client program will be called *StockItemClient.java* and, like the server program, will import package *Sales*. As with the client program in the previous example, it should also import *org.omg.CosNaming* and *org.omg.CORBA*. In addition to the steps executed by the client in the previous example, the steps listed below will be carried out.

- Several method calls will be made on the (pre-existing) *StockItem* object, rather than just the one made on the *Hello* object.
- A reference to the *StockItemFactory* object created and registered by the server will be obtained.
- The above reference will be used to create a new *StockItem* object by invoking method *createStockItem* (supplying the arguments required by the constructor).
- Methods of the new *StockItem* object will be invoked, to demonstrate once again that the object may be treated in just the same way as a local object.

The full code is shown below, with comments indicating the purpose of each operation.

```
import Sales.*;

import org.omg.CosNaming.*;
import org.omg.CORBA.*;

public class StockItemClient
{
   public static void main(String[] args)
   {
      try
      {
         //Create and initialise the ORB...
         ORB orb = ORB.init(args,null);

         //Get a reference to the root naming context...
         org.omg.CORBA.Object objectRef =
          orb.resolve_initial_references("NameService");
```

```
//'Downcast' the context reference…
NamingContext namingContext =
        NamingContextHelper.narrow(objectRef);

//Create a NameComponent object for the
//StockItem interface…
NameComponent nameComp =
               new NameComponent("Stock", "");

//Specify the path to the interface…
NameComponent[] stockPath = {nameComp};

//Get a reference to the interface (reusing
//existing reference)…
objectRef = namingContext.resolve(stockPath);

//'Downcast' the reference…
StockItem stockRef1 =
            StockItemHelper.narrow(objectRef);

//Now use this reference to call methods of the
//StockItem object…
System.out.println("\nStock code: "
                         + stockRef1.code());
System.out.println("Current level: "
                 + stockRef1.currentLevel());
stockRef1.addStock(58);
System.out.println("\nNew level: "
                 + stockRef1.currentLevel());

//Create a NameComponent object for the
//StockFactory interface…
NameComponent factoryNameComp =
        new NameComponent("StockFactory", "");

//Specify the path to the interface…
NameComponent[] factoryPath =
                         {factoryNameComp};

//Get a reference to the interface (reusing
//existing reference)…
objectRef = namingContext.resolve(factoryPath);

//'Downcast' the reference…
StockItemFactory stockFactoryRef =
     StockItemFactoryHelper.narrow(objectRef);
```

```
            /*
            Use factory reference to create a StockItem
            object on the server and return a reference to
            this StockItem (using method createStockItem
            within the StockItemFactory interface)…
            */
            StockItem stockRef2 =
             stockFactoryRef.createStockItem("S0002",200);

            //Now use this reference to call methods of the
            //new StockItem object…
            System.out.println("\nStock code: "
                                      + stockRef2.code());
            System.out.println("Current level: "
                              + stockRef2.currentLevel());
         }
         catch (Exception ex)
         {
            System.out.println("*** Client error! ***");
              ex.printStackTrace();
         }
      }
}
```

7. Compile the client.
From the directory above directory *Sales*, execute the following command:

```
javac StockItemClient.java
```

8. Run the application.
As before, this requires three steps…

(i) *Start the CORBA naming service (unless it is already running).*
Enter the following command:

```
tnameserv
```

Output should be as shown in Fig. 6.3.
N.B. Attempting to start (another instance of) the naming service when it is already running will generate an error message!

(ii) *Start the server in a new command window.*
The command for the current application will be:

```
java StockItemServer
```

Output should be as shown in Fig. 6.5.

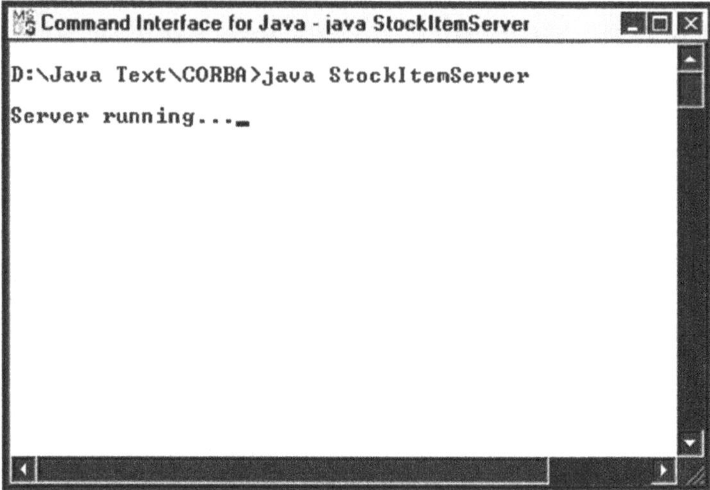

Fig. 6.5 Output from the *StockItemServer* program

(iii) *Start the client in a third command window.*
The command for this application will be:

```
java StockItemClient
```

The expected output should appear in the client window, as shown in Fig. 6.6.

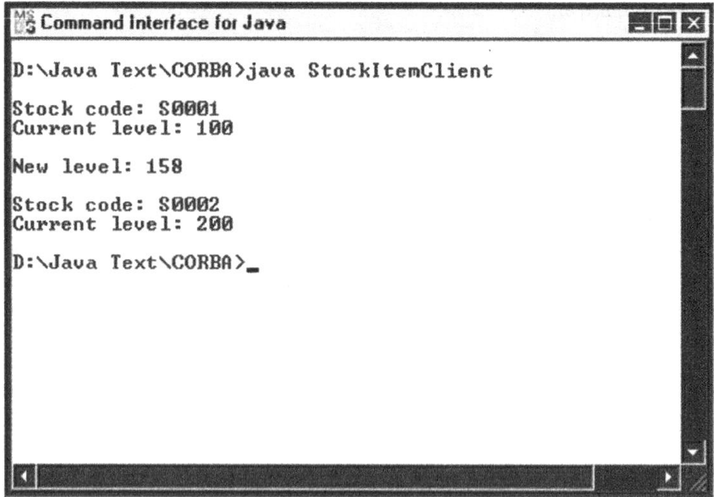

Fig. 6.6 Output from the *StockItemClient* program

The examples in this section and in the previous section have (for convenience) made use of *localhost* to run all the components associated with a CORBA application on the same machine. However, this need not have been the case. The ORB, nameserver and object server program could have been started on one host, whilst the client (or clients) could have been started on a different host (or hosts). Each client would then have needed to use the command line option `-ORBInitialHost` to specify the host machine for the ORB (and, if appropriate, the command line option `-ORBInitialPort` to specify the port).

6.5 Object Persistence

In commercial ORBs, object references **persist**. They can be saved by clients as strings and subsequently be recreated from those strings. The methods required to perform these operations are *object_to_string* and *string_to_object* respectively, both of which are methods of class *Orb*. With the latter method, an object of (CORBA) class *Object* is returned, which must then be 'downcast' into the original class via method *narrow* of the appropriate 'helper' class.

Example

Suppose that we have a reference to a *StockItem* object and that this reference is called *itemRef*. Suppose also that the ORB on which the object is registered is identified by the variable *orb*. The following Java statement would store this reference in a *String* object called *stockItemString*:

```
String stockItemString =
                        orb.object_to_string(itemRef);
```

The following statements could subsequently be used to convert this string back into a *StockItem* object reference:

```
org.omg.CORBA.Object obj =
           orb.string_to_object(stockItemString);
StockItem itemRef = StockItemHelper.narrow(obj);
```

Of course, the client would have needed to save the original string in some persistent form (probably within a disc file).

Since *Java IDL* supports **transient** objects only (i.e., objects that disappear when the server process closes down), the above technique is not possible. However, it **is** possible to implement an object so that it stores its state in a disc file, which may subsequently be used by the object's creation method to re-initialise the object.

6.6 RMI-IIOP

In order to overcome the language-specific disadvantages of RMI when compared with CORBA, Sun and IBM came together to produce RMI-IIOP (Remote Method Invocation over Internet Inter-Orb Protocol), which combines the best features of RMI with the best features of CORBA. Using IIOP as the transport mechanism, RMI-IIOP implements OMG standards to enable application components running on a Java platform to communicate with components written in a variety of languages (and vice-versa)—*but only if all the remote interfaces are originally defined as Java RMI interfaces*. RMI-IIOP was first released in June of 1999 and is an integral part of the Java SE from version 1.3 onwards. It is intended to be used by software developers who program objects in Java and wish to use RMI interfaces (written in Java) to communicate with CORBA objects written in other languages. It is of particular interest to programmers using *Enterprise JavaBeans* [see Chap. 11], since the remote object model for EJBs is RMI-based. Using RMI-IIOP, objects can be passed both by reference and by value over IIOP. However, the specific implementation details of RMI-IIOP are outside the scope of this text.

Exercises

6.1 Create a CORBA client/server application that handles student examination results as objects of class *Result*. This class is to have instance variables *studID* (holding an individual student's identity number as a Java *long*) and *mark* (holding the student's examination result as an integer 0–100). The former should be read-only, while the latter should allow read/write access. Have the server register an object of class *ResultFactoryServant* with the ORB and have the client use this factory object to create an array of five *Result* objects (supplying the constructor for each with appropriate data). Use a display routine to display a table of results on the client. Then use the 'set' method for the *mark* attribute to change a couple of the marks and re-display the table of results.
(You should be able to use the client and server programs for the *StockItem* example as a basis for your application.)

6.2 This exercise is a fairly lengthy one that implements the bank example from the preceding chapter and should allow you to compare the CORBA implementation with the corresponding RMI implementation (referring to *Method 1* from the preceding chapter, rather than *Method 2*). The IDL code for this application is supplied and is shown below. Note, in particular, that there is no direct equivalent of the *Vector* class in IDL, so a new type has been created via typedef:

```
typedef sequence<Account> BankAccts;
```

Thus, a *BankAccts* object is effectively an array of *Account* objects that is of indeterminate size.
In implementing the server, you should follow the advice given below.

- Create an *AccountFactoryServant* object and a *BankFactoryServant* object, but do not register these with the ORB, since clients will not need to use them.
- Declare and initialise three parallel arrays to hold the data for bank customers (surnames, first names and balances).
- Create an array of *Account* objects and use the *createAccount* method of the *AccountFactoryServant* object to create the members of this array, employing the data from the above three arrays in the construction of these members.
- Create a *BankServant* object, passing the above array to the constructor for this object, and register the object with the ORB.

In implementing the client, you should follow the advice given below.

- Use the above *BankServant* object to create a *Bank* reference.
- Retrieve the *BankAccts* attribute of this *Bank* reference (as an array of *Account* objects).
- Use the methods of class *Account* to display the contents of these *Account* objects.

```
module BankApp
{
   interface Account
   {
      readonly attribute long acctNum;
      attribute string surname;
      readonly attribute string firstNames;
      attribute double balance;

      string getName();
      double withdraw(in double amount);
      void deposit(in double amount);
   };

   interface AccountFactory

   {
      Account createAccount(in long newAcctNum,
                            in string newSurname,
                            in string newFirstNames,
                            in double newBalance);
   };

   typedef sequence<Account> BankAccts;

   interface Bank
   {
      attribute BankAccts accounts;
   };

   interface BankFactory

   {
      Bank createBank(in BankAccts newAccounts);
   };
};
```

Chapter 7
Java Database Connectivity (JDBC)

Learning Objectives

After reading this chapter, you should:

- be aware of what JDBC is and why it is needed;
- be aware of the differing versions of JDBC that are associated with the differing versions of Java;
- know how to use JDBC to make a connection to a database by employing Java's *DriverManager* class;
- know how to make use of the JDBC-ODBC bridge driver;
- know how to use JDBC to execute SQL queries and updates and how to handle the results returned;
- know how to use Apache Derby/Java DB to create and manipulate a relational database table;
- know how to carry out transaction processing via JDBC;
- know how to use JDBC to find out structural information about databases;
- know how to make use of a *JTable* to format the results of a database query;
- know how to use JDBC to move freely around the rows returned by a query;
- know how to use JDBC to modify databases via Java methods;
- know how to use JDBC to make a connection to a database by employing Java's *DataSource* interface;
- be aware of the advantages that the use of the *DataSource* interface has over the use of the *DriverManager* class.

The previous three chapters employed individual, 'flat' files to provide persistent data storage. Nowadays, of course, most organisations have the bulk of their data structured into **databases**, which often need to be accessed from more than one site. These databases are almost invariably **relational** databases. Programs written in Java are able to communicate with relational databases (whether local or remote) via the Java Database Connectivity (JDBC) API, which became part of the core Java distribution with JDK 1.1. In this chapter, we shall consider how such databases may be accessed via JDBC.

J. Graba, *An Introduction to Network Programming with Java: Java 7 Compatible*,
DOI 10.1007/978-1-4471-5254-5_7,

7.1 The Vendor Variation Problem

A fundamental problem that immediately presents itself when attempting to provide some general access method that will work for all relational databases is how to cope with the variation in internal format of such databases (and, consequently, the associated database API) from vendor to vendor. Thus, for example, the internal format of an Oracle database will be different from that of an Access database, while the format of a MySQL database will be different from both of these.

In order to use JDBC for the accessing of data from a particular type of relational database, it is necessary to provide some mediating software that will allow JDBC to communicate with the vendor-specific API for that database. Such software is referred to as a **driver**. Suitable drivers are usually supplied either by the database vendors themselves or by third parties. For information about JDBC 4 drivers for specific databases, visit http://docs.oracle.com/cd/E13222_01/wls/docs100/jdbc_drivers/index.html. JDBC drivers may be written purely in Java or in a combination of Java and Java Native Interface (JNI) methods. (JNI allows Java programmers to make use of code written in other programming languages.) However, the details are beyond the scope of this text and no further reference will be made to these differing categories.

Before Java came onto the scene, Microsoft had introduced its own solution to the problem of accessing databases that have different internal formats: Open Database Connectivity (ODBC). Though (not surprisingly) ODBC drivers were originally available only for Microsoft (MS) databases, other vendors and third party suppliers have since brought out ODBC drivers for most of the major non-MS databases. In recognition of this fact, Oracle provides the **JDBC-ODBC bridge driver** in package *sun.jdbc.odbc*, which is included in the Java Standard Edition (and has been present in Java from JDK 1.1). This driver converts the JDBC protocol into the corresponding ODBC one and allows Java programmers to access databases for which there are ODBC drivers. However, adding an extra conversion phase may lead to unacceptably long delays in some large, database-intensive applications. In fact, to quote from the JDBC API, "…the bridge driver included in the SDK is appropriate only for experimental use or when no other driver is available".

7.2 SQL and Versions of JDBC

The standard means of accessing a relational database is to use SQL (Structured Query Language). [Readers unfamiliar with SQL are advised to read the appendix on this subject before proceeding further with this chapter.] This is reflected in the fact that the package comprising the core JDBC API is called ***java.sql.***

The original JDBC that was released with JDK 1.1 was JDBC 1.0, which comprised package *java.sql*. Using this API, it is possible to access data not only from relational databases, but also from spreadsheets and flat files—i.e., from just about any data source. With JDBC 2.0, which appeared in J2SE 1.4, extra functionality was introduced with the additional package *javax.sql*. Probably the most notable feature of this version was the introduction of the *DataSource* interface, which now provides the preferred method of making a connection to a database, This is due to the fact that a *DataSource* object has properties that can be modified. Thus, for example, if the data source is moved to a different server, the property for the server can be changed without requiring the code accessing the data source to be changed. In spite of the fact that the use of a *DataSource* object is the official preferred method of making connection to a database, the old method of making a connection, which involves the use of the *DriverManager* class, is still quite commonly used. Both of these techniques will be covered in this chapter.

The latest version of the JDBC API (at the time of writing) is JDBC 4.1, which is included with Java SE 7, and most drivers nowadays adhere to the JDBC 4 standard, which has been included in the Java installation since Java SE 6 (launched in December of 2006). However, users of earlier versions can expect their code to continue to work under Java SE 7, since one of the guiding design principles of each new version has been that of maintaining compatibility with existing applications and drivers.

In the examples that follow in the next two sections, a simple MS Access database will be used for purposes of illustration, which means that the inbuilt JDBC-ODBC bridge driver can be employed (even though, as noted at the end of 7.1, this may not be the best strategy in many commercial applications). Convenient though this may be, in view of the widespread use and availability of MS Access and the inclusion of the JDBC-ODBC bridge driver in the Java installation, it does introduce a couple of complications: (i) we have to create an **ODBC Data Source** and (ii) we need to use the 32-bit version of Java, even though there is now a 64-bit version. The reason for the latter is that, although a 64-bit version of MS Access does now exist, even Microsoft is recommending that the 32-bit version be installed for the time being: "For these reasons, we recommend running 32-bit Office 2010 even on 64-bit Windows operating systems for better compatibility…When the 64-bit ecosystem for Office is more mature, you'll be able to easily migrate to 64-bit Office" [http://blogs.technet.com/b/office2010/archive/2010/02/23/understanding-64-bit-office.aspx].

The next section describes the process required to create an ODBC Data Source, with the two sections after that describing the steps required to make connection to the database and to retrieve or manipulate the contents of the database. Apart from creation of the ODBC Data Source, all steps are applicable to any type of relational database. Before starting the next section, though, it is worth mentioning that the reader who wishes to experiment with other databases (such as Oracle or MySQL) will probably find it necessary to place the appropriate JDBC driver within folder ***<Java_Home>\jre\lib\ext.***

As of Java SE 6, Java also has its own inbuilt database, known as either *Java DB* or *Apache Derby*. Use of this database will also be covered in a later section

7.3 Creating an ODBC Data Source

Before an ODBC-driven database can be accessed via a Java program, it is necessary to register the database as an ODBC Data Source. Once this has been done, the database can be referred to by its Data Source Name (DSN). Assuming that the database has already been created, the steps required to set up your own ODBC Data Source are shown below. (These instructions were used on a Windows 7 machine and the naming of some items may vary slightly with other MS operating systems, but the basic steps should remain much the same.)

1. Select *start* → *Run...*
2. Enter **cmd** and click on OK.
3. Enter **C:\windows\syswow64\odbcad32.exe**.
4. Ensure that the *User DSN* tab is selected.
5. Click on the *Add...* button to display the *Create New Data Source* window.
6. Select *Microsoft Access Driver (*.mdb, *.accdb)* and click on *Finish.*
7. To locate the required database within the directory structure, click on the **Select...** button.
8. Navigate through the directory structure and select your database.
9. Supply a name for the data source. ('Description' field is optional.)
10. If specifying a username and password (not mandatory and not necessary for the examples in this section), click on *Advanced Options* and key in the values, clicking **OK** when finished.
11. Click **OK** to finish registration.

N.B. Remember that the above procedure is required **only** for ODBC databases!

The next section describes how our Java code can make use of the database's DSN to retrieve data from the database and is applicable to **any** type of relational database.

7.4 Simple Database Access

In what follows, reference will be made to *Connection*, *Statement* and *ResultSet* objects. These three names actually refer to **interfaces**, rather than classes. Each JDBC driver must implement these three interfaces and the implementation classes may then be used to create objects that may conveniently be referred to as *Connection*, *Statement* and *ResultSet* objects respectively. Similar comments apply to interfaces *ResultSetMetaData* and *DatabaseMetaData* in Sect. 7.7. From now on, such terminology will be used freely and this point will not be laboured any further.

Using JDBC 4 to access a database requires several steps, as described below.

1. Establish a connection to the database.
2. Use the connection to create a *Statement* object and store a reference to this object.
3. Use the above *Statement* reference to run a specific query or update statement and accept the result(s).

4. Manipulate and display the results (if a query) or check/show number of database rows affected (for an update).
5. Repeat steps 4 and 5 as many times as required for further queries/updates.
6. Close the connection.

[If using an earlier version of JDBC, the following additional step is required before those above: Load the database driver.]

For purposes of illustration, we shall assume the existence of an MS Access database called *Finances.accdb* that holds a single table called *Accounts*. The structure of this simple table is as shown below.

Field name	MS access type	Java type
acctNum	Number	int
surname	Text	String
firstNames	Text	String
balance	Currency	float

We shall further assume that the DSN given to the database is *Finances*.

Let's take each of the above seven steps in turn for this database…

1. Establish a Connection to the Database

We declare a *Connection* reference and call static method *getConnection* of class *DriverManager* to return a *Connection* object for this reference. Method *getConnection* takes three *String* arguments:

- a URL-style address for the database;
- a user name;
- a password.

The JDBC API specification recommends that the database address have the following format:

```
jdbc:<sub-protocol>:<data-source>
```

Here, `<sub-protocol>` specifies a database connection service (i.e., a **driver**) and `<data-source>` provides all the information needed by the service to locate the database (typically, the URL path to the database). For a **local** ODBC database with data source name *Finances*, the sub-protocol is *odbc* and the final part of the address is simply the name of the data source:

```
jdbc:odbc:Finances
```

Assuming that our *Finances* database is indeed local and that we did not set a user name or password for this database, the line required to open a connection to the database would be similar to this:

```
Connection connection =
         DriverManager.getConnection(
                "jdbc:odbc:Finances", "", "");
```

If this same database were remote, then the above line would look something like this:

```
Connection connection =
  DriverManager.getConnection(
    "jdbc:odbc://AnyServer.SomethingElse.com/Finances",
                                                "", "");
```

However, the API-specified syntax is only a **recommendation** and database vendors are free to ignore this if they wish. Consequently, some drivers may specify sub-protocols and data sources with syntax that is different from that shown above. It is up to the *DriverManager* to query each loaded driver in turn to determine whether the driver recognises the type of database that is being addressed.

2. Create a Statement Object and Store Its Reference

A *Statement* object is created by calling the *createStatement* method of our *Connection* object (whose reference was saved in variable *link* in the previous step). The address of the object returned by this call to *createStatement* is saved in a *Statement* reference. In the line below, this reference is simply called *statement*.

```
Statement statement = connection.createStatement();
```

3. Run a Query or Update and Accept the Result(s)

DML (Data Manipulation Language) statements in SQL may be divided into two categories: those that retrieve data from a database (i.e., SELECT statements) and those that change the contents of the database in some way (viz., INSERT, DELETE and UPDATE statements). Class *Statement* has methods *executeQuery* and *executeUpdate* that are used to execute these two categories respectively. The former method returns a *ResultSet* object, while the latter returns an integer that indicates the number of database rows that have been affected by the updating operation. (We shall postpone consideration of method *executeUpdate* until the next section.)

It is common practice to store the SQL query in a *String* variable and then invoke *executeQuery* with this string as an argument, in order to avoid a rather cumbersome invocation line. This practice has been followed in the examples below.

Examples

```
(i)   String selectAll = "SELECT * FROM Accounts";
      ResultSet results =
                statement.executeQuery(selectAll);

(ii)  String selectFields =
               "SELECT acctNum, balance FROM Accounts";
      ResultSet results =
               statement.executeQuery(selectFields);

(iii) String selectRange = "SELECT * FROM Accounts"
                         + " WHERE balance >= 0"
                         + " AND balance <= 1000"
```

```
                                + " ORDER BY balance DESC";
        ResultSet results =
                  statement.executeQuery(selectRange);

  (iv)  String selectNames =
         "SELECT * FROM Accounts WHERE surname < Jones'";
        ResultSet results =
                  statement.executeQuery(selectNames);
```

Note the need for inverted commas around any string literals! (Speech marks cannot be used, of course, since the opening of speech marks for a string within an SQL query would be interpreted by the compiler as the closing of the query.) Inverted commas are not required for numbers, but no error is generated if they are used.

4. Manipulate/Display/Check Result(s)
The *ResultSet* object returned in response to a call of *executeQuery* contains the database rows that satisfy the query's search criteria. The *ResultSet* interface contains a **very** large number of methods for manipulating these rows, but the majority of these will not be discussed here. [see Sect. 7.9 for coverage of some of the other methods.] The only method that we need to make use of at present is *next*, which moves the *ResultSet* cursor/pointer to the next row in the set of rows referred to by that object.

Having moved to the particular row of interest via any of the above methods, we can retrieve data via either the field name or the field position. In doing so, we must use the appropriate *getXXX* method (where 'XXX' is replaced by the appropriate Java type).

Examples

- `int getInt(String <columnName>)`
- `int getInt(int <columnIndex>)`
- `String getString(String <columnName>)`
- `String getString(int <columnIndex>)`

Similar methods exist for the other types, in particular *getFloat*, *getLong* and *getDate*. Note that the last of these is a method of class *java.sql.Date,* not of class *java.util.Date*. The latter is, in fact, a subclass of the former. Note also that the number of a field is its position **within a *ResultSet* row**, not its position within a database row. Of course, if all fields of the database table have been selected by the query, then these two will be the same. However, if only a subset of the fields has been selected, they will not necessarily be the same!

Initially, the *ResultSet* cursor/pointer is positioned **before** the first row of the query results, so method *next* must be called before attempting to access the results. Such rows are commonly processed via a `while` loop that checks the Boolean return value of this method first (to determine whether there is any data at the selected position).

Example

```
String select = "SELECT * FROM Accounts";
ResultSet results =
            statement.executeQuery(select);
while (results.next())
{
   System.out.println("Account no."
                        + results.getInt(1));
   System.out.println("Account holder: "
                        + results.getString(3)
                        + " "
                        + results.getString(2));
   System.out.println("Balance: "
                        + results.getFloat(4));
   System.out.println ();
}
```

N.B. Column/field numbers start at **1**, not 0!
Alternatively, column/field names can be used. For example:

```
System.out.println("Account no."
                   + results.getInt("acctNum");
```

5. Repeat Steps 3 and 4, as Required
The *Statement* reference may be used to execute other queries (and updates).

6. Close the Connection
This is achieved by calling method *close* of our *Connection* object and should be carried out as soon as the processing of the database has finished. For example:

```
connection.close();
```

Statement objects may also be closed explicitly via the identically-named method of our *Statement* object. For example:

```
statement.close();
```

[Note: If using a version of JDBC that precedes version 4, then it will be necessary to load the JDBC driver explicitly before any of the six steps above are executed. This is done via static method *forName* of class *Class*(!):

```
E.g.,     Class.forName("<Driver name>");     ]
```

We are now almost ready to write our first database access program in Java. Before we do, though, there is one last issue to consider: exception-handling. Any of our SQL statements may generate an *SQLException*, which is a checked exception, so we must either handle such an exception or throw it.

Now let's bring everything together into a program that simply accesses our *Finances* database and displays the full contents of the *Accounts* table. In order to make use of JDBC (without cumbersome package references), of course, our program should import *java.sql*. In what follows, the lines corresponding to the above six steps have been commented to indicate the relevant step numbers.

Example

```
import java.sql.*;

public class JDBCSelect
{
   public static void main(String[] args)
   {
      Connection connection = null;
      Statement statement = null;
      ResultSet results = null;

      try
      {
         //Step 1…
         connection = DriverManager.getConnection(
                          "jdbc:odbc:Finances","","");
      }
      //For any of a number of reasons, it may not be
      //possible to establish a connection…
      catch(SQLException sqlEx)
      {
         System.out.println(
                     "* Cannot connect to database! *");
         System.exit(1);
      }

      try
      {
         //Step 2…
         statement = connection.createStatement();

         String select = "SELECT * FROM Accounts";
         //Step 3…
         results = statement.executeQuery(select);
      }
      catch(SQLException sqlEx)
      {
         System.out.println(
                      "* Cannot execute query! *");
         sqlEx.printStackTrace();
         System.exit(1);
      }
```

```
        try
        {
            System.out.println();

            //Step 4…
            while (results.next())
            {
                System.out.println("Account no. "
                                    + results.getInt(1));

                System.out.println("Account holder:  "
                                    + results.getString(3)
                                    + " "
                                    + results.getString(2));
                System.out.printf("Balance: %.2f %n%n"
                                     + results.getFloat(4));
            }
        }
        catch(SQLException sqlEx)
        {
            System.out.println(
                          "* Error retrieving data! *");
            sqlEx.printStackTrace();
            System.exit(1);
        }

        //(No further queries, so no Step 5!)

        try
        {
            //Step 6…
            connection.close();
        }
        catch(SQLException sqlEx)
        {
            System.out.println(
                         "* Unable to disconnect! *");
            sqlEx.printStackTrace();
            System.exit(1);
        }
    }
}
```

Alternatively, we could put everything into a single `try` block that is followed by code that handles all *SQLException*s. However, we would not then be able to give specific SQL error messages.

The output from this program when executed for an *Accounts* table that holds just three rows of data will be similar to that shown below (Fig. 7.1).

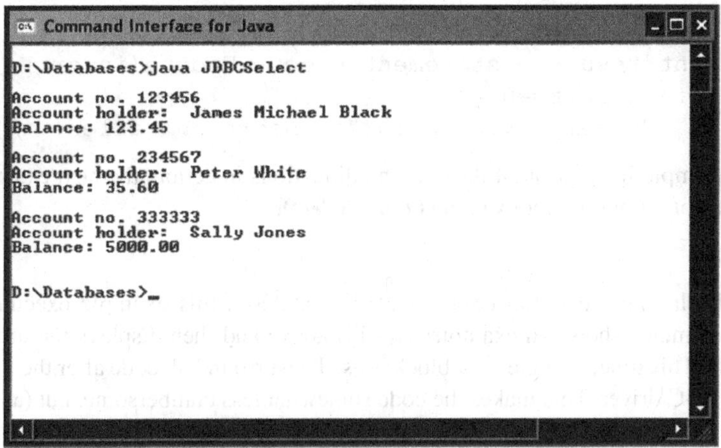

Fig. 7.1 Output from program *JDBCSelect*

7.5 Modifying the Database Contents

As mentioned in Sect. 7.4, DML (Data Manipulation Language) statements in SQL may be divided into two categories: those that retrieve data from a database (SELECT statements) and those that change the contents of the database in some way (INSERT, DELETE and UPDATE statements). So far, we have dealt only with the former, which has meant submitting our SQL statements via the *executeQuery* method. We shall now look at the latter category, for which we shall have to submit our SQL statements via the *executeUpdate* method. Some examples are shown below.

<u>Examples</u>

```
(i)    String insert = "INSERT INTO Accounts"
                     + " VALUES (123456,'Smith',"
                     + "'John James',752.85)";
       int result = statement.executeUpdate(insert);

(ii)   String change = "UPDATE Accounts"
                      + " SET surname = 'Bloggs',"
                      + "firstNames = 'Fred Joseph'"
                      + " WHERE acctNum = 123456";
       statement.executeUpdate(change);

(iii)  String remove = "DELETE FROM Accounts"
                      + " WHERE balance < 100";
       result = statement.executeUpdate(remove);
```

For the second of these examples, the value returned by *executeUpdate* has not been saved and is simply discarded by the runtime system. In practice, though, the integer returned is often used to check whether the update has been carried out.

Example

```
int result = statement.executeUpdate(insert);
if (result==0)
   System.out.println("* Insertion failed! *");
```

As a simple illustration of database modifications in action, the next example is an extension of our earlier example (*JDBCSelect*).

Example

After displaying the initial contents of the database, this example executes the SQL statements shown in examples (i)–(iii) above and then displays the modified database. This time, a single `try` block is used to surround all code after the loading of the JDBC driver. This makes the code somewhat less cumbersome, but (as noted at the end of the last example) does not allow us to display problem-specific SQL error messages. The only other change to the code is the introduction of method *displayTable*, which encapsulates the selection and display of all data from the table (in order to avoid code duplication).

```
import java.sql.*;

public class JDBCChange
{
   private static Statement statement;
   private static ResultSet results;

   public static void main(String[] args)
   {
      Connection connection = null;

      try
      {
         //Step 1…
         connection = DriverManager.getConnection(
                           "jdbc:odbc:Finances","","");
      }
      catch(ClassNotFoundException cnfEx)
      {
         System.out.println(
                           "* Unable to load driver! *");
         System.exit(1);
      }
      //For any of a number of reasons, it may not be
      //possible to establish a connection…

      catch(SQLException sqlEx)
      {
         System.out.println(
                       "* Cannot connect to database! *");
         System.exit(1);
      }
```

```
try
{
   //Step 2…
   statement = connection.createStatement();

   System.out.println(
                  "\nInitial contents of table:");
   //Steps 3 and 4…
   displayTable();

   //Start of step 5…
   String insert = "INSERT INTO Accounts"
                + " VALUES (123456,'Smith',"
                + "'John James',752.85)";
   int result = statement.executeUpdate(insert);
   if (result == 0)
      System.out.println(
                   "\nUnable to insert record!");

   String change = "UPDATE Accounts"
                      + " SET surname = 'Bloggs',"
                      + "firstNames='Fred Joseph'"
                      + " WHERE acctNum = 123456";
   result = statement.executeUpdate(change);
   if (result == 0)
      System.out.println(
                    "\nUnable to update record!");

   String remove = "DELETE FROM Accounts"
                       + " WHERE balance < 100";
   result = statement.executeUpdate(remove);
   if (result == 0)
      System.out.println(
                    "\nUnable to delete record!");

   System.out.println(
                    "\nNew contents of table:");
   displayTable();
   //End of step 5.

   //Step 6…
   connection.close();
}
catch(SQLException sqlEx)
{
   System.out.println(
                   "* SQL or connection error! *");
   sqlEx.printStackTrace();
   System.exit(1);
}
}
```

```
    public static void displayTable() throws SQLException
    {
        String select = "SELECT * FROM Accounts";

        results = statement.executeQuery(select);

        System.out.println();

        while (results.next())
        {
            System.out.println("Account no. "
                                    + results.getInt(1));

            System.out.println("Account holder:  "
                             + results.getString(3)
                             + " " + results.getString(2));
            System.out.printf("Balance: %.2f %n%n",
                                    results.getFloat(4));
        }
    }
}
```

The output from this program is shown in Fig. 7.2.

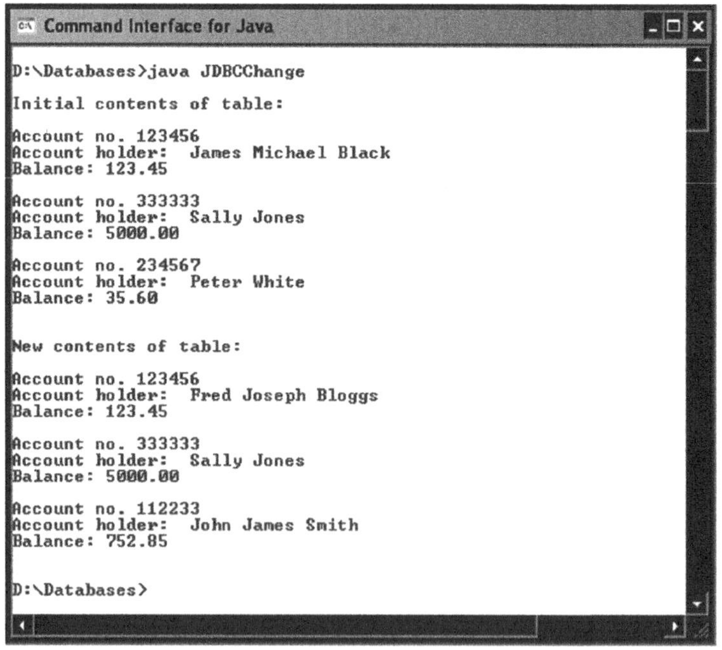

Fig. 7.2 Output from program *JDBCChange*

7.6 Java DB/Apache Derby

As of Java SE 6, Java has included its own inbuilt database, which originated in a small company called Cloudscape, this company subsequently being taken over by Informix Software and the latter itself then being taken over by IBM. In 2004, IBM donated the code to the Apache Software Foundation, which developed the product under the name *Derby*. When Sun released Java SE 6, it included the database product under the re-branded name of *Java DB*, although the Apache Foundation continues to make it available as open source software under the name *Apache Derby* and this (or simply *Derby*) is often the name that is used in a Java SE context. This component takes up an impressively small disc-space of 2 MB and allows Java programmers to embed a relational database system in their Java programs.

Also included in the product is a rather tersely and strangely named SQL scripting tool called **ij**. This can be used with either the *Derby* embedded JDBC driver or with a client JDBC driver such as *Derby Network Client*. In either case, the associated commands are entered into an MS-DOS command window. We'll use it with the embedded driver.

The steps required to create, populate and manipulate a Derby database are listed below.

1. Starting up ij

Enter the following command (into the command window):

```
java org.apache.derby.tools.ij
```

The output that is returned in response to this command should be similar to the following:

```
ij version 10.9
ij>  [Prompt]
```

The above prompt remains until the user quits in step 7.

2. Creating a Database

Use the `connect` command with a `create` attribute of `true` to specify the URL of the database, using the following format for this URL:

```
jdbc:derby:<DbPath&Name>
```

Examples

```
connect 'jdbc:derby:Finances;create=true';
connect 'jdbc:derby:C:\\Databases\\Finances;create=true';
```

3. Creating a Table

Example

```
create table Accounts(acctNum int primary key, surname
varchar(15), firstNames varchar(25), balance real);
```

[Note the setting of the primary key!]

4. Inserting Rows

Example

```
insert into Accounts values(123456, 'Black', 'James
Michael', 123.45);
```

5. Selecting, Updating and Deleting Rows

Examples

```
select * from Accounts;
update Accounts set balance=999.99 where acctNum=123456;
delete from Accounts where acctNum = 234567;
```

6. Disconnecting and Reconnecting

disconnect;
connect 'jdbc:derby:<DbPath&Name>';
Note that **relative addressing** may be used.

7. Quitting

```
exit;
```

8. Using Scripts

Unless dealing with only one or two SQL statements, one should always use ij scripts. First place all of the required SQL statements into a text file with an appropriate name (e.g., *AccountsScript.sql*). This file may then be run in any one of the following three ways…

(i) Use the ij command, supplying the input file as a command line argument.

Example

```
java org.apache.derby.tools.ij AccountsScript.sql
```

(ii) Redirect standard input [see Sect. 4.3] to come from the script file.

Example

```
java org.apache.derby.tools.ij < AccountsScript.sql
```

(iii) From the ij prompt, use the `run` command.

Example

```
run 'AccountsScript.sql';
```

7.7 Transactions

Industrial-strength databases (so **not** MS Access!) will normally incorporate **transaction processing**. A transaction is one or more SQL statements that may be grouped together as a single processing entity. This feature caters for situations in which a group of related statements needs to be carried out at the same time. If only some of the statements are executed, then the database is likely to be left in an inconsistent state. For example, an online ordering system may update the *Orders* table when a customer places an order and may also need to update the *Stock* table at the same time (in order to reflect the fact that stock has been set aside for the customer and cannot be ordered by another customer). In such a situation, we want either both statements or neither to be executed. Unfortunately, network problems may cause one of these statements to fail after the other has been executed. If this happens, then we want to undo the statement that has been executed.

The SQL statements used to implement transaction processing are COMMIT and ROLLBACK, which are mirrored in Java by the *Connection* interface methods *commit* and *rollback*. As their names imply, *commit* is used at the end of a transaction to commit/finalise the database changes, while *rollback* is used (in an error situation) to restore the database to the state it was in prior to the current transaction (by undoing any statements that may have been executed). By default, however, JDBC automatically commits each individual SQL statement that is applied to a database. In order to change this default behaviour so that transaction processing may be carried out, we must first execute *Connection* method *setAutoCommit* with an argument of `false` (to switch off auto-commit). We can then use methods *commit* and *rollback* to effect transaction processing.

Example

```
.............................
connection.setAutoCommit(false);
.............................
try
{
   //Assumes existence of 3 SQL update strings
   //called update1, update2 and update3.
   statement.executeUpdate(update1);
   statement.executeUpdate(update2);
   statement.executeUpdate(update3);
   connection.commit();
}
catch(SQLException sqlEx)
{
   connection.rollback();
   System.out.println(
               "* SQL error! Changes aborted... *");
}
.............................
```

7.8 Meta Data

Meta data is 'data about data'. There are two categories of meta data available through the JDBC API:

- data about the rows and columns returned by a query (i.e., data about *ResultSet* objects);
- data about the database as a whole.

The first of these is provided by interface *ResultSetMetaData*, an object of which is returned by the *ResultSet* method *getMetaData*. Information available from a *ResultSetMetaData* object includes the following:

- the number of fields/columns in a *ResultSet* object;
- the name of a specified field;
- the data type of a field;
- the maximum width of a field;
- the table to which a field belongs.

Data about the database as a whole is provided by interface *DatabaseMetaData*, an object of which is returned by the *Connection* method *getMetaData*. However, most Java developers will rarely find a need for *DatabaseMetaData* and no further mention will be made of it.

Before proceeding further, it is worth pointing out that the full range of SQL types is represented in class *java.sql.Types* as a series of 28 named static integer (*int*) constants. The 8 that are likely to be of most use are listed below.

- *DATE*
- *DECIMAL*
- *DOUBLE*
- *FLOAT*
- *INTEGER*
- *NUMERIC*
- *REAL*
- *VARCHAR*

INTEGER and *VARCHAR* are particularly commonplace, the latter of these corresponding to string values.

The example coming up makes use of the following *ResultSetMetaData* methods, which return properties of the database fields held in a *ResultSetMetaData* object.

- `int getColumnCount()`
- `String getColumnName(<colNumber>)`
- `int getColumnType(<colNumber>)`
- `String getColumnTypeName(<colNumber>)`

The basic purpose of each of these methods is fairly self-evident, but the distinction between the last two is worth clarifying. Method *getColumnType* returns the selected field's SQL type as an integer matching one of the named constants in class *java.sql.Types*, while method *getColumnTypeName* returns the string holding the database-specific type name for the selected field. Now for the example…

Example

This example uses the *Accounts* table in our *Finances* database to retrieve all data relating to account number 12345. It then uses the above methods to display the name of each field, its database-specific type name and the value held (after ascertaining the field's data type, so that the appropriate Java *getXXX* method can be called).

```
import java.sql.*;

public class JDBCMetaData
{
   private static Connection connection;
   private static Statement statement;
   private static ResultSet results;

   public static void main(String[] args)
   {
      try
      {
         //Step 1…
         connection = DriverManager.getConnection(
                              "jdbc:odbc:Finances","","");

      }
      catch(ClassNotFoundException cnfEx)
      {
         System.out.println(
                              "* Unable to load driver! *");
         System.exit(1);
      }
      catch(SQLException sqlEx)
      {
         System.out.println(
                         "* Cannot connect to database! *");
         System.exit(1);
      }

      try
      {
         //Step 2…
         statement = connection.createStatement();
```

```
String select = "SELECT * FROM Accounts"
                + " WHERE acctNum = 123456";
//Step 3…
results = statement.executeQuery(select);

//Start of step 4…
ResultSetMetaData metaData =
                        results.getMetaData();
int numFields = metaData.getColumnCount();

//Check that record has been found…
boolean found = results.next();

if (!found)
{
   //No point in continuing…
   System.out.println("\nNot found!");
   connection.close();
   return;
 }

//Cycle through the database fields, displaying
//meta data about each one…
for (int i=1; i<=numFields; i++)
 //N.B. Remember that count must start at 1!
{
   System.out.println("\nField name: "
                  + metaData.getColumnName(i));

   System.out.println("Field type:  "
              + metaData.getColumnTypeName(i));

   int colType = metaData.getColumnType(i);

   System.out.print("Value: ");

   //Select the appropriate getXXX method,
   //according to the SQL type of the field…
   switch (colType)
   {
      case Types.INTEGER:
                System.out.println(
                           results.getInt(i));
                break;
      case Types.VARCHAR:
                System.out.println(
                        results.getString(i));
                break;
      case Types.NUMERIC:
```

```
                          System.out.printf("%.2f %n%n",
                                   results.getFloat(i));
                          break;
                 default: System.out.println("Unknown");
              }
           }
           //End of step 4.

           //(No further queries, so no Step 5!)

           //Step 6…
           connection.close();
        }
        catch(SQLException ex)
        {
           System.out.println(
                          "* SQL or connection error! *");
           ex.printStackTrace();
           System.exit(1);
        }
    }
}
```

The output from this program is shown in Fig. 7.3. The only features of note concern the *balance* field. The MS Access-specific type for this field is *CURRENCY*, its SQL type is represented in Java by the integer constant *NUMERIC* and the value in this field has to be retrieved via method *getFloat*!

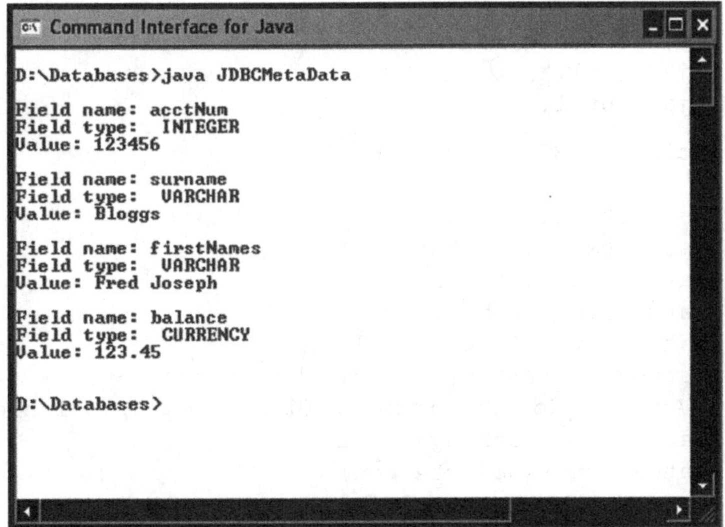

Fig. 7.3 Output from program *JDBCMetaData*

7.9 Using a GUI to Access a Database

All the programs in this chapter up to this point have been executed in command windows, with the values retrieved from the database being displayed in a rather primitive manner. Nowadays, of course we would expect such data to be displayed in tabular format, using a professional-looking GUI. This can be achieved in Java with very little extra code by making use of class *JTable*, which, as its name indicates, is one of the *Swing* classes. An object of this class displays data in a table format with column headings. The class has seven constructors, but we shall be concerned with only one of these, the one that has the following signature:

```
JTable(Vector <rowData>, Vector <colNames>)
```

The first argument holds the rows that are to be displayed (as a *Vector* of *Vector*s), while the second holds the names of the column headings. Since each row contains data of differing types, each of the 'inner' *Vector*s within our *Vector* of *Vector*s will need to be a heterogeneous *Vector*. That is to say, it will need to be of type *Vector<Object>*. This means that the full type for our *Vector* of *Vector*s will have the following rather unusual appearance: *Vector<Vector<Object>>*. The *Vector* holding the headings will, of course, have type *Vector<String>*.

To allow for scrolling of the rows in the table, it will be necessary to 'wrap' our *JTable* object in a *JScrollPane*, which will then be added to the application frame. The example below uses our *Accounts* table to illustrate how a *JTable* may be used to display the results of an SQL query.

Example

```
import java.awt.*;
import java.awt.event.*;
import javax.swing.*;
import java.sql.*;
import java.util.*;

public class JDBCGUI extends JFrame
{
   private static  Connection connection;
   private Statement statement;
   private ResultSet results;
   private JTable table;
   private JScrollPane scroller;
   private final String[] heading =
      {"Account No.","Surname","First Names","Balance"};
   private Vector<String> heads;
   private Vector<Object> row;
   private Vector<Vector<Object>> rows;

   public static void main(String[] args)
```

```
{
     JDBCGUI frame = new JDBCGUI();
     frame.setSize(400,200);
     frame.setVisible(true);

     frame.addWindowListener(
         new WindowAdapter()
         {
               public void windowClosing(
                                WindowEvent winEvent)
               {
                    try
                    {
                         connection.close();
                         System.exit(0);
                    }
                    catch(SQLException sqlEx)
                    {
                         System.out.println(
                          "*Error     on     closing
                          connection!*");
                    }
               }
         }
     );
}

public JDBCGUI()
{
     setTitle("Accounts Data");

     try
     {
          connection = DriverManager.getConnection(
                        "jdbc:odbc:Finances","","");
          statement = connection.createStatement();
          results = statement.executeQuery(
                          "SELECT * FROM Accounts");

          heads = new Vector<String>();
          for (int i=0; i<heading.length; i++)
          {
               heads.add(heading[i]);
          }

          rows = new Vector<Vector<Object>>();

          while (results.next())
```

```
                {
                    row = new Vector<Object>();
                    //Heterogeneous collection.

                    row.add(results.getInt(1));
                    row.add(results.getString(2));
                    row.add(results.getString(3));
                    row.add(results.getFloat(4));
                    rows.add(row);
                }
                table = new JTable(rows,heads);
                scroller = new JScrollPane(table);
                add(scroller, BorderLayout.CENTER);
            }
            catch(ClassNotFoundException cnfEx)
            {
                System.out.println(
                                "* Unable to load driver! *");
                System.exit(1);
            }
            catch(SQLException sqlEx)
            {
                System.out.println("* SQL error! *");
                System.exit(1);
            }
        }
    }
```

The output from the above program when run with our *Accounts* data is shown in Fig. 7.4.

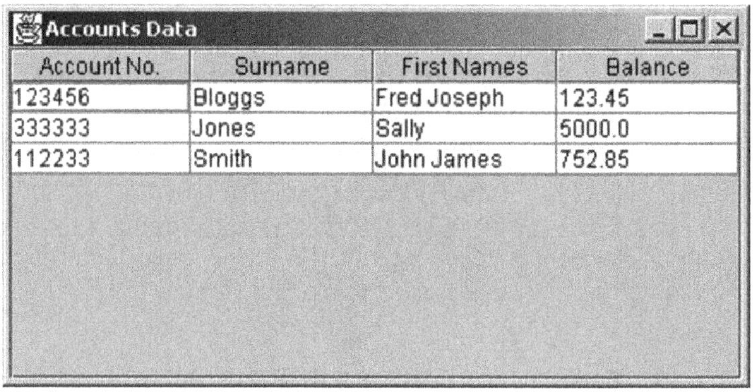

Accounts Data

Account No.	Surname	First Names	Balance
123456	Bloggs	Fred Joseph	123.45
333333	Jones	Sally	5000.0
112233	Smith	John James	752.85

Fig. 7.4 Output from program *JDBCGUI*

7.10 Scrollable *ResultSets*

In all our examples so far, movement through a *ResultSet* object has been confined to the forward direction only, and even that has been restricted to moving by one row at a time. In fact, JDBC 1 did not allow any other kind of movement, since the only method available for moving through a *ResultSet* was *next*. With the emergence of JDBC 2 in Java 2, however, a great deal more flexibility was made available to Java programmers by the introduction of the following *ResultSet* methods:

- `boolean first()`
- `boolean last()`
- `boolean previous()`
- `boolean relative (int <rows>)`
- `boolean absolute(int <rows>)`

As with method *next*, the return value in each case indicates whether or not there is data at the specified position. The purposes of most of these methods are pretty well self-evident from their names, but the last two probably need a little explanation. Method *relative* takes a signed argument and moves forwards/backwards the specified number of rows. For example:

```
results.relative(-3);   //Move back 3 rows.
```

Method *absolute* also takes a signed argument and moves to the specified absolute position, counting either from the start of the *ResultSet* (for a positive argument) or from the end of the *ResultSet* (for a negative argument). For example:

```
results.absolute(3);
//Move to row 3 (from start of ResultSet).
```

Before any of these new methods can be employed, however, it is necessary to create a **scrollable** *ResultSet*. This is achieved by using an overloaded form of the *Connection* method *createStatement* that takes two integer arguments. Here is the signature for this method:

```
Statement createStatement(int <resultSetType>,
                          int <resultSetConcurrency>)
```

There are three possible values that the first argument can take to specify the type of *ResultSet* object that is to be created. These three values are identified by the following static constants in interface *ResultSet*:

- *TYPE_FORWARD_ONLY*
- *TYPE_SCROLL_INSENSITIVE*
- *TYPE_SCROLL_SENSITIVE*

As might be guessed, the first option allows only forward movement through the *ResultSet*. The second and third options allow movement of the *ResultSet*'s cursor both forwards and backwards through the rows. The difference between these two is that *TYPE_SCROLL_SENSITIVE* causes any changes made to the data rows to be reflected dynamically in the *ResultSet* object, whilst *TYPE_SCROLL_INSENSITIVE* does not. [More about this in the next section.]

There are two possible values that the second argument to *createStatement* can take. These are identified by the following static constants in interface *ResultSet*:

- *CONCUR_READ_ONLY*
- *CONCUR_UPDATABLE*

As is probably obvious from their names, the first means that we cannot make changes to the *ResultSet* rows, whilst the second will allow changes to be made (and to be reflected in the database, as will be seen shortly!).

Example

For this first example involving a scrollable *ResultSet*, we shall simply modify the code for the earlier program *JDBCSelect* by inserting lines that will iterate through the *ResultSet* rows starting from the **last** row, displaying the contents of each row (immediately after traversing the *ResultSet* in the forward direction and displaying the contents, as in the original program). For ease of comparison with the original program, the new and changed lines relating to the introduction of a scrollable *ResultSet* will be shown in bold.

In order to avoid code duplication, the lines that display the contents of an individual row from the *ResultSet* have been place inside a method called *showRow* that is called from two places in the code, but these changes do not directly involve the scrollable *ResultSet* and have not been shown in bold.

```
import java.sql.*;

public class JDBCScrollableSelect
{
   private static Connection connection;
   private static Statement statement;
   private static ResultSet results;

   public static void main(String[] args)
   {
      try
      {
         connection = DriverManager.getConnection(
                                  "jdbc:odbc:Finances","","");
      }
```

```
catch(SQLException sqlEx)
{
   System.out.println(
               "* Cannot connect to database! *");
   System.exit(1);
}

try
{
   statement = connection.createStatement(
             ResultSet.TYPE_SCROLL_SENSITIVE,
             ResultSet.CONCUR_READ_ONLY);
   results = statement.executeQuery(
                       "SELECT * FROM Accounts");
}
catch(SQLException sqlEx)
{
   System.out.println(
                     "* Cannot execute query! *");
   sqlEx.printStackTrace();
   System.exit(1);
}

try
{
   while (results.next())
   //Iterate through the rows in the forward
   //direction, displaying the contents of each
   //row (as in the original program)…
      showRow();
}
catch(SQLException sqlEx)
{
   System.out.println(
                "* Error retrieving data! *");
   sqlEx.printStackTrace();
   System.exit(1);
}

try
{
   //Cursor for ResultSet is now positioned
   //just after last row, so we can make use
   //of method previous to access the data…
```

```
         while (results.previous())
         //Iterate through rows in reverse direction,
         //again displaying contents of each row...
            showRow();
      }
      catch(SQLException sqlEx)
      {
         System.out.println(
                        "* Error retrieving data! *");
         sqlEx.printStackTrace();
         System.exit(1);
      }

      try
      {
         connection.close();
      }
      catch(SQLException sqlEx)
      {
         System.out.println(
                        "* Unable to disconnect! *");
         sqlEx.printStackTrace();
      }
   }

   public static void showRow() throws SQLException
   {
      System.out.println();
      System.out.println("Account no. "
                           + results.getInt(1));
      System.out.println("Account holder:  "
                        + results.getString(3)
                        + " " + results.getString(2));
      System.out.printf("Balance: %.2f %n%n",
                              results.getFloat(4));
   }
}
```

The output from this program is shown in Fig. 7.5. For some reason, the initial ordering of rows when using the second version of method *createStatement* differs from that which occurs with the original version of *createStatement* (even though exactly the same query is used and movement through the data rows is in the forward direction in both cases). However, it can clearly be seen that the order of output when *previous* is used is the reverse of that which occurs in this program when *next* is used.

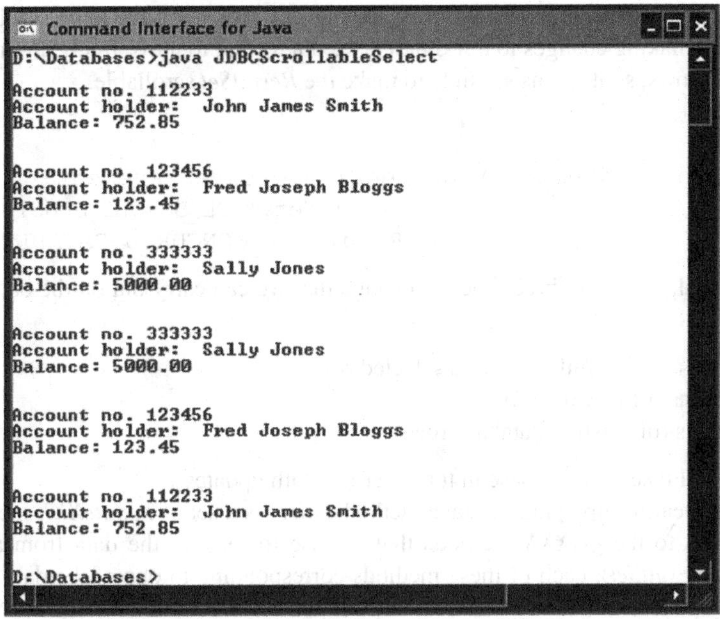

Fig. 7.5 Output from program *JDBCScrollableSelect*

In this example, we had no need to move explicitly past the end of the data rows before we started traversing the rows in reverse order, since the cursor was conveniently positioned beyond the last row at the end of the forward traversal. If this had not been the case, however, we could easily have positioned the cursor beyond the last row by invoking method *afterLast*. For example:

```
results.afterLast();
```

Analogous to this method, there is a method called *beforeFirst* that will position the cursor before the first row of the *ResultSet*. Another method that is occasionally useful is *getRow*, which returns the number of the current row.

7.11 Modifying Databases via Java Methods

Another very useful feature of the JDBC API is the ability to modify *ResultSet* rows directly via Java methods (rather than having to send SQL statements), **and to have those changes reflected in the database itself**! In order to do this, it is necessary to use the second version of *createStatement* again (i.e., the version that takes two integer arguments) and supply *ResultSet.CONCUR_UPDATABLE* as the second argument. The updateable *ResultSet* object does not **have** to be scrollable, but, when making changes to a *ResultSet*, we often want to move freely around the *ResultSet* rows, so it seems sensible to make the *ResultSet* scrollable.

Example

```
Statement statement = connection.createStatement(
                          ResultSet.TYPE_SCROLL_SENSITIVE,
                          ResultSet.CONCUR_UPDATABLE);
```

As usual, there are three types of change that we can carry out on the data in a database:

- updates (of some/all fields of a selected row);
- insertions (of new data rows);
- deletions (of existing database rows).

We shall take each of these in turn, starting with updates…

At the heart of updating via Java methods, there is a set of *updateXXX* methods (analogous to the *getXXX* methods that we use to retrieve the data from a row within a *ResultSet*), each of these methods corresponding to one of the data types that may be held in the database. For example, there are methods *updateString* and *updateInt* to update *String* and *int* data respectively. Each of these methods takes two arguments:

- a string specifying the name of the field to be updated;
- a value of the appropriate type that is to be assigned to the field.

There are three steps involved in the process of updating:

- position the *ResultSet* cursor at the required row;
- call the appropriate *updateXXX* method(s);
- call method *updateRow*.

It is this last method that commits the update(s) to the database and must be called before moving the cursor off the row (or the updates will be discarded).

Example

```
results.absolute(2);//Move to row 2 of ResultSet.
results.updateFloat("balance", 42.55f);
results.updateRow();
```

(Note here that an 'f' must be appended to the `float` literal, in order to prevent the compiler from interpreting the value as a `double`.)

For an insertion, the new row is initially stored within a special buffer called the ''insertion row' and there are three steps involved in the process:

- call method *moveToInsertRow*;
- call the appropriate *updateXXX* method for each field in the row;
- call method *insertRow*.

Example

```
results.moveToInsertRow();
results.updateInt("acctNum", 999999);
results.updateString("surname", "Harrison");
results.updateString("firstNames",
                                    "Christine Dawn");
results.updateFloat("balance", 2500f);
results.insertRow();
```

However, it is **possible** that *getXXX* methods called after insertion will not retrieve values for newly-inserted rows. If this is the case with a particular database, then it will be necessary to close the *ResultSet* and create a new one (using the original query), in order for the new insertions to be recognised.
To delete a row without using SQL, there are just two steps:

- move to the appropriate row;
- call method *deleteRow*.

Example

```
results.absolute(3);    //Move to row 3.
results.deleteRow();
```

Note that JDBC drivers can handle deletions differently. Some remove the row completely from the *ResultSet*, while others use a blank row as a placeholder. With the latter, the original row numbers are not changed.

Now to bring together all the above 'snippets' of code into one program…

Example

We shall use program *JDBCChange* from Sect. 7.5 as the starting point for this example and make the necessary modifications to it. The new lines will be shown in bold below

```
import java.sql.*;

public class JDBC2Mods
{
   private static Connection connection;
   private static Statement statement;
   private static ResultSet results;

   public static void main(String[] args)
   {
      try
```

```
{
   //Step 1…
   connection = DriverManager.getConnection(
                     "jdbc:odbc:Finances","","");
}

//For any of a number of reasons, it may not be
//possible to establish a connection…
catch(SQLException sqlEx)
{
   System.out.println(
                "* Cannot connect to database! *");
   System.exit(1);
}

try
{
   //Step 2…
   statement = connection.createStatement(
                     ResultSet.TYPE_SCROLL_SENSITIVE,
                     ResultSet.CONCUR_UPDATABLE);

   String select = "SELECT * FROM Accounts";

   System.out.println(
                 "\nInitial contents of table:\n");
   //Steps 3 and 4…
   displayTable();

   //Start of step 5…

   //First the update…
   results.absolute(2);
   //(Move to row 2 of ResultSet.)
   results.updateFloat("balance", 42.55f);
   results.updateRow();

   //Now the insertion…
   results.moveToInsertRow();
   results.updateInt("acctNum", 999999);
   results.updateString("surname", "Harrison");
   results.updateString("firstNames",
                                "Christine Dawn");
   results.updateFloat("balance", 2500f);
   results.insertRow();
```

```
         //Finally, the deletion...
         results.absolute(3);   //Move to row 3.
         results.deleteRow();

         System.out.println(
                      "\nNew contents of table:\n");
         displayTable();
         //End of step 5.

         //Step 6...
         connection.close();
      }
      catch(SQLException sqlEx)
      {
         System.out.println(
                      "* SQL or connection error! *");
         sqlEx.printStackTrace();
         System.exit(1);
      }
   }

   public static void displayTable() throws SQLException
   {
      String select = "SELECT * FROM Accounts";

      results = statement.executeQuery(select);

      System.out.println();

      while (results.next())
      {
         System.out.println("Account no. "
                          + results.getInt(1));

         System.out.println("Account holder:  "
                          + results.getString(3)
                          + " "
                          + results.getString(2));
         System.out.printf("Balance: %.2f %n%n",
                             results.getFloat(4));
      }
   }
}
```

The output from this program is shown in Fig. 7.6.

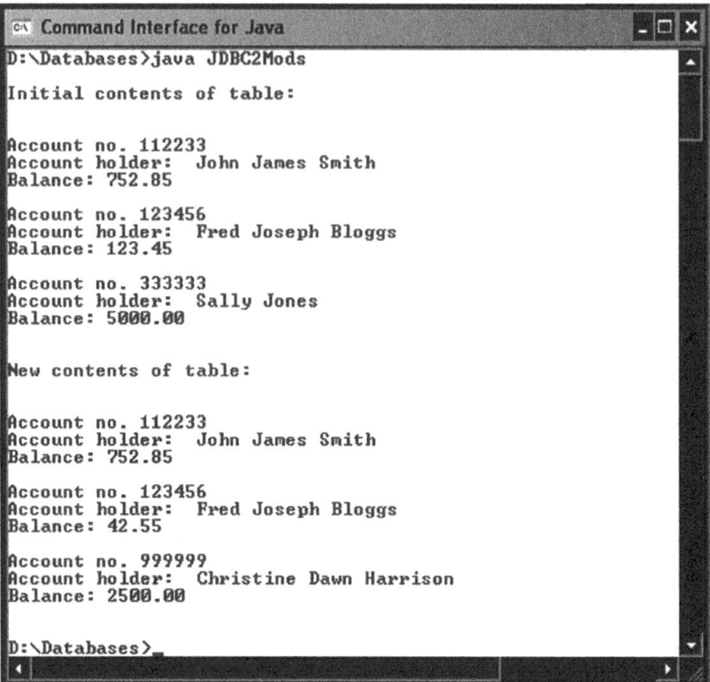

Fig. 7.6 Output from the **modified** *JDBC2Mods* program

7.12 Using the *DataSource* Interface

7.12.1 Overview and Support Software

As demonstrated in earlier sections of this chapter, the original method of accessing remote databases via JDBC involves making use of the *DriverManager* class. This is still the method used by many Java database programmers, but "the preferred method" (as it is described on the Oracle site) is to make use of the *DataSource* interface. This interface is contained in package *javax.sql* and has been part of the Standard Edition of Java since J2SE 1.4. The primary advantages of this method are twofold, as detailed below.

1. The password and connection string are handled by a Web application server, rather than being hard-coded into the application program. As a consequence, security is greatly enhanced.
2. At the heart of the method is a concept called **connection pooling** (as described briefly in Sect. 7.2). This is a much more efficient method of handling multiple database connections, and so is more applicable to real-world, commercial databases.

As indicated by point 1 above, we need the services of a Java-aware Web application server in order to make use of the *DataSource* interface. The server used here (and in later chapters) is **Tomcat**, a very popular open source server originally developed by the Apache Software Foundation's Jakarta project and controlled directly by Apache since the Jakarta project was retired on 21st December 2011. Apache Tomcat is also the servlet container that is used in the official Reference Implementation for the Java Servlet and JavaServer Pages technologies (as covered in the next two chapters).

The steps required to obtain a free download of the latest version of Tomcat, to install this server and to start and stop it are given in Sect. 8.2 of the next chapter. In order to understand fully the material in the current section, the reader must have some familiarity with servlets. If the reader does not have such familiarity, then he/she is advised to read the following chapter before continuing with the present section.

Tomcat includes a Database Connection Pool (DBCP) connection broker. DBCP is part of the Apache *commons* sub-project (previously the Jakarta *commons* sub-project). Apache *commons* can be found at http://commons.apache.org/. In order to use DBCP from within Tomcat, the following two files must be downloaded into folder *<CATALINA_HOME>\lib* (previously *<CATALINA_HOME>\common\lib*, but folder *commons* no longer exists):

- commons-dbcp-(1.4).jar
- commons-dbcp-(1.4)-sources.jar.

The brackets above are not any part of the file names, of course, but indicate version numbers that may be different in future. Remember that *CATALINA_HOME* is the Tomcat root directory. The steps required to download these two files are given below.

1. Go to http://commons.apache.org/.
2. In the left-hand frame, click on the link *Releases*, under the heading 'Releases'.
3. Click on <u>DBCP</u> link in the 'Downloads' list.
4. Under the 'Binaries' heading for the latest version of the DBCP (1.4, at the time of writing), click on:

   commons-dbcp-<Version no.>–bin.zip
   (E.g., commons-dbcp-1.4-bin.zip)

5. Using *WinZip* (or some other suitable utility), extract your zip file to *<CATALINA_HOME>\lib*. The documentation file *commons-dbcp-(1.4)-javadoc.jar* will also be extracted, along with the two main files.

Since DBCP uses JNDI (Java Naming and Directory Interface), it is necessary to configure the JNDI data source before it can be used. (If you are unfamiliar with JNDI, then don't be concerned. You won't really need to know anything about it in order to follow the material in this section.) Three steps are required in order to configure the JNDI data source. Here are the steps, with details provided in the sub-sections that follow…

1. Define a JNDI resource reference in the Web deployment descriptor, which is a file called *web.xml*. Every Web application requires the existence of such a file, which must be in *<CATALINA_HOME>\webapps\<WebAppName>\WEB-INF*.
2. Map the JNDI resource reference onto a real resource (a database) in the context of the application. This is done by creating a folder called *META-INF*, alongside *WEB-INF*, and placing a file called *context.xml* inside this folder. This file will contain the necessary tags for the mapping. [Normally, *META-INF* would be used only within a WAR (Web Archive) file, but it will work fine without such and will allow us to keep things as simple as possible.]
3. In the application code, look up the JNDI data source reference to obtain a pooled database connection. This connection may then be used in the same way that such connections were used after having been set up via the *DriverManager* class in the earlier sections of this chapter.

Details of the three steps listed above are given in the next few sub-sections. For purposes of illustration, we shall assume the existence of a MySQL database called *Finances* that holds a single table called *Accounts*. The structure of this simple table will be the same as that specified in Sect. 7.4 for the MS Access table that was used for illustration in earlier sections of this chapter, the only slight variation being in the names of the MySQL types. The structure of this is shown below.

Field name	MySQL type	Java type
acctNum	INTEGER	int
surname	VARCHAR(15)	String
firstNames	VARCHAR(15)	String
balance	FLOAT	float

7.12.2 Defining a JNDI Resource Reference

This is achieved by creating a *<resource-ref>* tag in *web.xml*. This tag must appear **after** the *<servlet-mapping>* tag(s) and has three named elements:

- *<res-ref-name>*, which specifies a name for the connection, this name commencing with *jdbc/*;
- *<res-type>*, which identifies the reference as being of type *javax.sql.DataSource* (i.e., a JDBC data source);
- *<res-auth>*, which specifies that resource authentication will be applied by the Web Container (Tomcat).

Example

```
<resource-ref>
   <res-ref-name>jdbc/Finances</res-ref-name>
   <res-type>javax.sql.DataSource</res-type>
   <res-auth>Container</res-auth>
</resource-ref>
```

7.12.3 Mapping the Resource Reference onto a Real Resource

First create folder *META-INF* alongside *WEB-INF* and then create folder *context.xml* inside *META-INF.* Within *context.xml*, create a <*Context*> tag and place within it a <*Resource*> tag. The <*Resource*> tag will have eight attributes:

- *name* (of the specific resource);
- *type* (which will be *javax.sql.DataSource*);
- *auth* (again specifying the Tomcat container, as in the *web.xml* file);
- *username*;
- *password*;
- *driverClassName* (the MySQL driver, in this case);
- *factory* (a fully qualified reference to the *DataSourceFactory* class);
- *url* (showing the required syntax for referencing the specific database on the specific host).

Of course, the reader will need to determine the appropriate values for the host (including port number) and database reference for the required database at his/her own site and use these in the *url* attribute.

Example

```
<Context path="/myapps" docBase="myapps" debug="0"
                                       reloadable="true">

     <Resource
          name="jdbc/Finances"
          type="javax.sql.DataSource"
          auth="Container"
          username="cmsjg3" password="opensesame"
          driverClassName="com.mysql.jdbc.Driver"
          url=
            "jdbc:mysql://ivy.shu.ac.uk:3306/"
                                  +"cmsjg3_Finances"

     />
</Context>
```

*** Note that the JAR file holding the database driver must be in <JAVA_ *HOME*>*\jre\lib\ext.*

7.12.4 Obtaining the Data Source Connection

In order to use JNDI, it is necessary to import *javax.naming*. The name used when referring to the data source within an application program must be identical to that used in the *<res-ref-name>* tag within the Web application's deployment descriptor (the *web.xml* file). In order to resolve the resource associated with this name, it is necessary to obtain the JNDI context for the Web application. Getting the context and resolving the resource requires the three steps shown below.

1. Get a reference to the 'initial context', which is the starting context for performing naming operations. This is done simply by creating an *InitialContext* object. For example:

   ```
   Context initialContext = new InitialContext();
   ```

2. Get a reference to the Java environment variables (the 'Java context') by calling method *lookup* on the above *InitialContext* object, supplying the method with the string "java:comp/env". This method will return an Object reference that must be typecast into a Context reference. For example:

   ```
   Context context =
       (Context)initialContext.lookup("java:comp/env");
   ```

3. Call method *lookup* on the Java *Context* object returned above, supplying it with the name of the required database, using the name that was supplied in the *<res-ref-name>* tag within the deployment descriptor. This will need to be typecast into a *DataSource* reference. For example:

   ```
   dataSource =
       (DataSource)context.lookup("jdbc/Finances");
   ```

Control code for the particular application will be provided by at least one servlet. The code above **can** be placed inside the servlet's *init* method, as shown in the example below.

Example

```
private DataSource dataSource;

public void init(ServletConfig config)
                               throws ServletException
{
     super.init(config);
                    //Carry out generic initialisation
     try
     {
          Context initialContext = new InitialContext();
          Context context =
               (Context)initialContext.lookup(
```

```
                                        "java:comp/env");
            dataSource =
              (DataSource)context.lookup("jdbc/Finances");
        }
        catch (NamingException namEx)
        {
            ......................
        }
}
```

This avoids incurring the overhead of JNDI operations being generated for every HTTP request. In the *doGet/doPost* method, a database connection can then be established via method *getConnection*. For example:

```
connection = dataSource.getConnection();
```

(Assuming here, of course, that *connection* is a pre-declared *Connection* reference.)

SQL statements can then be executed and results processed exactly as they would have been if the *DriverManager* class had been used to establish the connection.

However, this will mean that HTML presentation code and database access code are intermingled in the servlet, which is not a good idea from a design point of view. It is better to make use of a separate *Data Access Object (DAO)* to establish the connection. The creation and use of such objects will be described in the next sub-section.

7.12.5 Data Access Objects

These encapsulate access to databases so that the data manipulation code can be separated from the business logic and data presentation code. A DAO is written as a JavaBean. Though JavaBeans will not be covered formally until a later chapter, all that need be said right now is that a JavaBean is an ordinary Java class file with the following characteristics:

- it is unlikely to have a *main* method;
- it must be in a named package.

The DAO includes a constructor that contains the context-setting and connection code, along with any other methods required to access and/or manipulate the data source. Since servlets associated with a particular Web application are contained within *<CATALINA_HOME>\webapps\<WebAppName>\WEB-INF\classes* and the DAO must be in a named package easily accessible to the servlet that will use it, the DAO will be stored within a sub-folder of *classes* that has the same name as its package.

Example

This example establishes a connection to our example MySQL database *Finances* and provides an access method called *getAcctDetails* that returns all the data in the *Accounts* table, using an *ArrayList* of *Object*s to hold the heterogeneous data set.

```
package myDAOs;

import java.sql.*;
import javax.naming.*;
import javax.sql.*;
import java.util.*;

public class AccountsDAO implements java.io.Serializable
{
   private Connection connection;

   public AccountsDAO()
                 throws SQLException, NamingException
   {
        Context initialContext = new InitialContext();

        Context context =
       (Context)initialContext.lookup("java:comp/env");
        DataSource dataSource =
           (DataSource)context.lookup("jdbc/Finances");

        connection = dataSource.getConnection();
   }

   public ArrayList<Object> getAcctDetails()
                                      throws SQLException
   {
        ArrayList<Object> acctDetails = null;
        Statement statement = null;
        ResultSet results = null;

        statement = connection.createStatement();
        results = statement.executeQuery(
                             "SELECT * FROM Accounts");

        acctDetails = new ArrayList <Object>();
        while (results.next())
        {
             acctDetails.add(results.getInt(1));
             acctDetails.add(results.getString(3) + " "
                                 + results.getString(2));
             acctDetails.add(results.getFloat(4));
        }
```

```
        return acctDetails;
    }

    public void close() throws SQLException
    {
    //Any error on disconnecting is handled by servlet.
        connection.close();
    }
}
```

A simple example servlet that makes use of an instance of the above DAO class is shown below.

Example

This servlet calls method *getAcctDetails* on the DAO object and displays the results in an HTML table.

```
import myDAOs.*;
import java.io.*;
import java.util.*;
import javax.servlet.*;
import javax.servlet.http.*;
import javax.servlet.annotation.WebServlet;
import java.sql.*;
import javax.sql.*; //*** NOTE! ***
import javax.naming.*;

@WebServlet("/DataSourceTestServlet")
public class DAOTestServlet extends HttpServlet
{
    public void doGet(HttpServletRequest request,
                       HttpServletResponse response)
                   throws ServletException, IOException
    {
        try
        {
            processRequest(request, response);
        }
        catch (SQLException sqlEx)
        {
            System.out.println("Error: " + sqlEx);
            sqlEx.printStackTrace();
        }
    }

    public void doPost(HttpServletRequest request,
                       HttpServletResponse response)
                   throws ServletException, IOException
```

```
{
        try
        {
           processRequest(request, response);
        }
        catch (SQLException sqlEx)
        {
             System.out.println("Error: " + sqlEx);
             sqlEx.printStackTrace();
        }
}

public void processRequest(
                    HttpServletRequest request,
                    HttpServletResponse response)
  throws ServletException, IOException, SQLException
{
    response.setContentType("text/html");
    PrintWriter out = response.getWriter();

    out.println("<HTML>");
    out.println("<HEAD>");
    out.println("<TITLE>DAO Test</TITLE>");
    out.println("</HEAD>");
    out.println("<BODY><CENTER><BR><BR><BR>");
    out.println("<h1>Account Details</h1>");
    out.println("<TABLE BGCOLOR='aqua' BORDER=1>");
    out.println("<TR>");
    out.println(
           "<TH BGCOLOR='orange'>Acct.No.</TH>");
    out.println(
           "<TH BGCOLOR='orange'>Acct.Name</TH>");
    out.println(
           "<TH BGCOLOR='orange'>Balance</TH>");
    out.println("</TR>");

      AccountsDAO dao = null;
      try
      {
           dao = new AccountsDAO();
      }
      catch (NamingException namEx)
      {
           System.out.println("Error: " + namEx);
           namEx.printStackTrace();
           System.exit(1);
      }
```

```
            ArrayList<Object> accounts=dao.getAcctDetails();
            int acctNum;
            String acctName;
            float balance;
            String formattedBalance;
            final int NUM_FIELDS = 3;

            for (int i=0; i<accounts.size()/NUM_FIELDS; i++)
            {
                acctNum =
                    (Integer)accounts.get(i*NUM_FIELDS);
                acctName =
                   (String)accounts.get(i*NUM_FIELDS+1);
                balance =
                  (Float)accounts.get(i*NUM_FIELDS + 2);
                out.println("<TR>");
                out.println("<TD>" + acctNum + "</TD>");
                out.println("<TD>" + acctName + "</TD>");
                formattedBalance =
                        String.format("%.2f", balance);
                out.println("<TD>"+formattedBalance+"</TD>");

                out.println("</TR>");
            }
            out.println("</TABLE>");
            out.println("</CENTER>");

            out.println("</BODY>");
            out.println("</HTML>");

            out.close();

            dao.close();
    }
}
```

In order to access the above servlet, Tomcat must be started, either by double-clicking on file *startup.bat* (in *<CATALINA_HOME>\bin*) or by entering the following command into an MS DOS command window (assuming that *startup.bat* is on the *PATH*):

```
startup
```

By default, Tomcat runs on the local machine (identified by the name *localhost*) on port 8080. The URL that must be entered into your browser to execute the above servlet is http://localhost:8080/<WebAppName>/DAOTestServlet (replacing *<WebAppName>* with the name of the containing Web application, of course). This will generate output of the form shown in Fig. 7.7.

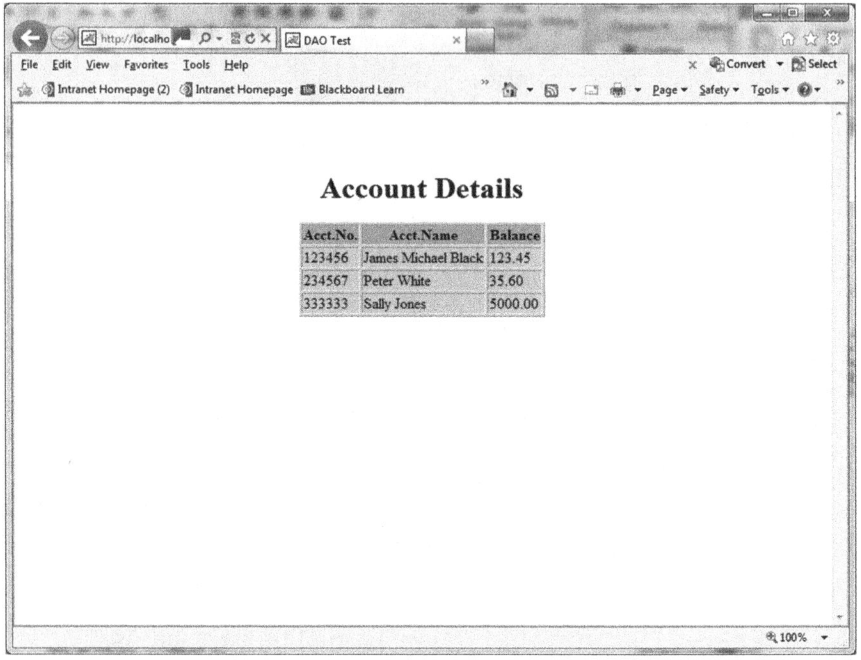

Fig. 7.7 Example output from the *DAOTestServlet* program

Exercises

When attempting the exercises below, you may use whichever type of database is convenient for you. If you are going to use an MS Access database, it will be appropriate to implement your solutions only via the *DriverManager* approach. If using any other type of database, however, it will probably be instructive to attempt to produce solutions both via the *DriverManager* approach and via the *DataSource* approach. (When implementing exercises 7.5 and 7.6 via the latter approach, of course, you should ignore the *JTable* and GUI references.)

7.1 (i) Ensure that either your database system has an accessible JDBC driver (using the URL supplied in Sect. 7.1, if necessary) or it has an ODBC driver (so that you can use the JDBC-ODBC bridge driver).

(ii) Create a database called *Sales* with a single table called *Stock*. Give it the structure shown below and enter a few rows of data for use in the later exercises. Make sure that there is at least one item for which the current level is at or below the reorder level.

Field name	Type
stockCode	Integer
description	Text/String
unitPrice	Real/Float/Currency
currentLevel	Integer
reorderLevel	Integer

(iii) If you need to use the JDBC-ODBC bridge driver, then follow the procedure outlined in Sect. 7.3 to create an ODBC DSN for your database.

7.2 (i) Write a program to display the stock code, unit price and current level for all items in table *Stock*.

(ii) Modify the above code to display description, current level and reorder level for all items whose current level is at or below reorder level.

7.3 Take a backup of your database. Then create a program (using SQL strings) that will insert one record, increase by 10 % the unit price of each item of stock and delete one record with specified stock code. The program should display stock codes and prices of all items both before and after the changes.

7.4 Restore your database to its original state by deleting it and then reinstating it with your backup copy. Modify the preceding program so that, instead of using SQL strings, it uses Java methods (as described in Sect. 7.10) to effect the same changes. If you are using an MS Access database, you should find that the insertion and updates don't work (possibly with all prices being changed to zero!), but the deletion should work fine.

7.5 Using a *ResultSetMetaData* object, write a program that displays the full contents of the *Stock* table in a *JTable*. (Field names should be retrieved via the *ResultSetMetaData* object.)

7.6 Write a simple GUI-driven program that will allow the user to retrieve the current stock level of any item whose stock code he/she enters (repeatedly, for as many items as the user wishes).

Chapter 8
Servlets

Learning Objectives

After reading this chapter, you should:

- understand what Java servlets are and how they are used;
- appreciate the power of Java servlets;
- know what software and installation steps are required before servlets can be created and tested;
- know how to create your own servlets for processing simple form data and returning results in a Web page;
- know how to create and use session variables with servlets;
- know how to redirect a user to any of several possible Web pages and/or servlets;
- know how to make use of cookies with servlets;
- know how to make use of servlets (and JDBC) to access a remote database.

HTML (HyperText Markup Language) is the tagging language used to create Web pages. In order to appreciate fully the material presented in this chapter, it will be necessary to have at least a rudimentary knowledge of HTML. If you do not have such knowledge, you are advised to consult the early chapters of one of the widely-available HTML texts before reading any further.

Through the introduction of HTML and its distribution system, the World Wide Web, use of the Internet has mushroomed at a phenomenal rate. However, HTML alone may be used to create ***static*** Web pages only—pages whose content is determined at the time of writing and which never changes. Though this is perfectly adequate for some applications, an increasing number of others have a requirement

J. Graba, *An Introduction to Network Programming with Java: Java 7 Compatible*,
DOI 10.1007/978-1-4471-5254-5_8, © Springer-Verlag London 2013

for ***dynamic*** web pages—pages whose content changes according to the particular user or in response to changing data. Some common examples are listed below.

- Results of a real-time, online survey.
- Results of a search operation.
- Contents of an electronic shopping cart.

One powerful way of satisfying this need is to use Java **servlets**.

8.1 Servlet Basics

A servlet is a program written in Java that runs on a Web server. It is executed in response to a client's (i.e., a browser's) HTTP request and creates a document (usually an HTML document) to be returned to the client by the server. It extends the functionality of the server, without the performance limitations associated with CGI programs. All the major Web servers now have support for servlets.

A servlet is Java code that is executed on the server, while an applet is Java code that is executed on the client. As such, a servlet may be considered to be the server-side equivalent of an applet. However, Java's servlet API is not part of Java SE (Standard Edition), though it **is** included in Java EE (Enterprise Edition). This means that non-Enterprise users must download an implementation of the Java servlet API.

8.2 Setting Up the Servlet API

The official Reference Implementation of the Java Servlet API (as mentioned in Sect. 7.12) is **Tomcat**, a very popular open source server produced by the Apache Software Foundation. The latest stable version of Tomcat at the time of writing is 7.0.34 and this is the version to which reference is made below, simply for the convenience of having some version number to use. This version will undoubtedly be different by the time the current text is published, but the required steps are likely to remain much the same, with the only notable changes being in the number of the version and the names of the associated installation folders. Obviously, the user will normally want to select the latest non-beta version.

1. Go to http://tomcat.apache.org/whichversion.html.
2. Click on the Tomcat 7.0 link in the *Download* column on the left of the screen.
3. Click on the 7.0.34 link.
4. Click on the zip link for your platform and architecture after the 'Core' bullet under *Binary Distributions*. If you have selected 64-bit Windows, this will cause file *apache-tomcat-7.0.34-windows-x64.zip* (size 8.53 MB) to be downloaded.
5. Click on *Save*, navigate to a suitable location (your Java SE folder?) and then click on *Save* again.

6. Click on *Open Folder*.
7. Use *WinZip* (or some other suitable utility program, such as *7-zip*) to extract the downloaded files, saving them in the current location.
8. Click on *OK*. This will create a sub-folder structure headed by a folder called *apache-tomcat-7.0.34-windows-x64*. This should probably be renamed to something shorter, such as *Tomcat7*.
9. Use the Control Panel to set up the three environment variables listed below. (If you are unsure of how to create environment variables, please refer to the details supplied following the steps below.)

   (i) *JAVA_HOME* (**Must** be in upper case!)
   This should hold the path to your Java SE folder
   E.g., C:\JavaSE7

   (ii) *CATALINA_HOME* (**Must** be in upper case!)
   This should hold the path to your Tomcat folder.
   E.g., C:\JavaSE7\Tomcat7

   (iii) *JRE_HOME* (**Must** be in upper case!)
   This should hold the path to your JRE folder.
   E.g., C:\JavaSE7

10. Add file *servlet-api.jar* to your *CLASSPATH* variable (again referring to the instructions following these steps if necessary). This file will be in <*CATALINA_HOME* >*lib*.
    E.g., C:\JavaSE7\Tomcat7\lib\servlet-api.jar.
11. Within your Tomcat folder is a folder called *bin*. Add the path to this folder to your *PATH* variable. (Once again, refer to the instructions following these steps if you are unsure of how to change this environment variable.) This step gives easy access to the *startup.bat* and *shutdown.bat* files mentioned below. Alternatively, of course, you can move into the above folder before using the *startup* and *shutdown* commands.
12. Click on *OK* three times, as you come out of the Control Panel.
13. Open up a command window and enter the following command:

    ```
    startup
    ```

    Four lines of output should appear in the window and a second command window should open and begin to fill up with output. When a line commencing *INFO: Server startup* appears in this second window, the Tomcat server is running.
14. To see information about Tomcat and to access example servlets and JSPs, open up a browser window and enter:

    ```
    http://localhost:8080
    ```

    This identifies port 8080 on the current machine as being the port upon which Tomcat will run. If the Tomcat Web page appears, the installation has been successful.

15. To stop Tomcat, enter the following command into the (first) command window:

    ```
    shutdown
    ```

    (This assumes, of course, that your *PATH* variable has been modified as described four steps earlier.)

For Windows 7 users, the *PATH* or *CLASSPATH* environment variable may be modified or a new environment variable created by following the steps given below. (The *CLASSPATH* environment variable may itself not exist before this, in which case it should be treated as a new environment.)

1. Select *Start-> Control Panel* from the bottom left corner of the desktop.
2. Click on the *System and Security* sub-heading.
3. Click on the *System* sub-heading.
4. Click on the *Advanced system settings* link in the left-hand pane.
5. Click on the *Environment Variables…* button in the bottom right corner.
6. **Either** select *Path* or *CLASSPATH* from *System Variables* and then click on *Edit* **or** click on *New* to create a new environment variable.
7. If adding a new path to *Path* or *CLASSPATH*, then either **prepend** the new path and a trailing semi-colon (<newPath>;<existingPath>) or **append** it with a leading semi-colon (<existingPath>;<newPath>). If creating a new environment variable, simply enter the name of the new variable and its associated path.
8. Click on *OK* and then again on *OK*.

For users of earlier versions of the Windows operating system, the steps will be somewhat similar to those given above, the only differences likely to be a reference to *Start->**Settings**->Control Panel* in the first step and **double-**clicking on a *System* icon in step 2.

For the remainder of this chapter, it is Tomcat that will be used for the execution of servlets.

8.3 Creating a Web Application

To set up your own servlets (and/or JSPs, as explained in the next chapter), you need to create a Web application under Tomcat (or make use of an existing one). To create a new Web application, you need to create the required folder structure immediately below the existing standard folder *webapps* in the Tomcat folder structure. The main part of the folder structure for a Web application called *MyWebApp* is:

MyWebApp->WEB-INF->classes

[N.B. Upper-case for '*WEB-INF' and lower-case for 'classes'* are **mandatory**.]

The rules governing what makes up a Web application and what goes where in such an application are listed below. For convenience, the name of the Web application here and through the rest of the chapter will be shown as *MyWebApp*, but this can be any name of your own choosing.

1. Place HTML files and JSPs (covered in the next chapter) within *MyWebApp*.
2. Place servlets within *MyWebApp\WEB-INF*. If packages are used, there must be a folder structure within *classes* to reflect this.
3. Create a file called *web.xml* within *WEB-INF*. This file is known as the **deployment descriptor** and specifies details of the Web application (as described below). In particular, it must contain *<servlet>* and *<servlet-mapping>* tags for each servlet.

The opening lines of the deployment descriptor are always the same and may simply be copied from one Web application to the next. In fact, it is highly advisable to copy these lines (i.e., via a wordprocessor, not by transcribing them), since it is very easy to make a mistake, particularly with the string identifying the XML schema location. The naive user may even place a line break in the middle of this.

The example below shows a deployment descriptor for a Web application containing a single servlet called *FirstServlet*. The servlet must have *<servlet>* and *<servlet-mapping>* tags that identify the associated Java *.class* file and the servlet's URL location (relative to the web application) respectively. These *<servlet>* and *<servlet-mapping>* tags will have exactly the same structure for any other servlet.

Example

```
<?xml version="1.0" encoding="ISO-8859-1"?>

   <web-app xmlns="http://java.sun.com/xml/ns/javaee"
     xmlns:xsi="http://www.w3.org/2001/XMLSchema-instance"
      xsi:schemaLocation="http://java.sun.com/xml/ns/javaee
   http://java.sun.com/xml/ns/javaee/web-app_3_0.xsd"
    version="3.0">

     <servlet>
       <servlet-name>FirstServlet</servlet-name>
       <servlet-class>FirstServlet</servlet-class>
     </servlet>

     <servlet-mapping>
         <servlet-name>FirstServlet</servlet-name>
         <url-pattern>/FirstServlet</url-pattern>
     </servlet-mapping>
 </web-app>
```

Note the use of a '/' in the *<url-pattern>* tag! This is easily omitted.

If any changes are made to servlet tags after Tomcat has started, it will be necessary to stop Tomcat (via `shutdown`) and re-start it (via `startup`). This is also necessary after changing any servlet.

8.4 The Servlet URL and the Invoking Web Page

Before we consider the structure of a servlet, recall that a servlet will be executed on a Web server only in response to a request from a user's browser. Though the servlet may be invoked directly by entering its URL into the browser (an example of which is shown at the end of the previous chapter), it is much more common for a servlet to be called from a preceding HTML page. This is usually achieved by the use of an HTML form, with the form's *METHOD* attribute specifying either *'GET'* or *'POST'* and its *ACTION* attribute specifying the address of the servlet. As noted in the previous section, each servlet must be held in folder *<CATALINA_HOME>\webapps\<WebAppName>\WEB-INF\classes*. The URL for such a servlet has the following format:

http://localhost:8080/<WebAppName>/<ServletName>

For example:

http://localhost:8080/MyWebApp/FirstServlet

Note the use of *localhost* above to refer to the current machine and *8080* to indicate that Tomcat uses port 8080. Usually, of course, client and server programs will be on separate machines, but this gives us a convenient test bed for our programs. The servlet above may then be invoked via the *ACTION* attribute of a *FORM* tag in a preceding HTML page as follows:

```
<FORM METHOD=GET ACTION="FirstServlet">
```

Note that the URL for the servlet is relative to the Web application that contains both the servlet and the HTML page.

To keep things as simple as possible for the time being, we shall start off with a Web page that calls up a servlet without actually sending it any data. The code for this simple Web page is shown below.

<u>Example</u>

```
<HTML>
   <HEAD>
      <TITLE>A First Servlet</TITLE>
      <STYLE>
            body{text-align:center;}
      </STYLE>
   </HEAD>

   <BODY>
      <BR><BR><BR>
      <FORM METHOD=GET ACTION="FirstServlet">
         <INPUT TYPE="Submit" VALUE = "Click me!">
      </FORM>
   </BODY>
</HTML>
```

Before we look at the output from this Web page, we need to consider just what our servlet will look like…

8.5 Servlet Structure

Servlets must import the following two packages:

- *javax.servlet*
- *javax.servlet.http*

As of Tomcat 7, it is also necessary to import the following annotation type:

- *javax.servlet.annotation.WebServlet*

In addition, since servlet output uses a *PrintWriter* stream, package java.io is required. Servlets that use the HTTP protocol (which means *all* servlets, at the present time) must extend class *HttpServlet* from package *java.servlet.http*. The two most common HTTP requests (as specified in the HTML pages that make use of servlets) are *GET* and *POST*. At the servlet end, method *service* will despatch either method *doGet* or method *doPost* in response to these requests. The programmer should override (at least) one of these two methods.

You should use the *POST* method for multiple data items and/or items that need to be transmitted securely. If you are transmitting just single items that have no security implications, then use *GET*. All three methods (*doGet*, *doPost* and *service*) have a *void* return type and take the following two arguments:

- an *HttpServletRequest* object;
- an *HttpServletResponse* object.

The former encapsulates the HTTP request from the browser and has several methods, but none will be required by our first servlet. The second argument holds the servlet's response to the client's request. There are just two methods of this *HttpServletResponse* object that are of interest to us at present and these are shown below.

- `void setContentType(String <type>)`
  This specifies the data type of the response. Normally, this will be "*text/HTML*".

- `PrintWriter getWriter()`
  Returns the output stream object to which the servlet can write character data to the client (using method *println*).

There are four basic steps in a servlet…

1. Execute the *setContentType* method with an argument of "*text/HTML*".
2. Execute the *getWriter* method to generate a *PrintWriter* object.
3. Retrieve any parameter(s) from the initial Web page.
   (Not required in our first servlet.)
4. Use the *println* method of the above *PrintWriter* object to create elements of the Web page to be 'served up' by our Web server.

The above steps are normally carried out by *doGet* or *doPost*. Note that these methods may generate *IOExceptions* and *ServletExceptions*, which are checked exceptions (and so must be either thrown or handled locally). Note also that step 4 involves a lot of tedious outputting of the required HTML tags.

Finally, as of Tomcat 7, a *WebServlet* annotation tag is required before the opening line of the servlet class. This tag indicates the name of the servlet and the path to it (relative to the *classes* folder) and has the following format:

@WebServlet("/<Path>/<ServletName>")

<u>Example</u>

This first servlet simply displays the message 'A Simple Servlet'.

[In passing, note that CSS scripts **will not work with servlets**, and so the conventional HTML tag *<CENTER>* (not supported in HTML 5) has had to be used below! The same comment applies to the *<FONT>* tag in later examples.]

```
import java.io.*;
import javax.servlet.*;
import javax.servlet.http.*;
import javax.servlet.annotation.WebServlet;

@WebServlet("/FirstServlet")
public class FirstServlet extends HttpServlet
{
   public void doGet(HttpServletRequest request,
                     HttpServletResponse response)
                throws IOException,ServletException
   {
      response.setContentType("text/HTML");

      PrintWriter out = response.getWriter();
      out.println("<HTML>");
      out.println("<HEAD>");
      out.println("<TITLE>Simple Servlet</TITLE>");
      out.println("</HEAD>");
      out.println("<BODY>");
      out.println("<BR><BR><BR>");
      out.println(
         "<CENTER><H1>A Simple Servlet</H1></CENTER>");
      out.println("</BODY>");
      out.println("</HTML>");
      out.flush();
   }
}
```

Note the use of method *flush* of the *PrintWriter* object to send data out of the object's buffer.

This servlet should now be compiled in the same way as any other Java program, either by using a development environment or by opening a command window and executing the Java compiler as follows:

```
javac FirstServlet.java
```

8.6 Testing a Servlet

In order to test our Web page and associated servlet, we first need to set Tomcat running. This may be done either by double-clicking on file *startup.bat* (in *<CATALINA_HOME>\bin*) or by entering the following command into an MS DOS command window (assuming that *startup.bat* is on the *PATH*):

```
startup
```

Four lines of output should appear in the current command window and a second command window will begin to fill up with output. When the line commencing *INFO: Server startup* appears in the second window, Tomcat is running.

Assuming that our initial Web page has been given the name *FirstServlet.html*, we can now open up our browser and enter the following address:

```
http://localhost:8080/FirstServlet.html
```

Figure 8.1 shows what this initial Web page looks like under the Firefox browser. Upon clicking on the page's button, the servlet is executed and the output shown in Fig. 8.2 is produced.

8.7 Passing Data

The previous example was very artificial, since no data was passed by the initial form and so there was no unpredictability about the contents of the page generated by the servlet. We might just as well have had two static Web pages, with a hyperlink connecting one to the other. Let's modify the initial form a little now, in order to make the example rather more realistic…

```
<FORM METHOD=GET ACTION="PersonalServlet">
   Enter your first name:
   <INPUT TYPE="Text" NAME="FirstName" VALUE="">
   <BR><BR>
   <INPUT TYPE="Submit" VALUE="Submit">
</FORM>
```

Now our form will accept the user's first name and, once the 'Submit' button is clicked, will pass the value entered to the servlet. The servlet may then make use of this value when constructing the page to be returned by the Web server.

It is now appropriate to consider the methods of *HttpServletRequest* that are responsible for handling values/parameters received by servlets. There are three such methods, as listed below.

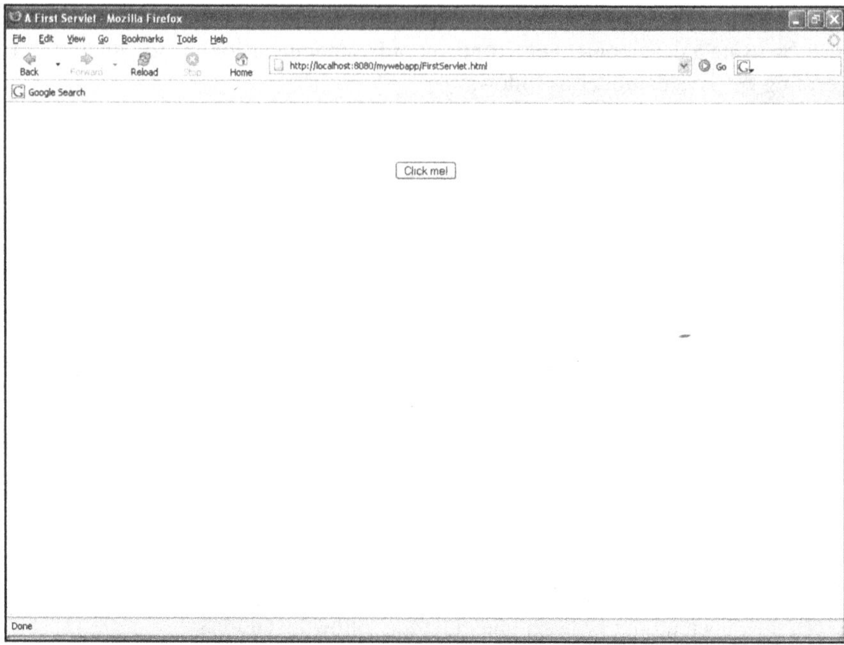

Fig. 8.1 Button to connect to servlet *FirstServlet*

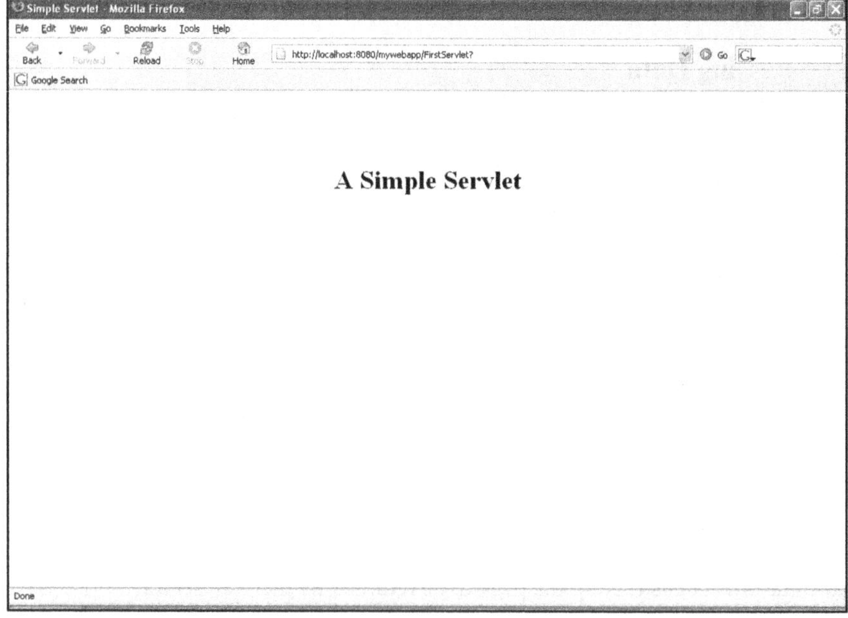

Fig. 8.2 Output from *FirstServlet* under Firefox 1.5

• *String getParameter(String <name>)*
Returns the value of a single parameter sent with GET or POST.
• *Enumeration getParameterNames()*
Returns the names of all parameters sent with POST.
• *String[] getParameterValues(String <name>)*
Returns the values for a parameter that may have more than one value.

Only the first of these methods is needed for a single parameter sent via *GET*, which is all we require for our current example. The code below shows our first servlet modified so that it adds the name entered by the user to the greeting that is displayed on the returned page. The code shown in bold type indicates the very few changes made to the original program.

Example

```
import java.io.*;
import javax.servlet.*;
import javax.servlet.http.*;
import javax.servlet.annotation.WebServlet;

@WebServlet("/PersonalServlet")
public class PersonalServlet extends HttpServlet
{
   public void doGet(HttpServletRequest request,
                     HttpServletResponse response)
                  throws IOException,ServletException
   {
      response.setContentType("text/HTML");

      PrintWriter out = response.getWriter();
      out.println("<HTML>");
      out.println("<HEAD>");
      out.println("<TITLE>Simple Servlet</TITLE>");
      out.println("</HEAD>");
      out.println("<BODY>");
      out.println("<BR><BR><BR>");
      String name = request.getParameter("FirstName");
      out.println("<H1> A Simple Servlet for ");
      out.println(name + "</H1></CENTER>");
      out.println("</BODY>");
      out.println("</HTML>");
      out.flush();
   }
}
```

This is what the initial page looks like (after a name has been entered into the text box) (Fig. 8.3):

The servlet-generated page (after the above button has been clicked) is shown in Fig. 8.4.

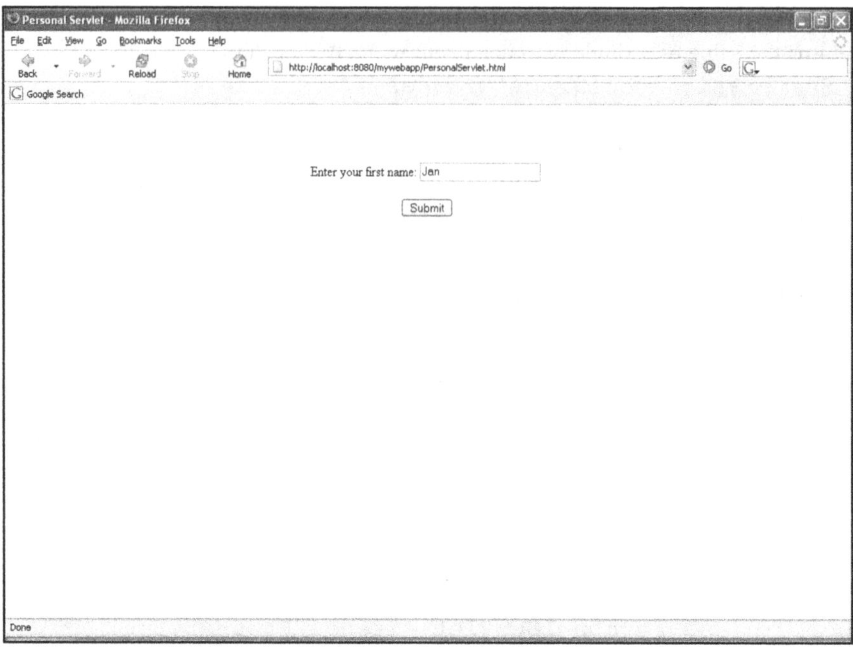

Fig. 8.3 Web page for passing a single data item to a servlet

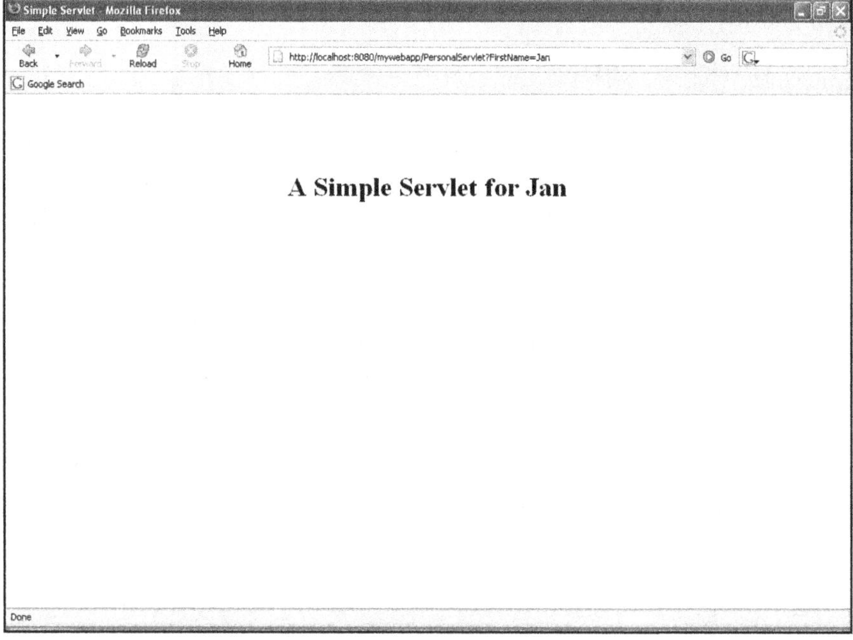

Fig. 8.4 Servlet output making use of data item received from initial Web page

One potential problem with this method is that, if the browser's 'Back' button is clicked to return to the opening Web page, the initial name entered is still visible. This doesn't really matter in this particular example, but, for other (repeated) data entry, it probably would. In order to overcome this problem, we need to force the browser to reload the original page, rather than retrieve it from its cache, when a return is made to this page. There is an HTML *META* tag that will do this, but the tag varies from browser to browser. However, the following set of tags will satisfy most of the major browsers:

```
<META HTTP-EQUIV="Pragma" CONTENT="no cache">
<META HTTP-EQUIV="Cache-control" CONTENT="no cache">
<META HTTP-EQUIV="Expires" CONTENT="0">
```

These should be placed immediately after the `<HEAD>` tag on the initial Web page.

Continuing now with the approach of gradually adding to the complexity of our servlets, the next step is to carry out some processing of the data entered and display the results of such processing. The next example accepts two numbers, adds them and then displays the result. Since there are multiple inputs, we shall use the *POST* method. In addition, an HTML table has been used for laying out the page elements neatly.

Example

Firstly, the code for the initial Web page…

```
<!-- SimpleAdder.html -->

<HTML>

   <HEAD>
        <META HTTP-EQUIV ="Pragma" CONTENT="no cache">
        <META HTTP-EQUIV ="Cache-control"
                                      CONTENT="no cache">
        <META HTTP-EQUIV ="Expires" CONTENT="0">
        <TITLE>Simple Adder</TITLE>
   <HEAD>

   <BODY>
        <CENTER>
        <FORM METHOD=POST ACTION="AdderServlet">
           <TABLE>
               <TR>
                  <TD>First number</TD>
                  <TD><INPUT TYPE="Text" NAME="Num1"
                                 VALUE="" SIZE=5></TD>
               </TR>
               <TR>
               <TD>Second number</TD>
               <TD><INPUT TYPE="Text"  NAME="Num2"
                                 VALUE="" SIZE=5></TD>
```

```
                </TR>
            </TABLE>
            <BR><BR><BR>
            <INPUT TYPE="Submit" VALUE = "Submit">
            <INPUT TYPE="Reset" VALUE="Clear">
        </FORM>
        </CENTER>
    </BODY>
</HTML>
```

Since the user may enter a non-numeric value, the servlet must cater for a possible *NumberFormatException*. In addition, method *getParameter* will need to convert the strings it receives into integers by using the *parseInt* method of the *Integer* wrapper class. Now for the code…

```
import java.io.*;
import javax.servlet.*;
import javax.servlet.http.*;
import javax.servlet.annotation.WebServlet;

@WebServlet("/AdderServlet")
public class AdderServlet extends HttpServlet
{
   public void doPost(HttpServletRequest request,
                      HttpServletResponse response)
                    throws IOException,ServletException
   {
      try
      {
         String value1 = request.getParameter("Num1");
         String value2 = request.getParameter("Num2");
         int num1 = Integer.parseInt(value1);
         int num2 = Integer.parseInt(value2);
         int sum = num1 + num2;

         sendPage(response,"Result = " + sum);
      }
      catch(NumberFormatException nfEx)
      {
         sendPage(response,"*** Invalid entry! ***");
      }
   }

   private void sendPage(HttpServletResponse reply,
                         String result) throws IOException
```

```
    {
        reply.setContentType("text/HTML");
        PrintWriter out = reply.getWriter();
        out.println("<HTML>");
        out.println("<HEAD>");
        out.println("<TITLE>Result</TITLE>");
        out.println("</HEAD>");
        out.println("<BODY>");
        out.println("<BR><BR><BR>");
        out.println("<CENTER><H1><FONT COLOR='blue'>");
        out.println("Result=" + result);
        out.println("</FONT></H1></CENTER>");
        out.println("</BODY>");
        out.println("</HTML>");
        out.flush();
    }
}
```

Note the convenient dual-purpose use of method *sendPage* to return either the result page or an error page (Figs. 8.5, 8.6 and 8.7).

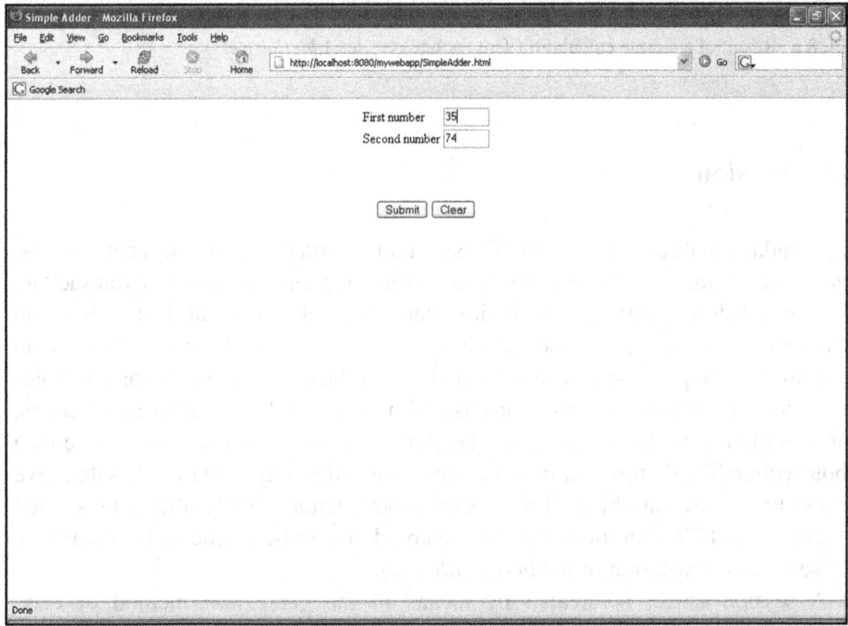

Fig. 8.5 Web page receiving two integers to be sent to a servlet

Output from the servlet:

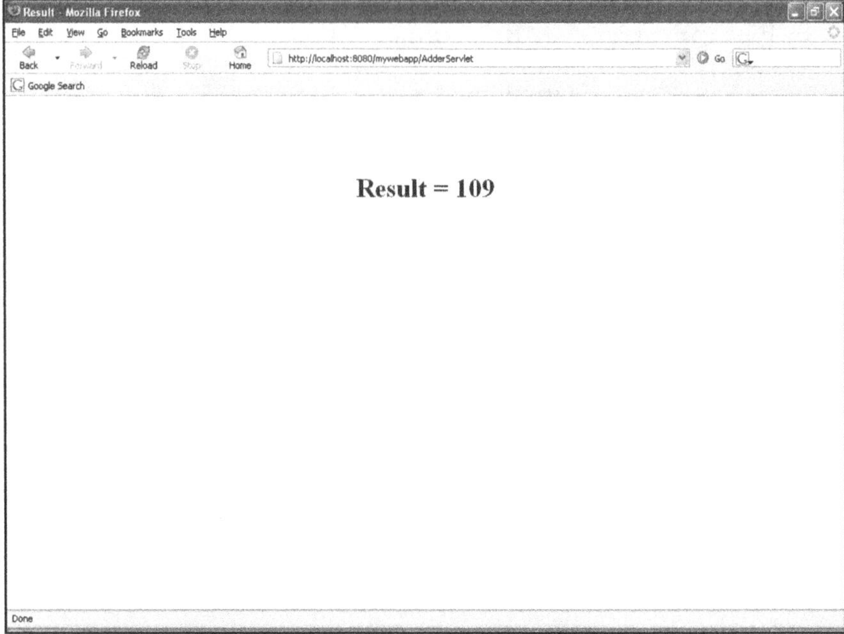

Fig. 8.6 Result of a simple calculation sent back by servlet *AdderServlet*

8.8 Sessions

One fundamental restriction of HTTP is that it is a *stateless* protocol. That is to say, each request and each response is a self-contained and independent transaction. However, different parts of a Web site often need to know about data gathered in other parts. For example, the contents of a customer's electronic cart on an e-commerce shopping site need to be updated as the customer visits various pages and selects purchases. To cater for this and a great number of other applications, servlets implement the concept of a **session**. A session is a container where data about a client's activities may be stored and accessed by any of the servlets that have access to the session object. The session expires automatically after a prescribed timeout period (30 min for Tomcat) has elapsed or may be invalidated explicitly by the servlet (by execution of method *invalidate*).

A session object is created by means of the *getSession* method of class *HttpServletRequest*. This method is overloaded:

- `HttpSession getSession()`
- `HttpSession getSession(boolean create)`

If the first version is used or the second version is used with an argument of `true`, then the server returns the current session if there is one; otherwise, it creates a new session object. For example:

```
HttpSession cart = request.getSession();
```

If the second version is used with an argument of `false`, then the current session is returned if there is one, but `null` is returned otherwise.

A session object contains a set of name-value pairs. Each name is of type *String* and each value is of type *Object*. Note that **objects added to a session must implement the** Serializable **interface**. (This is true for the *String* class and for the type wrapper classes such as *Integer*.) A servlet may add information to a session object via the following method:

```
void setAttribute(String <name>, Object <value>)
```

Example

```
String currentProduct = request.getParameter("Product");
HttpSession cart = request.getSession();
cart.setAttribute("currentProd",currentProduct);
```

The method to remove an item is *removeAttribute*, which has the following signature:

```
Object removeAttribute(String <name>)
```

For example:

```
cart.removeAttribute(currentProduct);
```

To retrieve a value, use:

```
Object getAttribute(String <name>)
```

Note that a *typecast* will usually be necessary after retrieval. For example:

```
String product =
      (String)cart.getAttribute("currentProd");
```

To get a list of all named values held, use:

```
String[] getAttributeNames()
```

For example:

```
String[] prodName = cart.getAttributeNames();
```

It's now time to put these individual pieces together into a full example application…

Example

This example involves a simplified shopping cart into which the user may place a specified weight of apples and/or a specified weight of pears. Three servlets are used, for the following purposes:

- selection of apples/pears;
- entry of required weight;
- checking out.

If one servlet needs to transfer execution to another, then method *sendRedirect* of class *HttpServletResponse* may be used. The initial HTML page makes use of radio buttons (`<INPUT TYPE="Radio"...........>`).

```
<!-- ShoppingCart.html
Home page for a very simple example of the use
of servlets in a shopping cart application.
Demonstrates the use of session variables.
-->

<HTML>

   <HEAD>
      <META HTTP-EQUIV ="Pragma" CONTENT="no cache">
      <META HTTP-EQUIV ="Cache-control"
                                       CONTENT="no cache">
      <META HTTP-EQUIV ="Expires" CONTENT="0">
      <TITLE>Shopping Cart</TITLE>
   </HEAD>

   <BODY>
      <CENTER>
      <H1><FONT COLOR=red>Simple Shopping Cart
      </FONT></H1>
      <BR><BR><BR><BR><BR>
      <FORM METHOD=POST ACTION="Selection">

         <TABLE>
            <TR>
               <TD><INPUT TYPE="Radio" NAME="Product"
                               VALUE = "Apples" CHECKED>
               <FONT COLOR=Blue>Apples</FONT></TD>

            </TR>
            <TR>
              <TD><INPUT TYPE="Radio" NAME="Product"
                                        VALUE = "Pears">
              <FONT COLOR=Blue>Pears</FONT></TD>
            </TR>
            <TR>
              <TD><INPUT TYPE="Radio" NAME="Product"
                                     VALUE = "Checkout">
              <FONT COLOR=Red>
              Go to checkout</P></TD>
```

```
            </TR>
          </TABLE>
          <BR><BR><BR>
          <INPUT TYPE="Submit" VALUE="Submit">
        </FORM>
        </CENTER>
    </BODY>
</HTML>
```

Here's what this initial Web page looks like (without colour!):

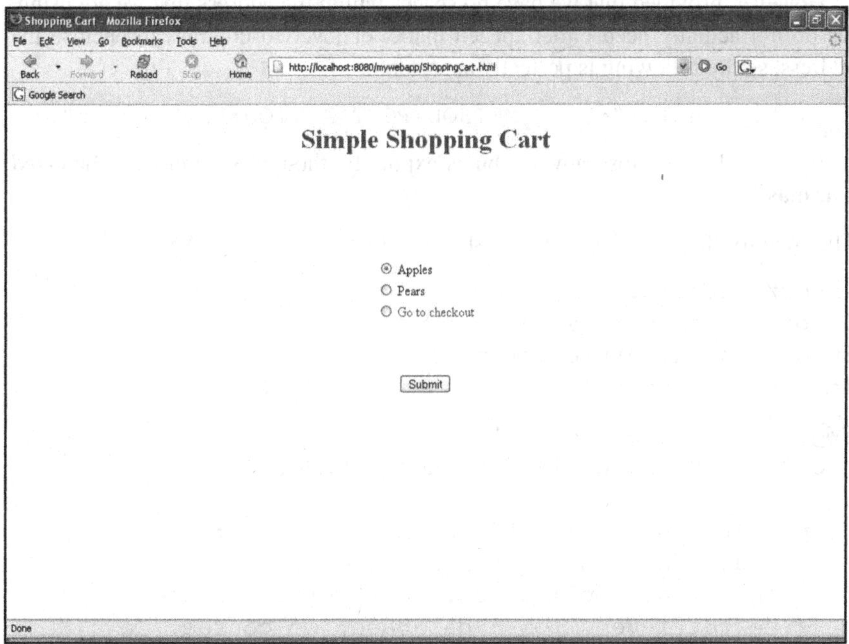

Fig. 8.7 Initial Web page for a simple shopping cart application

When a selection has been made and the user has clicked 'Submit', the *Selection* servlet is executed. Before we look at the code for this servlet, there is an apparent minor problem (that turns out not to be a problem at all) that needs to be considered…

As you are aware by now, a servlet builds up a Web page by outputting the required HTML tags in string form via method *println* of class *PrintWriter*. This means, of course, that any string literals must be enclosed by speech marks. For example:

```
println("<HTML>");
```

However, the next servlet needs to output a *FORM* tag with an *ACTION* attribute specifying the address of another servlet. This address, if we follow the convention from our previous examples, will already be enclosed by speech marks. If we try to include both sets of speech marks, then an error will be generated, since what is intended to be opening of the inner speech marks will be taken as closure of the outer speech marks. Here is an example of such invalid code:

```
out.println("<FORM METHOD=POST ACTION='AnyServlet'");
```

One solution to this apparent problem is to use inverted commas, instead of speech marks, for the inner enclosure:

```
out.println("<FORM METHOD=POST ACTION=AnyServlet");
```

However, provided that we have no spaces within the address that we are using, we do not actually need either speech marks or inverted commas to enclose the address, so the following is perfectly acceptable:

```
out.println("<FORM METHOD=POST ACTION=AnyServlet");
```

If we wish to enclose any attributes explicitly, though, we must use **inverted commas**.

The code for the *Selection* servlet is shown below.

```
import java.io.*;
import javax.servlet.*;
import javax.servlet.http.*;
import javax.servlet.annotation.WebServlet;

@WebServlet("/Selection")
public class Selection extends HttpServlet
{
   private final float APPLES_PRICE = 1.45F;
   private final float PEARS_PRICE = 1.75F;
   //In a real application, above prices would
   //be retrieved from a database, of course.
   public void doPost(HttpServletRequest request,
                      HttpServletResponse response)
                    throws IOException,ServletException
   {
      String currentProduct =
                        request.getParameter("Product");
      HttpSession cart = request.getSession();
      cart.putValue("currentProd",currentProduct);
      //Places user's selected product into the session
      //variable called 'cart'.
```

```
    //This product name will then be available to any
    //servlet that accesses this session variable.

    if (currentProduct.equals("Checkout"))
       response.sendRedirect("Checkout");
    else
       sendPage(response,currentProduct);
       //Creates page for selection of weight.
 }

 private void sendPage(HttpServletResponse reply,
                  String product) throws IOException
 {
    reply.setContentType("text/HTML");
    PrintWriter out = reply.getWriter();

    out.println("<HTML>");
    out.println("<HEAD>");
    out.println("<TITLE>" + product + "</TITLE>");
    out.println("</HEAD>");

    out.println("<BODY>");

    out.println("<CENTER>");
    out.println("<H1><FONT COLOR=Red>"
                  + product + "</FONT></H1>");
    out.println("<BR><BR><BR>");

    out.println("<FORM METHOD=POST ACTION='Weight'");

    out.println("<TABLE>");
    out.println("<TR>");
    out.println("   <TD>Quantity required (kg)");
    out.println("   <INPUT TYPE='Text' NAME='Qty'"
                       + " VALUE='' SIZE=5></TD>");
    out.println("</TR>");
    out.println("</TABLE>");
    out.println("<BR><BR><BR>");

    out.println("<TABLE>");

    out.println("<TR>");
    out.println("   <TD><INPUT TYPE='Radio'"
          + " NAME='Option' VALUE='Add' CHECKED>");
    out.println("  <FONT COLOR=blue>   "
                    + "Add to cart.</FONT></TD>");
    out.println("</TR>");
```

```
        out.println("<TR>");
        out.println("    <TD><INPUT TYPE='Radio'"
                    + " NAME='Option' VALUE='Remove'>");
        out.println("    <FONT COLOR=blue> " +
                  "Remove item from cart.</FONT></TD>");
        out.println("</TR>");

        out.println("<TR>");
        out.println("    <TD><INPUT TYPE='Radio'"
                      + " NAME='Option' VALUE='Next'>");
        out.println("    <FONT COLOR=blue> "
                     + "Choose next item.</FONT></TD>");
        out.println("</TR>");

        out.println("<TR>");
        out.println("    <TD><INPUT TYPE='Radio'"
                  + " NAME='Option' VALUE='Checkout'>");
        out.println("    <FONT COLOR=blue>    "
                       + "Go to checkout.</FONT></TD>");
        out.println("</TR>");

        out.println("</TABLE>");

        out.println("<BR><BR><BR>");
        out.println("<INPUT TYPE='Submit'
                                      VALUE='Submit'>");
        out.println("</FORM>");
        out.println("</CENTER>");

        out.println("</BODY>");
        out.println("</HTML>");
        out.flush();
    }
}
```

As an alternative to the use of *sendRedirect* to transfer control to another servlet (or HTML page), we can create a *RequestDispatcher* object and call its *forward* method.

Example

```
RequestDispatcher requestDispatcher =
               request.getRequestDispatcher("Checkout");
requestDispatcher.forward(request, response);
```

Provided that the user did not select 'Checkout' on the initial page [See later for coverage of this], the Web page shown in Fig. 8.8 is presented. As can be seen, a weight has been entered by the user.

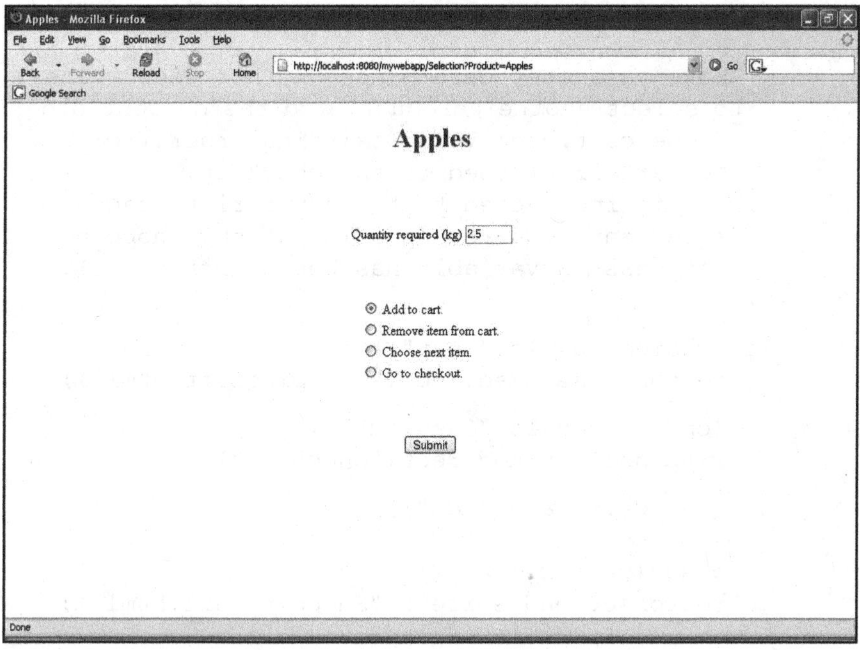

Fig. 8.8 Weight entry page for simple shopping cart application

When a selection has been made and 'Submit' clicked, the *Weight* servlet is executed. Here is the code for the *Weight* servlet:

```
import java.io.*;
import javax.servlet.*;
import javax.servlet.http.*;
import javax.servlet.annotation.WebServlet;

@WebServlet("/Weight")
public class Weight extends HttpServlet
{
   public void doPost(HttpServletRequest request,
                      HttpServletResponse response)
                   throws IOException,ServletException
   {
      HttpSession cart = request.getSession();
      String currentProduct =
               (String)cart.getAttribute("currentProd");
      //Current product ('Apples' or 'Pears') retrieved.
      //Note the necessity for a typecast from Object
      //into String.
```

```
    String choice = request.getParameter("Option");
    /*
      Above parameter determines whether user wishes
      to select another product, add the current order
      to the cart, remove an existing order from
      the cart or proceed to the checkout.
      User is redirected to the appropriate page
      (after any required updating of the shopping
      cart session variable has been carried out).
    */

    if (choice.equals("Next"))
       response.sendRedirect("ShoppingCart.html");

    if (choice.equals("Checkout"))
       response.sendRedirect("Checkout");

    if (choice.equals("Add"))
    {
       doAdd(cart,request);
       response.sendRedirect("ShoppingCart.html");
    }
    if (choice.equals("Remove"))
    //Not really possible for it to be
    //anything else, but play safe!
    {
       doRemove(cart);
       response.sendRedirect("ShoppingCart.html");
    }
 }

 private void doAdd(HttpSession cart,
                     HttpServletRequest request)
 {
    String currentProduct =
             (String)cart.getAttribute("currentProd");
    String qty = request.getParameter("Qty");
    //Value of weight entered by user retrieved here.

    if (qty!=null)
    //Check that user actually entered a value!
    {
       if (currentProduct.equals("Apples"))
          cart.setAttribute("Apples",qty);
       else
          cart.setAttribute("Pears",qty);
    }
 }
```

```
    private void doRemove(HttpSession cart)
    {
        String currentProduct =
                (String)cart.getAttribute("currentProd");
        Object product =
                        cart.getAttribute(currentProduct);
        //Note that there is no need for a typecast into
        //String, since we only need to know that there
        //is an order for the current product in the cart.

        if (product!=null)
        //Product found in cart.
            cart.removeAttribute(currentProduct);
    }
}
```

Once all product selections have been made and the 'Checkout' option has been taken, the *Checkout* servlet will be executed. Before we look at the code for this servlet, though, we need to consider the issue of **formatting decimal output**, since the *Checkout* servlet needs to show costs to precisely two decimal places and to allow a sensible maximum field size. We can't use *printf*, since this is a member of the *PrintStream* class, not of the *PrintWriter* class. However, the *PrintWriter* class does have the equivalent method *format* and it is this method that we shall use.

Now for the *Checkout* servlet code…

```
import java.io.*;
import javax.servlet.*;
import javax.servlet.http.*;
import java.util.Enumeration;
import javax.servlet.annotation.WebServlet;

@WebServlet("/Checkout")
public class Checkout extends HttpServlet
{
     private final float APPLES_PRICE = 1.45F;
     private final float PEARS_PRICE = 1.75F;
     //In a real application, the above prices would be
     //retrieved from a database, of course.

     public void service(HttpServletRequest request,
                         HttpServletResponse response)
                     throws IOException,ServletException
     {
          HttpSession cart = request.getSession();

          response.setContentType("text/HTML");

          PrintWriter out = response.getWriter();
```

```
out.println("<HTML>");
out.println("<HEAD>");
out.println("<TITLE>Checkout</TITLE>");
out.println("</STYLE>");
out.println("</HEAD>");

out.println("<BODY>");
out.println("<BR><BR><BR>");

out.println("<CENTER>");

out.println(
   "<H1><FONT COLOR=Red>Order List</FONT></H1>");
out.println("<BR><BR><BR>");

out.println("<TABLE BGCOLOR=Aqua BORDER=2>");
out.println("<TR>");
out.println("<TH>Item</TH>");
out.println("<TH>Weight(kg)</TH>");
out.println("<TH>Cost(£)</TH>");
out.println("</TR>");

cart.removeAttribute("currentProd");
Enumeration prodNames = cart.getAttributeNames();
float totalCost = 0;

int numProducts = 0;
while (prodNames.hasMoreElements())
{
     float wt=0,cost=0;
     String product =
              (String)prodNames.nextElement();
     String stringWt =
              (String)cart.getAttribute(product);

     wt = Float.parseFloat(stringWt);
     if (product.equals("Apples"))
         cost = APPLES_PRICE * wt;
     else if (product.equals("Pears"))
         cost = PEARS_PRICE * wt;

     out.println("<TR>");
     out.println("<TD>" + product + "</TD>");
     out.format("<TD> %4.2f </TD>%n",wt);
     out.format("<TD> %5.2f </TD>%n",cost);
     out.println("</TR>");
     totalCost+=cost;
     numProducts++;
}
if (numProducts == 0)
```

```
            {
               out.println(
                 "<TR STYLE='background-color:yellow'>");
               out.println(
                 "<TD>*** No orders placed! ***</TD></TR>");
            }
            else
            {
               out.println("<TR BGCOLOR=Yellow>");
               out.println("<TD></TD>"); //Blank cell.
               out.println("<TD>Total cost:</TD>");
               out.format("<TD> %5.2f </TD>%n",totalCost);
               out.println("</TR>");
            }
            out.println("</TABLE>");
            out.println("</CENTER>");

            out.println("</BODY>");
            out.println("</HTML>");

            out.flush();
        }
}
```

Example output from the *Checkout* servlet is shown in Fig. 8.9.

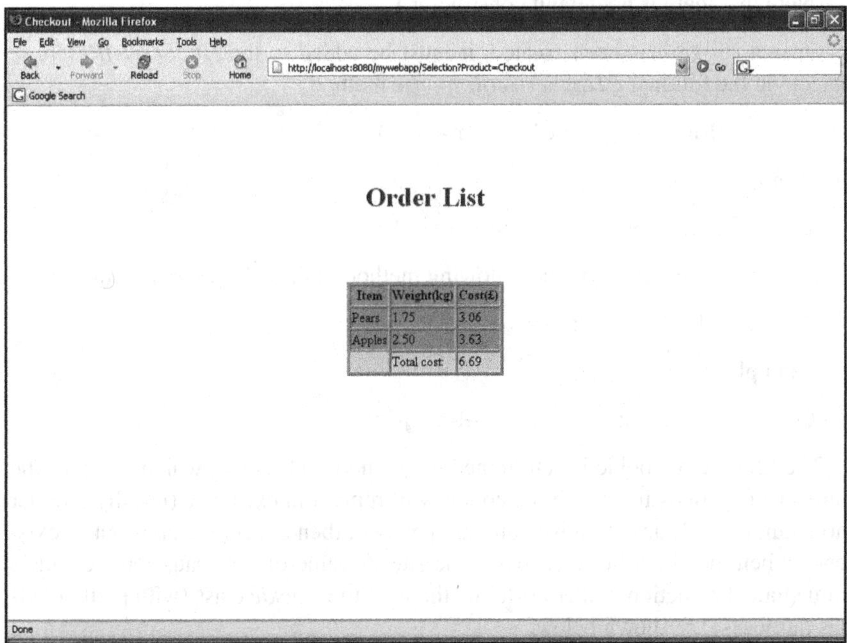

Fig. 8.9 Customer's order summary page for simple shopping cart application

Session variables allow much more interesting and dynamic Web sites to be created. However, they do not allow a user's personal details/preferences to be maintained between visits to the same site. The next section will show how this may be done.

8.9 Cookies

Cookies provide another means of storing a user's data for use whilst he/she is navigating a Web site. Whereas sessions provide data only for the duration of one visit to the site, though, cookies store information that may be retrieved on subsequent visits to the site. (In actual fact, *Session* objects make use of *Cookie* objects.) They can be used to personalise pages for the user and/or select his/her preferences. Cookies have been used by CGI programmers for years and the developers of Java's servlet API incorporated this de facto standard into the servlet specification. What **is** a cookie, though?

A cookie is an associated name-value pair in which both name and value are strings. (E.g., "username" and "Bill Johnson".) It is **possible** to maintain a cookie simply for the duration of a browsing session, but it is usually stored **on the client computer** for future use. Each cookie is held in a small file sent by the server to the client machine and retrieved by the server on subsequent visits by the user to the site. The constructor for a Java *Cookie* object **must** have this signature:

```
Cookie(String <name>, String <name>)
```

(Note that there is no default constructor.)

Once a cookie has been created, it must be added to the *HttpServletResponse* object via the following *HttpServletResponse* method :

```
void addCookie(Cookie <name>)
```

For example:

```
response.addCookie(myCookie);
```

Cookies are retrieved via the following method of class *HttpServletRequest*:

```
Cookie[] getCookies()
```

For example:

```
Cookie[] cookie = request.getCookies();
```

The lifetime of cookie is determined by method *setMaxAge*, which specifies the number of seconds for which the cookie will remain in existence (usually a rather large number!). If any negative value is specified, then the cookie goes out of existence when the client browser leaves the site. A value of zero causes the cookie's immediate destruction. Other useful methods of the *Cookie* class (with pretty obvious purposes) are shown below.

- `void setComment(String <value>)`
  (A comment is optionally used to describe the cookie.)
- `String getComment()`
- `String getName()`
- `String getValue()`
- `void setValue(String <value>)`
- `int getMaxAge()`

Example

This will be a modification of the earlier 'Simple Adder' example. On the user's first visit to the site, he/she will be prompted to enter his/her name and a choice of both foreground and background colours for the addition result page. These values will be saved in cookies, which will be retrieved on subsequent visits to the site. If the user fails to enter a name, there will be no personalised header. Failure to select a foreground colour will result in a default value of black being set, whilst failure to select a background colour will result in a default value of white being set. The only differences in the initial HTML file are in the lines giving the names of the two files involved:

```
<!-- CookieAdder.html -->
.............................................
.............................................
<FORM METHOD=POST ACTION="CookieAdder">
.............................................
.............................................
```

Servlet *CookieAdder* will set up a new *Session* object, retrieve the user's cookies and create session variables corresponding to those cookies. (A *Session* object is preferable, since three servlets will be involved, all of which require access to the data values. This saves each servlet from having to download the cookies separately.) In addition to the contents of the cookies, the result of the addition will need to be saved in a session variable. If the appropriate session variable indicates that this is the user's first visit to the site, method *sendRedirect* will be used to pass control to a preferences servlet. In order to avoid code duplication, control will also need to be redirected to a result-displaying servlet from both the initial servlet and the preferences servlet.

Here's the code for *CookieAdder* (the initial servlet):

```
import java.io.*;
import javax.servlet.*;
import javax.servlet.http.*;
import javax.servlet.annotation.WebServlet;

@WebServlet("/CookieAdder")
public class CookieAdder extends HttpServlet
{
   public void doPost(HttpServletRequest request,
                      HttpServletResponse response)
```

```
                throws IOException,ServletException
   {
      int sum=0;
      try
      {
         String value1 = request.getParameter("Num1");
         String value2 = request.getParameter("Num2");

         int num1=Integer.parseInt(value1);
         int num2=Integer.parseInt(value2);
         sum = num1 + num2;

      }
      catch(NumberFormatException nfEx)
      {
         sendPage(response, "*** Invalid entry! ***");
         return;
      }
      HttpSession adderSession = request.getSession();
      adderSession.putValue("sum",new Integer(sum));
      /*
      Second argument to putValue must be a class
      object, not a value of one of the primitive
      types, so an object of class Integer is
      created above.
      */

      Cookie[] cookie = request.getCookies();
      int numCookies = cookie.length;
      for (int i=0; i<numCookies; i++)
         adderSession.putValue(
             cookie[i].getName(),cookie[i].getValue());

      if (adderSession.getValue("firstVisit") == null)
      //First visit, soredirect to preferences servlet.
         response.sendRedirect("GetPreferences");
      else
         response.sendRedirect("ShowSum");
   }

   private void sendPage(HttpServletResponse reply,
                     String message) throws IOException
   {
      reply.setContentType("text/HTML");
      PrintWriter out = reply.getWriter();
      out.println("<HTML>");
      out.println("<HEAD>");
      out.println("<TITLE>Result</TITLE>");
```

```
        out.println("</STYLE>");
        out.println("</HEAD>");
        out.println("<BODY>");
        out.println("<BR><BR><BR>");
        out.println("<CENTER>" + message + "</CENTER>");
        out.println("</BODY>");
        out.println("</HTML>");
        out.flush();
    }
}
```

Note the addition of cookie values to the current session (making use of the *Cookie* class's *getName* and *getValue* methods). If this is the user's first visit to the site (indicated by a `null` value for session variable *firstVisit*), then the user is redirected to the *GetPreferences* servlet. Since the *GetPreferences* servlet is not receiving form data, it implements the *doGet* method…

```
import java.io.*;
import javax.servlet.*;
import javax.servlet.http.*;
import javax.servlet.annotation.WebServlet;

@WebServlet("/GetPreferences")
public class GetPreferences extends HttpServlet
{
    public void doGet(HttpServletRequest request,
                      HttpServletResponse response)
                throws IOException,ServletException
    {
        response.setContentType("text/HTML");

        HttpSession adderSession = request.getSession();

        adderSession.putValue("firstVisit","Yes");

        PrintWriter out = response.getWriter();
        out.println("<HTML>");
        out.println("<HEAD>");
        out.println("<TITLE>Preferences</TITLE>");
        out.println("</STYLE>");
        out.println("</HEAD>");

        out.println("<BODY>");
        out.println("<BR><BR><BR>");
        out.println("<CENTER>");
        out.println(
                "<FORM METHOD=POST ACTION='ShowSum'>");
        out.println("<FONT COLOR='Blue' SIZE=5>"
```

```
                            + "User Preferences</FONT>");
      out.println("<BR>");
      out.println("<TABLE>");
      out.println("<TR>");
      out.println("<TD>First name</TD>");
      out.println("<TD><INPUT  TYPE='Text' "
            + "NAME='Name' VALUE='' SIZE=15></TD>");
      out.println("</TR>");
      out.println("<TR>");
      out.println("<TD>Foreground colour</TD>");
      out.println("<TD><INPUT  TYPE='Text' "
                   + "NAME='ForeColour' VALUE=''"
                   + "SIZE=10></TD>");
      out.println("</TR>");
      out.println("<TR>");
      out.println("<TD>Background colour</TD>");
      out.println("<TD><INPUT  TYPE='Text' "
                   + "NAME='BackColour' VALUE=''"
                   + "SIZE=10></TD>");
      out.println("</TR>");
      out.println("</TABLE>");
      out.println("<BR><BR>");
      out.println("<INPUT  TYPE='Submit' "
                           + "VALUE = 'Submit'>");
      out.println("<INPUT  TYPE='Reset' "
                              + "VALUE='Clear'>");
      out.println("</CENTER>");

      out.println("</BODY>");
      out.println("</HTML>");
      out.flush();
   }
}
```

Note the setting of session variable *firstVisit* to 'Yes', for subsequent checking by the *ShowSum* servlet. Figure 8.10 shows the output generated by the *GetPreferences* servlet and some example user entry:

Servlet *ShowSum* may be called from either *GetPreferences* or *CookieAdder*. Since the former passes on form data and the latter doesn't, *ShowSum* implements neither *doPost* nor *doGet*, but method *service*. Before attempting to transmit the result page, the servlet checks the value of session variable *firstVisit*. If this variable has been set to 'Yes', the servlet retrieves the user's preferences (via the *HttpServletRequest* object), creates the appropriate cookies and updates the session variables (including the setting of the *firstVisit* cookie variable and session variable to 'No').

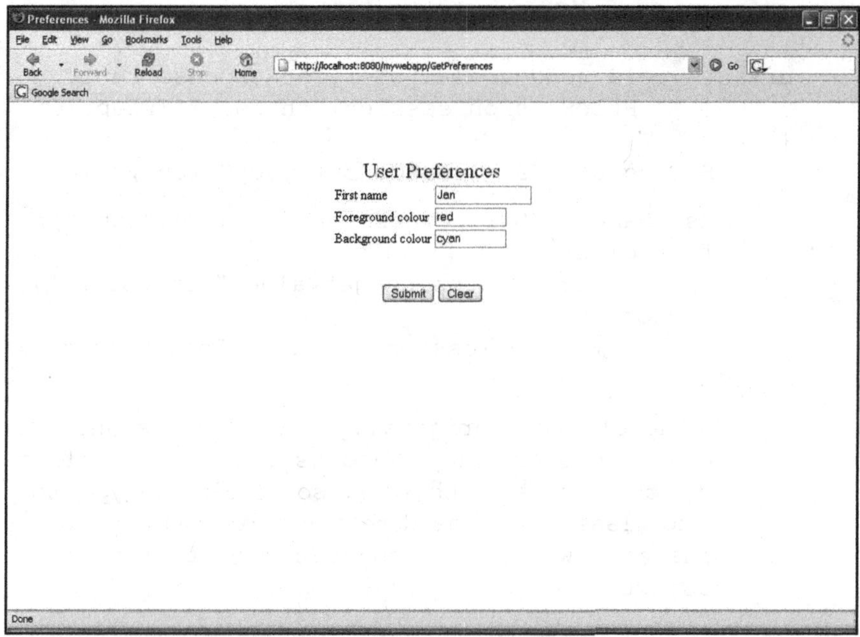

Fig. 8.10 A page to accept the user's preferences for storing in cookies

Here is the code for the *ShowSum* servlet:

```
import java.io.*;
import javax.servlet.*;
import javax.servlet.http.*;
import javax.servlet.annotation.WebServlet;

@WebServlet("/ShowSum")
public class ShowSum extends HttpServlet
{
     public void service(HttpServletRequest request,
                         HttpServletResponse response)
                    throws IOException,ServletException
     {
       HttpSession adderSession = request.getSession();

       String firstTime =
          (String)adderSession.getValue("firstVisit");
       if (firstTime.equals("Yes"))
            retrieveNewPreferences(
                      request,response,adderSession);
```

```
  sendPage(response,adderSession);
}
private void sendPage(HttpServletResponse reply,
          HttpSession session) throws IOException
{
     String userName,foreColour,backColour,sum;

     userName = (String)session.getValue("name");
     foreColour =
           (String)session.getValue("foreColour");
     backColour =
           (String)session.getValue("backColour");

     /*
     Value of 'sum' originally saved as instance of
     class Integer (and saved as instance of class
     Object in session object), so we cannot typecast
     into class String as done for three values above.
     Instead, we use method toString of class
     Object…
     */
     sum = session.getValue("sum").toString();

     reply.setContentType("text/HTML");
     PrintWriter out = reply.getWriter();
     out.println("<HTML>");
     out.println("<HEAD>");
     out.println("<TITLE>Result</TITLE>");
     out.println("</HEAD>");
     out.println("<BODY TEXT=" + foreColour
               + " BGCOLOR=" + backColour + ">");
     out.println("<CENTER>");
     if (!userName.equals(""))
       out.println("<H2>" + userName + "'s "
                              + "Result</H2>");
     out.println("<BR><BR><BR><H3>" + sum + "</H3>");
     out.println("</CENTER>");
     out.println("</BODY>");
     out.println("</HTML>");
     out.flush();
}

private void retrieveNewPreferences(
     HttpServletRequest request,
```

```
        HttpServletResponse response,HttpSession session)
    {
        final int AGE = 60;     //(60secs = 1min)

        String forename = request.getParameter("Name");
        if (forename==null) //Should never happen!
            return;

        if (!forename.equals(""))
        {
            Cookie nameCookie =
                        new Cookie("name",forename);
            nameCookie.setMaxAge(AGE);
            response.addCookie(nameCookie);
            session.putValue("name",forename);
        }

        String fColour =
                    request.getParameter("ForeColour");
        if (fColour.equals(""))
           fColour = "Black";
        Cookie foreColourCookie =
                       new Cookie("foreColour",fColour);
        foreColourCookie.setMaxAge(AGE);
        response.addCookie(foreColourCookie);
        session.putValue("foreColour",fColour);
        String bColour =
                  request.getParameter("BackColour");
        if (bColour.equals(""))
            bColour = "White";
        Cookie backColourCookie =
                  new Cookie("backColour",bColour);
        backColourCookie.setMaxAge(AGE);
        response.addCookie(backColourCookie);
        session.putValue("backColour",bColour);

        Cookie visitCookie =
                    new Cookie("firstVisit","No");
        visitCookie.setMaxAge(AGE);
        response.addCookie(visitCookie);
        session.putValue("firstVisit","No");
    }
}
```

Example output is shown in Fig. 8.11.

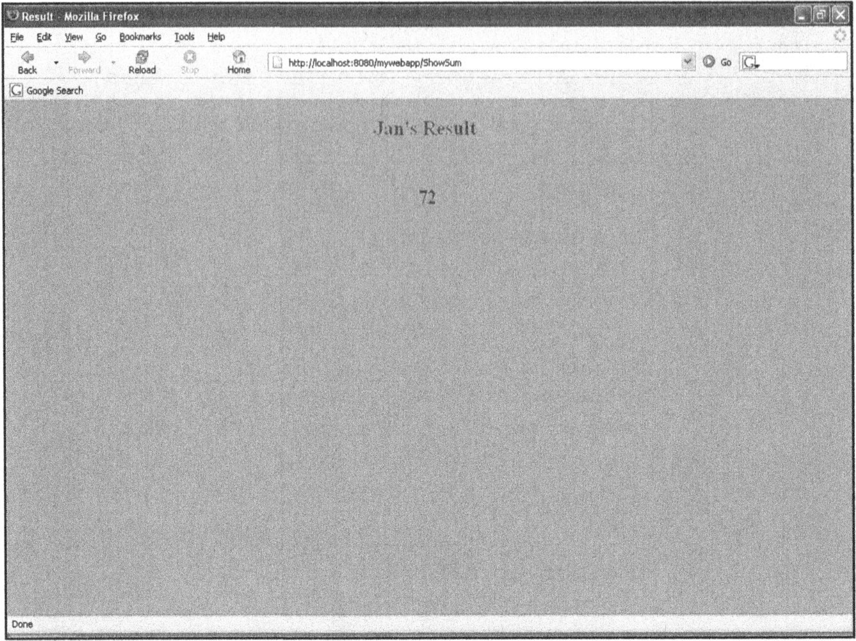

Fig. 8.11 Page output according to user's preferences (as specified in cookies)

8.10 Accessing a Database via a Servlet

Nowadays, accessing a database over the Internet or an intranet is a very common requirement. Using JDBC within a servlet allows us to do this. In fact, Sect. 7.11 from the preceding chapter demonstrated how to do this through use of the *DataSource* interface, which is the 'preferred method' of accessing a remote database via JDBC. However, the more traditional way of providing this access is to use the *DriverManager* class and this is still the method used by many Java database programmers. It is this approach that will be combined with the use of servlets in the current section.

The only additional servlet methods required are *init* and *destroy*. These are methods of interface *Servlet* and are implemented by class *HttpServlet*. Method *init* is called up once at the start of the servlet's execution (to carry out any required initialisation), while method *destroy* is called up once at the end of the servlet's execution (to carry out any required 'clean-up' operations, such as returning any allocated resources). We must provide an overriding definition of *init* that will load the JDBC driver and set up a database connection. Note that *init* should first make a call to *super*. We also override *destroy* by supplying a definition that closes the database connection. Both *init* and *destroy* must *throw* (or handle) *ServletExceptions*, of course.

Example

A Microsoft Access database called *HomeDB.mdb* contains a table called *PhoneNums*, which has fields *Surname*, *Forenames* and *PhoneNum*. A User DSN (Data Source Name) of *HomeDB* has been set up for the above database. (Refer back to Chap. 7 for details of how to do this.) The initial HTML page (*JDBCServletTest.html*) uses a form to accept a new record and then passes the values entered by the user to a servlet that adds a record to the phone numbers table and displays the new contents of this table. (Note that the use of the *<PRE>* tag below will produce slightly differing output in different browsers.)

The HTML code for the initial page is shown below.

```
<!-- JDBCServletTest.html -->
<HTML>

   <HEAD>
      <TITLE>Database Insertion Form</TITLE>
   </HEAD>

   <BODY>
      <H1><CENTER>Phonebook</CENTER><H1>
      <FORM METHOD=POST ACTION="DbServlet">
         <PRE>
          Surname:    <INPUT TYPE="Text" NAME="Surname">
          Forenames:    <INPUT TYPE="Text"
                                   NAME="Forenames">
          Phone number:    <INPUT TYPE="Text"
                                   NAME="PhoneNum">
         </PRE>
         <BR><BR>
         <CENTER><INPUT TYPE="Submit"
                          VALUE="Commit"></CENTER>
      </FORM>
   </BODY>

</HTML>
```

Here's the code for servlet *DbServlet*:

```
import java.io.*;
import javax.servlet.*;
import javax.servlet.http.*;
import java.sql.*;    //Don't forget this!
import javax.servlet.annotation.WebServlet;

@WebServlet("/DbServlet")
public class DbServlet extends HttpServlet
{
   private Statement statement;
```

```
private Connection link;
private String URL = "jdbc:odbc:HomeDB";

public void init() throws ServletException
{
   super.init();

   try
   {
      link = DriverManager.getConnection(URL,"","");
   }
   catch (SQLException ex)
   {
      ex.printStackTrace();
      System.exit(1);
   }
}
public void doPost(HttpServletRequest request,
                   HttpServletResponse response)
                throws ServletException,IOException
{
   String surname,forenames,telNum;

   surname = request.getParameter("Surname");
   forenames = request.getParameter("Forenames");
   telNum = request.getParameter("PhoneNum");
   response.setContentType("text/HTML");
   PrintWriter out = response.getWriter();
   out.println("<HTML>");
   out.println("<HEAD>");
   out.println("<TITLE>Servlet + JDBC</TITLE>");
   out.println("</HEAD>");
   out.println("<BODY>");

   String insertion = "INSERT INTO PhoneNums"
                + " VALUES('" + surname + "','"
                + forenames + "','" + telNum + "')";
   try
   {
      statement = link.createStatement();
      statement.executeUpdate(insertion);
      statement.close();   //Ensures committal.
   }
   catch (SQLException sqlEx)
   {
      out.println("<BR><CENTER><H2>Unable to execute"
                     + " insertion!</H2></CENTER>");
      out.println("</BODY>");
```

```
            out.println("</HTML>");
            out.flush();
            System.exit(1);
        }

        try
        {
            statement = link.createStatement();
            ResultSet results =
                    statement.executeQuery(
                            "SELECT * FROM PhoneNums");

            out.println("Updated table:");
            out.println("<BR><BR><CENTER>");
            out.println("<TABLE BORDER>");
            out.println("<TR><TH>Surname</TH>");
            out.println("<TH>Forename(s)</TH>");
            out.println("<TH>Phone No.</TH></TR>");

            while (results.next())
            {
                out.println("<TR>");
                out.println("<TD>");
                out.println(results.getString("Surname"));
                out.println("</TD>");
                out.println("<TD>");
                out.println(results.getString("Forenames"));
                out.println("</TD>");
                out.println("<TD>");
                out.println(results.getString("PhoneNum"));
                out.println("</TD>");
                out.println("</TR>");
            }
            out.println("</TABLE>");
        }
        catch(SQLException sqlEx)
        {
            out.println(
                "<BR><H2>Unable to retrieve data!</H2>");
            out.println("</BODY>");
            out.println("</HTML>");
            out.flush();
            System.exit(1);
        }

        out.println("</CENTER>");
        out.println("<BODY>");
```

```
      out.println("</HTML>");
      out.flush();
   }

   public void destroy()
   {
      try
      {
         link.close();
      }
      catch(Exception ex)
      {
         System.out.println(
                     "Error on closing database!");
         ex.printStackTrace();
         System.exit(1);
      }
   }
}
```

The output from *JDBCServletTest.html* and some example user data are shown in Fig. 8.12.

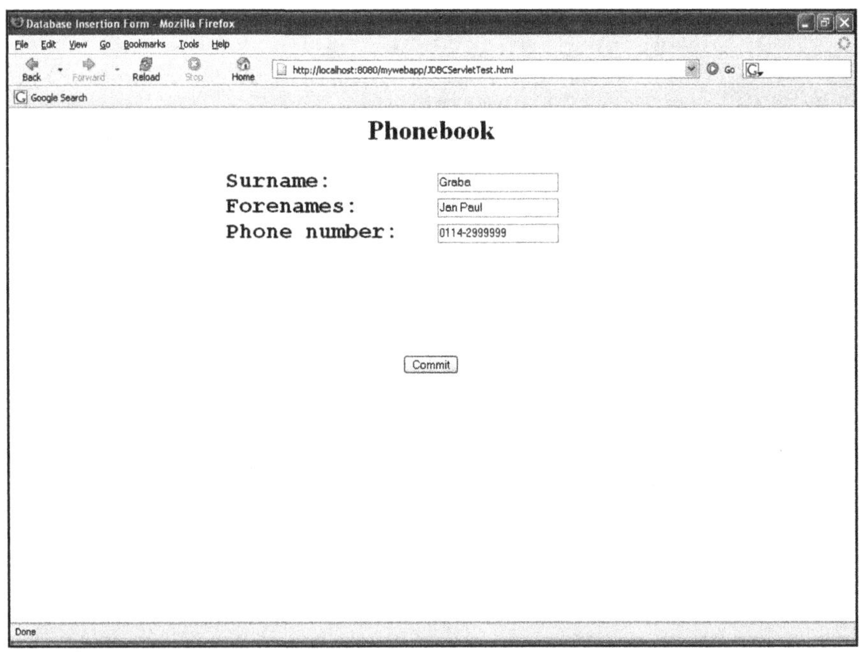

Fig. 8.12 Data entry for submission to a remote database via servlet and JDBC

The final output (after the entry of details for five records) is shown in Fig. 8.13.

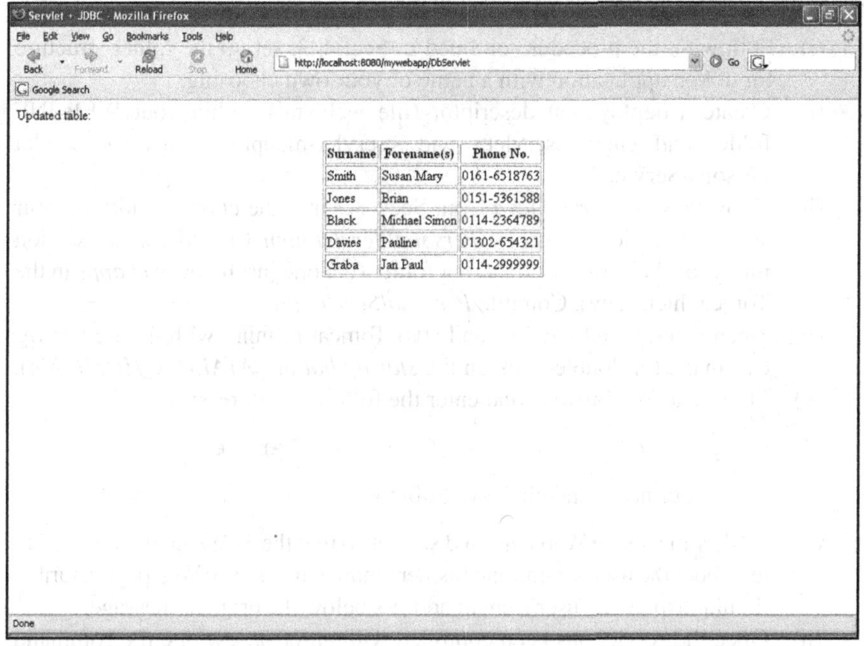

Fig. 8.13 Updated database table retrieved via servlet after insertion of record by same servlet

Exercises

Note that you will **not** be able to do any of the exercises listed below until you have set up the Java servlet API, as described in Sect. 8.2.

8.1 (i) Following the procedure outlined in Sect. 8.3, set up the folder structure for a Web application with a name of your own choosing.
(iv) Create a deployment descriptor (file web.xml) within your WEB-INF folder and enter <servlet> and <servlet-mapping> tags for servlet PersonalServlet.
(iii) Copy *PersonalServlet.java* from Sect. 8.7 into the *classes* folder of your Web application and copy *PersonalServlet.html* from the same section into your Web application's root folder (the one just below *webapps* in the Tomcat hierarchy). Compile *PersonalServlet.java.*
(iv) Open a command window and start Tomcat running with the `startup` command (or double-click on file *startup.bat* in *ÇATALINA_HOME\bin*).
(v) Start up a Web browser and enter the following address:

```
http://localhost:8080/PersonalServlet.html
```

(vi) Enter your name and click on 'Submit'.

8.2 (i) Modify the above Web page and servlet so that the *POST* method is used to send both the user's name and his/her email address. The Web page returned should display the user's email address below the original message.
(ii) Once the servlet has been compiled without error, execute the command `shutdown` in the initial command window and then re-start the server. Use your browser to test your new servlet.

8.3 (i) Copy *AdderServlet.java* from Sect. 8.7 into your *classes* folder and *SimpleAdder.html* from the same section into your Web app's root folder. Then compile the Java servlet.
(ii) Add the appropriate *<servlet>* and *<servlet-mapping>* tags for the above servlet to your deployment descriptor.
(iii) Start up Tomcat (stopping it first, if it is already running) and access the above Web page via any browser (as for the preceding programs).
(iv) Enter integers into the two text boxes, as prompted, and click on 'Submit'.

8.4 (i) Copy *ShoppingCart.html* from Sect. 8.8 into your Web app's root folder.
(ii) Create your own Selection servlet, placing it in the classes folder. This servlet should generate a Web page that simply displays the name of the product selected by the user.
(iii) Add the appropriate tags to your deployment descriptor and compile the servlet.
(iv) Start up Tomcat (stopping it first, if it is already running) and then test the servlet by accessing *ShoppingCart.html* in your browser window.

8.5 (i) Remove (or rename) the *Selection* servlet from the last task and then copy *Selection.java*, *Weight.java* and *Checkout.java* from Sect. 8.8 into the *classes* folder.

(ii) Add the appropriate tags to your deployment descriptor and compile the three servlets.

(iii) Start up Tomcat (stopping it first, if it is already running) and then access *ShoppingCart.html* via your browser. Experiment with this simple shopping cart application.

8.6 Extend the above application to cater for selection of bananas, as well as apples and pears.

8.7 Further extend the above application to allow the user to enter his/her name **the first time only** that he/she accesses the home page during a given session. Achieve this by redirecting the user on this first occasion to a simple HTML page called *GetName.html* that accepts the name and then passes control back to the *Selection* servlet. Ensure that the user's initial selection is still stored in the session, as well as his/her name and any subsequent selections. Display the user's name in the checkout heading.

8.8 (i) Copy *CookieAdder.html* into your Web app's root folder. Then copy *CookieAdder.java*, *GetPreferences.java* and *ShowSum.java* into the *classes* folder

(ii) Add the appropriate tags to your deployment descriptor and compile the three servlets.

(iii) Start up Tomcat (stopping it first, if it is already running) and then access the above Web page via your browser. Experiment with differing input to the Web page. Notice that you will not be permitted to change your preferences immediately after entering them. However, since the cookies will 'time out' after a minute, you will be able to experiment with other values if you wait for this timeout and then re-load the initial page.

(iv) Modify *ShowSum.java* so that the result page shows either the date and time of the user's last visit to the page or, if it is the user's first visit, a message to indicate this. [Use new to create a Date object (package java.util) and the Date object's *toString* method to place the date value into a cookie.] Re-compile the servlet.

(v) Stop Tomcat, re-start it and then re-test the above application with the modified servlet.

Chapter 9
JavaServer Pages (JSPs)

Learning Objectives

After reading this chapter, you should:

- appreciate why the JavaServer Pages technology was introduced and the circumstances under which JSPs should be used instead of servlets;
- appreciate when JSPs and servlets may appropriately be used together;
- be aware of the process that occurs when a JSP is referenced by a browser;
- know the basic structure and allowable contents of a JSP;
- know how to combine the above elements to produce a working JSP;
- know how to combine JSPs and servlets in an application;
- know how to set up a JSP error page to handle exceptions generated by a JSP.

The term *JavaServer Pages* is used to refer to both a technology and the individual software entities created by that technology (though reference is often made, somewhat redundantly, to 'JSP Pages', rather than simply JSPs). The technology was introduced in late 1999 as a new Java API and is an extension of servlet technology. Like servlets, JSPs (the software entities) generate HTML pages with dynamic content. Unlike servlets, though, JSPs are not Java programs, but HTML documents with embedded Java code supplied via HTML-style tags. A JSP file must have the suffix *.jsp*, which will allow the JSP to be recognised by any JSP-aware Web server, so that the JSP filename may be supplied in a URL to a browser or may appear in the address for a hyperlink on an HTML page (as, indeed, may any servlet). We can use Tomcat to test our JSPs, just as we used it to test our servlets.

9.1 The Rationale Behind JSPs

Since JSPs serve essentially the same purpose as servlets, it is natural to ask why there is a need for both. The simple answer is that servlets require the expertise of Java programmers, whilst the production of Web pages for anything more than a

J. Graba, *An Introduction to Network Programming with Java: Java 7 Compatible*, 269
DOI 10.1007/978-1-4471-5254-5_9, © Springer-Verlag London 2013

simple site is usually the responsibility of Web page authors, who often do not have such programming skills. The introduction of the JavaServer Pages technology attempts to return the job of Web page authoring to those people whose responsibility it is, whilst the Java programmers maintain responsibility for the software components used upon the Web pages. Using JSPs rather than servlets also removes the rather tedious repetition of *out.println* for HTML tags.

However, the original JSP API still required Web page authors to supply small 'snippets' of Java code in their JSPs. Since those early days, much work has gone into producing additional HTML-style tags that will further reduce the amount of programming required in JSPs. The major output of this effort has been the **JavaServer Pages Standard Tag Library (JSTL)**, which was developed by the JSR-052 expert group as part of the Java Community Process. JSTL provides support for iterations, conditions, the processing of XML documents, internationalisation and database access using SQL. At its heart is Expression Language (EL), which is designed specifically for Web authors, and an enhanced version of EL was integrated into the JSP 2.0 specification. The latest version of JSTL at the time of writing is 1.2, which was released as long ago as May of 2006. JSTL 1.2 was integrated into the Java EE 5 platform and is present in Java EE 6, though no further development appears to have been made. Coverage of JSTL goes beyond the scope of this text, however, and no further mention will be made of it.

Although the remainder of this chapter will be devoted to the use of scripting within JSPs, it is worth pointing out that the use of scripting code should be kept to a minimum. It is also worth mentioning in passing that such scripting code may actually be provided in other languages (such as Perl, JavaScript or VBScript), but Java is the natural vehicle to use.

JSPs don't make servlets redundant. Servlets are still useful for supplying overall control to all/part of a Web site. This is achieved by a servlet receiving HTTP requests, determining what action to take, carrying out the necessary background processing (e.g., opening up a connection to a remote database) and then passing control to a JSP or ordinary HTML page that provides the response to the initial browser request. This last stage may involve the servlet selecting the appropriate page from a number of possible pages. Thus, servlets and JSPs may be used together in a complementary and harmonious manner.

Before we consider the structure and contents of a JSP, we shall examine what happens behind the scenes when a JSP is called up by a server…

9.2 Compilation and Execution

JSPs are held in the same Web application server folder as that holding HTML files. (For Tomcat, of course, this means the root folder of the Web application.) When a JSP is first referenced by a Web server, it is actually converted into a servlet. This servlet is then compiled and the compiled code stored on the server for subsequent referencing. (For Tomcat, this compiled code is stored in *<CATALINA_HOME>\work*.) If the referencing by the server was in response to a request for the JSP from a browser, the compiled code would then be executed. All subsequent browser requests for this JSP would cause the compiled code to be executed on the server. This would continue to be the case until either the server was shut down (a rare event for most Web servers) or the JSP source code was changed. (The Web server detects a change by comparing dates of source and compiled files.)

A consequence of the above is that, if the first time that a JSP is referenced by the Web server occurs when a request is received from a browser, there is a noticeable delay for the user of the browser as the Web server goes through the conversion and translation phases before executing the compiled code. In order to avoid this first-time delay, **pre-compiled JSPs** may be used. One way of creating pre-compiled JSPs is for the Web page developer to use a development environment to go through all the JSPs on the site (causing the conversion-compilation-execution cycle to be performed) and then save the resultant *.class* files in the appropriate directory of the production version of the site. However, a more convenient way of producing the precompiled pages is provided by the JSP specification in the form of a special request parameter called *jsp_precompile*. Use of this parameter avoids the need to execute the associated JSP and may be used by a JSP container to produce the required *.class* file(s). Like any request parameter included within a URL, *jsp_precompile* is preceded by a question mark. The following example shows the format required to precompile a JSP called *MyPage.jsp*:

```
MyPage.jsp?jsp_precompile
```

The parameter *jsp_precompile* is a Boolean parameter, so the above line could alternatively end in `jsp_precompile=true` to make this explicit. However, this is not necessary, since the default value for this parameter is `true`.

When a browser calls up a Web page, the Web server executes the compiled JSP elements to produce HTML elements, merges these with the static HTML elements of the page and serves up the completed page to the browser. One important difference between testing servlets and testing JSPs is that it is **not** necessary to stop and restart the server when changes are made to a JSP.

9.3 JSP Tags

In addition to standard HTML tags and ordinary text, a number of JSP-specific tags may be used on a JavaServer Page. The differing categories of JSP tag are listed below. This list is followed by a description of the purpose of each category, its required syntax and associated brief examples.

- Directives.
- Declarations.
- Expressions.
- Scriptlets.
- Comments.
- Actions.

Note that all of the keywords used in the tags below must be in **lower case**.

9.3.1 *Directives*

There are three tags in this category:

- **`page`** (used to define the attributes of the Web page, via a number of other keywords such as `language`, `contentType` and `import`);
- **`include`** (specifying an external file to be inserted);
- **`taglib`** (specifying a custom tag library to be used).

These directives are processed by the JSP engine upon conversion of the JSP into a servlet. Such tags commence with `<%@` and end with `%>`. Note there must be **no spaces** between `%` and `@`!

<u>Examples</u>

```
<%@ page language="java" contentType="text/html"
import="java.util.*" %>
```

(The `language` and `contentType` settings above are actually superfluous, since they are the default values.)

```
<%@ include file="myFile.html" %>
```

```
<%@ taglib uri="myTagLib" %>
```

Note the use of the `import` attribute with the `page` tag to allow the usual abbreviated reference to the contents of any available Java package.

9.3.2 *Declarations*

These declare variables for subsequent use in expressions or scriptlets. (See below.) The tags commence with `<%!` and end with `%>`.

<u>Examples</u>

```
<%! int visitCount; %>
<%! Date today = new Date(); %>
```

Such declarations refer to instance variables of the servlet class that will be created from this JSP and will be recognised within any subsequent JSP tags on the page.

9.3.3 *Expressions*

These tags are used to specify Java expressions, the values of which will be calculated and inserted into the current page. Such an expression can involve any valid combination of literals, variables, operators and/or method calls that returns a value that can be displayed on a Web page. The tags commence with <%= and end with %>.

Examples

```
<%= origPrice*(1+VAT) %>
<%= today.getMonth() %>
```

Not that, unlike declarations (and scriptlets below), an expression must **not** be terminated with a semi-colon

9.3.4 Scriptlets

Scriptlets are blocks of Java code that are to be executed when the JSP is called up. It is possible to include large amounts of code via this method, but that would not be good practice. As noted in Sect. 9.1, such code should be kept to a minimum. It will be seen in the latter part of the next chapter that the bulk of such processing may be encapsulated within a JavaBean, the methods of which may then be called from the JSP. Methods of the standard Java classes may also be called, of course. Scriptlets tags commence with <% and end with %>.

Example

```
<%
   //'total' and 'numArray' are pre-declared.
   total = 0;
   for (int i=0; i<numArray.length; i++)
      total+=numArray[i];
%>
Total:
<%= total %>
```

The value of any output may be varied according to whether a particular condition is true or not.

Example

```
<%
   if today.getHours() < 12
   {
%>
Good morning!
<%
   }
   else
   {
%>
```

```
Good afternoon!
<%
    }
%>
```

Declarations may also be made within scriptlets and will be recognised within any subsequent JSP tags on the page.

9.3.5 *Comments*

These are similar to HTML comments, but are removed from the page before it is sent to the browser. They commence with `<%--` and end with `--%>`.

Example

```
<%-- Search algorithm --%>
```

Such tags are effective for only one line, so multi-line comments necessitate the repeated use of these tags.

Example

```
<%-- Search algorithm --%>
<%-- Implements Quicksort --%>
```

9.3.6 *Actions*

Action tags perform various functions that extend the standard capabilities of JSPs, such as making use of JavaBeans. The opening tag specifies a library and an action name, separated from each other by a colon. The closing ‘>’ is preceded by a forward slash (‘/’).

Example

```
<jsp:useBean id="manager" class="staff.Personnel"
scope="session" />
```

The reference to `useBean` and associated attributes here indicates the use of a JavaBean. (There will be extensive coverage of JavaBeans in the next chapter.)

9.4 Implicit JSP Objects

To provide the flexibility required by dynamic Web sites, a JSP-aware Web server automatically makes available a number of objects that may be used by JSPs without explicit declaration. There are nine such objects, as shown in Table 9.1. These implicit objects are instances of the classes defined by the servlet and JSP specifications. The last three objects are very rarely used. Variable *out* is also not often required.

Table 9.1 The implicit JSP objects

Variable	Type	Purpose
`request`	`HttpServletRequest`	Http request originally sent to server
`response`	`HttpServletResponse`	Http response to request
`session`	`HttpSession`	*Session* object associated with the above request and response
`application`	`ServletContext`	Holds references to other objects that more than one user may access, such as a database link
`out`	`JspWriter`	Object that writes to the response output stream
`exception`	`Throwable`	Contains information about a runtime error and is available only on error pages
`pageContext`	`PageContext`	Encapsulates the page context
`config`	`ServletConfig`	*ServletConfig* object for this JSP
`page`	`Object`	The *this* object reference in this JSP

ServletContext is an interface implemented by each servlet engine that provides a servlet with methods that allow it to find out about its environment (independent of any individual session). This interface has two methods that mirror the *Session* class's methods *getAttribute* and *setAttribute*. The two methods have names, arguments and return types that are identical to those of the corresponding *Session* methods. The signatures for these methods are repeated below.

- `public Object getAttribute(String <name>)`
- `public void setAttribute(String <name>,`
  `Object <attribute>)`

As shown in Table 9.1, the implicit object *application* is the *ServletContext* object that is created automatically for a JSP and allows the programmer to retrieve and set environment-level properties via the two methods above.

In the examples below, note the need for typecasting with *getAttribute*, since it returns an *Object* reference.

<u>Examples</u>

```
String userName =
          (String)application.getAttribute("name");
Float balanceObject =
        (Float)application.getAttribute("balance");
setAttribute("total", new Integer(0));
```

Other methods of object *application* that are sometimes useful are listed below and have purposes that are self-evident.

- `public Enumeration getAttributeNames()`
- `public void removeAttribute(String name)`

9.5 Collaborating with Servlets

Since servlets are often used in combination with JSPs, it is useful to consider the methods that can be made use of to allow the two to collaborate easily. The two major ways in which servlets and JSPs may wish to share information are the sharing of data related to an individual user's session and the sharing of data related to the application environment that is applicable to all users who visit the site. For JSPs, these two categories of information are provided by the implicit objects *session* and *application* respectively. We need to consider what objects will supply the same information via servlets and how this information may be passed between servlets and JSPs. It turns out that this is considerably easier than might at first be thought.

If a *Session* object has already been created by a servlet (in the same session) when a JSP is referenced, then the JSP implicit object *session* will contain any attribute-value pairs that were placed in the original *Session* object. Thus, object *session* may simply use its *getAttribute* method to retrieve any information stored by the servlet.

Class *HttpServlet* implements interface *ServletConfig* through its superclass, *GenericServlet*. This interface has a method called *getServletContext* that returns a *ServletContext* reference. In order to gain read/write access to environment-level information, then, a servlet first calls this method and stores the *ServletContext* reference that is returned. It then invokes methods *getAttribute* and *setAttribute* on the *ServletContext* reference, in the same way that those methods are invoked on the implicit object *application* in JSPs.

Example

```
ServletContext context = getServletContext();
String userName =
            (String)context.getAttribute("name");
```

Analogous to the situation with the sharing of session information, the object *application* created when the JSP is first referenced will automatically contain any attribute-value pairs that have been set up previously by a servlet.

9.6 JSPs in Action

Now that the basic structure of a JSP has been explained and the allowable contents identified, it is time to look at an example JSP application. To illustrate how JSPs may be used in collaboration with servlets, rather than having the dynamic content of a Web site provided entirely via servlets, the shopping cart example from the previous chapter will be re-implemented.

Example

The initial page will be renamed *ShoppingCartX.html*. The only change required for this page is the address for the form's *ACTION* attribute. Instead of specifying a servlet called *Selection*, this will now specify a JSP called *Selection.jsp*:

```
<FORM METHOD=POST ACTION="Selection.jsp">
```

The code for *Selection.jsp* is shown below, with JSP-specific content shown in bold. Note that, if the 'Checkout' option is selected by the user, control is now re-directed to another JSP (viz., *Checkout.jsp*), rather than to servlet *Checkout*. Note also how use is made of the implicit object *session* to store the value of the current product, without the necessity for creating a *Session* object explicitly (as was the case in the *selection* servlet).

In the servlet-only version of this application, control is then passed to a *Weight* servlet. Since this servlet's activities consist entirely of background processing and re-direction to the next appropriate page, with no Web page output being generated, this is an ideal opportunity for keeping the servlet. There are one or two minor changes that need to be made to this servlet (as will be identified shortly) and the modified servlet will be named *WeightX*. The reference to this servlet is also shown in bold type below.

```
<!-- Selection.jsp -->

<HTML>
   <HEAD>
      <TITLE><%= currentProduct %></TITLE>
      <STYLE>
         body{text-align=center; color=blue;}
      </STYLE>
   </HEAD>

   <BODY>

   <%
      String currentProduct;

      currentProduct = request.getParameter("Product");
      if (currentProduct.equals("Checkout"))
         response.sendRedirect("Checkout.jsp");
      else
         session.setAttribute(
                             "currentProd",currentProduct);
   %>
    <H1><P STYLE="color:red"><%= currentProduct %>
      </P></H1>
      <BR><BR><BR>
```

```
    <FORM METHOD=POST ACTION="WeightX">
      <TABLE>
         <TR>
            <TD>Quantity required (kg)
            <INPUT TYPE='Text' NAME=Qty VALUE=''
                                          SIZE=5></ TD>
         </TR>
      </TABLE>
      <BR><BR><BR>
      <TABLE>
         <TR>
            <TD><INPUT TYPE='Radio' NAME='Option'
                                    VALUE='Add' CHECKED>
            Add to cart.
         </TR>
         <TR>
            <TD><INPUT TYPE='Radio' NAME='Option'
                                         VALUE='Remove'>
            Remove item from cart.
         </TR>
         <TR>
            <TD><INPUT TYPE='Radio' NAME='Option'
                                           VALUE='Next'>
            Choose next item.
         </TR>
         <TR>
           <TD><INPUT TYPE='Radio' NAME='Option'
                                       VALUE='Checkout'>
            Go to checkout.
         </TR>
      </TABLE>
      <BR><BR><BR>
      <INPUT TYPE='Submit' VALUE='Submit'>
    </FORM>
  </BODY>
</HTML>
```

The only lines in the original *Weight* servlet requiring change are the class header line and those lines specifying URLs. The changed lines (with changes indicated in bold) are shown below.

```
public class WeightX extends HttpServlet
```

```
response.sendRedirect("ShoppingCartX.html");
```
(There are three occurrences of the above line.)

```
response.sendRedirect("Checkout.jsp");
```

File *WeightX.java*, which encapsulates this servlet, will need to be compiled before running the application, of course.

Finally, we come to the code for the JSP corresponding to the *Checkout* servlet (which, naturally enough, will be named *Checkout.jsp*). We can't use either *printf* (a method of the *PrintStream* class) or *format* (a method of the *PrintWriter* class) to format our decimal output, since we have neither a *PrintStream* object nor a *PrintWriter* object that we can use. Consequently, we shall have to use the static method *format* of the *String* class.

Since a reference to an object of class *Enumeration* (from package *java.util*) is returned by the *Session* class's *getAttributeNames* method, we shall make use of the `import` attribute of the JSP directive `page`. As in *Selection.jsp*, use will be made of the implicit JSP object *session*, rather than a *Session* object that has been created explicitly by this application. Once again, the JSP-specific code is shown in bold type…

```
<!-- Checkout.jsp -->

<%@ page import="java.util.Enumeration" %>

<HTML>
   <HEAD>
      <TITLE>Checkout</TITLE>
      <STYLE>
        body{text-align=center; }
        table,th,td{border:2px solid black;}
        table{background-color:aqua;}
     </STYLE>
   </HEAD>

   <BODY>
   <%
      final float APPLES_PRICE = 1.45F;
      final float PEARS_PRICE = 1.75F;
      //In a real application, the above prices would be
      //retrieved from a database, of course.
   %>
```

```
        <BR><BR><BR>

        <H1><P STYLE="color:red">Order List</P></H1>
        <BR><BR><BR>

        <TABLE>
           <TR>
              <TH>Item</TH>
              <TH>Weight(kg)</TH>
              <TH>Cost(£)</TH>
           </TR>

<!-- Now make use of the implicit object session -->
<!-- to retrieve the contents of the shopping cart… -->
<%
   session.removeAttribute("currentProd");
   //(Removes "Checkout".)

   Enumeration prodNames = session.getAttributeNames();
   float totalCost = 0;

   int numProducts = 0;
   while (prodNames.hasMoreElements())
   {
      float wt=0,cost=0;
      String product = (String)prodNames.nextElement();
      String stringWt =
                  (String)session.getAttribute(product);
      wt = Float.parseFloat(stringWt);
      if (product.equals("Apples"))
         cost = APPLES_PRICE * wt;
      else if (product.equals("Pears"))
         cost = PEARS_PRICE * wt;
%>

           <TR>
              <TD><%= product %></TD>
              <TD><%= wt %></TD>
              <TD><%= String.format("%.2f",cost) %></TD>
           </TR>

<%
      totalCost+=cost;
      numProducts++;
   }
%>
           <TR STYLE="background-color:yellow">
<%
   if (numProducts == 0)
   {
```

```
%>
            <TD>*** No orders placed! ***</TD>
        </TR>
<%
    }
    else
    {
%>
        <TR STYLE="background-color:yellow">
            <TD></TD>       <!-- Blank cell -->
            <TD>Total cost:</TD>
            <TD>
           <%= String.format("%.2f",totalCost) %></ TD>
        </TR>
<%
    }
%>

      </TABLE>

   </BODY>

</HTML>
```

Actually, there is really more Java code here than there should be in any JSP. The material on the use of **JavaBeans** in JSPs in the latter part of the next chapter should serve to demonstrate how this problem may be solved.

9.7 Error Pages

In common with other network software, JSPs can generate errors for a variety of reasons, even when all syntax errors have been eradicated. For example, a database connection can fail or the user can enter invalid data. Ideally, our software should be able to handle such situations in a graceful manner by supplying a meaningful message for the user and, if possible, providing him/her with a way to recover from the situation (possibly by re-entering data). As things stand at present in our shopping cart application, the generation of an exception by our code will result in a non-helpful error page being served up by Tomcat in the user's browser (often, but not always, relating to error 500). In fact, some JSP containers do not even provide this much assistance to the user.

Consequently, instead of relying upon the error-handling facilities provided by the JSP container (which will not be user-orientated), we should try to handle exceptions gracefully in our own code. We **could** use a servlet to build up an error page and redirect control to this page, but this is not necessary. A way of handling errors is provided by the JSP specification in the form of programmer-designated error pages, the contents of which are created by the programmer. To associate an error page with the current JSP, we make use of an attribute of the `page` directive that we have not yet encountered: `errorPage`. For example:

```
<%@ page errorPage="MyErrorPage.jsp" %>
```

To illustrate the use of such a page, the *AdderServlet* from Chap. 8 will now be converted into a JSP. As in previous examples, all JSP-specific code will be emboldened.

Example

Note the specification of the associated error page in the second line of code below.

```
<!-- Adder.jsp -->
<%@ page errorPage="NumError.jsp" %>
<%
      String value1 = request.getParameter("Num1");
      String value2 = request.getParameter("Num2");
      int num1 = Integer.parseInt(value1);
      int num2 = Integer.parseInt(value2);
      int sum = num1 + num2;
%>
<HTML>
   <HEAD>
      <TITLE>Result</TITLE>
   </HEAD>
   <BODY>
      <BR><BR><BR>
      <CENTER><H1><FONT COLOR='blue'>
      <%= "Result = " + sum %>
      </FONT></H1></CENTER>
   </BODY>
</HTML>
```

The initial Web page (originally called *SimpleAdder.html*) will need to have the URL of its form's *ACTION* attribute modified so that it refers to our JSP, of course:

```
<FORM METHOD=POST ACTION="Adder.jsp">
```

This opening file will itself be renamed *SimpleAdder*X*.html*.

All that remains now is to specify the code for the error page itself. This file must use attribute `isErrorPage` of the `page` directive to specify its error page status. This attribute is a Boolean value and should be set to the value *true*, specified as a string (i.e., enclosed by speech marks):

```
<%@ page isErrorPage="true" %>
```

In this simple application, it is highly likely that the error that has been generated has been caused by the user entering invalid (i.e., non-numeric) data. This being the case, all that we really want to do is display an appropriate error message and then give the user the opportunity to re-submit the data. However, this program will also be used to illustrate the use of the implicit JSP object *exception* (shown in Table 9.1 of Sect. 9.4). Though this object would normally be used only within the internal processing of our JSP, we shall make use of its *toString* method to display the name of the exception that has been generated. (This is unlikely to be of any interest to the user, of course, and would not normally be included in JSP output.) As usual, all JSP-specific code will be shown in bold text…

```
<!-- NumError.jsp -->

<%@ page isErrorPage="true" %>

<HTML>

   <HEAD>
      <TITLE>Error Page</TITLE>
   </HEAD>

   <BODY>
      <BR><BR><BR>
      <CENTER><H3>Data Entry Error<BR><BR>
      <FONT COLOR="red"><%= exception.toString() %>
      </FONT></H3>
      <BR><BR><BR>

      <FORM METHOD=GET ACTION="SimpleAdderX.html">
         <INPUT TYPE="Submit" VALUE="Try again">
      </FORM>
      <CENTER>
   </BODY>

</HTML>
```

The output from *SimpleAdderX.html* and *Adder.jsp* will be exactly the same as that generated by *SimpleAdder.html* and *AdderServlet* respectively, of course. Such output is illustrated in Figs. 8.5 and 8.6 of the previous chapter. An example of the output generated by *NumError.jsp* when the user enters a non-numeric value is shown in Fig. 9.1.

***** Warning! *****

When Internet Explorer 5.5 onwards is used with Tomcat 5 onwards, the default action for the browser when it receives an HTTP 500 error code ('Internal server error') is to display its own (rather unhelpful!) error page, rather than displaying the JSP error page. In order to correct this default action, it is necessary to amend the settings in Explorer as indicated below.

1. Select *Tools->Internet Options* from Explorer's menus.
2. Select the *Advanced* tab.

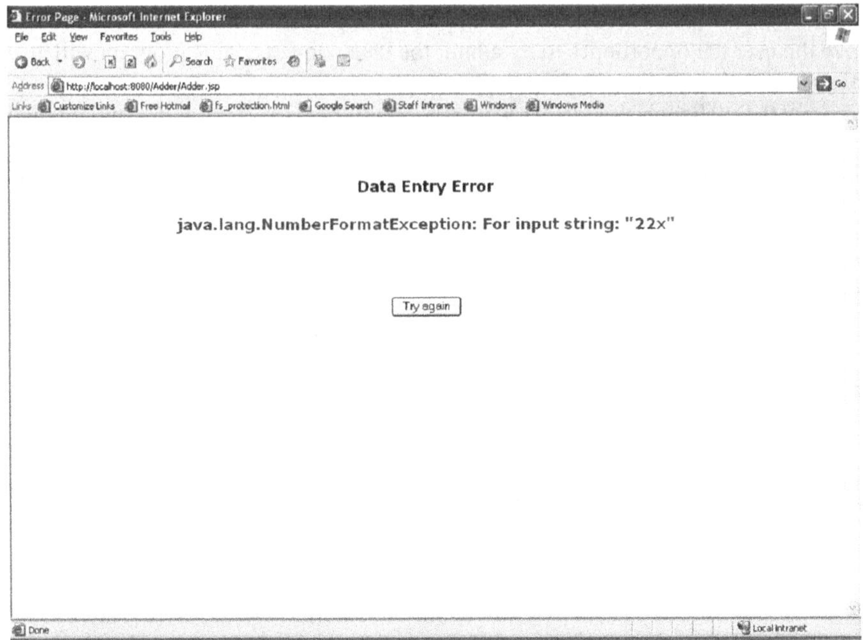

Fig. 9.1 JSP error page output

3. Scroll down the list of settings to locate 'Show friendly HTTP error messages'.
4. **Un**tick (!) this option and click on *OK*.

   Your JSP error pages should work fine after this.

9.8 Using JSPs to Access Remote Databases

One very powerful and increasingly popular application of JSPs is to provide Web access to databases. This can be done (via JDBC) in several ways:

- by placing the required Java statements into the JSP (producing an excessive amount of Java code in the JSP);
- by defining custom action tags (not covered in this text);
- by employing JavaBeans (probably the best way).

Since JavaBeans are not covered until the next chapter, it is not appropriate to describe the technique here. However, most of the latter part of the next chapter is devoted to the use of JavaBeans within JSPs, with the accessing of databases being used as the central vehicle for illustration.

Exercises

For the exercises below, it would be appropriate to create one or more Web applications. (One would be quite sufficient, but you might choose to create a separate one for each exercise.)

9.1 Write a JSP that simply displays the current date and time when it is opened.

9.2 Create a simple HTML page containing a single button that takes the user to a JSP called *Count1.jsp*. Now create a JSP with this name that uses a session variable (i.e., an attribute set up by object *session*) to display the number of times that the user has visited the page during this session. Add a button that takes the user back to the HTML page.

9.3 Extend *Count1.jsp* (copying and renaming it as *Count2.jsp*?) so that the *application* object is used to display the total number of times that the page has been visited by anybody (in all sessions). If you use a name for the JSP that is different from the one used in the previous question, remember to modify the initial HTML page (copying and renaming it?) so that pressing the button takes the user back to the correct JSP. When testing this program, open up two browser windows and observe the difference between the two counts in each pair and the difference between the contents of the two windows.

9.4 There is now too much Java code in the JSP of the previous exercise and this should really be moved to a servlet. Introduce a servlet that will do the background processing and then redirect control to the (reduced) JSP.

9.5 Re-write *PersonalServlet* (and its associated HTML page) from Chap. 8 so that a JSP is used instead of the servlet. (Use the implicit object *request*.)

9.6 Create an error page for the above JSP that displays a meaningful error message and allows the user to re-enter his/her name if no name was entered initially. Modify the original JSP so that (a) it registers the error page and (b) it throws a general *Exception* object if no name is entered by the user. (Once again, remember to modify the original HTML page to reflect any name change in your JSP.)

9.7 Re-write *AdderServlet* (and its associated HTML page) from Chap. 8 so that a JSP is used instead of the servlet. Create an error page that displays a meaningful error message if non-numeric data is entered and allows the user to re-enter the values.

9.8 (i) Create three *Exception* classes (using `extends Exception`) that correspond respectively to the following error situations:

- the first of the operands in the preceding exercise being non-numeric;
- the second being non-numeric;
- both being non-numeric.

Give these classes empty constructor bodies, define the *toString* method for each to return a meaningful error message and place the classes in a package called *errorExceptions*. Create a subdirectory of *classes* called *errorExceptions* and save these *Exception* classes (at least the *.class* files) into this directory.

(ii) Modify the JSP of the preceding exercise so that it imports package *errorExceptions* and throws an object of one of the three *Exception* classes just defined, according to whether the first operand, the second operand or both is/are non-numeric. (This involves some interesting logic that includes nested `try` blocks.) If you are going to change the name of your error page (which will require modification, as noted below), remember to change its name in this JSP's `page` directive.

(iii) Modify the associated JSP error page so that it makes use of the *toString* method of the implicit *exception* object (if it didn't already do so) and allows return to the correct JSP.

Chapter 10
JavaBeans

Learning Objectives

After reading this chapter, you should:

- understand the rationale behind JavaBeans;
- appreciate the potential offered by JavaBeans;
- know how to create a JavaBean and how to expose selected properties of the bean;
- know how to use a JAR file to package a JavaBean and its associated files;
- know how to cause changes in one bean's properties to have automatic effects on other beans;
- know how to make use of beans in an application program;
- know how to make use of beans in JSPs, both via direct invocation of bean methods and via HTML tags.

For a number of years, one of the primary goals of software engineering has been to create and make use of general-purpose software components that may be 'plugged' into a variety of applications. The internal workings of such components are hidden from the application developer and are of no concern to him/her. The only things that the developer needs to know are what purpose the component serves and what interface it provides (i.e., what parameters need to be passed to the component and what value(s) the component will return). The major advantages of such components are fairly obvious:

- greatly reduced time and expense for software development, as developers reuse software and avoid 'reinventing the wheel';
- much more reliable software (since the reused components will generally have been used in many other applications and will be 'tried and tested').

One of the most well known and widely used component models is Microsoft's ActiveX. Powerful though its capabilities are, it has one major drawback: it is dependent upon the MS Windows platform (though moves have been made to alleviate this situation). Java provides a platform-independent alternative to this with its JavaBeans component model.

J. Graba, *An Introduction to Network Programming with Java: Java 7 Compatible*, DOI 10.1007/978-1-4471-5254-5_10, © Springer-Verlag London 2013

JavaBeans was introduced into Java with JDK1.1. In recognition of the fact that other component models were already in existence, the designers of Java tried to ensure that JavaBeans components were interoperable with components designed under these other models. A notable example of this attempt is the ***ActiveX bridge***, which can be used to convert a JavaBean into an ActiveX component that can then be used on a Windows platform. (In addition, Microsoft has opened up the ActiveX technology to development in a range of languages, including Java.)

An individual JavaBeans component is often referred to as a JavaBean or simply a 'bean'. Before we look at the construction of JavaBeans, it will help in the understanding of what JavaBeans are and how useful they can be by pointing out an important fact that concerns most of the classes that we have used in our GUI programs: **all Swing and AWT components are JavaBeans**. GUI components make ideal JavaBeans, since they are required in a vast number of applications and would necessitate an enormous amount of tedious, repetitive coding if they did not exist. In keeping with the component technology ethos, the application programmer needs to know nothing of the internal workings of such components. All that he/she needs to know are what method names and arguments must be supplied and what values are returned by those methods.

10.1 Creating a JavaBean

A bean class has the same basic structure as an ordinary Java class, but with the particular characteristics listed below.

1. It **must** be within a named package (and so within a folder of the same name).
2. Each (non-library) public method should begin with either 'get' or 'set'.
3. It does not usually have a *main* method, but will have if some initial activity is required.

There are three basic steps in the creation of a bean, as stated below.

1. Write the program code for the required bean functionality.
2. Add any accessor and mutator ('get' and 'set') methods required to allow users to examine/change properties.
3. Compile the bean and possibly wrap it (and any required resource files) in a JAR (Java Archive) file. The latter operation is only really necessary if the bean is going to be 'fed' into an IDE.

Consideration of 'get' and 'set' methods will be postponed for the time being while we consider a JavaBean that (initially) makes no use of these methods.

Example

To make things a little more interesting than they might otherwise be, we'll set up a bean to run an animation that involves the Java mascot 'Duke' juggling some peanuts. A separate thread could be set up to handle the animation, but it is convenient to make use of an object of class *Timer* (a Swing class). Since the reader may be unfamiliar with aspects of this technique, a little time will be taken to explain the basic steps…

The *Timer* object takes two arguments:

- an integer delay (in milliseconds);
- a reference to an *ActionListener*.

The *Timer* object automatically calls method *actionPerformed* at intervals prescribed by the above delay. The *ActionListener* can conveniently be the application container itself, of course. Inside the *actionPerformed* method will simply be a call to *repaint*, which automatically calls method *paint* (which cannot itself be called directly). Each time that *paint* is called, it will display the next image from the sequence of frames making up the animation. Inbuilt methods *start* and *stop* will be called to start/stop the *Timer*.

The bean application class upon which the images will be displayed will extend class *JPanel*. The images themselves will be held in *ImageIcon*s and *paint* will display an individual image by calling *ImageIcon* method *paintIcon* on an individual image. This method takes four arguments:

- a reference to the component upon which the image will be displayed (usually *this*, for the application container);
- a reference to the *Graphics* object used to render this image (provided by the argument to *paint*);
- the x-coordinate of the upper-left corner of the image's display position;
- the y-coordinate of the upper-left corner of the image's display position.

There is one final point to note before we look at the code for this example:

- the *BeanBox* takes the size of the bean from method *getPreferredSize* of class *Component*, which takes a *Dimension* argument specifying the container's width and height.

Now for the code…

```
package animBeans;

import java.awt.*;
import java.awt.event.*;
import javax.swing.*;

public class AnimBean1 extends JPanel
                              implements ActionListener
{
   private ImageIcon[] image;

   private String imageName = "juggler";
   /*
   The above string forms the first part of the name for
```

```
each image in the sequence. Appended to this will be
an integer in the range 0-3, followed by the suffix
'.gif' (so names will be 'juggler0.gif', …,
'juggler3.gif').
*/

private final int NUM_FRAMES = 4;

private int currentImage = 0;
//Holds no. of current frame.

private final int DELAY = 100; //100/1000sec = 0.1sec
//(May need to be adjusted for different processors.)

private Timer animTimer;

public static void main(String[] args)
{
   AnimBean1 animation = new AnimBean1();

   //If panel size is set here, it is ignored!

   animation.setVisible(true);
}

public AnimBean1()
{
   //Set up array of images…
   image = new ImageIcon[NUM_FRAMES];

   for (int i=0; i<image.length; i++)
   {
      image[i] =
            new ImageIcon(imageName + i + ".gif");
   }

   animTimer = new Timer(DELAY,this);

   //Call inbuilt method start of Timer object…
   animTimer.start();
}

public void paint(Graphics g)
{

   //Display next frame in sequence…
   image[currentImage].paintIcon(this,g,0,0);

   //Update number of frame to be displayed, in
   //preparation for next call of this method…
   currentImage = (currentImage+1)%NUM_FRAMES;
}
```

```
    public void actionPerformed(ActionEvent event)
    {
        repaint();
    }
    public Dimension getPreferredSize()
    {

        //This is the method from which the
        //application panel gets its size…
        return new Dimension(140,120);
    }
}
```

Having created and compiled the above code, we **may** now need to package the bean (and any required GIF files) within a JAR file, so that the bean may be loaded into a particular IDE or transmitted easily across a network. (If this is not a requirement for you, then there is no need to do this.) JAR files are compressed by default, using the same format as ZIP files. To do the packaging, we make use of Java's *jar* utility. The syntax for executing this utility is:

```
jar <options> [<manifest>] <JAR_file> <file_list>
```

(Note that the order of parameters is not fixed. In particular, the second and third parameters may be reversed.)

The third parameter specifies the name of the JAR file, which will normally have the *.jar* extension. The final parameter specifies the files that are to go into this JAR file. The second parameter specifies the name of a manifest file that will hold information about the contents of the JAR file. The manifest is normally a very short text file. Though optional, it is good practice to include it, since it provides the user with an easy way of finding out the contents of the JAR file without actually running the associated JavaBean. At the very least, the manifest will have two lines specifying a bean class file by naming the file (via property *Name*) and stating explicitly (via Boolean property *Java-Bean*) that the file holds a JavaBean.

Example

```
Name: beanPackage/MyBean.class
Java-Bean: True
```

Any other class files will also be listed, each separated from the preceding class by a blank line.

Example

```
Name: beanPackage/MyBean.class
Java-Bean: True
Name: SupportClass1.class

Name: SupportClass2.class
```

(We could also have further beans in the same JAR file.)

If the bean contains a *main* method, the first line of the manifest will use a *Main-Class* specifier to name the containing class, followed by a blank line. The manifest for our animation bean is as follows:

```
Main-Class: AnimBean1

Name: animBeans/AnimBean1.class
Java-6: True
```

All that needs to be explained now before looking at full command lines that will create JAR files is the meaning of the first parameter supplied to the *jar* utility (the *options* parameter). 'Options' are single letters that appear consecutively. The possible values for such options are **c**, **f**, **m**, **t**, **v**, **x** and **0**. The meanings of these values are shown in Table 10.1.

Table 10.1 Option values for the *jar* utility

Option	Meaning
c	Create a new JAR file
f	If combined with 'c', specifies that file to be created is named on command line; if used with 't' or 'x', specifies that an existing file is named
m	Use manifest file named on command line
t	List table of contents for JAR file
v	'Verbose' output: generate additional output (file sizes, etc.)
x	Extract file named on command line or, if none specified, **all** files in directory
0	Suppress compression of files

Examples

1. `jar cmf MyManifest.mf MyBean.jar *.class`
   (Creates a JAR file called *MyBean.jar* containing all *.class* files in the current directory and allocates manifest file *MyManifest.mf* to the JAR file.)

2. `jar tf OldBean.jar`
   (Lists the contents of *OldBean.jar*.)

Assuming (i) that our manifest file is called *AnimManifest1.mf*, (ii) that we are executing the *jar* utility from the folder that holds the manifest file, (iii) the bean folder is immediately below the current folder and (iv) we wish to call our JAR file *Animation1.jar*, the required command line is:

```
jar cmf AnimManifest1.mf Animation1.jar animBeans\
AnimBean1.class
```

Note the use of a backslash for the Windows platform here, but the use of a forward slash in the manifest file! It is very easy to make a slip with this.

Having packaged our bean, we can open it up in an IDE (if our IDE has such a facility) or send the JAR file across a network. More commonly, we will probably leave the bean unpackaged and make use of it within an application. This will be covered in Sect. 10.4, but first we need to consider the mechanism for making use of a bean's properties.

10.2 Exposing a Bean's Properties

The users of a bean may be given read and/or write access to the properties (data values) of a bean via 'get' and 'set' (accessor and mutator) methods respectively that are built into the design of the bean. For a property with name *prop* of type *T*, the corresponding methods will have the following signatures:

- `public T getProp()`
- `public void setProp(T value)`

For example, if users of a bean with a property called *colour* are to be given read-and-write access to this property, then the bean designer would provide methods *getColour* and *setColour* as part of the bean's interface. If only read access is to be granted, then only the former method would be made available. If *prop* is a Boolean property, then method name *isProp* is used instead of *getProp* (and returns a *boolean* value, of course).

<u>Example</u>

For purposes of illustration, we'll expose properties *delay* and *imageName* of our animation bean, granting read-and-write access to both of these properties. Implementation of methods *getDelay*, *setDelay* and *getImageName* is reasonably straightforward, but the implementation of method set*ImageName* requires the erasing of the old image and the loading of frames for the new animation. Using our previous program (*AnimBean1.java*) as our starting point, the additions and modifications required to expose properties *delay* and *imageName* are shown in bold text below.

In order for this program to work, the GIF files used in any animation sequence must have names comprising a fixed string followed by an integer, with integer values covering the range 0…n−1 for a sequence of n frames. (E.g., *cartoon0*, *cartoon1*,…, *cartoon5* for a sequence of six frames.)

```
package animBeans;
import java.awt.*;
import java.awt.event.*;
import javax.swing.*;
import java.io.File;

public class AnimBean2 extends JPanel
                                    implements ActionListener
{
   private ImageIcon[] image;
   private String imageName = "juggler";

   private String oldImage = "juggler";
   //Need to save old image name so that code can
   //compare this with current image name and determine
   //whether user has changed the image name.
```

```
private int numFrames; //(No longer a constant.)
private int oldNumFrames;  //No. of frames in
                           //previous image.
private int currentImage = 0;
private int delay = 100;  //(No longer a constant.)
private Timer animTimer;

public static void main(String[] args)
{
   AnimBean2 anim = new AnimBean2();
   anim.setVisible(true);
}

public AnimBean2()
{
   //Loading of frames not done just once now,
   //so must be moved out of constructor…
   loadFrames();

   animTimer = new Timer(delay,this);
   animTimer.start();
}

private void loadFrames()
{
   //Check no. of frames in animation first…
   numFrames = 0;
   File fileName =
           new File(imageName + numFrames + ".gif");
   while (fileName.exists())
   {

      //Increment frame count for each image in
      //sequence that is found…
      numFrames++;

      //Update filename to check for next frame in
      //sequence…
      fileName =
           new File(imageName + numFrames + ".gif");
   }
   if (numFrames==0)   //No image found!
      return;          //Abandon loading of frames.

   //Following lines moved from constructor
   //(with no. of frames now variable)…
   image = new ImageIcon[numFrames];
   //Now load frames…
```

```
      for (int i=0; i<numFrames; i++)
      {
         image[i] =
                 new ImageIcon(imageName + i + ".gif");
      }
   }

   public void paint(Graphics g)
   {
      //Check whether user has changed
      //imageName property…
      if (!imageName.equals(oldImage))
      {
         //Load new frame sequence…
         loadFrames();
         if (numFrames==0)    //No image found!
         {
            //Reset image name and no. of frames
            //to their old values…
            setImageName(oldImage);
            numFrames = oldNumFrames;
         }
         else
         {
            oldImage = imageName;
            oldNumFrames = numFrames;
            //Retrieve background colour…
            g.setColor(getBackground());
            //Erase old image by filling old image area
            //with background colour…
            g.fillRect(0,0,getWidth(),getHeight());
            //Reset frame count to first frame in new
            //sequence…
            currentImage = 0;
         }
      }
      if (numFrames>0)
      {
         image[currentImage].paintIcon(this,g,0,0);
         currentImage = (currentImage+1)%numFrames;
      }
   }
```

```
    public void actionPerformed(ActionEvent event)
    {
        repaint();
    }

    public String getImageName()
    {
        return imageName;
    }

    public void setImageName(String name)
    {
        //Simple assignment for this property…
        imageName = name;
    }

    public int getDelay()
    {
        return delay;
    }

    public void setDelay(int delayIn)
    {
        delay = delayIn;

        //Also need to reset Timer delay for
        //this property…
        animTimer.setDelay(delay);
    }

    public Dimension getPreferredSize()
    {
        return new Dimension(140,120);
    }
}
```

Using a manifest called *AnimManifest2.mf* and JAR file called *Animation2.jar*, the command to package the above bean into a JAR file is:

```
jar cmf AnimManifest2.mf Animation2.jar animBeans\
AnimBean2.class
```

10.3 Making Beans Respond to Events

We can add some sophistication to our bean by introducing buttons that will allow the user to have greater control over the operation of the bean. As an example of this, we shall introduce buttons into our animation bean that will allow the user to stop and restart the animation whenever he/she wishes. In order to support this additional functionality, we shall have to introduce methods *stopAnimation* and *startAnimation* that will be executed in response to the button presses. The former will simply need to stop the *Timer* object, but the latter will need to check whether it is the first time that the animation is being started. If it is, then the *Timer* object will have to be created and started; if not, then the *Timer* method *restart* will have to be called if the animation is not currently running. The code for these two methods is shown below (and would be incorporated into bean *AnimBean*3).

```
public void startAnimation()
 {
    //Check whether this is first time during current
    //run of program that animation is being run...
    if (animTimer == null)
    {
        //First run of animation, so set current frame
       //to first one in sequence, create Timer and
       //start Timer running...
       currentImage = 0;
       animTimer = new Timer(delay,this);
       animTimer.start();
    }
    else
       //Not first time that animation is being run,
       //so check that it is not still running...
       if (!animTimer.isRunning())
       //Not currently running, so safe to restart...
          animTimer.restart();
 }
 public void stopAnimation()
 {
    animTimer.stop();
 }
```

As well as adding these two methods, we shall need to replace lines

```
animTimer = new Timer(delay,this);
animTimer.start();
```

in the constructor with the following line:

```
startAnimation();
```

10.4 Using JavaBeans Within an Application

Once a bean has been created and compiled, we can use it as we would any GUI component (though the program using it need not be a GUI). We should import the bean class explicitly, of course.

Example

This example simply places an instance of *AnimBean1* [See earlier part of this chapter] onto the application frame, whereupon the juggler animation commences. Note that the required GIF files must be on the system *PATH*.

```
import java.awt.*;
import java.awt.event.*;
import javax.swing.*;
import animBeans.AnimBean1;    //Note this inclusion.

public class AnimBeanApp1 extends JFrame
{
   public static void main(String[] args)
   {
      AnimBeanApp1 frame = new AnimBeanApp1();

      frame.setSize(150,150);
      frame.setVisible(true);

      frame.setDefaultCloseOperation(EXIT_ON_CLOSE);
   }
   public AnimBeanApp1()
   {
      AnimBean1 sequence = new AnimBean1();

      //Add bean to application frame…
      add(sequence);
   }
}
```

The resultant output is shown in Fig. 10.1.

Fig. 10.1 JavaBean animation running in a GUI

As an enhancement of this, we can make use of the 'set' methods in *AnimBean2* to change the animation images and/or animation delay…

Example

This example employs an instance of *AnimBean2* and two text fields. It allows the user to change the animation sequence and/or the frame delay via the text fields, by calling the bean's *setImageName*/*setDelay* method in response to the <Return> key being pressed at the end of entry into one of the text fields.

```
import java.awt.*;
import java.awt.event.*;
import javax.swing.*;
import animBeans.AnimBean2;

public class AnimBeanApp2 extends JFrame
                              implements ActionListener
{
   private AnimBean2 sequence;
   private JPanel speedControl, imageControl;
   private JLabel delayPrompt, imagePrompt;
   private JTextField delay, imageName;

   public static void main(String[] args)
   {
      AnimBeanApp2 frame = new AnimBeanApp2();

      frame.setSize(150,250);
      frame.setVisible(true);

      frame.setDefaultCloseOperation(EXIT_ON_CLOSE);
   }

   public AnimBeanApp2()
   {
      sequence = new AnimBean2();
      speedControl = new JPanel();
      delayPrompt = new JLabel("Delay(ms): ");
      delay = new JTextField(4);
      imageControl = new JPanel();
      imagePrompt = new JLabel("Image: ");
      imageName = new JTextField(8);

      add(sequence, BorderLayout.NORTH);
      speedControl.add(delayPrompt);
      speedControl.add(delay);
      delay.addActionListener(this);
      add(speedControl, BorderLayout.CENTER);

      imageControl.add(imagePrompt);
      imageControl.add(imageName);
      imageName.addActionListener(this);
      add(imageControl, BorderLayout.SOUTH);
   }

   public void actionPerformed(ActionEvent event)
   {
```

```
        if (event.getSource() == delay)
        {
           //<Return> key pressed at end of entry into
           //delay text field, so reset delay...
           int pause = Integer.parseInt(delay.getText());
           sequence.setDelay(pause);
           delay.setText("");
        }
        else
        {
           //<Return> key must have been pressed at end of
           //entry into image name text field, so change
           //animation...
           sequence.setImageName(imageName.getText());
           imageName.setText("");
        }
    }
}
```

Figure 10.2 shows the resultant output.

Fig. 10.2 Modified JavaBean animation running in a GUI

10.5 Bound Properties

A *bound property* causes the owner of the property (i.e., the component whose property it is) to notify other JavaBeans when the value of the property changes, potentially leading to changes within those beans. The values changed in these other beans must be of the **same type** as that of the bound property. The relevant classes to achieve this linkage are contained within package *java.beans*. The objects to be notified are registered as *PropertyChangeListeners*. A *PropertyChangeSupport* object maintains a list of these listeners. The constructor for this object takes one argument: the source bean. For example:

```
PropertyChangeSupport changeSupport =
                    new PropertyChangeSupport(this);
```

In this example, the *PropertyChangeSupport* object has been created within the source bean itself.

The *PropertyChangeSupport* object notifies any registered listeners of a change in the bound property via method *firePropertyChange*, which takes three arguments:

- a *String*, identifying the bound property;
- an *Object*, identifying the old value;
- an *Object*, identifying the new value.

Since the second and third arguments must be of type *Object* or a subclass of this (i.e., an object of **any** class), any primitive value must be converted into an object by the appropriate 'wrapper' class (*Integer*, *Float*, etc.). For example:

```
changeSupport.firePropertyChange(
  "boundProp",new Integer(oldVal),new Integer(newVal));
```

Execution of the above method causes *PropertyChangeEvent* objects to be generated automatically (and transparently).

The changes in the source bean required to achieve all this are summarised in the steps below.

1. Add the line : `import java.beans.*;`
2. Create a *PropertyChangeSupport* object, using *this* as the single argument to the constructor.
3. Define methods *addPropertyChangeListener* and *removePropertyChangeListener*, specifying a *PropertyChangeListener* argument and `void` return type. (Definitions of the above methods simply call up the corresponding methods of the *PropertyChangeSupport* object, passing a listener argument.)
4. Extend the 'set' method for the bound property to call method *firePropertyChange*.

Example

This is a further extension of our animation bean, using *imageName* as the bound property. The code changes are shown in bold text below.

```
package animBeans;

import java.awt.*;
import java.awt.event.*;
import javax.swing.*;
import java.io.File;
```

```
import java.beans.*;

public class AnimBean4 extends JPanel
                            implements ActionListener
{
   private ImageIcon[] image;
   private String imageName = "juggler";
   private String oldImage = "juggler";
   private int numFrames;
   private int oldNumFrames = 0;
   private int currentImage = 0;
   private int delay = 100;      //??
   private Timer animTimer;
   private PropertyChangeSupport changeSupport;

   public static void main(String[] args)

   {
      AnimBean4 anim = new AnimBean4();
      anim.setVisible(true);
   }

   public AnimBean4()
   {
      changeSupport = new PropertyChangeSupport(this);
      loadFrames();
      startAnimation();
   }

   private void loadFrames()
   {
      //Check no. of frames first…
      numFrames = 0;
      File fileName =
            new File(imageName + (numFrames) + ".gif");
      while (fileName.exists())
      {
         numFrames++;
         fileName =
            new File(imageName + (numFrames) + ".gif");
      }
      if (numFrames==0)    //No image found!
         return;           //Abandon loading of frames.

      image = new ImageIcon[numFrames];
      //Now load frames…
      for (int i=0; i<numFrames; i++)
      {
```

```
            image[i] =
                new ImageIcon(imageName + (i+1) + ".gif");
        }
    }

    public void startAnimation()
    {
        if (animTimer == null)
        {
            currentImage = 0;
            animTimer = new Timer(delay,this);
            animTimer.start();
        }
        else
            if (!animTimer.isRunning())
                animTimer.restart();
    }

    public void stopAnimation()
    {
        animTimer.stop();
    }
    public void paint(Graphics g)
    {
        if (!imageName.equals(oldImage))
        {
            loadFrames();
            if (numFrames==0)   //No image found!
            {
                //Reset image name and no. of
                //frames to their old values…
                setImageName(oldImage);
                numFrames = oldNumFrames;
            }
            else
            {
                oldImage = imageName;
                oldNumFrames = numFrames;
                g.setColor(getBackground());
                g.fillRect(0,0,getWidth(),getHeight());
                currentImage = 0;
            }
        }
        if (numFrames>0)      //Image exists.
        {
            image[currentImage].paintIcon(this,g,0,0);
            currentImage = (currentImage+1)%numFrames;
```

```
        }
    }
    public void actionPerformed(ActionEvent event)
    {
        repaint();
    }
    public String getImageName()
    {
        return imageName;
    }
    public void setImageName(String name)
    {
        String oldName = imageName;
        imageName = name;
        changeSupport.firePropertyChange(
                    "imageName", oldName, imageName);
    }
    public int getDelay()
    {
        return delay;
    }

    public void setDelay(int delayIn)
    {
        delay = delayIn;
        animTimer.setDelay(delay);
    }

    public Dimension getPreferredSize()
    {
        return new Dimension(140,120);
    }

    public void addPropertyChangeListener(
                    PropertyChangeListener listener)
    {
        changeSupport.addPropertyChangeListener(listener);
    }

    public void removePropertyChangeListener(
                    PropertyChangeListener listener)
    {
        changeSupport.removePropertyChangeListener(
                                            listener);
    }
}
```

It is a relatively simple matter to modify example *AnimBeanApp2* from the previous section to make use of the above bean, which is what the next example does.

Example

In this example, the application is going to act as a *PropertyChangeListener*, and so must implement method *propertyChange*. The application frame must be registered as a *PropertyChangeListener* for the bean by executing method *addPropertyChangeListener* on the bean, supplying an argument of *this*. When the String identifying the animation changes (i.e., when the value of property *imageName* changes), a *PropertyChangeEvent* will be generated and method *propertyChange* will be invoked. The simple action to be taken by this method will be to change the title of the application frame to reflect the change in property *imageName*. As usual, the changes from the original version of the program will be shown in bold text.

```
import java.awt.*;
import java.awt.event.*;
import javax.swing.*;
import java.beans.*;
import animBeans.AnimBean4;

public class AnimBeanApp3 extends JFrame
    implements ActionListener,PropertyChangeListener
{
     private AnimBean4 sequence;
     private JPanel speedControl, imageControl;
     private JLabel delayPrompt, imagePrompt;
     private JTextField delay, imageName;

     public static void main(String[] args)
     {
       AnimBeanApp3 frame = new AnimBeanApp3();

       frame.setSize(150,250);
       frame.setVisible(true);

       frame.setDefaultCloseOperation(EXIT_ON_CLOSE);
     }

     public AnimBeanApp3()
     {
       sequence = new AnimBean4();
       sequence.addPropertyChangeListener(this);
       setTitle(sequence.getImageName());
       speedControl = new JPanel();
       delayPrompt = new JLabel("Delay(ms): ");
       delay = new JTextField(4);
       imageControl = new JPanel();
       imagePrompt = new JLabel("Image: ");
       imageName = new JTextField(8);

       add(sequence, BorderLayout.NORTH);
       speedControl.add(delayPrompt);
```

```
        speedControl.add(delay);
        delay.addActionListener(this);
        add(speedControl, BorderLayout.CENTER);

        imageControl.add(imagePrompt);
        imageControl.add(imageName);
        imageName.addActionListener(this);
        add(imageControl, BorderLayout.SOUTH);
    }

    public void actionPerformed(ActionEvent event)
    {
        if (event.getSource() == delay)
        {
          //<Return> key pressed at end of entry into
          //delay text field, so reset delay…
          int pause =
                   Integer.parseInt(delay.getText());
          sequence.setDelay(pause);
          delay.setText("");
        }
        else
        {
            //<Return> key must have been pressed at end
            //of entry into image name text field, so
            //change animation…
            sequence.setImageName(imageName.getText());
            imageName.setText("");
        }
    }

    public void propertyChange(PropertyChangeEvent event)
    {
        setTitle(sequence.getImageName());
    }
}
```

Figure 10.3 shows the display from the above program just after the image name has changed from 'juggler' to 'poorpic'.

10.6 Using JavaBeans in JSPs

10.6.1 The Basic Procedure

This is a powerful combination that can be used to add further dynamism to Web pages. In order to be used by a JSP, a bean must have a default (i.e., no-argument)

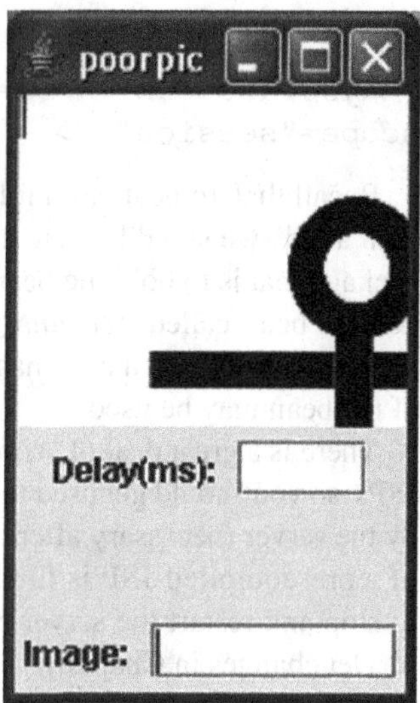

Fig. 10.3 Title change illustrating use of a bound property

constructor. Within the JSP, any bean that is to be used is identified by an action tag that specifies *jsp* as the library and *useBean* as the action name. Recall from the last chapter that an action tag shows the bean's library and action name, separated by a colon. Thus, the tag commences as follows:

```
<jsp:useBean
```

If the bean tag has no body (as is commonly the case), the closing angle bracket is preceded by a forward slash:

```
/>
```

The bean tag must also specify the following attributes:

- `id` (name for individual bean);
- `class` (specifying both package and class).

For example:

```
<jsp:useBean id="myAccount" class="bank.Account" />
```

In addition, there are three optional attributes:

- `scope`;
- `type`;
- `beanName`.

Only `scope` is of any real interest to us. This attribute specifies the access to/availability of the bean and takes one of the following four values:

- `page` (actions and scriptlets on the same page—the default);
- `request` (all pages servicing the same user request);
- `session` (all requests during the same user session);
- `application` (all users of the application).

For example:

```
<jsp:useBean   id="myAccount"   class="bank.Account"
scope="session" />
```

Recall that Tomcat has a folder called classes. For each bean that we wish to use with a JSP, we should create a sub-folder of *classes* that has the same name as the package that is to hold the bean. For instance, in the above example, directory *bank* holds a bean called *Account* (within package *bank*) and directory *bank* is placed inside *classes*. Once a bean has been placed inside a JSP, the 'get' and 'set' methods of the bean may be used.

There is a great deal of scope for things to go wrong when using JavaBeans from JSPs, so you should get used to seeing error pages. In addition to this, re-compilation by the server (necessary after any change to the JSP, of course) is **slow**! Re-loading of a pre-compiled JSP is fine, though. In addition, recall that it is not necessary to stop and restart the server every time a change is made to a JSP (as it was with servlet changes in Chap. 8).

10.6.2 Calling a Bean's Methods Directly

Example

This is a modification of one of our JDBC examples (*JDBCGUI.java*) from Chap. 7. It is advisable to specify an error page, of course, since several things can go wrong when accessing a database that could be remote.

There are several changes that need to be made to the original program, as listed below.

- Remove all references to GUI elements (substantially reducing the code in so doing).
- Remove all exception-handling code (since we shall be using a JSP error page).
- Since class *ResultSet* has no constructor and does not implement *Serializable*, introduce a *Vector* for transferring query results.
- Introduce a 'get' method for retrieving the contents of the *Vector* object.

The numeric values retrieved from the database and stored in a *Vector* will need to be typecast into objects of the type *Integer* and *Float* when the *Vector* is received by the JSP. Due to auto-unboxing, these values may be assigned directly to variables of type *int* and *float*.

Here is the code for the bean…

```
package jdbc;

import java.sql.*;
import java.util.Vector;

public class JDBCBean
```

```
{
    private Vector<Object> acctDetails;
    public JDBCBean() throws SQLException,
                                ClassNotFoundException
    {
        Connection connection = null;
        Statement statement = null;
        ResultSet results = null;

        connection = DriverManager.getConnection(
                        "jdbc:odbc:Finances","","");
        statement = connection.createStatement();
        results = statement.executeQuery(
                        "SELECT * FROM Accounts");

        acctDetails = new Vector<Object>();

        while (results.next())
        {
            acctDetails.add(results.getInt(1));
            acctDetails.add(results.getString(3)
                  + " " + results.getString(2));
            acctDetails.add(results.getFloat(4));
        }
        connection.close();
    }

    public Vector<Object> getAcctDetails()
    {
        return acctDetails;
    }
}
```

The code for the error page will be placed in file *JDBCError.jsp*. The code for the main JSP creates a local *Vector* that stores the query results returned by the appropriate 'get' method in the bean. The results are then displayed in a table. The code for the main JSP is shown below. Note that the bean to be used must be identified in the `useBean` tag by a concatenation of its package name and bean name (*jdbc.JDBCBean*).

```
<HTML>

   <%@ page language="java" contentType="text/html"
   import="java.util.*" errorPage="JDBCError.jsp" %>
   <jsp:useBean id="data" class="jdbc.JDBCBean" />

   <HEAD>
        <TITLE>JDBC Bean Test</TITLE>
        <STYLE>body{text-align:center;}</STYLE>
```

```
    </HEAD>

    <BODY>
         <H1>Results</H1>
         <BR><BR><BR>

         <TABLE STYLE="background-color:aqua" BORDER=1>
            <TR>
                <TH STYLE="background-color:orange">
                Acct.No.</TH>
                <TH STYLE="background-color:orange">
                Acct.Name</TH>
                <TH STYLE="background-color:orange">
                Balance</TH>
            </TR>
            <%
                Vector<Object> nums=data.getAcctDetails();
                int acctNum;
                String acctName;
                float balance;
                final int NUM_FIELDS = 3;

                for (int i=0;i<nums.size()/NUM_FIELDS;i++)
                {
                //Auto-unboxing doesn't work here!
                    acctNum = (Integer)nums.elementAt(
                                        i*NUM_FIELDS);
                    acctName = (String)nums.elementAt(
                                    i*NUM_FIELDS + 1);
                    balance = (Float)nums.elementAt(
                                      i*NUM_FIELDS + 2);
            %>
            <TR>
                <TD><%= acctNum %></TD>
                <TD><%= acctName %></TD>
                <TD>
                <%= String.format("%.2f",balance %></TD>
            </TR>

            <%
               }
            %>

         </TABLE>

     </BODY>

</HTML>
```

The output from this JSP is shown in Fig. 10.4.

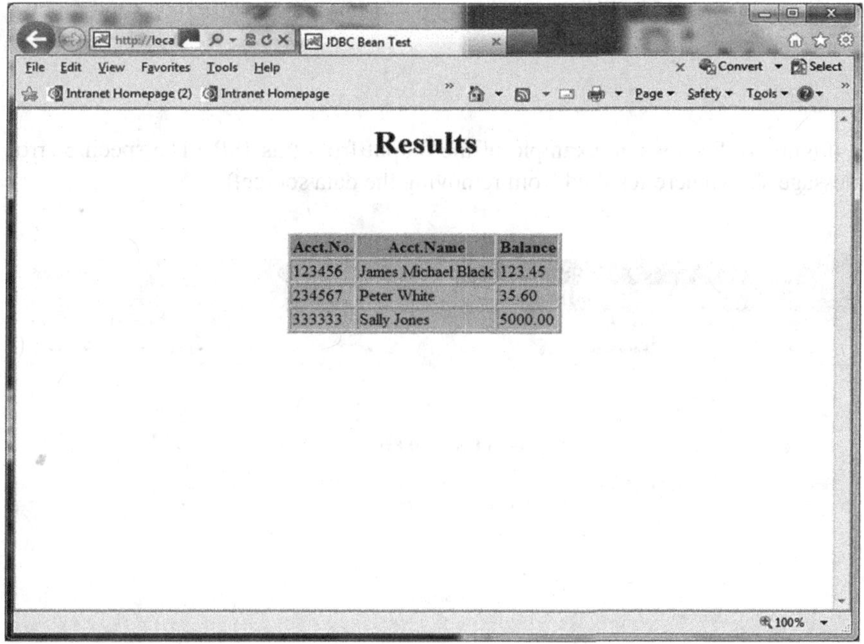

Fig. 10.4 Normal output from *JDBC.jsp*

As in an earlier example from the previous chapter, our error page will simply make use of the *exception* object's *toString* method to display the associated error message and then allow a fresh attempt at data retrieval. The code for the error page is shown below.

```
<!-- JDBCError.jsp -->

<%@ page isErrorPage="true" %>

<HTML>

     <HEAD>
          <TITLE>Error Page</TITLE>
          <STYLE>body{text-align:center;}</STYLE>
     </HEAD>

     <BODY>
          <BR><BR><BR>
          <H3>Data Retrieval Error<BR><BR>
          <P STYLE="color:red">
          <%= exception.toString() %></P></H3>
          <BR><BR><BR>
```

```
            <FORM METHOD=GET ACTION="JDBC.jsp">
                <INPUT TYPE="Submit" VALUE="Try again">
            </FORM>
        </BODY>
    </HTML>
```

Figure 10.5 shows an example of the output from this JSP. (The specific error message shown here resulted from removing the data source.)

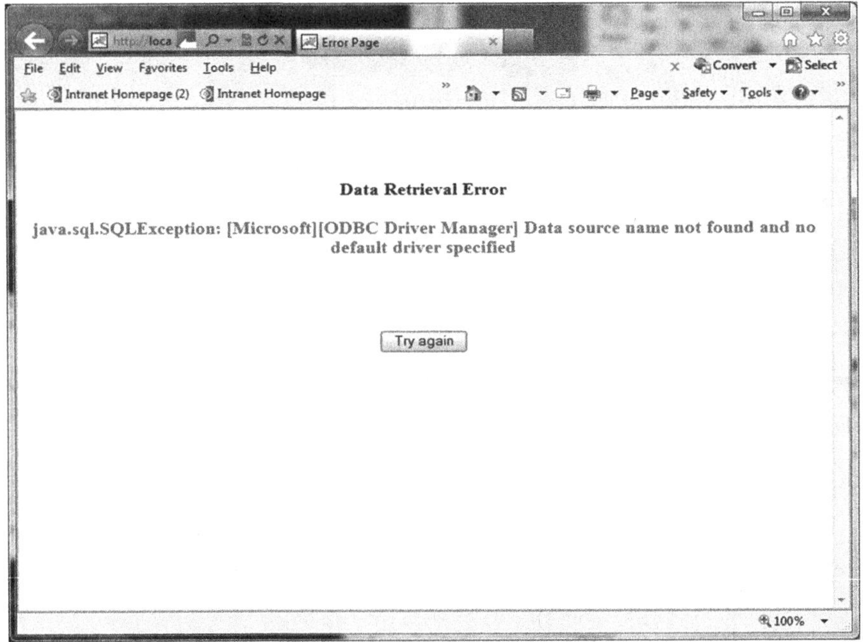

Fig. 10.5 Error output from *JDBC.jsp* (via *JDBCError.jsp*)

10.6.3 Using HTML Tags to Manipulate a Bean's Properties

In addition to using JSPs for reading and displaying data via JavaBeans, it is also possible to use them for manipulating bean properties directly (both reading and writing). This is achieved by using action tags `<jsp:getProperty>` and `<jsp:setProperty>`, which are used to 'get' and 'set' exposed bean properties respectively. This is particularly useful for non-programmers. For the `<jsp:getProperty>` tag, two attributes are required:

- `name` (specifying name of required bean);
- `property` (specifying name of property).

The value of the specified property will be displayed at the position in the Web page where this tag occurs. Note that a named property *X* does not actually have to exist as an attribute of the bean, but method *getX* must. This can be very useful for returning a calculated value, as the example below illustrates.

Example

This example simply extends *JDBCBean.java* by providing method *getNumAccounts*, which returns the number of account holders in table *Accounts* of our *Finances* database. The new version of the bean is called *JDBCBeanX.java*. For ease of comparison with the original bean, the code changes are shown in bold.

```
package jdbc;

import java.sql.*;
import java.util.*;

public class JDBCBeanX
{
    private static Connection link;
    private static Statement statement;
    private static ResultSet results;
    private static Vector<Object> acctDetails;
    private final int NUM_FIELDS = 3;

    public JDBCBeanX() throws SQLException,

    ClassNotFoundException
    {
        connection = DriverManager.getConnection(
                            "jdbc:odbc:Finances","","");
        statement = connection.createStatement();
        results = statement.executeQuery(
                            "SELECT * FROM Accounts");

        acctDetails = new Vector<Object>();

        while (results.next())
        {
            acctDetails.add(results.getInt(1));
            acctDetails.add(results.getString(3)
                    + " " + results.getString(2));
            acctDetails.add(results.getFloat(4));
        }
        connection.close();
    }
    public Vector<Object> getAcctDetails()
    {
```

```
            return acctDetails;
        }

        public int getNumAccounts()
        {
            /*
            Dividing the number of objects in the Vector
            holding the data by the number of table fields
            will produce the number of rows (and so the
            number of accounts) in the database table...
            */

            return acctDetails.size()/NUM_FIELDS;
        }
}
```

For consistency (and to save an unnecessary effort of imagination!), the corresponding JSP will be named *JDBCX.jsp*. The name of the error page will be changed in a similar fashion (with appropriate creation of this new, but identically-coded, error page) and the name of the bean will also be changed in the `<jsp:useBean>` tag. The lines containing these minor changes are shown below (with the changes marked in bold).

```
<%@ page language="java" contentType="text/html"
errorPage="JDBCXError.jsp" %>
<jsp:useBean id="data" class="jdbc.JDBCBeanX" />
```

In order to use the JSP to access the *numAccounts* property and display the result it returns, the following lines must be placed after the `</TABLE>` tag in the original JSP:

```
Number of accounts held:
<p STYLE="color:blue">
<jsp:getProperty name="data" property="numAccounts" />
</P>
```

The resultant output is shown in Fig. 10.6.

For the `<jsp:setProperty>` tag, three attributes are commonly required:

- `name` (of bean, as before);
- `property` (as before);
- `value` (to be assigned to the property).

The example below sets the *balance* property of a bean called *account* to 0.

```
<jsp:setProperty name="account" property="balance" value="0" />
```

Instead of setting the property to a literal value, though, we often need to set it to a parameter value passed to the JSP (possibly via a form), provided that the parameter has the same type as the property (or can be converted into that type). There are three ways of doing this…

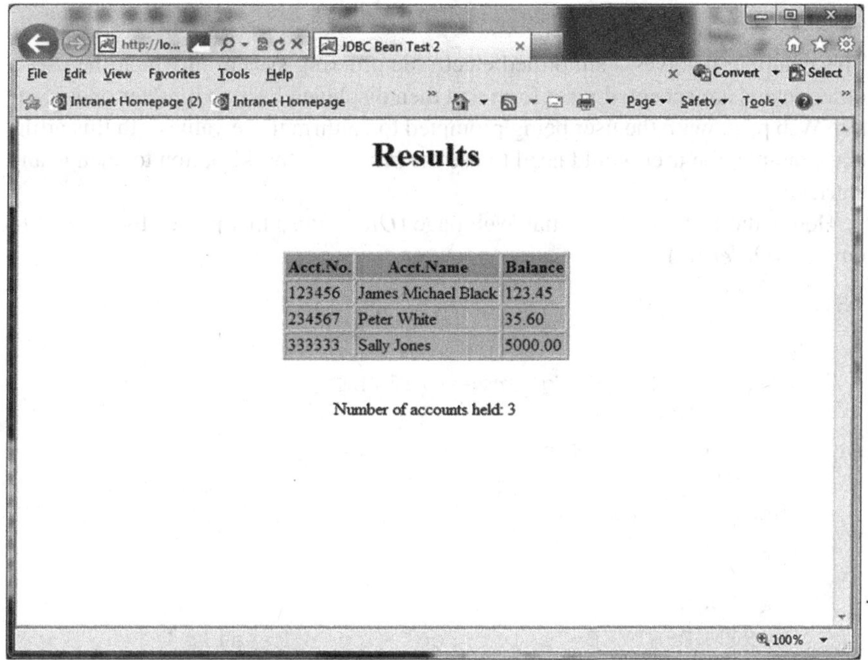

Fig. 10.6 Output from *JDBCX.jsp*

1. If the parameter has the same name as the property, simply omit the `value` attribute of that property. For example:

```
<jsp:setProperty name="account" property="balance" />
```

(Note that there is no need to call *getParameter* to retrieve the value of the parameter.)

2. Use a parameter with a different name, replacing the `value` attribute with a **`param`** attribute. For example:

```
<jsp:setProperty name="account" property="balance"
                                param="userEntry" />
```

3. Set **all** bean properties that have names matching those of parameters sent to the page (at the same time). In this variation, only attributes `name` and `property` can be used, with the latter being set to **"*"**. For example:

```
<jsp:setProperty name="account" property="*" />
```

(Parameters having names matching attributes of *account* are used to set values of those attributes.)

Now let's take a look at a complete JSP that makes use of a `<jsp:setProperty>` tag…

Example

This example involves a simplified electronic ordering system in which the user's order details are accepted via a form and then displayed back to him/her on a separate Web page, with the user being prompted to confirm those values. (In this artificial example, the user would need to use the browser's 'back' button to change any entries.)

Here's the code for the initial Web page (*Order.html*) that passes form input to our JSP (*Order.jsp*):

```
<HTML>

   <HEAD>
      <TITLE>Shopping Order</TITLE>
      <STYLE>
          body {text-align:center;}
      </STYLE>
   </HEAD>

   <BODY>

      <BR><BR>
      <H1><P STYLE="color:red">Order Details</P>
      </H1>
      <BR>

      <!-- Pass all form entries to Order.jsp... -->
      <FORM METHOD=POST ACTION="Order.jsp">

         <TABLE>
            <TR>
               <TD>Name:</TD>
               <TD><INPUT TYPE="text" NAME= "name"></ TD>
            </TR>
            <TR>
               <TD>Address line1:</TD>
               <TD><INPUT TYPE="text"
                             NAME= "addressLine1"></ TD>
            </TR>
            <TR>
               <TD>Address line2:</TD>
               <TD><INPUT TYPE="text"
                             NAME= "addressLine2"></ TD>
            </TR>
            <TR>
               <TD>Address line3:</TD>
               <TD><INPUT TYPE="text"
                             NAME= "addressLine3"></ TD>
            </TR>
            <TR>
```

```
                <TD>Post code:</TD>
                <TD><INPUT TYPE="text"
                                NAME= "postCode"></ TD>
            </TR>
            <TR>
                <TD>Order item:</TD>
                <TD><INPUT TYPE="text"
                                NAME= "orderItem"></ TD>
            </TR>
            <TR>
                <TD>Quantity:</TD>
                <TD><INPUT TYPE="text"
                                NAME= "quantity"></ TD>
            </TR>
        </TABLE>
        <BR><BR>
        <INPUT TYPE="submit" VALUE= "Send order">
    </FORM>
  </BODY>
</HTML>
```

An example featuring user input when the above page is displayed is shown in Fig. 10.7.

The bean to be used will simply hold instance variables corresponding to all form values shown on the above page (**with identical names**) and their corresponding accessor and mutator ('get' and 'set') methods.

We'll call our bean *OrderBean* and place it into package *shopping*...

```
package shopping;
import java.util.*;
public class OrderBean implements java.io.Serializable
{
   private String name;
   private String addressLine1, addressLine2,
                                         addressLine3;
   private String postCode;
   private String orderItem;
   private int quantity;
   private Date orderDate;
   public String getName()
   {
      return name;
   }
```

```
public void setName(String nameIn)
{
   name = nameIn;
}

public String getAddress()
{
   return (addressLine1 + "\n"
         + addressLine2 + "\n"
         + addressLine3 + "\n"
         + postCode);
}

public String getAddressLine1()
{
   return addressLine1;
}

public void setAddressLine1(String add1)
{
   addressLine1 = add1;
}
public String getAddressLine2()
{
   return addressLine2;
}

public void setAddressLine2(String add2)
{
   addressLine2 = add2;
}

public String getAddressLine3()
{
   return addressLine3;
}

public void setAddressLine3(String add3)
{
   addressLine3 = add3;
}

public String getPostCode()
{
   return postCode;
}

public void setPostCode(String code)
{
```

```
      postCode = code;
   }
   public String getOrderItem()
   {
      return orderItem;
   }
   public void setOrderItem(String item)
   {
      orderItem = item;
   }
   public int getQuantity()
   {
      return quantity;
   }
   public void setQuantity(int qty)
   {
      quantity = qty;
   }
}
```

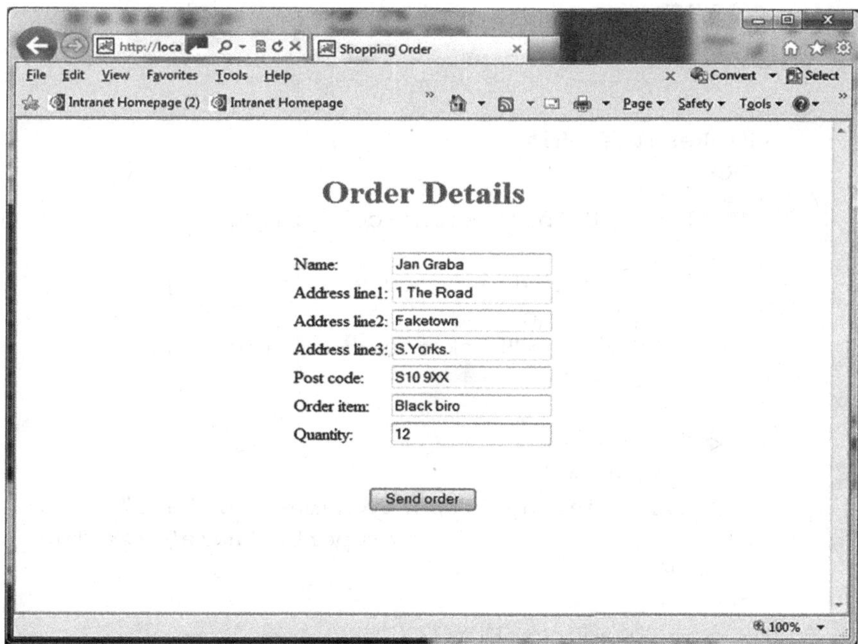

Fig. 10.7 Example I/O for *Order.html*

The required JSP will allow us to make use of a 'body' within the `<jsp:useBean>` tag for holding the `<jsp:setProperty>` tag and setting the bean properties to the form values. When a body is used, an explicit `</jsp:useBean>` closing tag is required. Assuming that our bean instance is to be called *purchase*, the opening lines of our JSP will be as follows:

```
<jsp:useBean id="purchase" class="shopping.OrderBean">
    <jsp:setProperty name="purchase" property="*" />
</jsp:useBean>
```

For retrieving and displaying properties, we can again make use of `<jsp:getProperty>` tags. To emphasise the setting of property values that has occurred, the names of bean properties will be displayed in the table output. Here's the code for the JSP…

```
<HTML>
<%@ page language="java" contentType="text/html" %>
<jsp:useBean id="purchase" class="shopping.OrderBean">
    <jsp:setProperty name="purchase" property="*" />
</jsp:useBean>

   <HEAD>
      <TITLE>Order Bean Test</TITLE>
      <STYLE>
             body {text-align:center;}
      </STYLE>

   </HEAD>

   <BODY>
      <H1>Results</H1>
      <BR>

      <TABLE STYLE="background-color:aqua">
         <TR>
            <TH STYLE="background-color:orange">
            Field Name</TH>
            <TH STYLE="background-color:orange">
            Value</TH>
         </TR>
         <TR>
            <TD>name</TD>
            <TD><jsp:getProperty name="purchase"
                                 property="name" /></TD>
         </TR>
         <TR>
            <TD>addressLine1</TD>
            <TD><jsp:getProperty name="purchase"
```

```
                    property="addressLine1" /></TD>
      </TR>
      <TR>
         <TD>addressLine2</TD>
         <TD><jsp:getProperty name="purchase"
                    property="addressLine2" /></TD>
      </TR>
      <TR>
         <TD>addressLine3</TD>
         <TD><jsp:getProperty name="purchase"
                    property="addressLine3" /></TD>
      </TR>

      <TR>
         <TD>postCode</TD>
         <TD><jsp:getProperty name="purchase"
                    property="postCode" /></TD>
      </TR>
      <TR>
         <TD>orderItem</TD>
         <TD><jsp:getProperty name="purchase"
                    property="orderItem" /></ TD>
      </TR>
      <TR>
         <TD>quantity</TD>
         <TD><jsp:getProperty name="purchase"
                    property="quantity" /></TD>
      </TR>
   </TABLE>

   <BR><BR>
   <FORM METHOD=GET ACTION="Acceptance.html">
   <!--
     When confirm button pressed,
     display Acceptance.html.
   -->
      <INPUT TYPE="submit" VALUE="Confirm">
   </FORM>

  </BODY>

</HTML>
```

Output is shown in Fig. 10.8. (As noted earlier, the user in this simple example can change the order only by using the browser's 'back' button!)

All that remains now is to show the code for a simple acceptance Web page (which really is minimalistic):

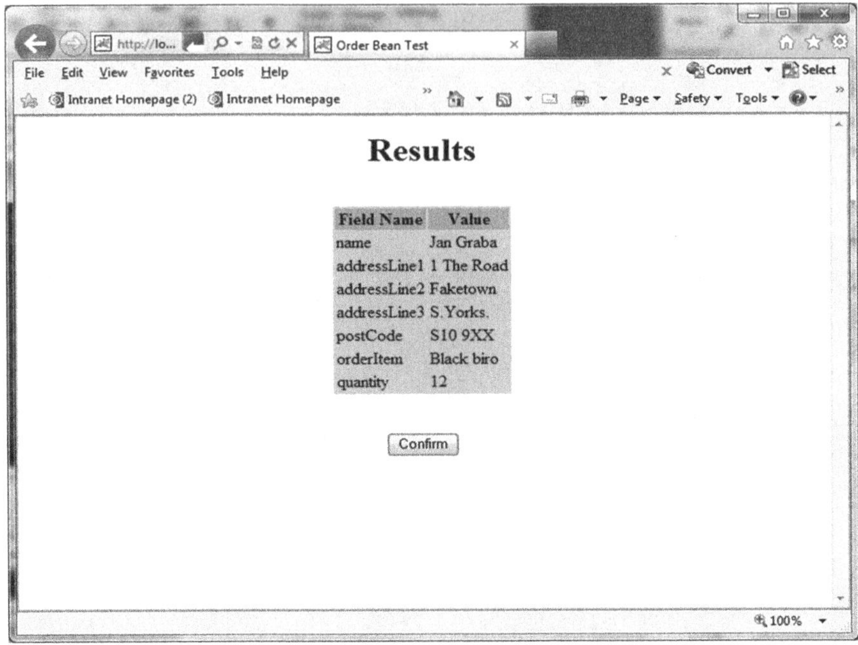

Fig. 10.8 Output from *Order.jsp*

```
<HTML>
   <HEAD>
      <TITLE>Order Acceptance</TITLE>
      <STYLE>
            body {text-align:center;}
      </STYLE>
   </HEAD>
   <BODY TEXT="red">
      <BR><BR><BR><BR>
      <H1>Order Accepted!</H1>
   </BODY>
</HTML>
```

Output from this final page is shown in Fig. 10.9.

Finally, listed below are some advanced aspects of JavaBeans not covered in this chapter.

- Custom event types.

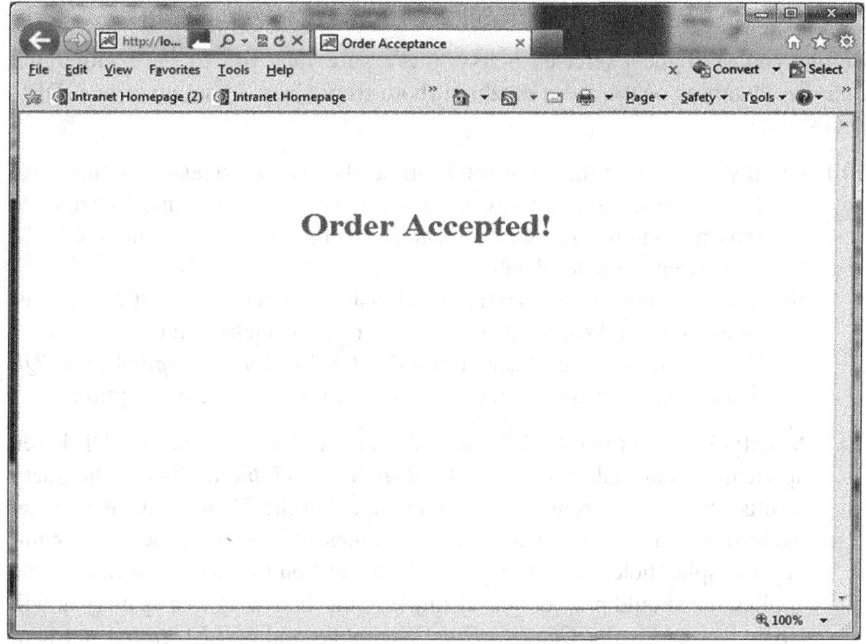

Fig. 10.9 Output from *Acceptance.html*

- *BeanInfo* classes, used to provide builder tools with more information about the characteristics of beans.
- Custom property editors (to provide greater sophistication than the default editors).

Exercises

Before you start the exercises below, make sure that you to have either the *Finances* database or the *Sales* database (both from Chap. 7) set up as an ODBC data source.

10.1 (i) If you are using the *Finances* database, then you need take no action here. If you are using the *Sales* database, however, you will need to re-code (and re-compile) *JDBCBean.java* so that the bean is accessing the *Stock* table from the *Sales* database.

(ii) Create a simple (non-GUI) application that makes use of *JDBCBean*. Your program should simply display the query results retrieved by the bean. Note that, since the bean 'throws' *ClassNotFoundException* and *SQL Exception*, your code will have to catch (or throw) these exceptions.

10.2 Modify the code for *JDBCGUI.java* from Sect. 7.9 to produce a GUI-driven application that makes use of *JDBCBean* and a *JTable* to display the query results. In so doing, remember (if you are using the *Finances* database) that the bean concatenates surname and first names, effectively reducing the number of display fields from four to three. In addition to the table of results, the application should provide just a simple 'Quit' button. (Once again, you will have to cater for the *ClassNotFoundException* and *SQLException* not handled by the bean.)

10.3 (i) Create a JavaBean that encapsulates a very simple calculator that will allow the user to enter an arithmetic expression involving two operands. The JavaBean should be implemented as a subclass of *JPanel* and the user should be able to carry out the four basic arithmetic operations (using operators '+', '–', 'x' and '/'). Two buttons should be provided, the first of these to calculate and display the result of the current calculation and the second to move the result into the field for the first operand (with subsequent fields being cleared), so that the user can carry out further operations on this result. The layout should look something like that shown below.

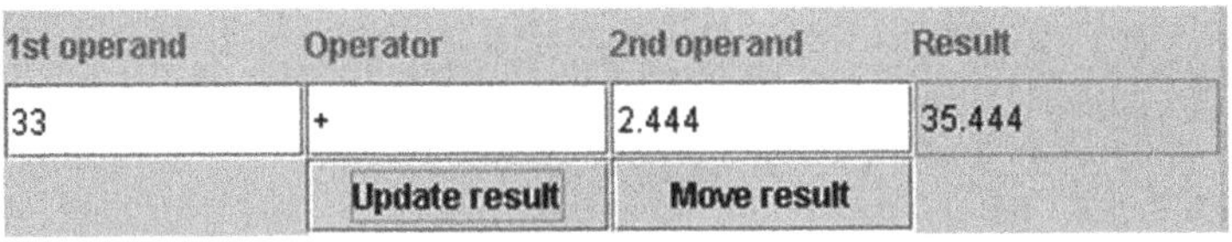

1st operand	Operator	2nd operand	Result
33	+	2.444	35.444
	Update result	Move result	

Note that no *main* method is required.

(ii) Create a manifest file for the above bean and package the bean and its manifest within a JAR file. Then execute the following command from the command line (substituting your own JAR file name, if yours is not called *Calculator.jar*):

```
jar tf Calculator.jar
```

Check that the contents listed are what they should be. If they aren't, then re-create your JAR file until you get the right output.

10.4 Create a simple GUI-driven application that makes use of the above bean (**not** the JAR file) to provide the user with a simple calculator. In addition to the bean itself, you need supply only a 'Quit' button.

10.5 Modify the calculator bean so that the user can set the background colour of the result box to red, green or blue, via method *setResultBground*. Then modify the code for the previous exercise by adding a button that allows the user to make use of method *setResultBground* (probably via method *JOptionPane.showInputDialog*).

10.6 (i) Create a bean called *JDBCQueryBean* that is a modification of *JDBCBean*. Instead of dealing only with a fixed query 'SELECT * FROM Accounts', this bean should be capable of processing any query directed at the *Accounts/Stock* table (depending upon which database you are using). The code for the major method *getQueryResults* is supplied at the end of this question. In addition to this method, the bean should provide read/write access to a property called *query* that holds the current query (and has a default value of 'SELECT * FROM Accounts'). Read access should also be provided to properties *numFields* (holding the number of fields in the query) and *numRows* (the number of rows in the query results).

(ii) Create a simple HTML page that uses a text field in a form to accept the user's query and pass it on to a JSP called *JDBCQuery.jsp*.

(iii) Possibly using *JDBC.jsp* as a starting point, produce a JSP that accepts the query from the above HTML page and then uses the bean to display the results of the query in a table.

```
public static Vector<Object> getQueryResults()
                                        throws SQLException
{
   results = statement.executeQuery(getQuery());
   metaData = results.getMetaData();
   numFields = metaData.getColumnCount();

   queryResults = new Vector<Object>();
   fieldNames = new Vector<String>();
   dataTypes = new Vector<String>();

   for (int i=1; i<=numFields; i++)
      fieldNames.add(metaData.getColumnName(i));

   while (results.next())
   {
      for (int i=1; i<=numFields; i++)
```

```
        {
            int colType = metaData.getColumnType(i);
            switch (colType)
            {
             case Types.INTEGER:
                queryResults.add(results.getInt(i));
                dataTypes.add("integer");
                break;
             case Types.VARCHAR:
                queryResults.add(
                               results.getString(i));
                dataTypes.add("string");
                break;
               case Types.NUMERIC:
                queryResults.add(
                                results.getFloat(i));
                dataTypes.add("float");
                break;
             default: //Hopefully, will never happen!
                queryResults.add(
                               results.getString(i));
                dataTypes.add("string");
          }
        }
     }
     return queryResults;
  }
```

Chapter 11
Multimedia

Learning Objectives

After reading this chapter, you should:

- know one multi-purpose method for transferring image, sound and video files across a network;
- know a second method for transferring image files only across a network;
- know two methods for displaying images in Java;
- know how to use Java for playing sound files;
- be aware of the API that needs to be downloaded for the playing of video files;
- know how to use the Java Media Framework for playing audio and video files.

In the early days of the Internet, the only type of data that could be transferred was text. Gradually, file formats that allowed the transfer of data associated with other media came onto the scene. Notable amongst these formats was GIF (*Graphics Interchange Format*), the most enduring graphics file format, which first appeared in 1987. However, it took the emergence of HTML and the World Wide Web in 1991 to awaken users to the full potential of the Internet as a vehicle for communication. As this potential dawned upon users, they began to crave more flexible, more varied and more complete ways of conveying and accessing information—which meant the transfer of data in all its media (textual, graphical, audio and video). The use of such **multimedia** data has since mushroomed, in spite of the technical problems related to file size and speed of transfer. These problems still exist, of course, but have been considerably alleviated by the greater bandwidth provided by many of today's networks and will undoubtedly continue to diminish over the coming years, as the technology advances.

One means of supplying multimedia information and entertainment over the Internet is provided by Java applets (which will be covered in the next chapter). Applets have been an integral part of Java since its earliest days and played a great part in the initial popularising of the language, though their use has waned considerably in recent years with the increasing popularity of scripting languages such as

J. Graba, *An Introduction to Network Programming with Java: Java 7 Compatible*, DOI 10.1007/978-1-4471-5254-5_11,

JavaScript, PHP and Python. In fact, the overhead of building up a Web page to use applets for transferring multimedia files over the Internet and the security restrictions placed upon applets can often make the transfer of files via Java applications preferable to the use of applets. In such applications, the use of interface *Serializable* (described in Sect. 4.6) is crucial.

Java's original support for audio was restricted to *Sun Audio file format* (***.au*** files). Nowadays, Windows *Wave* format (***.wav*** files), Macintosh *AIFF* format (***.aif*** files) and the *MIDI* format (***.mid*** or ***.rmf*** files) are all supported by the standard Java libraries. For the transfer of image files, the original release of Java accepted only GIF format (***.gif*** files). Support for the JPEG format (***.jpg*** and ***.jpeg*** files) was added in JDK1.1. In order to play video clips and most other file formats, however, it is necessary to download the Java Media Framework. This API will be covered in a later section of this chapter, but we shall restrict our attention to the standard Java SE provision for the time being.

11.1 Transferring and Displaying Images Easily

In Java, classes *Image* (from package *java.awt*) and *ImageIcon* (package *javax.swing*) are used for holding and manipulating images. Either may be used on its own, but *ImageIcon* is particularly useful for loading an image from the current directory into an application. For example:

```
ImageIcon image = new ImageIcon("pic.gif");
```

ImageIcon is also useful for transferring the image across a network, since it implements the *Serializable* interface. There are more ways than one of transferring image files across a network via Java. However, since *ImageIcon* implements *Serializable*, it is particularly convenient to use the method described below.

1. Create an *ObjectOutputStream* object from the relevant *Socket* object at the sending end.
2. Transmit the *ImageIcon* object via method *writeObject* of *ObjectOutputStream*.
3. Create an *ObjectInputStream* object from the relevant *Socket* object at the receiving end.
4. Receive the transmitted object via method *readObject* of *ObjectInputStream*.
5. Typecast the received object (from type *Object*) into *ImageIcon*.

As might be expected, there will often be a client-server relationship between the two ends of such a communication (though it may be that the two ends are actually peers and are using the client-server relationship merely as a convenience). The basic code for the two ends of the communication will be very similar to that which was featured in several of the examples in earlier chapters, of course. Because of that, such lines will not be commented or explained (again) here. The lines of code corresponding to steps 1–5 above, however, will be commented clearly in bold type.

Example

This example creates (a) a server process that transmits a fixed graphics file to any client that makes contact and (b) a client process that makes contact with the server and accepts the file that is transmitted.

Firstly, the server code…

```
import java.io.*;
import java.net.*;
import javax.swing.*;

public class ImageServer
{
   private static ServerSocket serverSocket;
   private static final int PORT = 1234;

   public static void main(String[] args)
     {
        System.out.println("Opening port…\n");
        try
        {
           serverSocket = new ServerSocket(PORT);
        }
        catch(IOException ioEx)
        {
           System.out.println(
                          "Unable to attach to port!");
           System.exit(1);
        }

        do
        {
          try
          {
             Socket connection = serverSocket.accept();

             //Step 1…
             ObjectOutputStream outStream =
                  new ObjectOutputStream(
                       connection.getOutputStream());

             //Step 2…
             outStream.writeObject(
                       new ImageIcon("beesting.jpg"));

             //To play safe, flush the output buffer…
             outStream.flush();
          }
          catch(IOException ioEx)
          {
```

```
                ioEx.printStackTrace();
            }
        }while (true);
    }
}
```

Before looking at the client code, it is appropriate to give consideration to how the image might be displayed when it has been received. The simplest way of doing this is to create a GUI (using a class that extends *JFrame*) and define method *paint* to specify the placement of the image upon the application. As was seen in the 'juggler' animation bean in Sect. 10.2 (though that application used a *JPanel*, rather than a *JFrame*), this will entail invoking the *ImageIcon* method *paintIcon*. The four arguments required by this method were stated in Sect. 10.2 and are repeated here:

- a reference to the component upon which the image will be displayed (usually *this*, for the application container);
- a reference to the *Graphics* object used to render this image (provided by the argument to *paint*);
- the x-coordinate of the upper-left corner of the image's display position;
- the y-coordinate of the upper-left corner of the image's display position.

Remember that we cannot call *paint* directly, so we must call *repaint* instead (and allow this latter method to call *paint* automatically). This call will be made at the end of the constructor for the client. Steps 3–5 from the original five steps are commented in bold type in the client program.

Now for the code…

```
import java.io.*;
import java.net.*;
import java.awt.*;
import java.awt.event.*;
import javax.swing.*;

public class ImageClient extends JFrame
{
   private InetAddress host;
   private final int PORT = 1234;
   private ImageIcon image;

   public static void main(String[] args)
   {
      ImageClient pictureFrame = new ImageClient();

      //Ideally, size of image should be
      //known in advance…
      pictureFrame.setSize(340,315);
      pictureFrame.setVisible(true);
      pictureFrame.setDefaultCloseOperation(
                                          EXIT_ON_CLOSE);
   }
```

```
   public ImageClient()
   {
      try
      {
         host = InetAddress.getLocalHost();
      }
      catch(UnknownHostException uhEx)
      {
         System.out.println("Host ID not found!");
         System.exit(1);
      }
      try
      {
         Socket connection = new Socket(host,PORT);

         //Step 3…
         ObjectInputStream inStream =
                  new ObjectInputStream(
                        connection.getInputStream());

         //Steps 4 and 5…
         image = (ImageIcon)inStream.readObject();

         //Remember to close the socket…
         connection.close();
      }
      catch(IOException ioEx)
      {
        ioEx.printStackTrace();
      }
      catch(ClassNotFoundException cnfEx)
      {
        cnfEx.printStackTrace();
      }

      //Now cause the paint method to be invoked…
      repaint();
   }
   public void paint(Graphics g)
   {
     //Define paint to display the image
     //upon the application frame…
      image.paintIcon(this,g,0,0);
   }
}
```

(Note that, though meaningful variable names are very much to be encouraged, the use of variable name 'g' above (a) is very common practice and (b) cannot really be misinterpreted, since it is glaringly obvious what it represents.)

Example output from the client program after it has successfully received an image from the server is shown in Fig. 11.1.

Fig. 11.1 Displaying a received image on a *JFrame*

An alternative to displaying the image directly onto the application frame is to make use of an overloaded form of the *JLabel* constructor that takes an *Icon* 'object' as its single argument. *Icon* is an interface that is implemented by class *ImageIcon*, making an *ImageIcon* object also an *Icon* 'object'. Thus, the only changes that need to be made to the client code above are as follows:

- declare the *JLabel* object;
- use `new` to create the above *JLabel*, supplying the *ImageIcon* as the argument to the constructor;
- add the *JLabel* to the application frame;
- remove the call to *repaint*;
- remove the re-definition of *paint*.

<u>Example</u> (of lines that need to be added)

```
JLabel imageLabel; //Amongst initial declarations.
.......................................
imageLabel = new JLabel(image);
add(imageLabel,BorderLayout.CENTER);
```

The resultant output will be virtually identical to that shown in Fig. 11.1.

11.2 Transferring Media Files

Unfortunately, there is no *Serializable* sound class corresponding to the *ImageIcon* class for images, so we need a different transfer method for sound files. One viable method involves transferring the file as an array of bytes (which is *Serializable*, since it is a stream of primitive-type elements). This method can also be applied to graphics files, which means that we can use the same method to transfer files that may be of mixed types. In some applications, this is likely to be very useful. Adopting a client-server approach again, the steps required at each end of the transmission will be considered in turn…

Server

1. Create a *Scanner* and associate it with the input stream from the socket connected to the client.
2. Create an *ObjectOutputStream* associated with the above *Socket* object.
3. Create a *FileInputStream*, supplying the name of the image/sound file as the single argument to the constructor.
4. Create a *File* object from the file name and use *File* method *length* to determine the size of the file. (The *File* object is not needed after this, so it can be anonymous.)
5. Convert the *long* value from step 3 into an *int* and declare a *byte* array of this size. (Method *length* has to return a *long*, but a *byte* array will accept only an *int* for specifying its size.)
6. Use the *FileInputStream* object's *read* method to read the contents of the *FileInputStream* into the *byte* array. (The *byte* array is supplied as the single argument to this method.)
7. Use method *writeObject* of the *ObjectOutputStream* created in step 1 to send the byte array to the client.

Client

1. Create an *ObjectInputStream* and a *PrintWriter* associated with the relevant *Socket* object.
2. Use the *PrintWriter* object to send a request to the server.
3. Use the *readObject* method of the *ObjectInputStream* to receive a file from the server.
4. Typecast the object received in step 3 (from type *Object*) into *byte[]*.
5. Create a *FileOutputStream* object, supplying a string file name for the file with which the *FileOutputStream* is to be associated.
6. Use the *FileOutputStream* object's *write* method to fill the file, supplying the name of the *byte* array as the argument to this method.

Hopefully, all of this will fall into place when you see the code for the following example…

Example

In this example, a server accepts connections from clients and returns to each client either an image file called *beesting.jpg* (if the client sent the single-word request 'IMAGE') or a sound file called *cuckoo.wav* (if the client sent the request 'SOUND'). Upon receipt of an image, the client saves it in a file called *image.jpg* (assuming, for simplicity's sake, that we know the file is going to be one in this format). Upon receipt of a sound file, the client saves it with the name *sound.wav* (again assuming that we know the file is going to be one in this format).

In the code that follows, the (now familiar?) convention of commenting in bold type each of the lines associated with one of the steps described above has been followed. The processing of the file to be transmitted (whether it be the image file or the sound file) is handled by method *sendFile*, whilst the processing of the received file is handled by method *getFile*.

Here's the code for the server…

```
import java.io.*;
import java.net.*;
import javax.swing.*;
import java.util.*;

public class MediaServer
{
   private static ServerSocket serverSocket;
   private static final int PORT = 1234;

   public static void main(String[] args)
   {
       System.out.println("Opening port…\n");

       try
       {
           serverSocket = new ServerSocket(PORT);
       }
       catch(IOException ioEx)
       {
           System.out.println(
                       "Unable to attach to port!");
           System.exit(1);
       }
       do
       {
           try
           {
               Socket connection = serverSocket.accept();

               //Step 1…
               Scanner inStream =
                 new Scanner(connection.getInputStream());

               //Step 2…
               ObjectOutputStream outStream =
                     new ObjectOutputStream(
                            connection.getOutputStream());

               String message = inStream.nextLine();

               if (message.equals("IMAGE"))
                   sendFile("beesting.jpg", outStream);
               if (message.equals("SOUND"))
                   sendFile("cuckoo.wav", outStream);
             }
             catch(IOException ioEx)
```

```
            {
                ioEx.printStackTrace();
            }
        }while (true);
    }

    private static void sendFile(String fileName,
       ObjectOutputStream outStream) throws IOException
    {
          //Step 3...
          FileInputStream fileIn =
                           new FileInputStream(fileName);
          //Step 4...
          long fileLen = (new File(fileName)).length();
          //Step 5...
          int intFileLen = (int)fileLen;
          //Step 5 (cont'd)...
          byte[] byteArray = new byte[intFileLen];
          //Step 6...
          fileIn.read(byteArray);
          //Now that we have finished
          //with the FileInputStream...
          fileIn.close();
          //Step 7...
          outStream.writeObject(byteArray);
          outStream.flush();
    }
}
```

Now for the client code…

```
import java.io.*;
import java.net.*;
import java.awt.*;
import java.awt.event.*;
import javax.swing.*;
import java.util.*;

public class MediaClient
{
   private static InetAddress host;
   private static final int PORT = 1234;

   public static void main(String[] args)
```

```
{
   try
   {
         host = InetAddress.getLocalHost();
   }
   catch(UnknownHostException uhEx)
   {
         System.out.println("Host ID not found!");
         System.exit(1);
   }

   try
   {
         String message;
         Socket connection = new Socket(host,PORT);

         //Step 1…
         ObjectInputStream inStream =
                new ObjectInputStream(
                       connection.getInputStream());

         //Step 1 (cont'd)…
         PrintWriter outStream =
               new PrintWriter(
                       connection.getOutputStream(),true);

         //Set up stream for keyboard entry…
         Scanner userEntry = new Scanner(System.in);
         System.out.print(
                       "Enter request (IMAGE/SOUND): ");
         message = userEntry.nextLine();
         while(!message.equals("IMAGE")
                           && !message.equals("SOUND"))
         {
            System.out.println("\nTry again!\n");
            System.out.print(
                       "Enter request (IMAGE/SOUND): ");
            message = userEntry.nextLine();
         }

           //Step 2…
           outStream.println(message);

           getFile(inStream,message);

           connection.close();
      }
```

```
            catch(IOException ioEx)
            {
                ioEx.printStackTrace();
            }
            catch(ClassNotFoundException cnfEx)
            {
                cnfEx.printStackTrace();
            }
        }

    private static void getFile(
                ObjectInputStream inStream, String fileType)
                    throws IOException, ClassNotFoundException
    {
        //Steps 3 and 4...
        //(Note the unusual appearance of the typecast!)
        byte[] byteArray = (byte[])inStream.readObject();
        FileOutputStream mediaStream;

        if (fileType.equals("IMAGE"))
        //Step 5...
            mediaStream =
                        new FileOutputStream("image.gif");
        else
        //Must be a sound file...
        //Step 5...
            mediaStream =
                        new FileOutputStream("sound.au");

        //Step 6...
        mediaStream.write(byteArray);
    }
}
```

If the request were for an image file and we wanted to display that image in our application (without saving it to file), then we could create an *ImageIcon* object holding the image by using an overloaded form of the *ImageIcon* constructor that takes a byte array as its single argument:

```
ImageIcon image = new ImageIcon(byteArray);
```

Since ways of displaying image files once they have been downloaded have already been covered, these methods will not be repeated here. However, we have not yet looked at how sound files may be played. The next section deals with this issue.

As might be expected, the above method also allows us to send and receive video files. The playing of such files, however, is not possible with the core Java SE and will be covered in Sect. 11.4.

11.3 Playing Sound Files

The standard Java classes provide two basic ways of playing sound files (otherwise known as audio clips):

- the *play* method of class *Applet* (from the *java.applet* package);
- the *play* method of the *AudioClip* interface (also from the *applet* package).

The former should be used for a sound that is to be played just once from an applet. For a sound that is to be played more than once or a sound that is to be played from an application (rather than from an applet), an *AudioClip* reference should be used. Since we shall be concerned only with applications in this chapter, no further mention will be made of the *play* method of class *Applet* here.

It may seem strange to use a class from package *applet* within an application, but *AudioClip* allows us to do just this. What is even stranger is that we use a method of class *Applet* to generate the *AudioClip* object! Method *newAudioClip* of class *Applet* takes a URL as its single argument and generates the required *AudioClip* object. The reason that we are able to use this class in an application, of course, is that it is a `static` method (and so can be used without the creation of an *Applet* object). Here is the signature for method *newAudioClip*:

```
public static final AudioClip newAudioClip(URL url)
```

The fact that a URL has to be supplied as the argument does **not** mean that we must refer to a remote file (though we can, as will be seen with applets in the next chapter). We can refer to a local file by supplying a URL that uses the *file* protocol. For example:

```
AudioClip clip =
   Applet.newAudioClip("file:///c:/mydir/mysound.au");
```

(Note the use of the *Applet* class name, since the method is static.)

Once the clip has been created, the following three methods are available and serve purposes that are self-evident from their names:

- `void play();`
- `void stop();`
- `void loop().`

These three methods may then be made use of in a Java GUI by associating them with different buttons.

<u>Example</u>

This simple example provides three buttons that will allow the user to play, stop and continuously loop through a specified sound file. (The third option is likely to get annoying pretty quickly!) The code is very straightforward and requires almost no commenting.

```
import java.applet.*;
import java.awt.*;
import java.awt.event.*;
import javax.swing.*;
import java.net.*;

public class SimpleSound extends JFrame
                        implements ActionListener
{
   private AudioClip clip;
   private JButton play, stop, loop;
   private JPanel buttonPanel;

   public static void main(String[] args)
   {
      SimpleSound frame = new SimpleSound();

      frame.setSize(300,200);
      frame.setVisible(true);

      frame.setDefaultCloseOperation(EXIT_ON_CLOSE);
   }

   public SimpleSound()
   {
      setTitle("Simple Sound Demo");
      try
      {
         //Obviously, the path given below is simply an
         //example and could be anywhere in the user's
         //file system.
          clip = Applet.newAudioClip(
             new URL("file:///C:/Sounds/cuckoo.wav"));
      }
      catch(MalformedURLException muEx)
      {
          System.out.println("*** Invalid URL! ***");
          System.exit(1);
      }

      play = new JButton("Play");
      play.addActionListener(this);
      stop = new JButton("Stop");
      stop.addActionListener(this);
      loop = new JButton("Loop");
      loop.addActionListener(this);

      buttonPanel = new JPanel();
```

```
        buttonPanel.add(play);
        buttonPanel.add(stop);
        buttonPanel.add(loop);

        add(buttonPanel,BorderLayout.SOUTH);
    }

    public void actionPerformed(ActionEvent event)
    {
        if (event.getSource() == play)
            clip.play();
        if (event.getSource() == stop)
            clip.stop();
        if (event.getSource() == loop)
            clip.loop();
    }
}
```

There is very little to see with this simple interface, of course, but what there is shown in Fig. 11.2.

Fig. 11.2 Interface for program *SimpleSound*

11.4 The Java Media Framework

As noted at the start of this chapter, the playing of video files requires the downloading of an extra API: the *Java Media Framework (JMF)*. This API may be downloaded (for free) from the following URL:

http://www.oracle.com/technetwork/java/javase/download-142937.html

*****Please note*****

Unfortunately, this very useful API has received no development in over a decade! As a consequence of this, there is no 64-bit version and anybody wishing to use the JMF must use the 32-bit version.

Class *Player* from the JMF is capable of playing all the audio formats already mentioned, as well as a number of others. In addition, it can play a variety of video formats, such as *AVI* (***.avi*** files), *GSM* (***.gsm*** files), *MPEG-1* (***.mpg*** files) and Apple *QuickTime* (***.mov*** files). (Unfortunately, it does not also display image files.) This class is held in package ***javax.media***, which should be imported into application programs. The basic steps required for a program that is to play a sound or video file are given below.

1. Accept a file name (including the path, if the file is not in the same directory as the program) and create a *File* object, supplying the file name as the constructor's single argument.
2. Use the *File* class's *exists* method to check that the file exists.
3. Create a *Player* object via static method *createPlayer* of class *Manager* (also from package *javax.media*). This method takes a single URL argument that can be generated via the *File* class's *toURL* method.
4. Use the exception-handling mechanism (catching any *Exception* object) to check that the file is of a valid type.
5. Provide a *ControllerListener* (package *javax.media*) for the media player.
6. Supply a definition for method *controllerUpdate* of the above *ControllerListener* object. This method (which takes a *ControllerEvent* argument) will usually generate any required visual and/or control panel components via *Player* methods *getVisualComponent* and *getControlPanelComponent* and then add those components to the content pane. As its last step, it should execute the *doLayout* method on the content pane.
7. Execute the *Player* object's *start* method.

Class *ControllerEvent* actually has 21 (!) direct and indirect subclasses, but the one that is likely to be of most use is class *RealizeCompleteEvent*. This is the type of object passed to *controllerUpdate* when the *Player* object has determined the clip's medium type and has loaded the clip. Inbuilt operator *instanceof* may be used to check the specific subtype of the *ControllerEvent* object that has been generated. Method *getVisualComponent* will return *null* for an audio clip (since an audio clip has no associated display component) and non-null for a video clip.

Example

The following program creates a *Player* object that plays any audio or video clip for which the name is entered by the user. As ever, the program lines corresponding to the above steps are indicated by emboldened comments that specify the associated step numbers.

Note that the JMF API has not been updated to allow adding of *its* GUI components directly to the application frame, as was introduced for all AWT and Swing components in J2SE 5.0. Instead, it is necessary to get a reference to the application's content pane (as a *Container* reference) and add GUI components that are part of the JMF to the content pane (as was the practice for all GUI components before Java 5). All other GUI components can, of course, be added directly to the application frame.

```
import java.awt.*;
import java.awt.event.*;
import java.io.*;
import javax.swing.*;

//Note the new import…
import javax.media.*;

public class MediaPlayer extends JFrame
       implements ActionListener, ControllerListener
//The application frame itself has undertaken to provide
//a definition for the controllerUpdate method of the
//ControllerListener interface.
{
   private JLabel prompt;
   private JTextField fileName;
   private JPanel inputPanel;

   private File file;

   //Here is the declaration for the
   //central media player object…
   private Player player;

   public static void main(String args[])
   {
      MediaPlayer frame= new MediaPlayer();

      frame.setSize(600, 400);
      frame.setVisible(true);

      frame.setDefaultCloseOperation(EXIT_ON_CLOSE);
   }

   public MediaPlayer ()
   {

      setTitle( "Java Media Player Frame" );

      inputPanel = new JPanel();
      prompt = new JLabel("Audio/video file name: ");
      fileName = new JTextField(25);
      inputPanel.add(prompt);
      inputPanel.add(fileName);
      add(inputPanel,BorderLayout.NORTH);
      fileName.addActionListener(this);
   }

   public void actionPerformed(ActionEvent event)
   {
      try
      {
```

```
        getFile();
        createPlayer();
    }
    catch(FileNotFoundException fnfEx)
    {
        JOptionPane.showMessageDialog(this,
                "File not found!", "Invalid file name",
                        JOptionPane.ERROR_MESSAGE);
    }

    //Step 4…
    catch (Exception ex)
    {
        JOptionPane.showMessageDialog(this,
            "Unable to load file!", "Invalid file type",
                        JOptionPane.ERROR_MESSAGE );
    }
}

private void getFile() throws FileNotFoundException
{
    //Step 1…
    file = new File(fileName.getText());

    //Step 2…
    if (!file.exists())
        throw new FileNotFoundException();
}

private void createPlayer() throws Exception
{
    //Step 3…
    player = Manager.createPlayer(file.toURL());
    //Note use of File class's toURL method to
    //convert a File object into a URL object.

    //Step 5…
    player.addControllerListener(this);

    //Step 7…
    player.start();
    fileName.setEnabled(false);
}

//Step 6…
public void controllerUpdate(ControllerEvent event)
{
    Container pane = getContentPane();
    //Needed for adding JMF GUI components to the
    //application (as explained before example).
```

```
      //Use operator instanceof to check subtype
      //of ControllerEvent object…
      if (event instanceof RealizeCompleteEvent)
      {
         //Attempt to create a visual component for the
         //file type…
         Component visualComponent =
                      player.getVisualComponent();

         if (visualComponent != null)
         //(Must be a video clip.)
            pane.add(visualComponent,
                         BorderLayout.CENTER);

         Component controlsComponent =
                   player.getControlPanelComponent();
         if (controlsComponent != null)
            pane.add(controlsComponent,
                        BorderLayout.SOUTH);

         //Need to tell content pane to rearrange its
         //components according to the new layout…
         pane.doLayout();
      }
   }
}
```

Example output is shown in Figs. 11.3 and 11.4.

If subsequent files are to be loaded, then the previous *Player* object must be closed down via the following steps:

- retrieve the visual and control panel components via *getVisualComponent* and *getControlPanelComponent*;
- execute method *remove* of the container pane for each of the above components (e.g., `pane.remove(visualComponent);`);
- execute the *Player* object's *stop* method.
  (Remember to check that the *Player* object is non-null first!)

Fig. 11.3 Video file output for program *MediaPlayer* (Microsoft product screenshot reprinted with permission from Microsoft Corporation)

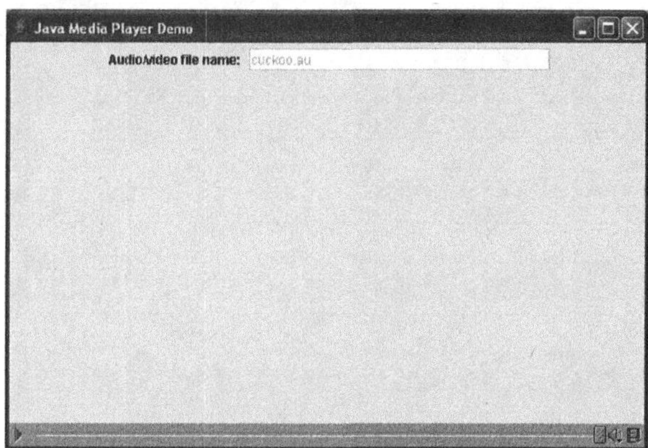

Fig. 11.4 Audio file output for program *MediaPlayer*

Exercises

You will find sound, image and video files that may be used with these and other multimedia programs on the CD-ROM supplied with this text.

11.1 Compile *ImageServer.java* and *ImageClient.java* from the first example in this chapter. Make sure that file *beesting.jpg* is accessible to the server and then run this application.

11.2 Modify *MediaClient.java* so that it creates an *ImageIcon* from the byte array received from the server and then uses a *JLabel* to display the image received. Compile the source code for the two program files (*MediaClient.java* and *MediaServer.java*) and then run the application.

11.3 Modify the code for *SimpleSound.java* so that the user can specify the number of 'cuckoos' when 'play' is pressed. (For separate chimes, you will need to insert an empty delay loop with a **very** large upper count value.)

11.4 (i) Compile and run the *MediaPlayer* program from the end of the chapter, experimenting with the video and sound files supplied on the CD-ROM.

(ii) Modify the above program so that the user can repeatedly specify further sound and/or video files (without necessarily waiting for the previous file to finish playing).

Chapter 12
Applets

Learning Objectives

After reading this chapter, you should:

- know what applets are and how they are used;
- be aware of the internal sequence of method invocations that occurs when an applet is executed;
- know how to use images applets;
- know how to use sound in applets.

As was mentioned at the start of the last chapter, Java applets were responsible for much of the initial popularisation of the Java language. This is because Java was introduced at a time when the World Wide Web was in its infancy and needed a platform-independent language in order to achieve its full potential. Java, through its applets, satisfied this need. This led to a large number of users thinking of Java entirely in terms of applets for the first few years of the language's existence. Indeed, many of the early Java authors covered Java exclusively or very largely in terms of applets. As the reader who has worked through the preceding 11 chapters of this book cannot fail to appreciate, there is far, far more to Java than just applets. In fact, what can be done with applets is only a subset of what can be done with Java applications, largely due to security restrictions that are placed on applets. However, this does not mean that Java applications can be used to replace applets. What, then, **are** applets?

Java applets are programs designed to be run from HTML documents by Java-aware Web browsers. They are server-side entities that need to be downloaded and run by the user's Web browser when the HTML documents (the Web pages) encapsulating them are referenced This being the case, it is important that the user is not discouraged from accessing the associated Web pages by irritatingly long download times. Consequently, applets are usually very small programs performing very specific tasks. Unlike a Java application, an applet **must** have a GUI, because it always runs in a graphical environment.

J. Graba, *An Introduction to Network Programming with Java: Java 7 Compatible*,
DOI 10.1007/978-1-4471-5254-5_12, © Springer-Verlag London 2013

12.1 *Applets* and *JApplets*

Though an applet must have a GUI, its containing class does not extend *JFrame*. This is hardly surprising, of course, since applets pre-date the Swing classes, but the applet's containing class does not extend class *Frame* either. Before the Swing classes appeared, an applet consisted of a class that extended class *Applet* (from package *java.applet*). The introduction of the Swing classes brought in class *JApplet* (package *javax.swing*), which extends class *Applet* and makes use of the other Swing classes. Thus, later applets **should** extend class *JApplet*. Unfortunately, there are **major** differences of operation between applets that use only pre-Swing classes and those that use the Swing classes. 'Differences in operation' is actually putting it very mildly. A lot of Swing applets will simply not work in some of the earlier versions of Internet Explorer and Netscape! However, this problem has been eradicated in the latest versions of the major browsers, as will be seen in the next section. Since the Swing classes have been around for so long now, most of what follows will refer to Swing applets only, and the term 'applets' will be used without qualification. In 12.4.1, two pre-Swing examples are used, but these are identified as such explicitly.

12.2 Applet Basics and the Development Process

When developing applets, it can be quite tedious having to go into and out of a Web browser in order to access the Web page containing the applet as changes are made to that applet. In recognition of this fact, Oracle provides a utility program called the **appletviewer** as part of the Java SE. This utility executes an applet when an HTML document containing the applet is opened by the program. The appletviewer itself is executed from a command window and must be supplied with the name of the appropriate HTML file as a command line parameter. For example:

```
appletviewer example.html
```

Class *Applet* (and, through it, class *JApplet*) extends *Panel*, rather than class *Frame*. The fact that an applet is a *Panel* object is a deliberate design decision, related to security. This means that an applet looks like part of an HTML page, rather than a standalone application. For example, the size of the applet window is fixed. This prevents programmers from spoofing users. If an applet were an extension of a *JFrame*, it could be made to resemble an application residing on a client's system that could then accept data from the user and transmit it to its host system. Though a frame window **can** be created from within an applet (simply by instantiating class *JFrame*), the browser adds a warning message to any such window.

Applets can respond to events, but do not have a *main* method to drive them. Instead, they are under the control of the browser or the appletviewer. As with GUI applications, packages *java.awt* and *javax.swing* should be imported into applets. In pre-Swing applets (which would not have imported *javax.swing*, of course), the programmer had to place the required drawing calls inside the inbuilt applet method *paint*. This method takes a *Graphics* object as its single argument and is not called directly by the applet, but is executed by the Web browser. In Swing applets, however, the required components are added to the applet's surface within method *init* (also executed implicitly by the browser) and **no painting should be specified** (though there is nothing that actually prevents us from doing so).

Example

Taking the simplest possible example, we'll create an applet that displays a greeting to the user. In order to avoid specifying painting onto the applet's window, we can use a *JLabel* and add this to the applet (within method *init*, of course), just as we would do for the application *JFrame* in a GUI application.

Remember that the applet class must extend class *JApplet*.

```
import java.awt.*;
import javax.swing.*;

public class AppletGreeting extends JApplet
{
   public void init()
   {
      JLabel message =
             new JLabel("Greetings!",JLabel.CENTER);

      //Default layout manager for JApplet is
      //BorderLayout...
      add(message,BorderLayout.CENTER);
   }
}
```

Just as we would do for a Java application, we save this applet with the name *AppletGreeting.java*. We then compile it in the usual way:

```
javac AppletGreeting.java
```

However, before we can run it, we must place it in an HTML page via the **<APPLET>** tag. This tag has three mandatory attributes (as well as a number of optional ones):6

- `CODE` (specifying the name of the applet's *.class* file);
- `WIDTH` (specifying the width of the applet, in pixels);
- `HEIGHT`(specifying height of the applet, in pixels).

As will be the case for all subsequent applets in this chapter, we shall employ a minimal HTML page:

```
<HTML>
   <APPLET CODE = "AppletGreeting.class"
           WIDTH = 300
           HEIGHT = 150>
   </APPLET>
</HTML>
```

If this HTML page is saved with the name *Greeting.html*, then the contained applet may be executed by loading the HTML page into the appletviewer with the following command:

```
appletviewer Greeting.html
```

N.B. This example assumes that both *Greeting.html* and *AppletGreeting.class* are in the current folder. If *AppletGreeting.class* is in a sub-folder, then the *CODE* attribute must specify the relative path. For example:

```
CODE = "folder1\folder2\AppletGreeting.class"
```

For a directory elsewhere, attribute ***CODEBASE*** must be used to specify that directory. For example:

```
CODEBASE = "..\otherfolder"
```

(Attribute *CODE* must still also be used to specify the applet's *.class* file, of course.)

The output from this applet under the appletviewer is shown in Fig. 12.1 below.

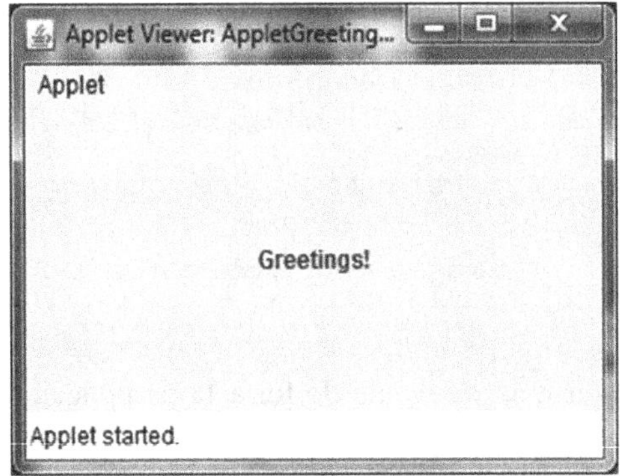

Fig. 12.1 Output from *AppletGreeting* under the appletviewer

In order to run a Swing applet in a browser, we must have the **Java Plug-in** installed and the browser must know that it is to use this plug-in (rather than the JVM). Both Chrome and IE9 will automatically use the Java Plug-in when accessing Swing applets. The output from each of these when referencing *Greeting.html* is shown in Figs. 12.2 and 12.3. (Note the grey background, as for the appletviewer, now serving the purpose of distinguishing the applet from the HTML page.)

12.3 The Internal Operation of Applets

As its name implies, method *init* carries out any initialisation required by the applet, such as initialisation of variables or loading of images. Since applets cannot call the *paint* method directly, it is necessary to circumvent direct painting via the following steps:

- create a subclass of *JPanel* (within the applet body) and place the painting code inside method *paintComponent* of this class;

- create an object of this class inside the applet's *init* method;
- use method *setContentPane* of class *JApplet* to make the above object the content pane for the applet.

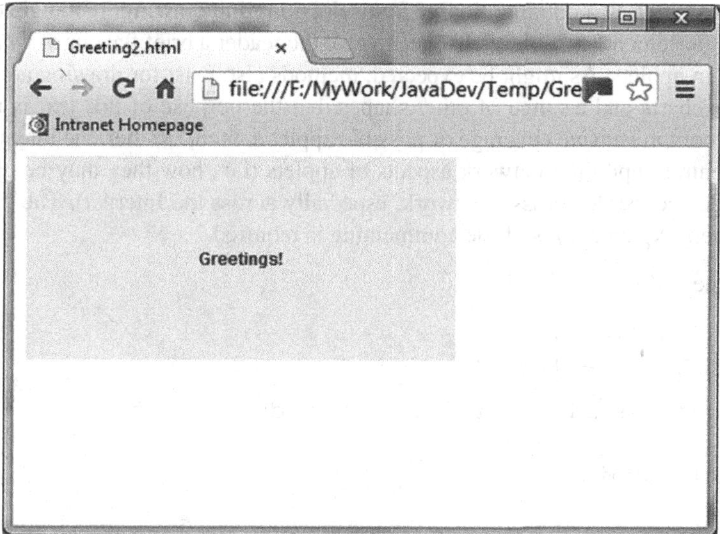

Fig. 12.2 Output from *AppletGreeting* under Google Chrome

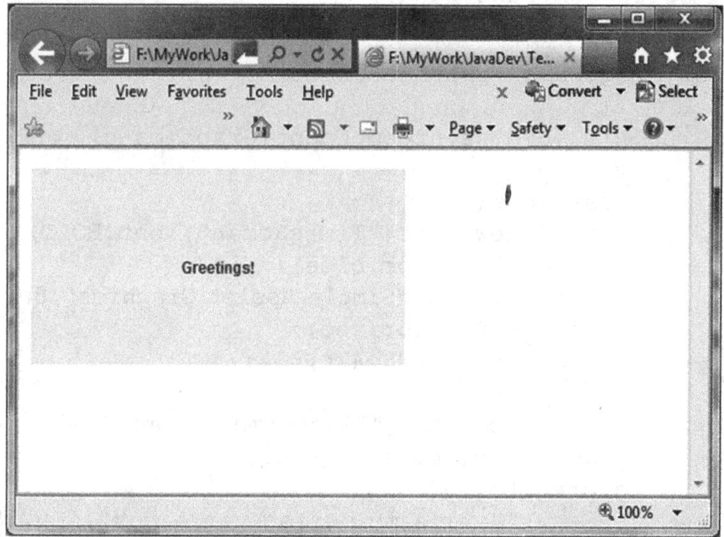

Fig. 12.3 Output from *AppletGreeting* under IE9

Method *paintComponent* is executed automatically by the browser.

Now that the reader is familiar with the basic creation of an applet, it seems appropriate to introduce a slightly more sophisticated example. Since applets will usually make use of graphics and colours, the next example illustrates some of these facilities (though still in a rather artificial way)

Example

This example uses a combination of font selection, line drawing, rectangle drawing, text placement and colour changes to give the reader a brief flavour of what can be done in applets. As might be expected, methods also exist for drawing arcs, circles, bar charts and a range of other shapes, but the purpose of this text is not to provide comprehensive coverage of possible applet content. Rather, the intention is to concentrate upon the network aspects of applets (i.e., how they may be created and made accessible across a network, especially across the Internet). The code is mostly self-explanatory, so little commenting is required.

Here's the code…

```
import java.awt.*;
import javax.swing.*;

public class SimpleGraphics extends JApplet
{
   public void init()
   {
       ImagePanel pane = new ImagePanel();

       //Make above panel the current content pane...
       setContentPane(pane);
   }

   class ImagePanel extends JPanel
   {
        public void paintComponent(Graphics g)
        {
           g.setFont(
                  new Font("TimesRoman",Font.BOLD,36));
           g.setColor(Color.blue);
             g.drawString("Simple Applet Graphics",50,80);
           g.setColor(Color.red);
           g.drawLine(50,85,410,85);
           g.setFont(
                  new Font("TimesRoman",Font.PLAIN,24));
           g.setColor(Color.magenta);
           g.drawString(
                  "Here's my message in a box",110,150);
           g.setColor(Color.green);
           g.drawRect(100,120,280,50);
        }
   }
}
```

Here is the minimal HTML code required to access the applet:

```
<HTML>
   <APPLET   CODE="SimpleGraphics.class"
             WIDTH = 500
             HEIGHT = 250>
   </APPLET>
</HTML>
```

Here's the output from the appletviewer (Fig. 12.4):

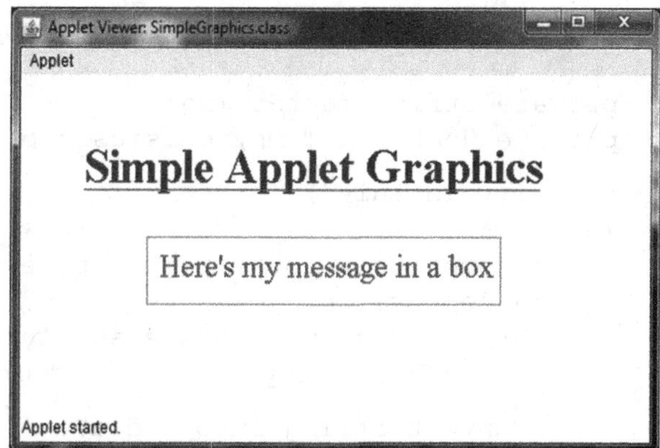

Fig. 12.4 Output from *SimpleGraphics* under the appletviewer

The output from IE9 is shown in Fig. 12.5.

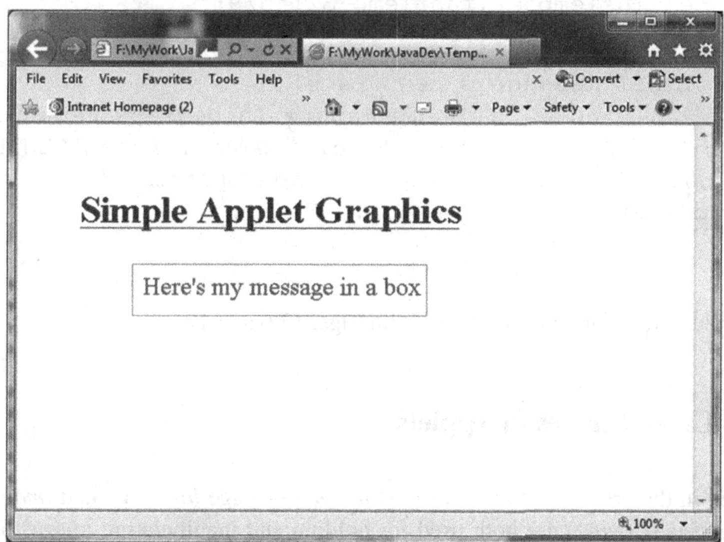

Fig. 12.5 Output from the *SimpleGraphics* applet under IE9

The above example does little more than could be achieved with HTML alone. In particular, there is no interaction with the user. The next example is a rather more practical applet that involves some interaction with the user.

Example

This applet accepts a Fahrenheit temperature from the user and converts it into the corresponding Celsius temperature. Following the convention established in earlier examples, the associated minimal HTML file (not shown below) will have the same name as the applet, but with a suffix of *.html*.

```
import java.awt.*;
import javax.swing.*;

public class FahrToCelsius extends JApplet
{
   private String fahrString;
   private float fahrTemp, celsiusTemp;

   public void init()
   {
      //Prompt user for a temperature and
      //accept value…
      fahrString = JOptionPane.showInputDialog(
            "Enter temperature in degrees Fahrenheit");

      //Convert string into a float…
      fahrTemp = Float.parseFloat(fahrString);

      //Carry out the conversion…
      celsiusTemp = (fahrTemp-32)*5/9;

      //Set up the response within a JLabel…
      JLabel message = new JLabel(
                    "Temperature in degrees Celsius: "
                         + celsiusTemp,JLabel.CENTER);
      //Add the above label to the applet…
     add(message,BorderLayout.CENTER);
  }
}
```

Sample output for Chrome is shown in Figs. 12.6 and 12.7.

12.4 Using Images in Applets

As noted in the previous chapter, classes *Image* (package *java.awt*) and *ImageIcon* (package *javax.swing*) are both used for holding and manipulating images. Either may be used on its own, but *ImageIcon* is particularly useful for loading an image into an application from the current directory. In theory, *ImageIcon* should be just as useful in applets. However, there is a problem that considerably restricts the usefulness of *ImageIcon*s in applets. Since explanation of this problem involves a

Fig. 12.6 User entry into applet *FahrToCelsius* under Google Chrome

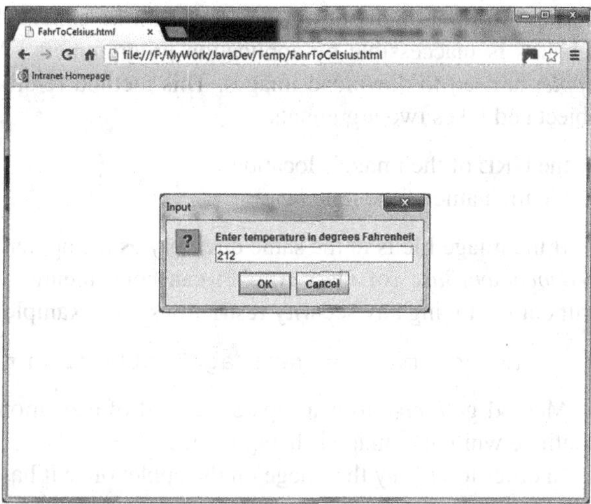

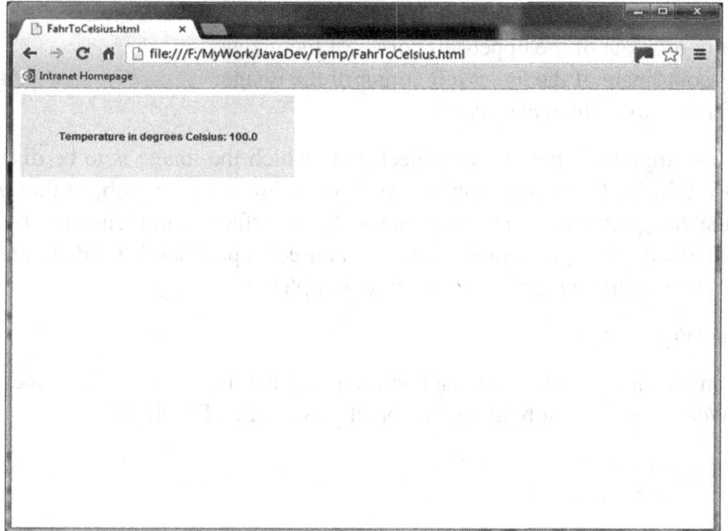

Fig. 12.7 Final output from applet *FahrToCelsius2* under Google Chrome

comparison with the corresponding technique for using class *Image*, however, it is appropriate to consider the use of this latter class first…

12.4.1 Using Class Image

Image is an abstract class, so we cannot directly create an instance of this class, but we can use an *Image* reference for the image that is downloaded. (To achieve platform independence, each Java platform provides its own subclass of *Image* for storing information about images. As might be expected, this platform-dependent subclass is inaccessible by application programmers.) Method *getImage* of class *Applet* is used to download images. This method returns a reference to an *Image* object and takes two arguments:

- the URL of the image's location;
- the file name of the image.

If the image file is in the same directory as the applet's HTML file, then method *getDocumentBase* (of class *Applet*) can conveniently provide the required URL without infringing any security restrictions. For example:

```
Image image = getImage(getDocumentBase(),"pic.gif");
```

Method *getImage* uses a separate thread of execution, allowing the program to continue while the image is being loaded.

In order to display the image on the applet once it has been downloaded, we use the *drawImage* method of class *Graphics*. This method takes four arguments:

- a reference to the image;
- the x-coordinate of the upper-left corner of the image;
- the y-coordinate of the upper left corner of the image;
- a reference to an *ImageObserver*.

The last argument specifies an object upon which the image is to be displayed (usually = *this*, for the current applet). An *ImageObserver* is any object that implements the *ImageObserver* interface. Since this interface is implemented by class *Component*, one of *Applet*'s (and *JApplet*'s) indirect superclasses, we do not need to specify '*implements ImageObserver*' for our applets.

Example (Pre-Swing)

This example simply loads and displays an image that is located in the same folder on the Web server as that holding the applet's associated HTML file.

```
import java.awt.*;
import java.applet.*;

public class ImageTest1a extends Applet
{
   private Image image;

   public void init()
   {
      image =
        getImage(getDocumentBase(),"cutekittie.gif");
   }

   public void paint(Graphics g)
   {
```

```
        //Draw image in top left corner of applet, using
        //applet itself as the ImageObserver…
        g.drawImage(image, 0, 0, this);
    }
}
```

The results of submitting the above applet's HTML page to Chrome and IE9 are shown in Figs. 12.8 and 12.9 respectively.

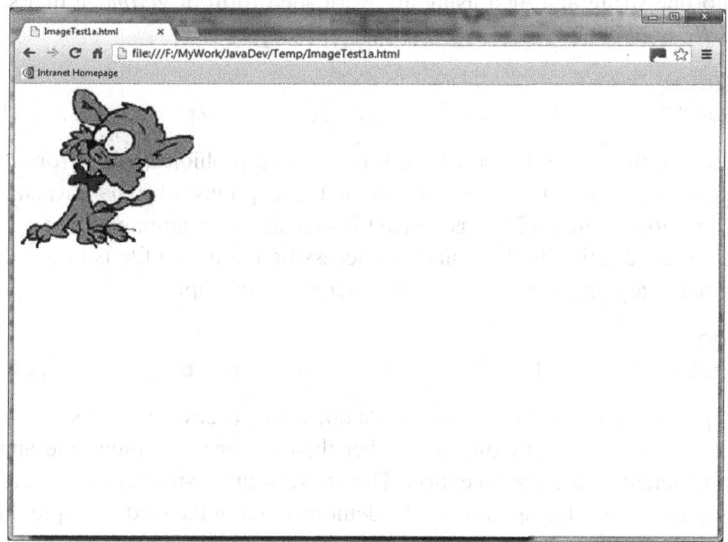

Fig. 12.8 Output from applet *ImageTest1a* under Google Chrome

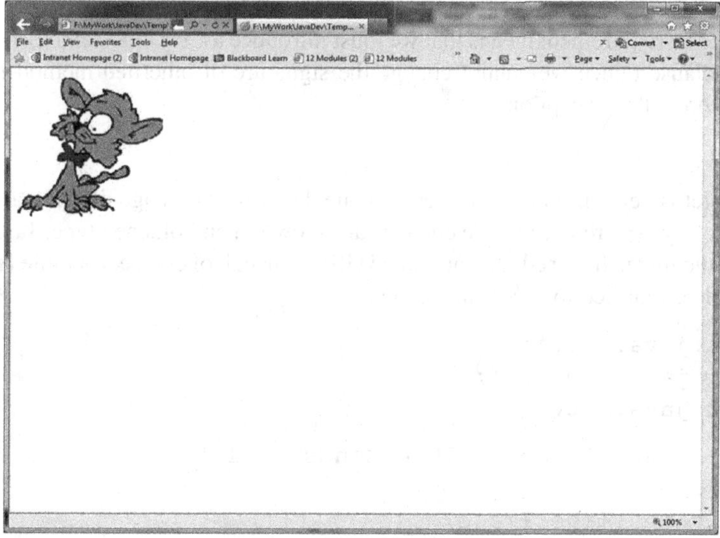

Fig. 12.9 Output from applet *ImageTest1a* under IE9

As an alternative to using method *getDocumentBase* (which returns a *URL* reference), we may create our own *URL* object directly from the image file's path and use this as the first argument to method *getImage*. For example:

```
image =
   getImage(new URL("http://somesite/pics/"),"pic.gif");
```

(Note that the '/' at the end of the URL path is mandatory.)

The above syntax may be abbreviated slightly by concatenating the path and file name into one string and then using an overloaded form of *getImage* that simply takes a *URL* argument:

```
image =
    getImage(new URL("http://somesite/pics/pic.gif"));
```

In practice, though, most sites have firewalls that prohibit applets from having such open access to their file systems and exceptions of type *java.security.AccessControlException* will be generated if such access is attempted.

Yet another variation in the syntax for accessing the image file is to use the *file* protocol in the argument to the *URL* constructor. For example:

```
image =
  getImage(new URL("file:///c:/webfiles/pics/pic.gif"));
```

As might be expected, this also does not allow free access to a site's file system. In fact, trying to access any directory other than the one containing the applet is likely to generate a security exception. The above syntax (stipulating the directory containing the associated applet) will be demonstrated in the next example. Firstly, though, it needs to be pointed out that our code:

- should import package *java.net*;
- must deal with exceptions of type *MalformedURLException*.

The latter requirement means that we must introduce a `try` block and associated `catch` clause (since we cannot change the signature of inherited method *init* to make it throw this exception).

Example (Pre-Swing)

This applet is very similar to the previous one, but now the image file is in a specified directory. The required code changes are shown in emboldened type. Just for a change, the image file used is an animated GIF. As usual, of course, a simple HTML page will be required to access the applet.

```
import.java.awt.*;
import java.applet.*;
import java.net.*;

public class ImageTest1b extends Applet
{
   private Image image;
   public void init()
```

```
{
   try
   {
      image = getImage(new URL(
                          "file:///d:/Applet Stuff/"
                          + "Pre-Swing/earth.gif"));
      /*
      Obviously, you will need to change the above
      URL to match up to your local directory
      structure if you wish to test the operation
      of this applet.
      */
     }
   catch (MalformedURLException muEx)
   {
      System.out.println("Invalid URL!");
      System.exit(1);
   }
 }

 public void paint(Graphics g)
 {
     g.drawImage(image,0,0,this);
 }
}
```

This applet runs without problem in the appletviewer and the two browsers, but **only** if both applet file and image file are in the same directory as the associated HTML file. (Output is shown in Figs. 12.10 and 12.11.) If the files are in different directories, a security exception is generated. This would appear to make the use of a path redundant, of course. Indeed, it turns out that using the string "file:///d:earth.gif" works just as well as using the full path "file:///d:/Applet Stuff/Pre-Swing/earth.

Fig. 12.10 Output from applet *ImageTest1b* under the appletviewer

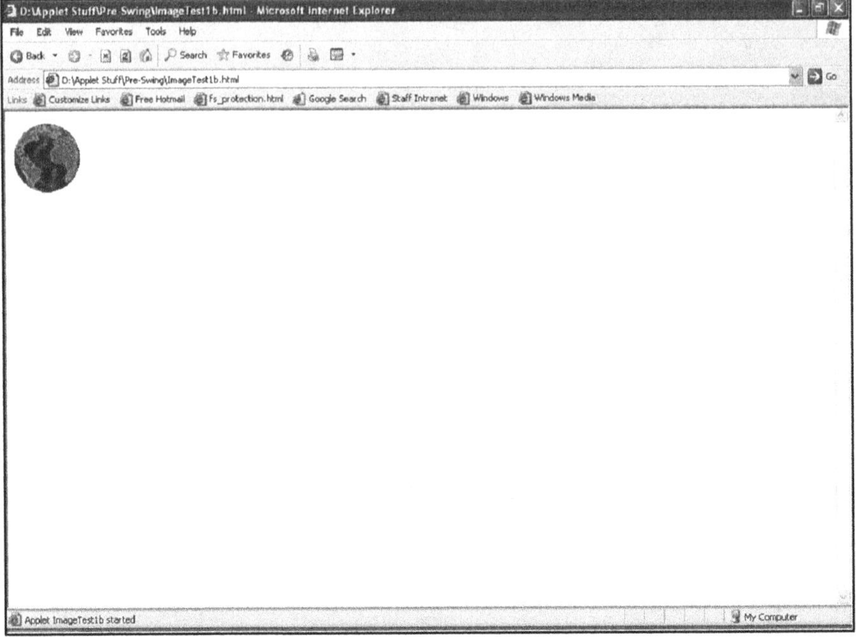

Fig. 12.11 Output from applet *ImageTest1b* under IE9

gif' in the appletviewer. However, the use of the abbreviated string fails to work in each of Chrome and IE9, each displaying an empty page.

As will be seen in the next sub-section, *ImageIcon*s offer no more flexibility than Images (and, in fact, are even more restrictive). It would appear that the only reliable way of using images in applets is to locate both images and applets in the same directory on the Web server. In most cases, however, this is unlikely to be a particularly inconvenient restriction.

12.4.2 Using Class ImageIcon

Now we can return to consideration of the problem with *ImageIcon*s referred to at the start of Sect. 12.4…

The *ImageIcon* constructor has nine different signatures, one of which takes the following two arguments:

- a URL, specifying the folder of the associated image;
- the file name of the image.

It would appear from this that we can make use of method *getDocumentBase* to specify the directory for an image file that is located in the same folder on the Web server as the associated Web page (just as we did with method *getImage* in the previous section).

<u>Example</u>

The applet below attempts to load an image (from the associated Web page's folder) into an *ImageIcon* and then use the *ImageIcon*'s *paintIcon* method to display the image on the applet window.

```
import java.awt.*;
import javax.swing.*;
import java.net.*;

public class ImageTest2a extends JApplet
{
   private ImageIcon image;
   public void init()
   {
     image =
       new ImageIcon(getDocumentBase(), " earth.gif");
   }

   public void paint(Graphics g)
   {
       image.paintIcon(this,g,0,0);
     }
}
```

Surprisingly, the above applet produces an empty display in the appletviewer and in IE9! Chrome is also empty of any image, but shows a grey rectangle in the top left corner, where the applet output would be, as shown in Fig. 12.12.

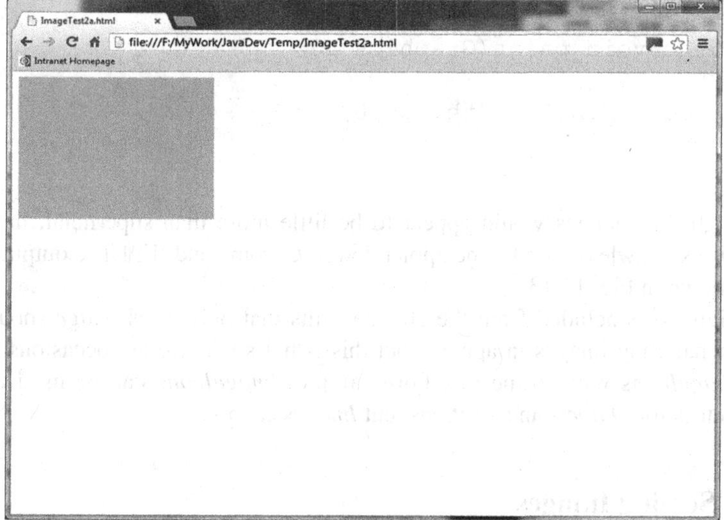

Fig. 12.12 Output from applet *ImageTest2a* under Chrome when path to image file removed

Now consider the code in the applet below. This is very similar to the code above, but declares an *Image* reference called *image* (changing the name of the *ImageIcon* object to *icon*) and replaces the line

```
image = new ImageIcon(getDocumentBase(), "earth.gif");
```

with the following two lines:

```
image = getImage(getDocumentBase(), "earth.gif");
icon = new ImageIcon(image);
```

Thus, instead of the call to *getDocumentBase* being within the constructor for the *ImageIcon* object, it is used by method *getImage* to return an *Image* object. The reference to this object is then used to construct an *ImageIcon* for the image. Essentially, the only difference is that it is now *getImage* that is making the call to *getDocumentBase*, rather than the *ImageIcon* constructor.

```
import java.awt.*;
import javax.swing.*;
import java.net.*;

public class ImageTest2b extends JApplet
{
   private Image image;
   private ImageIcon icon;

   public void init()
   {
      image = getImage(getDocumentBase(), "earth.gif");
      icon = new ImageIcon(image);
   }

   public void paint(Graphics g)
   {
      icon.paintIcon(this,g,0,0);
   }
}
```

Though the changes would appear to be little more than superficial, the new applet works flawlessly under the appletviewer, Chrome and IE9! The output from IE9 is shown in Fig. 12.13.

It might be concluded from the above results that only class *Image* should be used for handling images in applets, but this is not so. There are occasions when only *ImageIcons* will do the job. For example, *ImageIcons* can be used in the constructors for *JLabels* and *JButtons*, but *Images* cannot.

12.5 Scaling Images

An overloaded form of method *drawImage* takes six arguments, the two extra arguments being positioned immediately before the *ImageObserver* argument. These extra arguments specify the width and height of the image.

Fig. 12.13 Output from applet *ImageTest2b* under IE9

The size of the image is automatically scaled to fit these dimensions. For example:

```
g.drawImage(image,100,100,200,150,this);
```

By using methods *getWidth* and *getHeight* of class *Component*, the image may also be drawn relative to the size of the applet, which can enhance the layout of the Web page significantly. For example:

```
g.drawImage (
      image,50,60,getWidth()-100,getHeight()-120,this);
```

In the above example, the image will be scaled to fit within an area that is 50 pixels in from left and right sides of the applet window and 60 pixels in from the top and bottom of the window. *ImageIcons* have no direct scaling mechanism. However, *ImageIcon* has a *getImage* method that returns an *Image* reference which can then be used as above by *drawImage*.

12.6 Using Sound in Applets

As noted in the previous chapter, the standard Java classes provide two methods for the playing of audio clips:

- method *play* of class *Applet*;
- method *play* of the *AudioClip* interface.

Since we were concerned solely with applications (as opposed to applets) in the previous chapter, only the latter method was of any interest to us. This is still likely to be of greater use to us in applets, but the former method is convenient for a sound that needs to be played only once. This method has the following two forms:

- `public void play(
                URL <location>, String <soundFile>)`
- `public void play(URL <soundURL>)`

For the first version, the first argument is normally the value returned by a call to the applet's *getDocumentBase* method or its *getCodeBase* method. For example:

```
play(getDocumentBase(), "bell.au");
```

For a sound that is to be played more than once, an *AudioClip* reference should be used. The address to be held in this reference is returned by method *getAudioClip* of class *Applet*. This method has two forms that take the same arguments as the above signatures for method *play*:

- `public AudioClip getAudioClip(
                URL <location>, String <soundFile>)`
- `public AudioClip getAudioClip(URL <soundURL>)`

Once the clip has been loaded via *getAudioClip*, the same three methods that were listed in the previous chapter are available for manipulating the sound file:

- `void play();`
- `void stop();`
- `void loop().`

Example

The applet below provides three buttons that will allow the user to play, stop and loop a specified sound file. It mirrors the *SimpleSound* application example from the previous chapter and requires little commenting. To avoid having to circumvent the applet's security restrictions, the sound file is held in the same folder as the applet.

```
import java.applet.*;
import java.awt.*;
import java.awt.event.*;
import javax.swing.*;
import java.net.*;

public class SimpleSoundApplet extends JApplet
                              implements ActionListener
{
     private AudioClip clip;
     private JButton play, stop, loop;
     private JPanel buttonPanel;

     public void init()
     {
        try
```

```
        {
          clip = getAudioClip(
                       new URL(getDocumentBase(),
                                          "cuckoo.wav"));
        }
        catch(MalformedURLException muEx)
        {
            System.out.println("*** Invalid URL! ***");
            System.exit(1);
        }

        play = new JButton("Play");
        play.addActionListener(this);
        stop = new JButton("Stop");
        stop.addActionListener(this);
        loop = new JButton("Loop");
        loop.addActionListener(this);

        buttonPanel = new JPanel();

        buttonPanel.add(play);
        buttonPanel.add(stop);
        buttonPanel.add(loop);
        add(buttonPanel,BorderLayout.SOUTH);
    }

    public void stop()
    {
       clip.stop(); //Prevents sound from continuing
    }              //after applet has been stopped.

    public void actionPerformed(ActionEvent event)
    {

       if (event.getSource() == play)
          clip.play();
       if (event.getSource() == stop)
          clip.stop();
       if (event.getSource() == loop)
          clip.loop();
    }
}
```

Here's the code for the minimal Web page that will be used to contain the applet:

```
<HTML>
   <APPLET CODE="SimpleSoundApplet.class"
           WIDTH = 300
           HEIGHT = 200>
   </APPLET>
</HTML>
```

The output from Chrome is shown in Fig. 12.14.

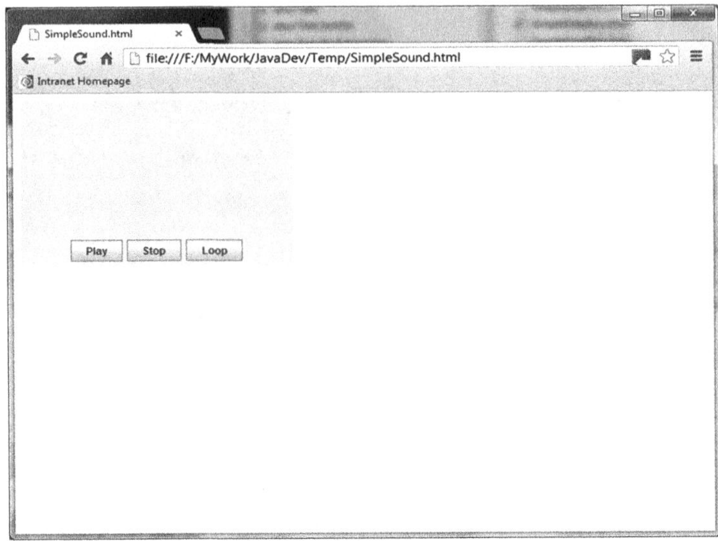

Fig. 12.14 Output from *SimpleSoundApplet* under Google Chrome

Exercises

To complete the following exercises, you will require access to a Java-aware browser. In order to run the Swing applets, this browser will also have to have the Java Plug-In installed. This plug-in should have been installed automatically when you installed Java SE.

12.1 From the Internet site associated with this book, copy the *.class* and *.html* files for the *AppletGreeting*, *SimpleGraphics*, *ImageTest1a* and *ImageTest1b* examples, along with image files *cute kittie.gif* and *earth.gif*. Ensuring that the files are in the current folder, load up each of the HTML files into the appletviewer and your browser, in turn, observing the results.

12.2 (i) From the Internet site associated with this book, copy the *.class* and *.html* files for the *ImageTest2a*, *ImageTest2b*, *FahrToCelsius* and *SimpleSoundApplet* examples, along with sound file *cuckoo.wav*.

(ii) Do the same for the four HTML files above as you did for the four HTML files in exercise 12.1 (again ensuring that all files are in the current folder). You should find that applet *ImageTest2a* will not run in either the appletviewer or your browser

For each of the next three exercises, you should create a minimal HTML page and test this page in both the appletviewer (while developing) and your browser (for the finished product).

12.3 Create an applet with a single button that holds an image. (Use the *JButton* constructor that takes an *ImageIcon* as its single argument.) Whenever the button/image is pressed a single 'cuckoo' should sound.

12.4 Specifying an area of size 300 pixels × 300 pixels in your HTML file, create an applet that holds an image that is positioned and scaled so that it occupies an area 40 pixels in from each side of the applet window. In order that the applet window can be distinguished from the Web page, change the colour of the applet's background to any colour of your choice.

12.5 Create an applet that displays a simple drawing of a house.

Appendix: Structured Query Language (SQL)

SQL is a language for communicating with relational databases and originates in work carried out by IBM in the mid-1970s. Since then, both ANSI (the American National Standards Institute) and the ISO (International Standards Organisation) have attempted to produce an SQL standard, with SQL3 being the latest, but most users still working with SQL2. Though each major database vendor adds its own specific extensions to 'standard' SQL, the most commonly required SQL statements are widely accepted, with little or no variation between vendors. In this very brief introduction to SQL, it is only these common statements that are of concern to us. Please note that there is **much** more to SQL than can be covered in this brief introduction, but this coverage will enable you to understand the contents of Chap. 7 and to create your own statements for the most common database manipulation activities.

In what follows, the *Sales* database from the exercises at the end of Chap. 7 will be used for illustration purposes. Recall that this database had a single table called *Stock*. Here's table *Stock* containing some test data (Fig. A.1):

	stockCode	description	unitPrice	currentLevel	reorderLevel
▶	111111	Pencil	£0.32	1517	1200
	333333	A4 pad narrow feint	£1.45	121	150
	444444	A4 pad wide feint	£1.45	123	120
	555555	Ruler	£0.69	80	80
	666666	Stapler	£2.65	72	60
*	0		£0.00	0	0

Fig. A.1 Test data contents of *Stock.mdb*

J. Graba, *An Introduction to Network Programming with Java: Java 7 Compatible*,
DOI 10.1007/978-1-4471-5254-5, © Springer-Verlag London 2013

SQL statements may be divided into two broad categories:

- Data Manipulation Language (DML) statements;
- Data Definition Language (DDL) statements.

It is primarily the first of these with which we shall be concerned, but each will be covered below. Whether a DML statement or a DDL statement, every SQL statement is terminated with a semi-colon. It is also conventional for the SQL keywords to appear in upper case, attributes (fields) in lower case and table names in lower case commencing with a capital letter.

A.1 DDL Statements

These are statements that affect the **structure** of a table by creating/deleting attributes or whole tables. Since these activities are usually much more conveniently and appropriately carried out via a GUI that is provided by the database vendor, not much attention will be paid to these statements, but the syntax for each is shown below, with examples relating to our *Stock* table.

A.1.1 Creating a Table

This is achieved via the `CREATE TABLE` statement. Syntax:

```
CREATE TABLE <TableName>(<fieldName> <fieldType>
                          {,<fieldName> <fieldType>});
```

For example:

```
CREATE TABLE Stock(stockCode INTEGER,
                   description VARCHAR(20),
                   unitPrice REAL,
                   currentLevel INTEGER,
                   reorderLevel INTEGER);
```

Just to complicate things, some databases would use `FLOAT`, `DECIMAL (<n>,<d>)` or `NUMERIC` instead of `REAL` above. (The ‘n’ and ‘d’ refer to the total number of figures and number of figures after the decimal point respectively.)

A.1.2 Deleting a Table

This is very straightforward via the `DROP` statement. Syntax:

```
DROP TABLE <TableName>;
```

For example:

```
DROP TABLE Stock;
```

A.1.3 Adding Attributes

The required statement is ALTER TABLE. Syntax:

```
ALTER TABLE <TableName> ADD <fieldName> <fieldType>
                              {,<fieldName> <fieldType>};
```

For example:

```
ALTER TABLE Stock ADD supplier VARCHAR(30);
```

A.1.4 Removing Attributes

As above, the required statement is ALTER TABLE, but now with a DROP clause. Syntax:

```
ALTER TABLE <TableName> DROP <fieldName> {,<fieldName>};
```

For example:

```
ALTER TABLE Stock DROP supplier;
```

A.2 DML Statements

These statements manipulate the rows (or 'tuples') of a database table. The primary DML statements are:

- SELECT
- INSERT
- DELETE
- UPDATE

DELETE must be used in combination with a WHERE clause, which contains a Boolean expression that specifies which rows of the table are to be affected. SELECT and UPDATE are also very often used with a WHERE clause for the same purpose, but do not require one. If no WHERE clause is supplied, then the SELECT/UPDATE acts upon **all** the rows of the specified table. The next few sections give details and examples relating to the four statements above.

A.2.1 SELECT

As its name implies, this statement is used to select values from a table. It is by **far** the most commonly used SQL statement. Basic syntax:

```
SELECT <fieldName> {,<fieldName>} FROM <TableName>
                                    [WHERE <condition>]};
```

This will return the named attribute(s) for all rows in the named table satisfying the specified condition. Often, all attributes are required, so the asterisk character (*) is provided to allow this requirement to be expressed in a shorthand form.

<u>Examples</u>

1. `SELECT * FROM Stock;`
   Here, all attributes in all rows are returned.

2. `SELECT stockCode, description FROM Stock;`
   Result returned for our test data:

```
111111   Pencil
333333   A4 pad narrow feint
444444   A4 pad wide feint
555555   Ruler
666666   Stapler
```

3. `SELECT stockCode,currentLevel,reorderLevel FROM Stock`
   `WHERE currentLevel <= reorderLevel;`
   Result returned for our test data:

```
333333   121   150
555555    80    80
```

Keywords AND and OR can also be used, to produce compound conditions. For example:

```
SELECT stockCode, unitPrice FROM Stock
             WHERE unitPrice> 1 AND unitPrice <1.5;
```

(Does not have to be the same attribute in both sub-conditions.)
Result returned:

```
333333   1.45
444444   1.45
```

By default, the order will be ascending (which can be specified explicitly by adding the `ORDER BY` clause with the qualifier `ASC`). If we want descending order, then we can use the `ORDER BY` clause with the specifier `DESC`. For example:

```
SELECT * FROM Stock ORDER BY unitPrice DESC;
```

A.2.2 INSERT

This statement is used to insert an individual row into a table. Syntax:

```
INSERT INTO <TableName> [<fieldName>{,<fieldName>}]
                                VALUES (<value>{,<value>});
```

If any attributes are missing, then the row created has default values for these. The most common default value is `NULL`. If no attributes are listed, then values for **all** attributes must be supplied. For example:

```
INSERT INTO Stock VALUES(222222,'Rubber',0.57,315,200);
```

A.2.3 DELETE

This statement is used to delete one or more rows from a specified table. Syntax:

```
DELETE FROM <TableName> WHERE <condition>;
```

It is most commonly used to delete a single row from a table, usually by specifying its primary key in the condition. For example:

```
DELETE FROM Stock WHERE stockCode = 222222;
```

Several rows may be deleted at once if multiple rows satisfy the condition. For example:

```
DELETE FROM Stock WHERE unitPrice < 1;
```

A.2.4 UPDATE

This statement is used to modify one or more rows in a specified table. Syntax:

```
UPDATE <TableName> SET <fieldName = value>
        {,<fieldName = value >} [WHERE <condition>];
```

For example:

```
UPDATE Stock SET unitPrice = 1 WHERE unitPrice < 1;
```

This would cause the prices of pencils and rulers to rise from 32p and 69p respectively to £1 each.

If all rows are to be affected, then the `WHERE` clause is omitted.

Index

J. Graba, *An Introduction to Network Programming with Java: Java 7 Compatible*,
DOI 10.1007/978-1-4471-5254-5, © Springer-Verlag London 2013

L

M

N